ST. JOHN AT PATMOS

I John, who also am your brother . . . was in the isle that is called Patmos . . .
(Revelation 1: 9)

Gustave Doré's "St. John on Patmos" (1866)

ADVANCE PRAISE FOR
A FOURTH MAN IN THE FURNACE

When it comes to eschatology in general and the book of Revelation in particular, it would be a miracle if two scholars agreed on every definition, detail, or disputed point. That said, I find much to commend in the first volume of Dr. Shultz's commentary on Revelation. Written from a classic premillennial perspective but sensitive to contemporary exegetical and eschatological discussions, Shultz provides a helpful orientation to his Historic Premillennial position while engaging with more recent developments like New Creation Millennialism. Shultz's commentary comes across as a dialogue with Scripture, theology, history, and present scholarship, not as a dogmatic declaration or the final say on the matter. As such, it serves to further continuing conversation regarding our common eschatological hope – regardless of where we may differ on some of the details.

– Michael J. Svigel, PhD.
Department Chair and Professor of Theological Studies,
Dallas Theological Seminary.
Author of *The Fathers on the Future: A 2nd Century Eschatology for the 21st Century Church.*

This work represents a distinguished contribution to biblical scholarship, characterized by a rigorous engagement with the original Greek manuscript of the Book of Revelation. Dr. Shultz skillfully synthesizes the analytical strengths of the four primary interpretive frameworks, resulting in a nuanced and multifaceted exegetical study.

Furthermore, the volume is highly recommended for its articulation of a historic premillennialist eschatology that eschews dogmatic militancy in favor of a collegial and irenic tone. By maintaining academic rigor while demonstrating intellectual generosity toward divergent viewpoints, Shultz provides a model for constructive theological discourse.

– Sung Wook Chung, D.Phil.
Professor of Christian Theology,
Denver Seminary.

This commentary opens with a fair and necessary question: Why another commentary on Revelation? It then proceeds to answer that question convincingly, explaining both the need for this work and the distinct contribution it seeks to make. In my judgment, it succeeds admirably in accomplishing its stated aim.

Michael Shultz has once again demonstrated why I consider him to be one of the brightest young ministers preaching today. He writes with the mind of a scholar and the heart of a pastor, combining careful exegesis with an evident concern for the church. Throughout the commentary, he engages the major contemporary debates surrounding the text with clarity, charity, and precision. Are there points at which we disagree? Certainly. As one who holds to an Amillennial perspective, I anticipated arriving at different conclusions in some areas. Yet I was encouraged to find that we agreed on far more than we differed.

Regardless of one's interpretive framework, I am confident that this commentary will prove to be a valuable and well-used addition to any pastor's library.

– **M. Keith Foskey, D.Min.**
Pastor,
Sovereign Grace Family Church.

Michael Shultz has an encouraging way of explaining the book of Revelation from a deeply pastoral perspective while retaining theological precision. He treats the prophecy with a Christ-centered focus, leading readers to eagerly await the unveiling of His glory at His return. Shultz emphasizes that Christ is exalted now and reigns over His church.

Readers will benefit from his careful attentiveness to apocalyptic symbolism rooted in Old Testament foundations. This commentary consistently grounds the present and certain triumph of Christ's sovereign rule. Shultz captures Revelation in a way that does not intimidate believers but highlights how Revelation 1:3 is meant to promise blessing.

This work stands as a thoughtful and edifying contribution, directing Christians away from an excessive fixation on timelines and toward a deeper confidence in our sovereign and victorious King.

– **Jeremiah Nortier**
Pastor and Elder,
Twelve 5 Church.
Director of The Apologetic Dog.

One of the central tensions of the book of Revelation is how the "already" fulfillments and the "not yet" prophecies relate to one another. Michael Shultz helps readers navigate this tension by providing an accessible window into the relationships of Revelation's apocalyptic imagery. With an eye toward exegetical clarity and contemporary application, Shultz navigates contemporary debates concerning eschatological frameworks from an explicitly premillennial perspective, and his introductory excursus highlights his hermeneutical commitments for the commentary which follows.

Shultz's commentary is both academically thoughtful and practically beneficial; his engagement with a great variety of intertextual connections from both the Old and New Testaments makes this work an excellent conversation partner for the preacher in the study. I highly recommend this volume for pastors, teachers, and students of the book of Revelation.

– David W. Bunce
Associate Pastor,
Geist Community Church
PhD Candidate,
The Southern Baptist Theological Seminary.

Many commentaries on the book of Revelation tend to become so absorbed in the details that they lose a clear sense of application and direction. Conversely, others lean so heavily into application that the text itself recedes into the background. Michael Shultz's commentary skillfully maintains the proper balance between careful exegesis and meaningful application.

I especially appreciate his clear articulation of the historic premillennial position. Although I do not share his millennial view, I have benefitted greatly from his work and found it highly valuable. Michael Shultz has produced an excellent commentary.

– Rev. Kenny E. Hilliard III
Chancellor,
Ambassador International University.

A FOURTH MAN IN THE FURNACE:

An Eclecticist Commentary on the Book of Revelation

Volume 1

Introduction and Revelation 1:1-3:22

H. Michael Shultz Jr.

Laureatus Academic
Nashville, Tennessee.

Grateful acknowledgement is made to the following publishers for permission to reprint from copyrighted material: *Nestle-Aland, Novum Testamentum Graece, 28th Revised Edition,* edited by Barbara and Kurt Aland, Johannes Karavidopoulos, Carlo M. Martini, and Bruce M. Metzger in cooperation with the Institute for New Testament Textual Research, Münster/Westphalia, © 2012 Deutsche Bibelgesellschaft, Stuttgart. Used by permission.; The ESV® Bible (The Holy Bible, English Standard Version®), © 2001 by Crossway, a publishing ministry of Good News Publishers.

First edition.

An original publication of Laureatus Academic. Nashville, TN. 2026.

ISBN: 979-8-9951598-0-3

Library of Congress Catalog Card Number: 2026905914

Front and Rear Cover Art: “Shadrach, Meshach and Abednego in the Furnace” by Gustave Doré (1832–1883). Public Domain.

Table of Contents

PART I: INTRODUCING THE APOCALYPSE OF JOHN

PART II: INTRODUCING THE TRIBULATION

Figures		
Fig.	**Content**	**Page #**
1.1	Witness Evidence for Domitianic and Neronic Dating	27
1.2	Old Testament Descriptors of God Applied to Christ in Revelation	41
2.1	Lundian Examples of Parallelism	56
2.2	The Chiastic Recapitulative Approach to Revelation	64
2.3	Manuscripts Consulted by Erasmus	65
2.4	Erasmian Departures from the Codex Reuchlini	69-70
2.5	King James Diversion from the *Textus Receptus*	72
2.6	Instances of the Textus Receptus Omitting/Deleting the Text	73
2.7	Instances of the Textus Receptus Taking Minority Positions	74-75
2.8	Noteworthy Historic Premillennialists Since the Reformation	92-94
4.1	Excurses: "Keys"	132-133
4.2	Proposed Translation of Rev. 1:19	135
5.1	Excurses: "Clean Garments"	216-217

PREFACE

One question publishers typically ask when an author proposes a book for publication is, "What qualifies you to write this book?" It is my opinion that such a question serving as a prerequisite to the publication of a commentary on Revelation would prove prohibitive to one ever being published. Who could possibly be qualified to write such a book? An expert in *Koine* Greek? Perhaps, but indeed, the Greek grammar is rather vulgar and a knowledge of grammatical mechanics can hardly assist one in interpreting the book. An expert in Hermeneutics? Perhaps, but truly, how can one expect to interpret the book based on any established rules when there are no other Biblical examples of Apocalyptic-Epistolary literature? The same goes for historians (as I clutch my pearls), who despite having a solid grasp on the ins-and-outs of what was originally being referred to will likely have difficulty understanding the applicability of these writings to subsequent generations, let alone our own.

In my humble opinion, there must be a conglomeration of these fields to qualify a person to write about Revelation. One must be familiar with the Greek while also having a firm grasp on hermeneutical approaches; they must have thorough historical knowledge of the era and people involved in John's Revelation, whilst also maintaining the ability to apply these truths to subsequent and ongoing generations. In short, it is my opinion that anyone who is going to explain the Revelation must be someone who believes the Bible, loves the Bible, vigorously studies the Bible, understands the Bible, devotes himself to the proper handling of the Bible, and who has spent years consulting with other Spirit-filled individuals to confirm that his lone view is not a renegade position but an historical, orthodox, Christian understanding. After all, there are no new ideas; just old errors.

With those things said, I pray that God has qualified me for the task undertaken. Having spent the last 20 years of my life in the ministry, preaching, studying, and teaching in regions from Missoula to Accra, Berlin to Nashville, I feel I can only now begin to truly convey what I believe to be the truth of John's Apocalypse.

It must be admitted that even after many years in the ministry and many more years in college and seminary, the greatest learning experience of my life has come in the past decade as the husband of my precious wife, Storm. No one has pushed me to a greater extent than you, my angel. You have always encouraged me, and it is an understatement to say that without you this commentary would not have been finished. Indeed, it would never have begun.

I must also thank those individuals who invested in me for so long. Marty Goforth, whose willingness to take doctrinal positions in the minority if they were Biblically defensible empowered me to look with fresh eyes at the Scriptures myself; Ron Cook, whose reliance on the Scriptures and steadfast commitment to inerrancy and infallibility fortified in me a commitment to these crucial doctrines that has held strong for decades; and Johnny Carr, whose capacity to balance Biblical teaching with loving compassion taught me how to be more than a preacher – but a pastor.

Educationally, I owe special thanks to Harley Howard, whose New Testament Exegesis courses taught me how to eat an elephant – *one bite at a time*. The writings of James (Jim) Hamilton have influenced me greatly, although none have played a larger influence on me than the late-George Eldon Ladd. To this monarch of the field and faith, I give my thanks.

Finally, to my great friend and comrade in the fight, Austin Rouse, whose conviction as a postmillennialist led me to reconsider many of my own assumptions, and whose commitment to the Scriptures reminded me that those who differ from me are equally dedicated to God and His Word as myself – I give eternal thanks.

Hats off to the past; Coats off to the future.
- George Washington Truett

This page intentionally blank

This page intentionally blank.

Part 1:

Introducing the Apocalypse of John

Introduction:

Why Another Revelation Commentary?

After almost 2000 years of interpretation and millions of pages littered with various theories and approaches, why would anyone think it necessary or helpful to have *another* commentary on Revelation? It is not the author's opinion that there are no good commentaries on Revelation for readers to use. That would be a gross misunderstanding. In fact, any reader considering this text would be encouraged to read it alongside historical commentaries from individuals like John Gill, more modern commentaries like that of George E. Ladd, or the most recent commentaries of men like Robert Mounce or Thomas Schreiner. Any one of these individuals would helpfully and thoroughly walk readers through the book with great success.

The intention of this author is not to recreate the wheel. Rather, the author intends to bring readers a commentary which accurately represents the text and at least one orthodox interpretation of it, and which is applicable in ways that other commentaries may not be. This latter effort will hopefully be the distinguishing factor for this commentary when held over against others, as the interpretation given will be influenced by the eclectic approach of the author in such a way that what is written will unavoidably bear in it the direct applications of each thought to the reader.

This is, in a real sense, the original intention of the book of Revelation. John records Jesus as saying in Revelation 1:11 that the book has a broad and sweeping addressal, which shows that the ensuing text was intended to be read and understood not by one single historical church, but by several churches in their direct context and in the surrounding contexts, both geographically and historically. Jesus did not leave it at that, however, as He closes the book in Revelation 22:16 with a reaffirmation of the direct application of what had been written to the church. He reminds John, "I, Jesus, have sent my angel to testify to you about these things *for the churches*." The Revelation of John is intended for the Church. God gave us the Revelation to be understood, not confusing. He gave us this book for our edification in application, not for us to pour over in studies without ever making real changes to our lives.

So, why another commentary on Revelation? In one sense, it is because there are some interpretive distinctives that the present author believes need to be put to paper for future generations to consider. But more importantly, it is because there seems to be a general disconnect between Christians and Revelation regarding application. Many past generations fell under the influence that the bulk of Revelation did not matter for the church since the church would not be here past chapter 3. More recent doctrinal movements have shifted Christians towards seeing much of Revelation as being fulfilled in AD 70. Many of the Reformers and pre-modern theologians saw Revelation as being fulfilled in their past, even if not in AD 70. But the present author thinks it crucial for Christians of this generation and those to follow to accept that the Revelation, while prophetic as well as historical (or epistolary), has a direct application and use for Christians of every generation. That, of course, includes John's generation which saw the fall of Jerusalem, but it also includes the final generation before Christ's return, and every generation between them. Reader, the Revelation of St. John matters for your life and it should be understood and responded to. It is my prayer that this commentary will be instructive on how to do that.

Chapter 1:
Canonicity

There is perhaps no more intriguing book in the Bible than the Revelation of St. John. For many, the symbolism is thought-provoking; for others, the apocalypticism strokes that part of them that loves a conspiracy theory; for still others, the fact that there are so many differing and widespread interpretations of the book makes it seemingly subject to their own fancies in ways that other books are not. It should be fascinating, then, to know that there is great speculation surrounding the book's place in the canon of Scripture. Therefore, before looking into the Revelation itself, it is appropriate to first devote time to establishing the right of the text to be found within the Bible, in order for the reader to understand *why* this book is worth studying.

The intrigue surrounding the book of Revelation is not new. In fact, as long as the book has existed there seems to have been a great deal of interest and speculation surrounding it. There is some evidence to support the argument that in the first and second centuries the book was less popular than some other New Testament books in no small part because of its seeming ambiguity.[1] Elaine Pagels, the current Harrington Spear Paine Professor of Religion at Princeton University, was recently quoted speaking about the relative lack of consensus on the book, saying that Revelation was "squeezed into the canon in the fourth century" having "barely made it into the 27-book lineup."[2] One has to wonder, though, is this a correct reflection on the situation that saw Revelation recognized as Holy Scripture fit to be in the canon? And if it is true that this book was barely squeezed in, is the intrigue surrounding it unwarranted?

In truth, it is not obvious that there was any more reason to reject the canonicity of the book of Revelation than there was to reject any other New Testament book – but the fact remains that many today do not know the standards by which a text was graded in order to be admitted or omitted from the canon. In a recent book on the history of the New Testament, Daniel Becerra forwards what he calls the "three criteria by which

---

[1] Daniel Becerra, "The Canonization of the New Testament" in *New Testament History, Culture, and Society*, Lincoln Blumell, ed., 773.

[2] Quoted in Corydon Ireland, "Revelations on Revelation" *The Harvard Gazette* (7 December 2009).

canonicity was determined: apostolicity, orthodoxy, and widespread use."[3] This last point, "widespread use" will herein be dubbed "Catholicity" as the word implies usage across the whole of the Christian church. The next several pages will be devoted to examining whether or not the book of Revelation met the Becerraean standards of canonization put forward.

A. Apostolicity

It is with great disappointment but little surprise that the modern situation finds many scholars giving way to the speculative theory that the book of Revelation was not written by the Apostle John. Readers will shockingly find a great deal of leeway given to this theory in discussions of the author even in very conservative commentaries such as that produced by Thomas Schreiner, who maintains only the certainty that the author was named John, saying, "he doesn't introduce himself as an apostle, and it may be another John."[4]

Modern academic credibility may dictate an openness to this idea, as Schreiner is far from alone with many other well-respected conservative scholars such as Robert Mounce and G.K. Beale not only entertaining this theory, but allowing the debate over the issue to force them into a position of unclarity and even apathy about the topic.[5] Beale goes so far as to say, "The issue [authorship] is not important to settle since it does not affect the message of the book."[6] One would be wise to argue the inverse. For example, one may look no further than Revelation 1:17 when the author says that upon seeing Christ in His glorified state, he "fell at his feet as though dead." If the author is the Apostle John, does this not say something of the unbearable glory of Christ, that even the disciple who leaned on His chest at the Last Supper, the man known as the "beloved disciple," would be so struck by His glory that he would fall at Christ' feet as dead?

It seems that the author's identity *does* impact the message of the book. But even if it did not, is this truly to be believed as the only thing that is lost if the Apostle John did not author the book? Certainly not. The first criteria put forward for canonization is apostolicity, which generally means that the book was either penned by an Apostle or

---

[3] Becerra, "The Canonization," 780.

[4] Thomas Schreiner, *Revelation* BECNT, 95.

[5] Robert H. Mounce, *The Book of Revelation* NICNT, 8.

[6] G.K. Beale, *The Book of Revelation* NIGTC, 35.

was penned under the oversight of an Apostle.[7] If the Apostle John did not author the book of Revelation, question marks suddenly appear surrounding Revelation's deservedness to be within the canon. Surely such an issue could never be labelled as "not important."

A.1 *Speculative Rejection*

While there has never been any compelling challenge to the authorship of the Apostle John, it is true that there have been many who have doubted his authoring Revelation from very early on in the Christian tradition.[8] Perhaps the first example of a Christian doubting or denying the apostolicity of the book of Revelation is found in Eusebius' *Historia Ecclesiastica* (AD 313) which reports Dionysius of Alexandria's (d. 265) denial of Johannine authorship.[9] Modern scholars have argued that Dionysius (and others like him) denied the apostolicity of the book "because of its difficulty and supposed millenarianism."[10] Whatever the cause, it is undeniable that speculation began early on, with some postulating that the author of the Revelation was John Mark who travelled with Paul and Barnabas, while others speculated that there was some otherwise unknown figure known as "Elder John" who has since been lost to history.[11]

It should be emphasized from the outset that the first individuals to reject the Apostolic authorship of Revelation did not do so because of some evidence they had, but because they disdained that which was taught in the book itself. There was never an appeal made to any evidence for another author.[12] When other authors have been proposed, their candidacy was based purely off of speculation, as there is no early testimony for any other author than the Apostle John.[13] There is simply no historical argument to be made for denying the apostolicity of the book of Revelation, and those

[7] Luke, for example, was not an Apostle, but his books (the Gospel of Luke and the Acts of the Apostles) are historically recognized as being overseen by Apostles such as Paul, Peter, or John.
[8] Becerra, "The Canonization," 780.
[9] Eusebius, *Historia Ecclesiastica*, 7:25-26. For the date of Eusebius' *Historia Ecclesiastica*, see Andrew Louth's "The Date of Eusebius' *Historia Ecclesiastica*" in *Journal of Theological Studies* 41:1 (1990): 111-123.
[10] Stephen S. Smalley, *Thunder and Love*, 38.
[11] Eusebius, *Hist Eccl.*, 7:25:15, 3:39:4.
[12] Eusebius seems to quote Papias, but in reality, all he does is say that Papias mentioned another John in Asia Minor in the era and presupposes based on his own evident desire for the Apostle to not be the author of Revelation that this must certainly be the John who penned the book.
[13] Isbon Beckwith, *The Apocalypse of John*, 350.

who do reject its apostolicity blatantly ignore the whole of the external testimony, as well as a great deal of significant internal testimony regarding the author's identity.[14]

A.2 *External Testimony*

The early testimony regarding the Apostle John's authorship of Revelation is readily admitted by many. George Ladd, in his commentary on Revelation, notes without argument that "the early church generally accepted [the author] as the apostle of Jesus Christ, the author of the Fourth Gospel."[15] Despite Ladd's assumption of this as a matter of historical fact, there are many in recent years who have not been convinced that this was the case, and are certainly not ready to admit that such would merit believing in the apostolicity of the book anyway.

Thus, let it first be argued that the early church *did* recognize the book as having been written by the Apostle John – the same Apostle who wrote the fourth Gospel and the three epistles. Justin Martyr, for example, writes in his *Dialogue with Trypho* (AD 160),

> There was a certain man with us, whose name was John, one of the apostles of Christ, who prophesied, by a revelation that was made to him, that those who believed in our Christ would dwell a thousand years in Jerusalem.[16]

It can scarcely be denied that this is a reference to Revelation 20, and Justin Martyr makes perfectly clear that the author of that text is "John, one of the apostles of Christ." This alone ought to be sufficient proof that other speculative identities proposed, such as John Mark or some random non-apostolic figure known only as "Elder John," are unlikely.

Irenaeus echoes Justin Martyr's affirmation of the Revelation's apostolicity in his *Against Heresies* (AD 180), saying, "John also, the Lord's disciple, when beholding the sacerdotal and glorious advent of His kingdom, says in the Apocalypse…"[17] These men were not alone, nor were they among a small group of early advocates for apostolic authorship. Hippolytus explicitly identifies the same John as being the author of both the

---

[14] Smalley provides a very helpful overview of the arguments on both sides, ultimately concluding that "there is no significant reason to question the relatively early ascription of the Apocalypse to John the Apostle." Smalley, *Thunder and Love*, 39.

[15] George E. Ladd, *A Commentary on Revelation*, 7.

[16] Justin Martyr, *Dialogue With Trypho*, 81:4. For dating (and other information on the *Dialogue*), see Craig Allert's *Revelation, Truth, Canon and Interpretation*.

[17] Irenaeus, *Against Heresies*, 4:20:11.

Revelation and the Fourth Gospel in his late-second century *Commentary on Daniel*.[18] Scholars have also defended the apostolicity of Revelation by appealing to Cyril of Alexandria (d. 444), Basil of Caesarea (d. 379), Athanasius (d. 373), Tertullian (b. 160), Clement of Alexandria (b. 150), and perhaps most consequentially among these, Origen (b. 185).[19]

Origen is of particular interest because he discipled Dionysius, the first known denier of the apostolicity of Revelation. Contrary to his student, Origen explicitly affirms that it was the Apostle John who wrote the Revelation, saying in his *Commentary on the Gospel of John*, "John, who left one Gospel… wrote also the Apocalypse." In this same context, Origen notes that there are some who doubt the legitimacy of the second and third epistles attributed to John, but he notes no such speculation regarding the apostolicity of Revelation.[20] Origen might laugh if he knew of modern speculations in which the legitimacy of the Johannine Epistles is accepted and indeed used as ammunition for denying the apostolicity of the Revelation.[21] Why or how Dionysius came to reject the apostolicity of Revelation, given his mentor's affirmation of it and extensive expertise given his commentaries on New Testament books, remains a mystery. Whatever catalyzed his rejection is unknown, but he did reject it, and Eusebius seems to have fallen in with him leading down a line of ungrounded speculations on other proposed authors.[22]

It can also be argued persuasively that the modern church, despite its great advancements in ability, wealth of ancient literature, and access to archaeological information has found nothing to lead to the conclusion that anyone other than the Apostle John wrote the book of Revelation. Little has changed regarding the external testimony on Revelation which caused several scholars of the last century to come down hard on this issue. Isbon Beckwith writes in his lengthy study of Revelation, "So much external testimony to the personality of the author, traceable back to almost contemporaneous sources, is found in the case of almost no other book of the New Testament."[23] B.W. Bacon echoes this sentiment, in his broader text on the whole New Testament, saying, "There is no book in the entire New Testament whose external

[18] Hippolytus, *Commentary on Daniel*, 4:24:5 (cf. 4:23:6).
[19] Smalley, *Thunder and Love*, 36-37.
[20] Origen, *Commentary on the Gospel of John*, 5:3.
[21] Beale, *Revelation*, 35.
[22] Smalley, *Thunder and Love*, 38.
[23] Beckwith, *Apocalypse*, 351.

attestation can compare with that of Revelation in nearness, clearness, definiteness, and positiveness of statement."[24]

To make brief mention of new developments in the field, everything that has changed has only further solidified the position for apostolic authorship, as Robert Mounce details the 1945 discovery of the *Apocryphon of John* which attributes the Revelation to "John, the brother of James, these who are the sons of Zebedee."[25] Charles Hill, in his 2004 book *The Johannine Corpus in the Early Church* argues that the widespread acceptance of the Apostle John as the author of Revelation in the second century is a major contributor to the book's popularity and circulation.[26] This view is affirmed and emphasized by experts like Larry Hurtado when examining the most recent discoveries of early manuscripts and fragments.[27] It seems that the more Biblical evidence is found, the more evidence there is for the Johannine (and therefore apostolic) authorship of Revelation.

A.3 *Internal Testimony*

If the external evidence remains relatively definitive, what arguments are made in the modern age for denying the apostolicity of the Revelation? Being absent of essentially any compelling external evidence against the apostolicity of the book, the arguments turn to internal evidence. One argument is the difference in style between the Revelation and other Johannine literature. Another argument is that the language used differs greatly from that of the other Johannine literature. The final argument, which is rarely used in a *deductive* sense but regularly used in an *inductive* sense, involves the identification of the author within the text itself.

This first argument, that the style differs, is a very difficult argument to make persuasively. First of all, it is not obvious that the styles are greatly different. S.S. Smalley states outright that "the supposed differences between the Apocalypse and the Fourth Gospel, at least, are not after all so immense."[28] And yet, if one does agree that there are overwhelming stylistic differences between the Revelation and the other Johannine literature, one would have to admit that the very nature of the book of Revelation when compared to the other Johannine literature, being the Gospel and three epistles,

---

[24] B.W. Bacon, *The Making of the New Testament*, 190.
[25] Mounce, *Revelation*, 11.
[26] Charles E. Hill, *The Johannine Corpus in the Early Church*, 469-470.
[27] Larry W. Hurtado, *The Earliest Christian Artifacts*, 32.
[28] Smalley, *Thunder and Love*, 20.

obviously requires a different style of writing. Even G.K. Beale, who entertains the arguments against apostolicity, concludes definitively,

> Differences in writing style... from the Johannine Gospel and Epistles cannot be determinative for nonapostolic authorship because such variation would be expected in a writing of a different (apocalyptic-prophetic) genre. Furthermore, differences of occasion and purpose in writing can significantly affect writing style.[29]

Thus, it seems obvious to an almost undeniable extent that a change in style between books of different genres, occasions, and purposes would be expected, and would in no way imply a change in author. It would be absurd for someone in the modern day to reject that C.S. Lewis wrote *Mere Christianity* because they also read the *Chronicles of Narnia*, concluding that such a difference in style could not possibly have been penned by the same author.

The second argument, while no more compelling, at least has a bit more substance and historical precedent behind it. Eusebius (in line with Dionysius) argued that the presence of some "forms" and "expressions" in Revelation which are altogether absent from other Johannine literature, especially grammatical preferences, led him to "judge... that it is not [the Apostle John's]."[30] This argument was not compelling to the ancient Greek readers, and it is not any more compelling today. Vern Poythress, for example, masterfully and with unparalleled brevity combats this argument in an article he published in the *Westminster Theological Journal*.[31] Poythress approaches the Revelation, noting that the first three chapters of Revelation are the most proper to compare with the other Johannine literature, since they bear close similarity to epistolary literature rather than the standard apocalyptic literature typical to the Revelation. After examining this passage in comparison to John's Gospel and epistles, Poythress concludes, "my judgment at this time is that the pattern tends strongly to confirm unity of authorship."[32] Other historical authors have pointed out that the choice of certain terms and phrases by the author indicates that he was likely a Hebrew-speaking Palestinian Jew

---

[29] Beale, *The Book of Revelation*, 34-35.

[30] Eusebius, *Hist. Eccl.*, 7:25:7-8.

[31] Vern S. Poythress, "Johannine Authorship and the Use of Intersentence Conjunctions in the Book of Revelation," *Westminster Theological Journal* 47 (1985): 329-336.

[32] Poythress, "Johannine Authorship," 332.

who was a native of Galilee.[33] It should come as no surprise, then, that in each of the Synoptic Gospels, the Apostle John is introduced as a fisherman from Galilee, and the fourth Gospel notes that the Apostle John was "known to the high priest" indicating that he was a Hebrew-speaking, Palestinian Jew.[34]

Another line of thought in this second argument is the use or presence of "solecisms," or a somewhat mistaken use of standard grammar. Eusebius mentions the use of solecisms in Revelation as an implication of a separate author.[35] Oddly enough, more recent scholarship has concluded that the inclusion of solecisms is, instead, evidence *for* apostolic authorship.[36] R.H. Charles argues that one cannot reasonably contend that the solecisms were placed in the text accidentally or unknowingly, as the author also pens "law and order underlying the seeming grammatical lawlessness of the seer" which could not possibly be written by someone of such little intellect as to miss basic grammatical rules.[37] Instead, the author is shown by Charles to be "a great spiritual genius... of profound insight and the widest sympathies" and "intimate acquaintance with the Hebrew text of the OT." He is said to have "clearly thought in Hebrew and translated idioms literally into Greek" which came out as "unlike any Greek that was ever penned by mortal man." Charles claims that rather than an author who is ignorant of the grammatical idiosyncrasies he commits, the author of Revelation "proceeds according to certain rules of the author's own devising."[38] More recently, G.K. Beale has reflected on such solecisms in much the same way, claiming that "commentators generally acknowledge that the 'incorrect' grammar is intentional" and is often maintained "in order to highlight it as an allusion" to Old Testament (i.e., Hebrew as Charles termed it) references.[39]

The final argument against apostolicity follows the line of thought that since the author of Revelation never identifies himself as the Apostle John, therefore, it is unlikely (at least) that the Apostle John is the author. Eusebius, again, seems to have first come upon this line of thinking, as he writes "that he who wrote these things was called John

---

[33] R.H. Charles, *A Critical and Exegetical Commentary on the Revelation of St. John* I, xliv.
[34] Matthew 4:18-22; Mark 1:16-20; Luke 5:1-11; John 18:15.
[35] Eusebius, *Hist. Eccl.*, 7:25:25-26.
[36] Andrea J. Kostenberger, L. Scott Kellum, Charles L. Quarles, *The Cradle, The Cross, and the Crown* 2, 930. In the corresponding footnote (n.16), the authors write that "most (if not all) of these solecisms are intentional."
[37] Charles, *A Critical and Exegetical Commentary*, xl.
[38] Ibid., xliv.
[39] Beale, *Revelation*, 188. Beale identifies these as intentional "Hebraisms" and gives the examples of 1:5; 2:20; 3:12; and 9:14.

must be believed, as he says it; but who he was does not appear."[40] Indeed, the author of Revelation does identify himself four separate times within the text as "John" (1:1; 1:4; 1:9; 22:8). Those giving credence to the non-apostolic authorship theory are quick to make note of the fact that John, whoever he was, does not call himself an apostle, nor does he present himself as particularly esteemed.[41]

However, this point is (just as was the case with the last argument) as much a *proof* of the Apostle John's authorship as it is a disproof. Many have made the point that evidently, this John who wrote the Revelation did not think it necessary to identify himself by any other title than "John" implying that the readers would certainly not misidentify who wrote the book. The author's identity was expected to be so clear as to require no further explanation. If a 19th Century British preacher told his church that he had received a letter from "Brother Spurgeon," one would scarcely have to ask, "which Brother Spurgeon?" What a ridiculous question that would be! Of what other Spurgeon would he possibly be speaking than Charles? If an American preacher in the 20th Century announced proudly to his church that he had received a letter from "Dr. Graham" commending their church, what fool in the crowd would say, "Which Dr. Graham?" Of course, he would be speaking of Billy Graham! Of equal absurdity would be a 1st Century Christian (specifically those in Asia Minor where he was particularly well-known) getting a letter from "John" claiming to have received a revelation from Jesus Christ, asking, "which John?"[42] One can almost picture the incredulity of those around, turning to look at this simpleton, saying with widened eyes, "Who do you think? Who do you think would send all the churches of Asia Minor a letter like this? Who do you think would be chosen to receive a revelation from our Lord? Who else but the beloved disciple? Who else but the Apostle John? What a ridiculous question!" The clear familiarity of the author with Asia Minor, as well as his knowledge of the Hebrew Old Testament and Jewish apocalyptic literature all points readers to the clear conclusion that the author was the Apostle John.[43]

The identification of the Apostle as the author by every early figure prior to Dionysius shows that there was no confusion on the author on the basis of his not referring to himself as "the Apostle," and yet the absence of this identifier *does* serve as a

---

[40] Eusebius, *Hist. Eccl.*, 7:25:12.

[41] Mounce, *The Book of Revelation*, 8.

[42] Kostenberger, Kellum, Quarles, *The Cradle*, 929.

[43] Smalley, *Thunder and Love*, 39.

proof of the legitimacy of the book. Beale is keen to point out that "if an unknown author were attempting to identify himself with a well-known Christian figure like the apostle John, he would probably call himself not just 'John' but 'John the apostle.' This the author does not do."[44]

In conclusion, there is simply no good argument to be made that the author of Revelation is anyone other than the Apostle John, the beloved disciple and author of the fourth Gospel and three epistles. In fact, every argument that can be raised against apostolic authorship, whether early external, modern external, or internal, is either on its face less likely than the alternative, or is equally likely to be used as an *affirmative proof* of the book's apostolicity. It would do modern scholars and theologians a lot of good if they would stop treating this issue as if it were unimportant, or entertaining and presenting as plausible theories that are patently false and dangerous to the case of the book's canonicity.

B. Catholicity

It is inarguable that the book of Revelation has been subject to neglect throughout church history. Sometimes, this neglect came in an implicit way, such as the case with John Calvin who wrote commentaries on almost every book of the Bible except Revelation.[45] Other times were more explicit, as in the case of Martin Luther who identified the book as non-canonical.[46] Becerra posits that the book of Revelation was slow to be accepted in the early Eastern church because of "disputes over the apostolic origins of the book and disagreements regarding whether the events therein should be understood literally or symbolically," but writes that it ultimately was accepted because of its widespread usage in the Western church.[47] Mounce tempers this claim by saying the Eastern church did not shirk at the book until the mid-third century when Dionysius

---

[44] Beale, *The Book of Revelation*, 34.

[45] T.H.L. Parker, *Calvin's New Testament Commentaries* 2, 116-119. Parker notes that Calvin's omission of Revelation "is a surprising omission" and ultimately concludes that "whatever his reasons, the fact remains that Calvin had the opportunity to complete his New Testament commentaries with 1 and 2 John and Revelation when he came to the end of the epistles, but preferred to ignore them and go on to the historical books and the Old Testament. To that extent, therefore, we may say that he was imposing a practical canon on the New Testament."

[46] Bruce M. Metzger, *The Canon of the New Testament*, 244-245. In an edition of the Bible following Luther's tradition, the New Testament was divided into three categories: "Gospel and Acts, Epistles and Holy Apostles, and Apocryphal New Testament." Revelation was included in this final category.

[47] Becerra, "The Canonization," 776, 781. This concept is corroborated by F.F. Bruce, "The Earliest Latin Commentary on the Apocalypse," *The Evangelical Quarterly* 10 (1938), 352.

began disputing the apostolic authorship of the text. Prior to that, he argues, "it cannot be disputed that the Apocalypse was widely accepted."[48] Michael Kruger notes that "Revelation's early reception was outstanding" saying "we have evidence for an early, widespread, and consistent reception of Revelation."[49]

So, regardless of how the book has been *treated* by Christians who already had access to it, the question remains in the discussion of its fitness for canonization whether it was widely distributed, read, and believed within the early church. In order to fully answer this question, though, one first has to answer the question of when the book was written. Popularity, recognition, and general circulation cannot rightly be judged unless one has a grasp of how long the book had been available.

Excursus: Date of Revelation

It is an unfortunate truth, rarely admitted but easily recognized, that modern disputes over when the book of Revelation was penned have more to do with one's eschatological position than any evidence surrounding the matter. There are essentially two camps, those advocating for an "early" (or sometimes "Neronian") date figure its authorship at some time around A.D. 64-68. Those advocating for a "late" (or sometimes "Domitianic") date figure its authorship at some time around AD 94-96. These secondary titles are derived from the names of the Roman Emperors ruling at the proposed time of authorship, Nero (A.D. 54-68) or Domitian (A.D. 81-96).

Thomas Ice writes scathingly of those advocating an early date who, in his perspective, are needlessly causing this dispute, saying,

> Since a preterist interpretation of Revelation requires an early date of the final book in the Bible, preterists go to great lengths in their attempts to make their view appear viable… It appears the major reason that preterists believe in an early date for Revelation is that their system requires it. In this instance, the saying is true that necessity is the mother of invention.[50]

Ice is correct. The preterist view holds as a central tenet that many (if not all) of the prophecies in the Bible came to fulfillment by or through the destruction of Jerusalem in

---

[48] Mounce, *Revelation*, 12.

[49] Michael J. Kruger, "The Book of Revelation: How Difficult Was Its Journey into the Canon?" *Canon Fodder* (12 February 2014). Accessed 28 March 2023 via michaeljkruger.com.

[50] Thomas D. Ice, "The Date of the Book of Revelation," *Article Archives* (May 2009), 79.

A.D. 70.[51] Naturally, if the book of Revelation was written after A.D. 70, then (as a prophetic book) the system is immediately undermined if not completely disproven.[52] Robert Thomas comes to precisely the same conclusion – that the advocates of what is known as an early date of the book of Revelation do so because of a desire to maintain the plausibility of their own systems of interpretation.[53]

Ken Gentry, a well-known preterist, in a review of a preterist commentary on Revelation says with some level of expectancy, "The author presents an evangelical preterist approach and quite naturally adopts an early date of composition: A.D. 65-66." He goes on to note that this issue is "essential to grasping the specific message of Revelation."[54] The inverse was also found to be true, as in a review of Gentry's book *Before Jerusalem Fell*, Grover Gunn wrote, "This book's dating dramatically affects its interpretation."[55] Notably, in referencing other scholars who agree with Gentry's dating of Revelation, Gunn lists Greg Bahnsen, Marcellus Kik, Jay Adams, and B.B. Warfield – all of whom he evidently assumed were in agreement because they were either preterists or postmillennialists.[56] However, Gunn must not have been aware that although B.B. Warfield was a postmillennialist, he was not an early date advocate. Warfield wrote, "The Canon of the New Testament was completed when the last authoritative book was given to any church by the apostles, and that was when John wrote the apocalypse, about A.D. 98."[57]

---

[51] It should be stated that Full-Preterists (those believing that all prophecies, including the return of Christ, came to pass before the end of the generation living in Christ's era) are heretics and have departed the orthodox Christian faith, while Partial-Preterists hold to nothing that necessarily excludes them from orthodoxy. However, it is maintained that while there are certainly application points in the book which seem most directly pertinent for John's generation (as the Preterist is keen to highlight), there are also application points for every generation throughout the inter-advent age (historicism, futurism, idealism, *eclecticism*). The point here is that Preterism is the only position which requires a specific date to operate, and when an interpretation begins to dictate upon the text, the interpretation must be doubted.

[52] Howard Winters, *Commentary on Revelation*, 15-16. Winters comments definitively, "If the late date is correct, the whole approach that assigns Revelation as a prophecy fulfilled in the destruction of Jerusalem is false and must be totally rejected." Winters rejects the early date theory himself, saying that it is "built upon a sandy foundation."

[53] Robert L. Thomas, "Theonomy and the Dating of Revelation," *The Masters Seminary Journal* (Fall 1994), 185.

[54] Kenneth L. Gentry, "Book Review: The Avenging of the Apostles: A Commentary on Revelation by Arthur M. Ogden," *The Counsel of Chalcedon* (April 1995), 11.

[55] Grover Gunn, "Book Review: Before Jerusalem Fell: Dating the Book of Revelation by Ken Gentry," *The Counsel of Chalcedon* (March 1990), 22.

[56] Ibid.

[57] B.B. Warfield, "The Formation of the Canon of the New Testament," in *The Inspiration and Authority of the Bible*, 415.

This gaffe proves the point, which is that there is an essential connection between assuming an early date and holding a preterist interpretation of the book of Revelation which does not exist in any other conviction. This single point is devastating, because there is much in partial-preterism which properly identifies referents to symbols and events, but which is also bound to incorrect conclusions because of this unadvisable insistence on an early date that is not historically accurate. To give an example, even Preterists like Keith Mathison recognize that it is a trait of Old Testament prophetic and other apocalyptic literature to reference major events which had recently taken place in order to give illustrations of end-times events.[58] Thus, when Preterists see symbols or allusions that appear to depict Nero (such as the number of the beast), one wishes to agree with them and say, "yes, John is likely referring to that in order to draw pictures in the minds of his readers that they will understand, such that they would be able to recognize the coming antichrist figure who was prefigured by those actions of Nero."

But this sort of approach is not possible to the pure-Preterist (that is, one denying an *eclecticist* approach) because they are unable to hold that Nero was being referred to as an example of something the readers would remember as occurring in the past. They *must* maintain that these things were prophetically predicted as future events, and why? Because of an inexplicable allegiance to the unhistorical claim that Revelation was written in an era prior to the destruction of Jerusalem. The true claims of Preterism can be maintained without such an intellectually degrading position, and it is this author's hope that the Preterists will see that and come alongside the eclecticist in a wholly stronger position which maintains their strengths and adds many more.

It is the opinion of this author that there is nothing irreconcilably dividing these two views, unless the extrapolation of Robert Thomas is correct. Thomas claims that the inclination to maintain this unhistorical position is:

> "... a desire for an undiluted rationale to support Christian social and political involvement. [Ken Gentry and other Preterists are] looking for an escape from the tension between the cultural mandate given to Christians and a realization that the prophecy of Revelation dictates that the culture

[58] Mathison, *From Age to Age*, 652.

will inevitably go downhill despite the best efforts of God's people to reverse the trend.[59]

Regrettably, if it is not the case that they are guided by their desired outcome more than a realistic reckoning with the facts, preterists are doing a very poor job proving that they are not doing that. Indeed, when they defend their position on an early date of Revelation they often readily admit that they are less concerned with the external evidence testifying of the book's date of authorship than they are about the internal evidence taken as supporting their view (based on their own interpretation).[60] In their view, everything written about the timing of Revelation's authorship is to be cast aside if the content of the book implies a contrary dating because the book itself is inspired and the historical testimonies are not. This logic would seem, at its face, to be a straightforward Christian way of thinking, but it is predicated on the fact that one will read the content of the book of Revelation *from the perspective of a preterist*. Any internal evidence antithetical to their perspective is also discredited as somehow relying on external evidence, which is of course, discredited.

Comically, this approach is only taken when it is convenient. For example, Gentry uses as a point of argument in favor of preterism, that "during the greater part of the nineteenth century there was a strong majority of critics in favour [sic] of a date" prior to A.D. 70.[61] He repeats this point no fewer than three separate times in his defense of preterism, bringing its importance as a single point of argument parallel to the level of anything else presented in the book.[62] So, it would appear that to a preterist reader, when the historical narrative rejects the early date of Revelation then the external evidence is not to be valued on par with the internal evidence, but when it affirms the early date, then the value of the external evidence must be emphasized again and again. This is the definition of confirmation bias.

Using one's interpretation of Scripture to deny historically validated facts, and then claiming that anyone refusing to adhere to such an interpretation is valuing uninspired literature over the Word of God is abuse of the Scripture; and yet it is not without repeated historical precedent. Historically minded individuals might recall the days when Christians were expected to check their brains at the door upon entering the

---

[59] Thomas, "Theonomy and the Dating of Revelation," 187-188.
[60] Gunn, "Book Review: Before Jerusalem Fell," 22.
[61] Kenneth Gentry, *Before Jerusalem Fell: Dating the Book of Revelation*, 28.
[62] Ibid., 60, 115, 259, 343, 352 n.66.

church, and as a result, Galileo Galilei encountered ardent opposition when the church of his day interpreted Scripture to teach geocentricism despite Galileo telling them to look through his telescope and see for themselves that the Earth was, in fact, not in the center of the universe. Afraid to lay down their flawed interpretation because of the proud assumption that if their interpretation was wrong then the Bible was wrong, they refused to accept the clear testimony of the evidence before them. Instead, they hid behind the same defense that preterists frequently make: to deny our interpretation of the text is to deny the text.

Perhaps a better analogy in describing how preterists approach Biblical history is found in how Landmarkists in the 19th and 20th centuries approached the study of Baptist history. Leon McBeth reflects on Landmarkists in his *Baptist Heritage*, saying,

> The Landmark view of Baptist history is based upon an assumption, not upon the evidence of historical research. Landmarkers assumed on the basis of doctrine that Baptist churches must have existed since New Testament times, no matter what the evidence may show. Instead of drawing conclusions from the historical data, they looked for historical evidence to support their a priori conclusions.[63]

This statement not only accurately describes Landmarkers in relationship to Baptist history, but it also accurately describes pure-preterists in relationship to Christian history. No matter what the evidence may show, they have begun their examination not with a question but with an assumption. Their doctrine determines what evidence they are allowed to admit as credible, and their conclusions are already determined before their search for an answer ever commences.

Excursus: *External Evidence*

As is standard with most any historical endeavor to establish the date of a document, one will be best served to look seriously at the external evidence. As a historical practice known to most any high school sophomore, primary source materials are to be preferred over secondary sources – meaning the testimony of those sources most contemporaneously close to the document in consideration are to be considered more weightily than those written after lengthy distances of time.

---

[63] H. Leon McBeth, *The Baptist Heritage*, 459.

For generations, Irenaeus was considered the earliest testifier to the date of Revelation, with his *Against Heresies* being written around A.D. 180. However, Hugh Lawlor produced a study of Eusebius' *Ecclesiastical History* which introduced an even earlier possibility in the person of Hegesippus (A.D. 120-190). Through a close examination of Eusebius' *Ecclesiastical History*, he concludes,

> Eusebius drew from Hegesippus the account of Domitian in chapter xvii and the statement of chapter xviii that the Apostle St. John was banished under Domitian to Patmos; and we have extended it by tracing to the same source the further statement in chapter xx that the Apostle returned to Ephesus in the reign of Nerva.[64]

This view was favorably endorsed by John A.T. Robinson in 1976, F.F. Bruce in 1979, Simon Kistemaker in 2001, and most recently by Mark Hitchcock in 2005.[65] Hitchcock expanded Lawlor's argument in his 2005 doctoral dissertation (which was largely a direct refutation of Gentry's *Before Jerusalem Fell*), concluding "in the context there is no other plausible conclusion except that Eusebius is referring to Hegesippus."[66] Thus, the testimony of Revelation being written under the reign of Domitian (i.e. at the earliest in A.D. 81) extends back to the writings of Hegesippus, written sometime between A.D. 175 and 180.[67]

Irenaeus (A.D. 120-202) wrote his *Against Heresies* around the time of this higher threshold, usually believed to have been around A.D. 180.[68] While Hegesippus may have won out by a few years on first testifying to the late date of Revelation's authorship, Irenaeus is by far the most definitive. His oft-quoted comment is worth seeing again,

> We will not, however, incur the risk of pronouncing positively as to the name of Antichrist; for if it were necessary that his name should be

---

[64] Hugh J. Lawlor, *Eusebiana: Essays on the Ecclesiastical History of Eusebius Bishop of Caesarea*, 53.

[65] John A.T. Robinson, *Redating the New Testament* (Philadelphia: Westminster Press, 1976), 223.; F.F. Bruce, *Peter, Stephen, James, and John*, 128.; Simon J. Kistemaker, *Revelation*, 28.

[66] Mark L. Hitchcock, "A Defense of the Domitianic Date of the Book of Revelation" (PhD Dissertation, Dallas Theological Seminary, 2005), 11-16. As a point of emphasis, Gentry's work is also thoroughly debunked in Bryan C. Hodge, *Problems with Preterism*, 213-267.

[67] Timothy Gervais marks A.D. 175 as the earliest plausible date, which is agreed to by Jonathan Bernier. Timothy Gervais, "The Fragments of Hegesippus and 1 Clement: Succession Crisis, Heresy and Apostasy," *Intermountain West Journal of Religious Studies* 8:1 (Fall 2017), 4.; Jonathan Bernier, "From Papias to Hegesippus," *Theoforum* 42:1 (2011), 40. William Telfer places the late date at 180. William Telfer, "Was Hegesippus a Jew?" *Harvard Theological Review* 53:2 (April 1960), 145.

[68] Hitchcock, "A Defense of the Domitianic Date," 19.

> distinctly revealed in this present time, it would have been announced by him who beheld the apocalyptic vision. For that was seen no very long time since, but almost in our day, towards the end of Domitian's reign.[69]

What is missing from the testimony of Hegesippus as reported through Eusebius is entirely provided by his contemporary in Irenaeus. Irenaeus leaves absolutely no doubt or room for equivocation on what document he is referring to or when it was put together. He is without argument referring to John's Apocalypse (Revelation), and states outright that it was not only penned in Domitian's reign, but "towards the end" of it. His testimony on this was so clear, and his affiliation to John so close (based not only on his temporal proximity but his geographical proximity as a fellow inhabitant of Asia Minor) that "no other tradition relating to the date of Revelation developed or gained a following in this part of the world."[70] Ice points out that this is a remarkable fact, given that if the book of Revelation had been written in the time of Nero, "it would have had a 30-year head start to establish itself within the early church tradition."[71]

Clement of Alexandria (A.D. 155-220), writing in the late-second century (or perhaps the very early third century) is also taken as holding to the late date of authorship, noting that the Apostle John "on the tyrant's death, returned to Ephesus from the isle of Patmos…"[72] While Gentry puts recognizable effort into identifying this "tyrant" as Nero, the earliest interpreters of this text positively identified the "tyrant" in question as Domitian.[73] Contemporary scholars have recognized that to identify this "tyrant" as anyone but Domitian departs from any known tradition in the early church.[74]

Another early author is Victorinus whose birth date is unknown, but whose writing dates to the late-third century just prior to his death in 303. His commentary on Revelation remains the earliest complete commentary on Revelation, and the first in Latin.[75] In his commentary, he writes, "When John said these things he was in the island of Patmos, condemned to the labour [sic] of the mines by Caesar Domitian. There,

---

[69] Irenaeus, *Against Heresies*, 5:30:3.

[70] Ice, "The Date of the Book of Revelation," 4.

[71] Ibid.

[72] Clement of Alexandria, *Salvation of the Rich Man*, 42. Accessed via ccel.org.

[73] Eusebius, *Eccl. Hist.*, 3:23:2-19.

[74] D.A. Carson and Douglas Moo, *An Introduction to the New Testament* 2, 708.

[75] Bruce, "The Earliest Latin Commentary, 352.

therefore, he saw the Apocalypse; and when grown old... Domitian being killed, all his judgments were discharged."[76]

One could wax on and on of the various early sources that testify in like manner, including earlier authors such as Tertullian (A.D. 160-220) and Origen (A.D. 185-253) who are noted for their being careful students of the New Testament and especially the Apostle John.[77] Further mention could also be made of later authors such as Eusebius (A.D. 260-340) and Jerome (A.D. 340-419).[78] Jerome is so specific as to even clarify which year in Domitian's reign John wrote the Revelation, citing Justin Martyr and Irenaeus as his most valued sources on the matter.[79] And yet, the argument simply cannot be made any more firm in the mind of those who reject it by external evidence. As previously noted, detractors and advocates of the early date will never be swayed by any amount of external evidence, and indeed they will only be made more and more confident in their position as they believe they are letting "God be true and every man a liar." (Rom. 3:4)

As a closing note on this section regarding the external evidence for a late date, let a brief point simply be made for the utter scarcity of any external evidence for an early date. Advocates for an early date will find absolutely no explicit teaching of their position until that of Epiphanius in the fourth century.[80] And yet, Epiphanius does no good to those seeking an early endorsement of Neronian dating, as Epiphanius twice dates John's banishment to the time of Claudius (A.D. 41-54), the predecessor of Nero.[81] This would not work in the standard preterist schema, as a large part of their internal argument is based directly on Nero himself being described in Revelation. Gentry embarrassingly appeals to pure speculation, suggesting that Epiphanius "may have meant the notorious Nero" which is certainly incorrect, as Apringius of Beja, a contemporary of Epiphanius who drew from his work, also claimed that the Apostle wrote Revelation under Claudius Caesar.[82] In an attempt to gain some credibility for this speculation, Gentry claims that

---

[76] Victorinus, *Commentary on the Apocalypse*, 10:11. Also quoted in Bruce, "The Earliest Latin Commentary," 358.
[77] Smalley, *Thunder and Love*, 37.
[78] The list is not comprehensive. It should also be noted that the Muratorian Canon (A.D. 170), Dio Cassius, Sulpicius Severus (A.D. 400), Primasius (A.D. 540), and Andreas (A.D. 600) all testify to the Domitianic Date. Hitchcock, "A Defense of the Domitianic Date," 49-66.
[79] Jerome, *De Viris Illustribus*, 9.
[80] Smalley, *Thunder and Love*, 42.
[81] Johannes van Oort and Einar Thomassen, eds., *The Panarion of Epiphanius of Salamis* 2, 37, 66. In Epiphanius' original *Against Heresies*, these references were found in 51:12:2 and 51:33:9, respectively.
[82] Gentry, *Before Jerusalem Fell*, 104.; William Weinrich, ed., *Latin Commentaries on Revelation*, xxix, 26.

this view is also endorsed by Robert Mounce in his commentary on Revelation, but Mounce does not endorse such a view. Instead, he maintains that Epiphanius meant Claudius, and notes that some have argued that it represents Nero.[83] An admission of the existence of an argument is certainly not an endorsement, nor even a recognition of plausibility. It is very unfortunate (for early-date advocates) that this early source does not fit with their framework, as the next earliest sources affirming anything like their contention come in the form of the Syriac witnesses of the sixth and seventh centuries, perhaps Arethas of the tenth century, and Theophylact of the twelfth century.[84]

Despite this clearly one-sided balance of evidence in favor of a late date, early-date advocates shake this off in stride, never reconsidering their position at all despite their absolute lack of evidence. One particularly unashamed preterist author, J. Christian Wilson, openly dismissed Irenaeus without any evidence for doing so, simply because "Irenaeus does not tell us any source for his information."[85] To be frank, this statement would beggar belief from the academic historical community. Any reputable historian would be elated to find a second century author attesting to events in the late-first century, and to claim (despite all the rest of the affirmative historical testimony) that this source could not be trusted because it does not cite its own sources would be historically sophomoric to a level unfathomable in the field.

Wilson does not stop there, though. He goes on to even more boldly state that there is no reason to "prefer the date of Irenaeus to that in the prefaces of both the Old Syriac versions and also in Theophylact."[86] Again, this assertion would be unthinkable to any trained historian. To fail to recognize why the second century testimony of Irenaeus (affirmed by countless other early figures in the third through sixth centuries) should be trusted over the sixth and seventh century Syriac versions of the New Testament is stunning. This is made even more unbelievable by the fact that the fifth century version of the Syriac Vulgate did not include Revelation at all, showing that whatever assertions the sixth and seventh century versions made about the book were original to those centuries.[87]

---

[83] Mounce, *Revelation*, 15.
[84] Hitchcock, "A Defense of the Domitianic Date," 73.
[85] J. Christian Wilson, "The Problem of the Domitianic Date of Revelation," *New Testament Studies* 39:4 (October 1993), 598.
[86] Ibid.
[87] Gentry, *Before Jerusalem Fell*, 106.

The writings of Theophylact appear in the early twelfth century, more than a millennia after Revelation was written.[88] If there is any scholar alive who does not understand why the testimony of Irenaeus should be trusted over a text written one thousand years later, they should be stripped of their degrees. The willful blindness of preterist authors when it comes to the external evidence for the late date of Revelation's authorship, combined with their complete comfort with generally discarding all contrary evidence to their own belief, should be reason enough to disavow their view in the mind of any self-respecting student of history – which all Christians ought to be. To place the point in one final visual before examining the internal evidence for a late date, examine the chart produced in Hitchcock's dissertation:

Witness Evidence for Domitianic and Neronic Dating	
Witnesses for the Domitianic Date	**Witnesses for the Neronic Date**
Irenaeus (ca. 180)	
Victorinus (ca. 300)	
Eusebius (ca. 300)	
Jerome (ca. 400)	
Sulpicius Severus (ca. 400)	
Primasius (ca. 540)	
Isidore of Seville (ca. 600)	
The Acts of John (ca. 650)	Syriac Witnesses (6th and 7th centuries)
Orosius (ca. 600)	
Andreas (ca. 600)	
Venerable Bede (ca. 700)	
	Arethas (ca. 900)
	Theophylact (d. 1107)

Fig. 1.1[89]

Excursus: *Internal Evidence*

Before embarking on the discussion of the internal evidences for a late date, let it first be stated that internal evidence in this case is not considered of more weight than external evidence for two primary reasons: First, much of the internal evidence argued by

[88] Hitchcock, "A Defense of the Domitianic Date," 74.

[89] Ibid., 73. Notably, Hegesippus could also have been included in this list. For more on this debate, see Jason L. Quintern and H. Michael Shultz Jr., *Revelation in Focus: Two Perspectives on Its Meaning and Timing*.

preterists is part and parcel of the apocalyptic imagery used by the Apostle in what could easily be argued as the most highly symbolic sections of the book. While they will regularly open discussions of Revelation with the necessity to consider it as apocalyptic literature (implying that anything seeming to clearly mean something might not mean what it seems), they will also take other images as absolutely essential to interpret one and only one way in order to establish their precise date of the book.

Second, the nature of the problem seeking to be solved (dating the book) is one of history rather than theology. To be quite blunt, the fact that the preterists must have a certain *historical* answer in order to maintain their *theological* doctrines is their own problem.[90] It is not the responsibility of the rest of the academic community to shift the way in which research is performed in order to accommodate the preconceived outcome of those who may indeed be wrong from the outset. A difference of thirty years is very difficult to deduce from the internal details of any document. Imagine attempting to date Victor Hugo's *Les Miserables* based on internal evidence. One might deduce that it was a primary account written during the 1832 June Rebellion which it depicts. However, in reality, it was penned in 1862. Robert Mounce, detailing the comparative value of internal and external evidence when considering apostolic authorship, greatly disagrees with the general preterist mindset, saying, "the unusually strong and early external evidence supporting apostolic authorship should cause us to hesitate before accepting a conclusion based on subjective appraisal of internal considerations."[91] His conclusion on how to determine the author of the text is doubly true for determining its date. Unusually strong and early external evidence supporting a late date of authorship should at the very least cause us to hesitate before accepting the conclusions of subjective theories produced on a small number of internal considerations.

Despite the questionability of the internal evidence when weighed against the external, the arguments made by preterists as proof of an early date are still very brief. There are usually only two points of argument in the entire book of Revelation.[92] Steve Gregg courteously presents three points of argument, noting the presence of the Temple in chapter 11, the identity of the sixth king in chapter 17, and the number of the beast in

---

[90] One may argue that the position taken in this text is predicated on the inverse conclusion, but that is incorrect. J. Barton Payne comes to the same understanding of Revelation as that endorsed herein while also holding to the Neronic date. Payne, *Encyclopedia of Biblical Prophecy*, 592.
[91] Mounce, *Revelation*, 15.
[92] Thomas, "Theonomy," 198.

chapter 13.[93] The point has already been made that these passages are (not coincidentally) found in some of the most loftily symbolic passages in the entire book, and it is therefore very difficult to present a conclusive or even compelling case against an inherently subjective argument.[94] Thus, rather than refuting the early-date arguments by delving into a pool of subjective interpretations, a few points of internal evidence will be made for a late-date and each of these points will be taken from less symbolic passages within Revelation. Surely, if the internal evidence for a late date is even equal to the evidence for an early date, then the overwhelming external evidence for a late date will leave readers with no choice but to admit the greater argument for the late date.

First, consider the reference to the martyrdom of Antipas in Revelation 2:13. In speaking to the church at Pergamum, Christ commends them for holding fast to His name and not denying the faith "even in the days of Antipas my faithful witness, who was killed among you, where Satan dwells." Paul Duff (in line with typical early-date advocates) argues that Antipas was martyred in 68 A.D. and that the language used implies that the martyrdom of Antipas is something that occurred in the distant past.[95] Absent from the historical record is *any* indication of this being true. In fact, Steven Friesen presents a compelling argument for precisely the opposite conclusion based on an examination of the language and surrounding context.[96] This goes to show that no matter what the situation, judging dates based on internal evidence is likely to cause more questions than it answers. Much to the chagrin of the early-date advocates, the inquirer is forced to turn to external evidence to evaluate the internal evidence.

Tertullian mentions Antipas, but says nothing of the time of his martyrdom.[97] It is not until the sixth century that authors began speaking of his martyrdom in any depth. And yet, *every single account* of the martyrdom of Antipas that references a date, records it distinctly as being in the time of Domitian. Andreas of Caesarea (A.D. 563-614) claims to

[93] Steve Gregg, *Revelation: Four Views*, 27-28. These three points are argued by Gentry in *Before Jerusalem Fell*.

[94] Werner G. Kummel, *Introduction to the New Testament*, trans. Howard C. Kee, 469. Kummel writes of this point, saying, "The secret number 666 cannot be introduced for dating purposes, since its solution is completely uncertain, and with good grounds several imperial names could be proposed." He also points out that the sixth king in Rev. 17 could easily be identified as Domitian, and provides several other compelling arguments against the early date (pp. 466-469).

[95] Paul B. Duff, *Who Rides the Beast?*, 38-39.

[96] Steven J. Friesen, "Satan's Throne, Imperial Cults and the Social Settings of Revelation," *Journal for the Study of the New Testament* 27:3 (2005), 365, n.42.

[97] Tertullian, *Adversus Gnosticos Scorpiace*, XII.

have read the account of Antipas' martyrdom, implying that some record or tradition had been handed down by his time.[98] By the ninth century, Symeon the Metaphrastes (a title meaning "translator" which was granted him for his invaluable work translating the many *Lives of the Saints* falling into degradation in his time) reports the story of Antipas' martyrdom. W. Robertson Nicoll, reporting what Symeon handed down, writes in his 1910 *Expositor's Greek Testament* that Antipas "was an old, intrepid bishop of Pergamos whose prestige drew upon him the honour of being burned to death in a brazen bull during Domitian's reign."[99] No fewer than three historical sources were found testifying to the fact that Antipas was martyred during the reign of Domitian before the end of the twentieth century.[100]

Furthermore, one may reflect on the date of the authorship of this passage in the verbiage used. It could be compellingly argued that the Greek word μάρτυς (*martys*) is only used to refer to martyrs in the New Testament in the book of Revelation. Of the 35 times that it is used, only one usage outside of Revelation could plausibly be taken as referring to martyrs as the word is now intended (Hebrews 12:1) and that is rather unlikely given the context. The word *martys* did not commonly refer to those who had died for the faith in the first century.[101] In fact, the first extrabiblical usage of this word in reference to those who had died for the faith was in the *Martyrdom of Polycarp* which dates either to A.D. 167 (per Eusebius) or 155 (according to internal evidence).[102] The fact that this word was not used to represent those who had died for the faith until the second century, and yet is used this way perhaps three times in Revelation (1:5, 2:13, 17:6) at least suggests that the writing of this text was late in the first century. Not only that, but the fact that the first extrabiblical usage of this word in this way is in a letter written from a church in Asia Minor (Smyrna) to another church in Asia Minor (Philomelium) proports well with the conception that John's Revelation revolutionized the term in his region.[103] Thus, if one considers the reference to Antipas, whether in

---

[98] *Andrew of Caesarea: Commentary on the Apocalpyse*, Eugenia S. Constantinou, trans., 67-68.
[99] W. Robertson Nicoll, ed., *The Expositor's Greek Testament* V (New York: Dodd, Mead, and Co., 1910), 356.
[100] Francois Halkin, *Bibliotheca Hagiographica Graeca*, 48. On Antipas, it is recorded "Persecution instigated by Domitian"…"Domitian holding the scepter of the Romans"…"Domitian the ruler of the sceptor of the kingdom." [Author's translation]
[101] Thomas Schreiner, *Revelation* BECNT, 83.; Keener, *NIV Application Commentary: Revelation*, 64-65.
[102] E.A. Sophocles, *Greek Lexicon of the Roman and Byzantine Periods*, 735.; For dates, see Michael W. Holmes, ed., *The Apostolic Fathers* 3, 301-302.
[103] Holmes, *Apostolic Fathers*, 298.

consideration of the internal or external evidence regarding him and his martyrdom, it seems that the comment about him fits overwhelmingly into the late date conception.

Second, Christ's comments regarding Laodicea seem to fit better with the late date. Christ says to the church at Laodicea, "You say, I am rich, I have prospered, and I need nothing, not realizing you are wretched, pitiable, poor, blind, and naked." (Rev. 3:17) While much ink has been spilt elaborating on the banking industries and water pipes and many other aspects of Laodicean culture in the first century, it is of particular importance in understanding this statement by Christ to know about an earthquake that rocked the city in A.D. 60. This earthquake destroyed much of the city, and the Roman historian Tacitus reports of the rebuilding process, "without any relief from us, [Laodicea] recovered itself by its own resources."[104] It would be impressive and certainly exemplary of their wealth and prosperity "needing nothing" if they had done so in the period between A.D. 60 and the proposed early date of 64-68. However, history tells another story. It did not take the Laodiceans five years to rebuild; it took them twenty-five years.[105] It cannot possibly be imagined that within the first ten years of a twenty-five-year reconstruction project to rebuild from a devastating earthquake the people of Laodicea would have imagined themselves as having prospered and being in need of nothing. This mindset would be much more likely found in someone who had, without the Roman Empire's assistance, rebuilt after a long time of independent fundraising and construction such as history records.[106]

Allow two sub-points before moving on to the final internal argument, on the topic of the letters to the seven churches. First of all, if the book of Revelation was written before the destruction of Jerusalem, and the judgments therein refer to that AD 70 event, why would seven churches of largely Gentile Christians in Asia Minor care? They were not Jews, nor did they place any emphasis on the value of the Temple after the time of Christ's death and resurrection. For Christ to spend time writing seven letters to seven churches full of Gentiles from cities that are nowhere near Jerusalem, only to tell them of an impending judgment on a city they had nothing to do with is nonsense. When Jesus promises the church at Ephesus that He would come to them if they did not repent (2:5), what would they care if this "coming" pertained to the destruction of some

---

[104] Tacitus, *Annals* 14:27.
[105] Ice, "The Date of Revelation", 3.
[106] This point has been noted as a convincing point for the late date argument by several noteworthy scholars, including Robert Mounce, *Revelation*, 35-37; and Kummel, *Introduction to the New Testament,* 469.

other city than their own? When Jesus promised to "come soon" and destroy the people of Pergamum with the sword of His mouth (3:16), what sense would it make if the fulfillment of that was the destruction of any city other than Pergamum? When He promised to come "like a thief" to the church at Sardis (3:3) what would it matter to them if His coming was to Jerusalem and not Sardis? When He tells the church at Philadelphia that He is "coming soon" (3:11), would it not be ridiculous to say that if He meant a "spiritual coming to Jerusalem?"

A second sub-point from the seven letters comes from the fact that early date advocates defend the view that the Revelation was penned around the same time the Apostle Paul was martyred under Nero in the late A.D. 60's. The letters to the churches produce a serious problem for this theory, as one of the letters – that to the church at Smyrna – naturally assumes that there *is* a church at Smyrna. In fact, the very praise they receive is commendation for their perseverance, implying that they have been enduring for some time. The problem with this is that Polycarp, a disciple of the Apostle John and bishop of Smyrna, claims that in Paul's time there was no church in Smyrna.[107] This is a most humiliating admission, and leaves the early date advocate with no choice but to (1) once again ignore the clear historical narrative, (2) develop some speculative theory about an underground church Polycarp was unaware of, or (3) abandon their view. This second view seems unlikely, since John's letter itself would have been instructive to Polycarp, his disciple, as to the existence of a church in Smyrna in the time of Paul if John's letter were written in that period. Thus, only the first and third options remain viable.

Returning to the third main argument surrounding internal evidence, one may look again at the precise language that John uses throughout the book. It has already been noted at length that the Greek used by John is considered abnormal, with its inclusion of solecisms. Some advocates of an early date have argued that the presence of solecisms indicates that John wrote the Revelation in the 60s, prior to attaining a mastery of the Greek language, and only later wrote his Gospel and Epistles.[108] However, this again presumes the early date and seeks to support it with the available data. R.H. Charles does the same thing in reverse, arguing based on the presumption that the book was composed at a late date that the solecisms indicate that the author "never mastered

---

[107] Polycarp, *Epistle to the Philippians*, 11:3.

[108] Samuel A. Cartledge, *A Conservative Introduction to the New Testament* 7, 198.

the ordinary Greek of his own times, [and] that he came to acquire whatever knowledge he had of this language when somewhat advanced in years."[109] Because both arguments are based on presuppositions that seek to support themselves with data rather than derive themselves from data, neither argument is particularly persuasive.

Furthermore, the specific solecisms themselves have been shown to be closer to contemporary usage in the time of writing than has often been admitted. For example, many experts have addressed the fact that in Revelation 14:19 John uses the Greek word μέγαν (*great*) to describe the ληνὸν (*winepress*) of the wrath of God. The issue is that the words differ in gender, with "great" being masculine and "winepress" being feminine. This is grammatically improper and was seen for generations as an embarrassing fluke. However, in the early 20th century, Greek scholars studying Koine Greek papyri found this same grammatical form of misgendering adjectives and nouns to be "common among the middle classes of the first century" leading one Biblical literature scholar to conclude that "this is one of the greatest discoveries that have been made."[110] It therefore makes little sense to conclude for an early or late date based on solecisms.

One final piece of internal evidence (though not to be taken as the strongest or weakest) is Revelation 4:11 and the usage of the phrase, "Our Lord and God." It is an established historical fact that Domitian demanded to be called *dominus et deus*, "lord and god" not only in conversation but in writing.[111] One early Roman historian reported that this was not simply a one-time event or rumor, but instead, it was a regular practice.[112] He was the first emperor to do this, so it is impossible to misattribute this particular claim to Nero.[113] It is also an agreed upon fact that John admitted language into his writings to directly counter this practice, proclaiming Christ as Lord and God.[114] It is therefore almost undeniable in linguistic terms, and in terms of scholarly agreement, that John included the proclamation of the one on the throne as "Lord and God" to directly reject the self-deification and imposed emperor worship of Domitian.[115]

---

[109] Charles, *A Critical and Exegetical Commentary*, xliv.

[110] Camden M. Cobern, *The New Archaeological Discoveries and Their Bearing Upon the New Testament*, 111. For a thorough explanation of this specific discovery, see James H. Moulton, *A Grammar of New Testament Greek,* Vol. 1, 60.

[111] Seutonius, *Domitianus*, 13:2.

[112] Cassius Dio, *History of Rome*, 67:4:7; 67:13:4.

[113] Bruce Metzger, *Breaking the Code: Understanding the Book of Revelation*, 16.; Mounce, *Revelation*, 140.

[114] N.T. Wright, *Paul and the Faithfulness of God*, 341.

[115] There are too many scholars endorsing this view to list them all, but to name a few: Beale, *Revelation*, 9-10.; Mounce, *Revelation*, 140.; Metzger, *Breaking the Code*, 51. A worthwhile overview of the argument

There are, just as can be done with those advocating for an early (Neronian) date, several places in which one could make speculative arguments for signs of a specific time frame. Just as early-date advocates interpret Revelation 13:18 as pointing to contemporary thoughts of Nero, late-date advocates have argued that Revelation 6:6 points to contemporary edicts of Domitian, which he made prohibiting vines in AD 92.[116] These sorts of interpretive arguments are speculative at best, and certainly should direct readers to relying on better methods of dating such as external evidence or direct internal indicators of date (such as martyrdoms, the existence of churches, or the status of cities).

In any case, it is shown that there is strong internal evidence for endorsement of the late date of Revelation, at least as strong as any internal evidence available to advocates of an early date. Without spending time disputing the two-to-three main points of internal evidence for a Neronian date, one can nevertheless see that there are at least as many or more points of internal evidence for a Domitian date. Therefore, if one is comparing evidence "apples to apples," the internal evidence is at best equally compelling for each side – although several scholars have concluded that even the internal evidence "while less than conclusive, also tends to support a later date."[117] This leaves readers and curious speculators with only one option: examine the external evidence. This option, for the early date advocate, is a non-starter and a complete nightmare as has already been shown.[118]

Interweaving Excursus: *Identifying Quantifiable Measurements of Early Circulation*

This late date only serves to further emphasize the veritable popularity of Revelation across the whole of the early church. Having established a defensible position on the dating of the Revelation, it is now possible to begin examining how widely used the text was in the early church. There are at least three different ways to measure the Catholicity of Revelation: manuscript evidence, widespread geographical footprint, and patristic use and endorsement.

---

surrounding this phrase can be found in Floyd O. Parker Jr., "'Our Lord and God' in Rev 4,11: Evidence for the Late Date of Revelation?" *Biblica* 82:2 (2001): 207-231. While Parker ultimately disagrees with the conclusion herein argued, his overview of the argument is helpful to understand the various implications if this contention is believed.

[116] Hemer, *Letters to the Seven Churches*, 175.

[117] Kostenberger, Kellum, Quarles, *The Cradle*, 942.

[118] For a fuller and more direct engagement of this issue, please read Bryan C. Hodge, *Problems with Preterism*, 213-267.

B.1 *Manuscript Evidence*

Judging by current manuscript discoveries, Revelation appears to be one of the most popular books of the New Testament in the early church. There are presently over sixty extant manuscripts, partial or whole, of the New Testament from the second and third centuries.[119] A point that is often emphasized among Christian apologists but rarely appreciated in the broader historical community is the fact that, as Michael Kruger notes, "the total number of New Testament manuscripts far outpaces any other texts from antiquity."[120] And still, among the much more common New Testament manuscripts, there are more extant copies of Revelation than all the other books of the New Testament except Matthew, Luke, John, and Acts.[121] To use a modern analogy, this implies that in its day Revelation would have been a *New York Times* best-seller; a "most popular" of the most popular books in the second and third centuries.

Of particular interest among these copies of Revelation is one labelled P.IFAO 2.31, or more commonly referred to as 𝔓98.[122] It is a papyrus fragment dating to the second century, currently held at the French Institute of Oriental Archaeology in Cairo. 𝔓98 is a very unique mid-second century fragment that was written on a scroll despite the early church showing a clear preference for writing in codices.[123] What is even more remarkable is that it may be the only New Testament text penned on a roll rather than a codex.[124] The roll is what is known as an opisthograph, which is a scroll that was reused in order to write a new text (usually) on the back of a previously used roll. While experts believe that ancient recyclers did not make a "conscious decision to use a roll," recent discoveries of other opisthographs has proven enlightening as to the purpose for which they were made.[125] Larry Hurtado, an early Christian artifact expert, claims the primary purpose attributed to the creation of these manuscripts is "to make personal copies of

---

[119] Michael J. Kruger, *The Question of Canon*, 97.
[120] Ibid.
[121] Larry W. Hurtado, *The Earliest Christian Artifacts*, 20-21.
[122] For extended study on this manuscript, see Peter Malik, "Another Look at P.IFAO II 31: An Updated Transcription and Textual Analysis" *Novum Testamentus* 58 (2016): 204-217.
[123] Hurtado, *The Earliest Christian Artifacts*, 55-56.
[124] Ibid.; Recent discoveries may disprove this concept, as per Geoffrey Smith who argues that a section of Hebrews has been found written on a roll, and perhaps even a section of the Gospel of John on another. Geoffrey Smith, "The Willoughby Papyrus: A New Fragment of John 1:49-2:1 (P134) and an Unidentified Christian Text" *Journal of Biblical Literature* 137:4 (Winter 2018), 949.
[125] Kruger, *Question of Canon*, 101, n.135.; For information on recent discoveries, see Scott D. Charlesworth, "A Reused Roll or a 'Curious Christian Codex'? Reconsidering British Library Papyrus 2053 (P.Oxy. 8.1075 + P.Oxy. 8.1079)" *Buried History* 53 (2017): 35-44.

texts for study purposes."[126] In his discussion of this scroll and others like it, he concludes that they are "probably best taken as artifacts reflecting interests of some second-century Christians in having edifying texts for their own reading."[127] This shows that in the early church there was already a desire to personally study the book of Revelation.

The sheer frequency of the book of Revelation across the second and third century manuscript collections, along with the uniqueness of its being copied for personal use and study, points modern readers to the fact that the book was widely appreciated and desired in the early church. Reflecting on this combination of facts, Hurtado helpfully comments,

> In spite of the lengthy time that it took for Revelation to be accepted as part of the emerging New Testament canon, particularly in the East, it appears to have enjoyed a reasonable popularity, at least among Christian circles reflected in the earliest extant papyri. [128]

B.2 *Widespread Geographical Footprint*

The slowness of the Eastern church to accept the book of Revelation as legitimate is a thorn in the side of the canonization argument for the text. After all, even though the Western Church exercised some influence in the early canonization effort, Revelation did not secure a "firm place in the canon" of the Eastern (Greek) church until the 10th century.[129] And yet, does this mean that there were large swaths of land in which the Revelation was not known or accepted?

Quite the contrary appears to be the case. The patristic evidence solidly supports the conclusion that by the end of the second century, the book of Revelation was both known and accepted as canonical in "Asia, Africa, and Europe."[130] It seems quite natural that the churches in Asia minor who are directly addressed in the Revelation would be familiar with the text, as evidenced by an early commentary on the book being written by Melito, the late-second century Bishop of Sardis.[131] Similarly, Justin Martyr, who is

---

[126] Hurtado, *Earliest Christian Artifacts*, 54.
[127] Ibid., 55.
[128] Ibid., 32.
[129] Wilhelm Schneemelcher, *New Testament Apocrypha* I, R. McL. Wilson, trans., 32.
[130] Smalley, *Thunder and Love*, 36.
[131] Charles, *A Critical and Exegetical Commentary* I, xcviii.

noted as having lived in Ephesus before his going to Rome, wrote of the book very early on.[132]

The book is attested to very early in church history outside of Asia Minor as well. Much further north in Phrygia (modern Anatolia, Turkey), Apollonius writes in the early third century, assuming the authority of the Revelation.[133] Theophilus, the bishop of Antioch in the late second century also quotes the Revelation in a work of correction and refutation.[134] Further west, in Rome, some scholars have gone so far as to say Revelation was "universally recognized" even over against other apocalyptic writings.[135] This point should be noted, at least in passing – that there were other apocalyptic writings in the era. Smalley contends that the widespread usage of the unqualified phrase "the Apocalypse" to refer to John's Revelation when there were several other apocalypses shows the overwhelming popularity of the text and the familiarity that its readers would have had with it, so as to not confuse it even with other texts of the same name.[136] Hippolytus (the Roman theologian of the second and third centuries) repeatedly quotes the Revelation in his *Commentary on Daniel.*[137] Much further west, and more famously, Irenaeus the Bishop of Lyons (modern France) wrote in the late-second century repeatedly quoting the Revelation.[138] Just prior to the publication of Irenaeus' *Against Heresies*, the churches of the region (Vienne and Lyons) wrote letters to the churches in Asia and Phrygia regularly quoting Revelation.[139]

The testimony of Revelation is also found further south in Alexandria, where Clement quotes from the Revelation in his late-second century *Paedagogus*.[140] Even the skeptical Dionysius, who in the third century made waves by becoming the first to reject the apostolicity of Revelation, was forced to do so because his opponents were seeking to prove their millenarianism by appealing to the Revelation.[141] Egypt was not the end of Revelation's expansive travels in Northern Africa, as Tertullian of Carthage constantly quotes Revelation, referencing the book ten times in just one of his writings, his late-

---

[132] Justin Martyr, *Dialogue with Trypho*, 81.
[133] Eusebius, *Hist. Eccl.*, 5:18:13.
[134] Eusebius, *Hist. Eccl.*, 4:24:1
[135] Charles, *A Critical and Exegetical Commentary* I, xcix.
[136] Smalley, *Thunder and Love*, 36.
[137] Hippolytus, *Commentary on Daniel*, 3:9:10; 4:22:3; 4:23:5; 4:49:1-3.
[138] Irenaeus, *Against Heresies*, 4:20:11.
[139] Charles, *A Critical and Exegetical Commentary* I, xcix.
[140] Clement of Alexandria, *Paedagogus*, 2:11.
[141] Eusebius, *Eccl. Hist.*, 7:24:2-3.

second to early-third century apology, *De Resurrectione Carnis* (On the Resurrection of the Flesh).[142] With evidence of Revelation's popularity throughout all of the Roman world, R.H. Charles appropriately concludes, "throughout the Christian church during the 2nd Century there is hardly any other book of the N.T. so well attested and received as Revelation."[143]

B.3 *Patristic Use and Endorsement*

Finally, in order to show that the book of Revelation was not simply distributed broadly and considered as an interesting apocryphal text, there must be evidence testifying to the widespread endorsement of the book by reputable early sources. Indeed, there is. Aside from all of those named above (as quotations can serve as endorsements, though not always), Andreas, writing in the late-sixth century, claims to preserve the tradition of Papias (a disciple of the Apostle John). If Andreas is to be believed, Papias not only affirmed the apostolicity of the Revelation, but affirmed its inspiration as well.[144]

If Andreas is doubted, however, it is of little effect in negating the early endorsements of Revelation. Clement of Alexandria, for example, in the late-second century compiled what could be called a *proto*-canon, including the book of Revelation.[145] Eusebius, in his early-fourth century *History of the Church*, notably written in the generation prior to the Councils of Hippo and Carthage which would first formally recognize a Biblical canon, wrote that the Apocalypse was sometimes rejected and sometimes recognized.[146] Importantly, he personally believed that the book should be recognized as within the canon of Scripture.[147]

To conclude, let two final pieces of famous literature be offered for examination, as they are much earlier than that offered by Eusebius. First, the Muratorian Canon is typically identified as dating to the A.D. 160's or 170's, and is therefore one of (if not the) earliest lists of authoritative books.[148] Bruce Metzger, in examining the content of the list, notes, "the list concludes with the mention of two apocalypses, that of John and that of

---

[142] Tertullian, *De Resurrectione Carnis*, 22, 25, 27, 38, 58.
[143] Charles, *A Critical and Exegetical Commentary* I, xcix.
[144] *Andrew of Caesarea: Commentary on the Apocalypse*, 142.
[145] Schneemelcher, *New Testament Apocrypha* I, 27.
[146] Eusebius, *Hist. Eccl.*, 3:25:4.
[147] Eusebius, *Hist. Eccl.*, 7:25:4.
[148] C.E. Hill, "The Debate Over the Muratorian Fragment and the Development of the Canon" *Westminster Theological Journal* 57:2 (Fall 1995), 445, 450.

Peter" and yet, a statement is included within the text that reads, "some of us are not willing that the latter should be read in church."[149] Thus, as early as the mid-second century, John's Revelation was considered inspired and canonical above other apocalyptic literature.

Finally, note must be made of the *Shepherd of Hermas*. The Muratorian Canon mentions the Shepherd of Hermas being written "recently" during the time of Pius, then-Bishop of Rome (A.D. 140-154).[150] What is particularly interesting about the *Shepherd* is that it repeatedly uses the imagery of John's Revelation, sometimes in slight variations and other times in complete mimicry.[151] This sort of similarity is certainly not coincidental, and the frequency with which it occurs leads one to imagine that the author of the *Shepherd* was either very familiar with Revelation in a way that implies regular personal study, or that the author actually had a copy of Revelation open before him while writing. Either way, no greater endorsement could be given.

C. Orthodoxy

The very genre of the book of Revelation has rendered it somewhat difficult to interpret and understand. Apocalyptic literature, as has briefly been mentioned, was a genre that had some level of popularity and commonality in the early church (as a remnant of the Jewish influence on early Christianity).[152] However, there is a prevalent belief which must be immediately dispelled, namely, that the book of Revelation *cannot* be understood – and that indeed it was written in such a mysterious way as to never be intended to be understood. This concept is not only false, it is anti-Christian.

In 1 Corinthians 14, Paul combats the concept that the Corinthians who abused their ability to speak in tongues could glorify God in doing so because, as he says, "God is not a God of confusion..." (1 Cor. 14:33) If it was inappropriate for the Corinthians to make the Word of God seem confusing or even unintelligible by their method of conveyance, it is doubly impermissible for modern Christians to make the Word of God

---

[149] Bruce Metzger, *The Canon of the New Testament*, 198.

[150] Bart D. Ehrman, ed., *The Apostolic Fathers* II, 168. Quoting from Eusebius *Eccl. Hist.*, 4:11:1, 6-7. There are significant studies arguing that *The Shepherd* is much earlier, but for our purposes this date suffices.

[151] Charles, *A Critical and Exegetical Commentary* I, xcvii, n.2.

[152] For a brief introduction to the connection between Jewish Apocalyptic literature and John's Revelation, see Sarah Robinson, "The Origins of Jewish Apocalyptic Literature: Prophecy, Babylon, and 1 Enoch" (M.A. Thesis, University of South Florida, 2005). For a more comprehensive overview of the apocalyptic literature and the early church, see Benjamin Reynolds and Loren Stuckenbruck, eds., *The Jewish Apocalyptic Tradition and the Shaping of the New Testament Thought*.

in the book of Revelation seem as though it is unfathomably confusing or even undecipherable. Furthermore, if God gave the book of Revelation to the Church to be used as Scripture, then it should be "profitable for teaching, for reproof, for correction, and for training in righteousness..." (2 Timothy 3:16-17) How could a book be those things if its meaning is so unclear as to never be understood? Certainly, God would not give His people a book that they would never (and could never) understand. The book is meant to be understood.

This does not mean that all things are going to be equally clear, but it does mean that there will be overarching concepts that are easily deduced and interpreted. In those cases, the concepts themselves should be expected to be in line with the rest of Scripture, whether understood in broad or narrow contexts. Is that the case with Revelation? Absolutely. This can be shown by exploring four points of orthodox unity between Revelation and the other Biblical texts: Christology, Ecclesiology, Eschatology, and Typology.[153] To establish each of these categories within Revelation as orthodox, they will be graded on their consistency with the other texts now recognized as inspired in the Old and New Testaments.

C.1 *Christological Orthodoxy*

To begin, the Old Testament parallels in the book of Revelation are unavoidable. In fact, one might argue that the book of Revelation cannot be rightly understood without a proper understanding of the Old Testament. Take, for an initial example, Revelation 3:7, "And to the angel of the church in Philadelphia write: 'The word of the holy one, the true one, who has the key of David, who opens and no one will shut, who shuts and no one opens." The statement that opens this letter to the Philadelphian church is entirely composed of Old Testament references pointed towards the identity of Christ.

John's calling Christ the one "who has the key of David" is agreed by most as an allusion to Isaiah 22:20-25.[154] In Isaiah, the passage refers to Eliakim who was made second-in-command over the Davidic kingdom (v. 21). Eliakim was to have the right to

---

[153] This is an adaptation of five categories proposed in Caley Tse, "Unity Between the Book of Revelation and the Gospel of John" (MTS Essay, Taylor Seminary, 2018). Tse's categorization is modified for use here in order to offer a broader approach than is often taken. See, for a counter-example, Mark Wilson, *Charts on the Book of Revelation*, 38-40 and 108, in which the Revelation is shown to have thematic parallels with the Gospel of John, Jude, and 2 Peter, as well as sharing literary parallels with Genesis.

[154] Gregg, *Revelation*, 109.

refuse entrance or grant admission to the Davidic Kingdom (representative of the Kingdom of God in its day). Revelation takes this image and applies it to Jesus, who as Messiah has the authority to refuse entrance or grant admission to God's true Kingdom, the New Jerusalem.[155] Far from the only reference in Revelation of Christ being the Davidic Messiah, the book is littered with such appeals. One other example of note is Christ's identification as the "root of David" (Rev. 5:5; 22:16), which is a reference to Isaiah 11:1 and 11:10 where the Messiah is said to be both the origin of David's strength and the place from which David's line will once again rise to power.[156]

What makes John's depiction of Christ unique from the Old Testament in his Revelation is that he so seamlessly weaves together imagery of the Davidic Messiah with imagery of God Himself. For example, in this same verse (Rev. 3:7), John opens with the identification of Christ, the Messiah, as "the holy one, the true one." In the Old Testament, these titles are reserved for God, as in Isaiah 40:25 or Habakkuk 3:3. This is a practice that one must become comfortable with: John regularly applies Old Testament descriptors of God to Jesus Christ. See the following chart for a few examples:

Old Testament Descriptors of God Applied to Christ in Revelation

Trait	Revelation	Old Testament
Searching Minds and Hearts	2:23	Jeremiah 11:20
Judging in Righteousness	19:11	Isaiah 11:4
Shepherding Sheep to Living Water	7:17	Ezekiel 34:23
Hair White like Wool	1:14	Daniel 7:9
Possessing the Book of Life	3:5; 13:8; 17:8; 20:12,15; 21:27	Exodus 32:32; Psalm 69:29; Daniel 12:1

Fig. 1.2[157]

---

[155] Mounce, *Revelation*, 100.

[156] Ekkehardt Mueller, "Christological Concepts in the Book of Revelation – Part 1: Jesus in the Apocalypse" *JATS* 21:1 (2010), 291.; Mounce, *Revelation*, 131. Mueller only refers to Isaiah 11:10 as being in reference, but Mounce explains further the relation to 11:1.

[157] Many of these and other examples can be found in Leopold Sabourin, *Christology: Basic Texts in Focus*, 169.

Regarding Revelation's Christological consistency with the rest of the New Testament literature, it is hard to narrow down the examples to a concise few. Scholars overwhelmingly agree that John's Christology is consistent throughout his works, and it aligns with the rest of the New Testament well. Leopold Sabourin, in his helpful book *Christology*, notes that "The Christ of the Apocalypse is not radically different from the Christ known through the other NT writings, but some features are characteristically underlined in Revelation."[158] Others also recognize that Revelation's Christology is consistent with the rest of the New Testament, despite it being "expressed in highly individualistic terms."[159] The consistent Christology (unique in expression though it may be) was recognized by the early Church, and should be recognized in the modern day as not only Biblically consistent, but in fact representing the culmination of Biblical Christology.[160] Nowhere in the Bible is Christ seen as gloriously as He is in the book of Revelation, and yet this is done without positing anything *new* about Him. Rather, Revelation emphasizes and highlights attributes of Christ to a degree yet unexplored in other New Testament texts.

Obviously, John's other writings feature Christ in similar ways as his Revelation. Jesus is presented as being one who brings both judgment and salvation (John 5:30, 3:16ff).[161] He is referred to as the "Word of God" (Rev. 19:13) which is a typically Johannine title (John 1:1).[162] But it is not only the Johannine corpus that is consistent with Revelation's Christology. The book bears striking resemblances to Paul's writings as well. It could be said that the identification of Christ as the "root of David" is a quotation of Paul in Romans 15:12, who was himself quoting Isaiah 11. More directly Pauline is the claim that Christ is the "firstborn of the dead" (Rev. 1:5; Colossians 1:18).[163] Furthermore, Paul's conception of Christ bringing about the consummation of the Kingdom of God in the world (Rom. 8:19-23) seems to be in line with what is presented in Revelation, with the admission that Revelation supplies some details that are not found in the Pauline literature.[164]

---

[158] Sabourin, *Christology*, 163.

[159] Donald Guthrie, "The Christology of Revelation" in *Jesus of Nazareth Lord and Christ: Essays on the Historical Jesus and New Testament Christology*, Joel Green and Max Turner, eds., 408.

[160] Ibid., 409.

[161] Ibid., 405.

[162] Ibid., 402.; Tse, "Unity", 9.

[163] Mueller, "Christological Concepts: Pt. 1", 288.

[164] Guthrie, "Christology in Revelation", 406.

Along with this is the repeated attribution of Christ as the Lamb. Paul refers to Christ as the Passover Lamb (1 Cor. 5:7) and in Revelation he is repeatedly described as the Lamb, and specifically as the Lamb which was slain to ransom the people of God. (Rev. 5:9-10; 13:8). This icon is used of Christ in the Johannine literature as well (John 1:29-36) and is perhaps the most significant label placed on Jesus in Revelation, occurring over 30 times in that book alone.[165]

Revelation's Christology is also very similar to that portrayed in the book of Hebrews as well as the Petrine literature. In Hebrews, the efficacy of Christ's blood is highlighted as a particularly significant factor in the redemption of mankind, and this carries through into Revelation. In Peter's writings, the Shepherd is depicted as redeeming His sheep (1 Pet. 1:18; 2:28; and 5:2), and the world as we know it is ultimately destroyed by the coming of Christ in glory (2 Pet. 3:10).[166]

Finally, John's Revelation does not neglect the humanity of Christ despite its great emphasis on His deity and authority. John notes that Jesus was genuinely killed (Rev. 5:9) and existed in death (1:18) at one point. He even makes a point to describe the manner in which Christ died, describing Him as being "crucified" (11:8) and "pierced." (1:7) Thus, the humanity, death, and even humility of Christ in the manner of death He endured are all distinctly present in Revelation.[167] All of this is simply to show that the Christ presented in the book of Revelation only differs from the Christ of the rest of the New Testament in degree of explanation. His glory is not elevated above that found in other New Testament texts in any way, but is maximally examined; and yet, His humanity is not neglected or hidden either, it is amply recognized.

C.2 *Ecclesiological Orthodoxy*

Chul Hae Kim makes a fascinating statement that is sure to hold great truth when he writes, "No eschatology can be separated from Christology... [and] the Christology of the book of Revelation also cannot be separated from the doctrine of the church."[168] His argument peaks the interest of most any systematician, as he contends that one's eschatology (the purpose for which most individuals look to Revelation) cannot be

---

[165] Tse, "Unity", 8.

[166] Guthrie, "Christology in Revelation", 408.

[167] Ekkehardt Mueller, "Christological Concepts in the Book of Revelation – Part 3: The Lamb Christology" *JATS* 22:2 (2011), 49.

[168] Chul Hae Kim, "Ecclesiology and Christology in the First Three Chapters of the Book of Revelation" *Torch Trinity Journal* 6:1 (2003), 133.

understood rightly without understanding the Christology of that same book, and the Christology of that book cannot be understood properly without understanding the ecclesiology of the book as well. Thus, to have a consistent grasp on one's beliefs about the end times, one must first look to what Revelation teaches about Christ and His Church.

In terms of ecclesiology, the book of Revelation is rivaled only by the Pastoral Epistles in its attention to how to maintain purity in the New Testament Church. The second and third chapters are obviously pertinent to this discussion, but they are far from John's only discussion of the Church in the text. In fact, the second and third chapters (depending largely on one's stance on preterism) could be argued as pertaining only to the local churches to which they were addressed. Even if that were true, which is not conceded, the lessons learned from Christ's instructions to those churches would certainly be worth learning and applying to ourselves.[169] In any case, one may conclude (much to the chagrin of many "online church" advocates) that Christ's definition of a "church" in Revelation 2-3 is the same as elsewhere identified in the Bible. An *Ekklesia* (as referenced each time a new letter begins and recognized by the English rendering, "church") in Christ's reckoning is a "local church."[170] This is clear, as He identifies each church not by its identity in the global or universal body of believers, but by its location. He writes "to the angel of the church of Ephesus... Smyrna... Pergamos...Thyatira... Sardis... Philadelphia... Laodicea...." Each time, Christ assumes that there is a locally operating – and perhaps (on the basis of his lack of appeal to any single authoritative figure) an autonomous and independent – body of believers with their own pastor (which may well be who the "angel" of each church is), their own congregations, their own church discipline, and their own responsibility for the maintenance of these things.

And yet, while consistent in its treatment of *what* a church is, the book of Revelation is also consistent with the rest of the New Testament in concern to *who* the church is operating under. As previously mentioned, the letters to these churches in Revelation 2-3 are not sent to a pope or bishop, but seem to be meant to be read before the assembled congregation for their mutual benefit. This goes to show that it was not a pope nor a bishop who was set over the church (either local or universal), but the one

[169] This assumes that one is following the standard practice of proper Biblical interpretation: Exegesis, Exposition, Application.
[170] Wesley J. Perschbacher, ed., *The New Analytical Greek Lexicon*, 127.; Sophocles, *Greek Lexicon of the Roman and Byzantine Periods,* 436.

who dictated the letters.[171] Christ is the "sovereign Controller... who walks around the church, taking care of the church" and as a result, argues Chul Hae Kim, "what the church should do is keep the right relationship with the Lamb."[172]

Dispensationalists are quick to point out that, in their reckoning, the church is absent from Revelation 4-18.[173] Much like the preterist, this is simply the result of only seeing what is compatible with the presuppositions of one's eschatological view. It has been recognized by various scholars that the church is referred to throughout the Revelation as various things, including but not limited to: *Ekklesia*, Saints, the 144,000, the Great Multitude, the Remnant, etc.[174] It has been powerfully defended that the most common way that believers are referred to is by the title "servants."[175] To argue on the basis of the absence of a single term that is often used to identify the Church that the whole of the Church is altogether removed from the storyline in some supernatural way is odd to the degree of defying comparison.

Other themes relating to the church in Revelation further exemplify its standard orthodoxy in line with other New Testament texts. The fact that John identifies himself as the brother of those in the churches (Rev. 1:9) implies his affirmation of the doctrine of adoption as taught in both the Johannine literature (John 1:12; 1 John 3:1), and Pauline literature. (Romans 8:15-16; Ephesians 1:5) While Christ's imagery of the churches as lamps is more typological of Old Testament symbols, the concept of the Church being the light of the world is certainly consistent with the New Testament teaching of the Church. (Matthew 5:14-16) Some have even noted how that the Church is envisioned in Revelation as the new and true Israel, an ecclesiological concept finding its origins in the Pauline epistles.[176]

A recurring theme that is often overlooked in Revelation is the theme of love that permeates the Church throughout the book. John's writings may focus on love as much as any others in the Bible, with the famous phrase "God is love" coming from the pen of

---

[171] Kim, "Ecclesiology and Christology", 144.
[172] Ibid., 142.
[173] John Walvoord, *The Rapture Question*, 260-261.
[174] Ekkehardt Mueller, "Introduction to the Ecclesiology of the Book of Revelation" *JATS* 12:2 (Autumn 2001), 200-205.; Edwin Reynolds, "The True and the False in the Ecclesiology of Revelation" *JATS* 17:2 (Autumn 2006), 20-22.
[175] Tse, "Unity", 9.
[176] Robert H. Gundry, "The New Jerusalem People as Place, Not Place for People" *Novum Testamentum* 29 (1987): 254-264.

John himself. (1 John 4:8) Thus, it should not be surprising (although it is to many) that John's Revelation is also a book filled with references to love in the community of the people of God. A few quick examples come in Revelation 2, as Jesus reprimands the church at Ephesus for abandoning their "first love" in 2:4. Christ then commends the church at Thyatira as He reflects on their "love and faith and service and patient endurance" in 2:19. And this brings to light what Ekkehardt Mueller says "stands out" about the people of God in Revelation, which is their love and service. He points out, however, that there is one slight change, writing, "while in other NT writings believers are called to serve one another and fellow humans, Revelation even more strongly emphasizes service to God/the Lamb."[177]

One final characteristic of the Church throughout the book of Revelation is its identity as those who are "made war upon" and not those who "make war."[178] The identity of the Church is found in its "conquering" and yet the manner in which they conquer is not through bloodshed or defending themselves, but purely by "the blood of the Lamb, and by the word of their testimony, for they loved not their lives even unto the end."[179] (Rev. 12:11) Their victory is found in their faithfulness to God, not triumph in the world. Indeed, it is Christ who makes war (Rev. 19:11), not the Church.

C.3 *Eschatological Orthodoxy*

Discussing whether the book of Revelation is eschatologically orthodox might seem like a very difficulty task, as many consider Revelation to be the most vivid and thorough eschatological text in the Bible. Perhaps that is true, but that is not to say that the other books of the Bible do not establish an eschatology which should be expected of the Revelation in order for it to be considered orthodox. To avoid chasing rabbits out into the weeds (which is very easy to do when discussing eschatology in general), the boundaries to define orthodox eschatology will be found through the historical conception of the "Four Last Things" (historically known as the *quattuaor novissima*). These four items have been generally agreed upon as being "death, judgment, hell, and eternal life."[180] It is true that, as with any attempt to define Christian orthodoxy, this

---

[177] Mueller, "Christological Concepts Pt. 3", 63.
[178] Lee Griffith, *The War on Terrorism and the Terror of God*, 205.
[179] This concept, while slightly different in her formulation, is well-developed by Barbara Rossing, "Apocalyptic Violence and Politics: End Times Fiction for Jews and Christians," *Contesting Texts* (2007), 67-77.
[180] Markus Muhling, *T&T Clark Handbook of Christian Eschatology*, Jennifer Adams-Massman and David A. Gilland, trans., 4.

configuration has historically been subject to various proposed reconfigurations with some elements taken out and others added in, such as the addition of resurrection of the dead and the annihilation of the world.[181] Yet, in general these four aspects have been accepted since the medieval ages when Anselm endorsed them, through the Puritan era when John Bunyan wrote extensively on them, and now into the modern era wherein they have recently been used as a tool to examine pieces of historical literature for Christian influence.[182]

Let a view first, then, be given to how the book of Revelation addresses death. The book is vivid in its description and illustrative usage of death, using the Greek term *thanatos* in no fewer than 15 unique verses.[183] This term is used frequently in three different ways. Sometimes it is used to refer to a status (or perhaps place), such as 1:18 when Jesus claims to have the "keys of *Death* and Hades" or similarly 20:13, when the sea gives up the dead, and they proceed out of "*Death* and Hades" for the judgment. Elsewhere, the phrase refers to that event which occurs at the end of human life, as in 2:10 when the Christians are commended to "be faithful unto *death*" so that they may receive the crown of life, or in 9:6 when the miserable masses "will seek death and will not find it." The last usage of the phrase seems to be in reference to eternal damnation in Hell (20:14-15), as reflected by the repeated usage of the phrase "second death" (ref., 2:11; 20:6; 21:8).

The chief characteristic of death in each of these three manners which maintains absolute orthodoxy is that God is shown to be in complete control of death at every turn. God the Son is said to have the keys to death (1:18) asserting His control over it and those who enter into it. His barring some from being able to physically die when otherwise it appears that they would shows His authority over physical death (9:6). His promises to those who are faithful against the threat of the second death assert that He also has control over who is affected by spiritual death (2:11; 20:6).

---

[181] These two additions are made by Sigurd Hjelde in *Das Eschaton und die Eschata: Eine Studie uber Sprachgebrauch und Sprachverwirrung in protestantischer Theologie von der Orthodoxie bis zur Gegenwart*, 41-47, and also by Johann Gerhard as quoted in Jeffrey G. Silcock, "A Lutheran Approach to Eschatology" *Lutheran Quarterly* 31 (2017), 373. Catholic scholars have also proposed that Purgatory should be included, though this is clearly unique to their tradition and is not indicative of orthodoxy. See, Reginald Garrigou-Lagrange, *Life Everlasting and the Immensity of the Soul*.

[182] John R. Fortin, "Saint Anselm and the Four Last Things" *The American Benedictine Review* 61:2 (2010): 183-203.; John Bunyan, *One Thing Is Needful: Serious Meditations on the Four Last Things* 3.; Maia Stepenberg, "Dostoevsky's *Crime and Punishment* in the Light of Eschatology" in *Quaestio Rossica* 7:4 (2019): 1160-1171.

[183] Rev. 1:18; 2:10; 2:11; 2:23; 6:8; 9:6; 12:11; 13:3; 13:12; 18:8; 20:6; 20:13; 20:14; 21:4; 21:8.

A secondary characteristic concerning death that maintains orthodoxy when held over against the rest of Scripture is the fact that death is shown to be a universal human experience. Not only is the death of Jesus Christ Himself affirmed when He says, "*I died*, and behold I am alive forever…" (1:18) but the death of every person is assumed, regardless of their righteousness or lack thereof, as God promises deliverance to those who are "faithful unto death" (2:10). Importantly, He promises to deliver them from the second death, which is implied as being the default position for all people unless Christ saves them, and He goes further to promise the banishment of all forms of death in the eternal state of the redeemed (21:4).

Next, it is clear that the concept of judgment is repeatedly forwarded as a major theme throughout the book. There are two types of judgment referenced in the Revelation, one being a form more akin to cursing and condemnation while the other is more akin to legal examination. One may reflect on the saints crying from beneath the altar, "O Sovereign Lord, holy and true, how long before you will *judge* and avenge our blood on those who dwell on the earth?" (6:10) These saints seem to be asking for something temporal, and some element of God's judgment is seen to fall in the procession leading to the Day of the Lord, as noted in 16:5, 18:8, 19:2, and most famously, 19:11. These punishments do, evidently, extend into the eternal state and are still considered a similar fashion of "judgment" as those poured out in time. For example, in 11:18 the punishment of God during the "time of the dead" in which he pours wrath on His enemies and rewards on His servants, prophets, and saints, is said to be the "time for the dead to be judged."

Alongside these is the famous "judgment" scene of Revelation 20, wherein God Himself sits as the judge on a "great white throne" and opens "the books" to judge mankind on the basis of their works. (20:12) The significance of this court seems to be of eternal consequence, as those whose names are not found in the "book of life" are thrown into the lake of fire.

The subject of Hell in the book of Revelation is nuanced, to say the least. While the Greek word typically rendered "hell" throughout the Bible (*hades*) is used four separate times (1:18; 6:8; 20:13; 20:14), it is used in conjunction with "Death" each time, a figure which is sometimes implied to be a status or place (1:18), but elsewhere takes on personified characteristics such as being referred to as a "rider" (6:8) or as being capable of delivering the dead and being thrown into the lake of fire itself. Thus, the word Hades is not rendered as Hell as it is elsewhere even in the English Standard Version (such as Matthew 16:18).

Adding to the difficulty is the fourfold reference to a hitherto unheard of "lake of fire" which evidently serves as the place most think of when considering Hell. It is this place which is called the "second death" and it is this place where the beast is sent (19:20), to be followed later by "Death and Hades" after the great white throne judgment. (20:14)

In any case, the conception of Hell (a place of eternal conscious torment) pervades the book of Revelation from the beginning in 1:18 when Christ affirms His authority over such a place, through to the end in 21:8 when the enemies of God are said to receive "their portion" in this place in the second death.

Finally, the concept of eternal life is so central to the message of the Revelation that one scarcely has to defend its presence. Not only does Christ introduce Himself as being the one who is "alive forevermore" (1:18), nor is it only said that God the Father "lives forever and ever" (4:9-10; 5:14; 10:6; 15:7), but Christ repeatedly promises His people that if they persevere, He will let them "eat of the tree of life" (2:7), and consequently they "will not be hurt by the second death" (2:11) but will have their names always written in the book of life (3:5), and will be endowed with authority (2:26) even to the degree of sitting with Christ on the Father's throne (3:21). They will dwell with God forever, where there shall never be any death, mourning, crying, or pain. (21:4)

In all of this, the elements of orthodox eschatology are not only maintained, but the power and authority of God over these is so elevated that the Revelation becomes a unique text in how it holds both eschatological truth and theological glorification. There is nothing in this book which is intended to "frighten" for the sake of frightening. The book is intended to glorify God and show readers that He is in absolute control over all things eschatological, whether death, judgment, hell, or heaven (eternal life). God is sovereign and powerful over each of these elements, and all things will end in His good timing for His good pleasure.

That the eschatological nature of Revelation is intended to elevate the reader's glorification of Christ is not an original thought. Anselm saw each of these four last things as specifically proceeding from Christ Himself – as Christ died and resurrected, and now issues out eternal life to His people as well as judgment in Hell to His enemies.[184] This perhaps serves as a reminder of what Kim has already been quoted saying, "no eschatology can be separated from Christology."[185] Kim is certainly correct, for eschatology has been largely neglected in the modern European scene and, as a result, their other central theological distinctives have withered away. Jean-Claude Larchet, a modern church historian in France, recently reflected on the status of the church in France and its relationship with eschatology, saying, "the clergy quite abruptly stopped speaking about all these delicate subjects, as if they had stopped believing in it themselves."[186] He goes on to argue that since they failed to convey these crucial doctrines, the logical Christian framework became irredeemably undermined, and has all but died in their setting.

C.4 *Typological Orthodoxy*

Perhaps the only category more difficult than eschatology to narrow down when discussing Revelation is typology.[187] As with any apocalyptic literature, the imagery that is given is highly symbolic, and with Revelation in particular, the types that John uses are often references to other Biblical texts that John does not courteously identify as being such (as Paul would do with his helpful, "for it is written"). John assumes that his readers will be familiar with typology and other Biblical texts, and therefore does not take the time to explain the images that he uses. He frequently uses symbols such as light, lamps, water, bread, and marriage, but to go through each of these and show the cross references with other Biblical texts would take an entire commentary on its own.[188] For the sake of brevity with clarity, permit three types to be examined.

First, there is the frequent usage of harvest/reaping language used throughout Revelation (though most vividly in Revelation 14:14-20). It is similar to the language used by Christ in John's Gospel (John 4:36-42) as well as Matthew's. (Matthew 13:24-30)

---

[184] Fortin, "Saint Anselm and the Four Last Things", 185.

[185] Kim, "Ecclesiology", 133.

[186] Jean-Claude Larchet de Guillaume Cuchet, *Comment notre monde a cessé d'être chrétien: Anatomie d'un effondrement*, 195. [Author's translation]

[187] For those unfamiliar with the study of typology or who desire a better grasp of how to interpret types, please read Aubrey Sequeira and Samuel Emadi, "Biblical-Theological Exegesis and the Nature of Typology" *SBJT* 21:1 (2017): 11-34.

[188] These symbols are pointed out by Alan Culpepper, *Anatomy of the Fourth Gospel: A Study in Literary Design*, 193. For one example of a cross-reference in this line, Culpepper believes that the banquet of John 2 would make contemporary readers think of the messianic eschatological banquet.

Other imagery associated with reaping and harvesting, such as wine, fruit, and vines, is frequently found in and through the text.[189]

Second, and perhaps associated with harvest and reaping imagery, is the frequent type or symbol of blood – specifically the blood of "the Lamb" or of Christ. This phrase is explicitly used in 7:14, 12:11 and is implied in 5:9. In each of these passages the blood of Christ (or the Lamb) is said to be effective to the washing clean of those who have their clothes stained with sins.[190] This is a theme that is found in other Johannine writings (1 John 1:7) as well as other non-Johannine texts. (Hebrews 9:22) Certainly, this usage of the phrase "the blood of the Lamb" hearkens back to earlier Old Testament types, not the least of which would be the Passover lamb whose blood delivered God's people from the judgment coming on the Egyptians at the hand of the Angel of Death.

This last note introduces the final typological theme in the book of Revelation, which is slightly less explicit though no less recognizable – the typology of Exodus symbolism.[191] Once more, for the sake of brevity, allow an examination of only three chapters to be given as evidence for the presence of this motif. In Revelation 12, the central characters (both protagonists and antagonists), the conflict between them, the song sung by God's people, the ensuing chase, the deliverance of God's people, and the maintenance of a remnant through persecution have all been shown to be clear allusions or references to the Exodus narrative.[192]

Similarly, Revelation 15 and 16 discuss the presentation and outpouring of the "Seven bowls" of God's judgment on His enemies, as well as His deliverance of His people. The bowl imagery itself could be seen as referential to Old Testament passages (such as Jeremiah 25:16 or Psalm 116:12-19) but it is more specifically the plagues of the Exodus narrative which come out of them.[193] Further, the imagery of the "sea of glass mixed with fire" is noted by some scholars as making "clear that John obviously has exodus imagery in mind."[194] Once again, the people of God sing a song, and this time it

---

[189] Tse, "Unity", 14.
[190] Mueller, "Christological Concepts Pt. 3", 50-51.
[191] Jay Smith Casey has written a wonderful Ph.D. dissertation on just this topic entitled "Exodus Typology in the Book of Revelation" (Southern Baptist Theological Seminary, 1981). For more easily accessible information on Exodus typology in Revelation, please see James Hamilton, *Revelation: The Spirit Speaks to the Churches*.
[192] David S. Gifford, "The Exodus Motif in Revelation 12: Divine Deliverance for the 21st Century", 10-17.
[193] Laslo Gallus, "The Exodus Motif in Revelation 15-16: It's Background and Nature" *Andrews University Seminary Studies* 46:1 (2008), 35-42.
[194] Ibid., 31.

is explicitly called the "Song of Moses" (Revelation 15:3) leaving no room for doubt of the reference. It is only further solidified that this is Exodus imagery when the heavenly temple is referred to as the "tent of witness", a phrase which echoes the Exodus-era tabernacle.[195]

It is worth noting that the author believes the Exodus narrative is instructive for understanding the macronarrative of Revelation as a whole. The general stories both contain these central elements: God's people enter the story as an oppressed people enduring hardship in a sinful atmosphere; God catalyzes a series of severe punishments on the oppressors of His people – and though His people are still present, they are in some sense preserved from the punishments by the sovereign power of God; At last, God's chosen deliverer guides His people out of that sinful atmosphere and into the land that has long been promised. These similarities between Exodus and Revelation seem to be clear – at least clear enough that no further explanation of the antecedents of these referential points is required in order for the reader to understand the analogy.

Conclusion

It has therefore been shown without any further room for doubt that the book of Revelation belongs in the Christian canon on the basis of its fitting the criteria of Apostolicity, Catholicity, and Orthodoxy. The arguments for its Apostolicity have been made on the grounds of both external and internal evidence, as well as through a refutation of known theories rejecting apostolic authorship. Its Catholicity has been shown by first establishing the dating in which it was composed (as concluded through an examination of the external and internal evidence), followed by an examination of the physical manuscript evidence, widespread geographical footprint, and patristic endorsement, all showing the widespread usage of the text across the Christian world. Finally, the orthodoxy of the book has been shown by examining its alignment with other canonical texts in four major categories: Christology, Ecclesiology, Eschatology, and Typology. With all of this in place, surely there is no room left for doubt regarding the canonicity of John's Revelation.

---

[195] Ibid., 34.

Chapter 2:

Intent of Analysis

I was once brought a commentary on Daniel and Revelation by a senior member of my church who said he had not read it, but thought it would be something good for me since it was very thorough. It was quite old and the cover was very warn – even falling apart. I began reading it and indeed found it to be interesting and unique in its own ways, with some valuable insights and other odd takes. At one point, when discussing the return of Christ, the commentator referred to His return in the past tense. Stunned, I began flipping through looking at other passages of the like, and indeed this author seemed to believe that Christ had already returned. Upon closer inspection of the opening pages of the book, I found the commentary to have been written by Uriah Smith, a major Seventh-Day Adventist author. I put the book down considering it to have been a massive waste of time.

Since then, it has been clear to me that a commentary on Revelation should include some disclaimer on the various approaches that will be taken in interpreting the text itself *prior* to beginning the exposition. Even within orthodox Christianity, it should be clear to a fledgling postmillennialist reader that they are reading a premillennial commentary from the outset, lest they confuse themselves and make a muck of their own view. A confused postmillennialist does not a premillennialist make. If one reads this commentary and comes away confused, the exercise was a failure, not a success. It would be much preferred if an amillennialist or postmillennialist read this commentary fully-aware from the outset that the author's intent was to approach this text as a premillennialist. That way, they could properly judge the text as sensical or nonsensical, not on the rubric of their own eschatological position, but on the rubric of my own. Furthermore, if a person finds the approach and arguments presented in this commentary to be logical (or even, dare I say, compelling) then it should be acceptable to expect them to admit the validity of the position, or even affirm it themselves.

Thus, let a few disclaimers be given and then thoroughly examined and defended. First, the author fully intends to do what he has never seen done before – to produce a premillennial commentary on Revelation that espouses a recapitulative approach to the structure of the book. Second, the author will explain and defend his preference in text, as all major quotations (excepting perhaps a few for expanded understanding) will be taken from the English Standard Version. Finally, the author's eschatological (i.e., millennial) position itself will be briefly explained and distinguished from close parallel views.

A. Approach to Structure

When approaching the book of Revelation, there is from the outset a certain necessity to know *how* the book is to be approached. One would have to agree that it is quite a unique text, being the only prophetic text in the New Testament and a genre of very odd nature as an apocalyptic writing. Unfortunately, many surrender their own right of "rightly handling the word of truth" in exchange for simply accepting the schema presented by a given eschatological framework. To be fair, this is the safer approach – and most would be wise to take it. If every man's hat was his own church (as Winthrop Hudson famously put it) then the broader Church of Christ would become a mess very quickly.[196] Tradition and frameworks are helpful.

Where problems arise is when those traditions and frameworks intersect and overlap. What is one to do when they see multiple approaches being accurate in a given situation, or as a whole? Robert Mounce helpfully reflects on the struggle, saying, "it is readily apparent that each approach has some important contribution to a full understanding of Revelation and that no single approach is sufficient in itself."[197] Thus, when approaching the book of Revelation, it is not quite fair to ask the interpreter to fall into a given category, asking, "Do you interpret it literally or figuratively?" or "Do you approach it as if it is chronological or recapitulative?" As will be shown, these categories simply do not convey the level of specificity that many wish they did.

Literal or Figurative

When answering the question of whether the book of Revelation should be handled "literally" or not, one is forced to admit from the outset that the word "literally" does not properly identify the position held by those who espouse it. There are simply *no* Christians who interpret the book of Revelation *literally*. No Christian is awaiting a literal monster-like animal to arise out of the ocean with a leopard/bear/lion body, seven heads (one dead) and ten horns (somehow oddly distributed), to receive power from a literal dragon. (Rev. 13:1-3) Even those accused of being the most sophomoric interpreters do not take that passage as literal – it is approached as something to be

---

[196] Winthrop Hudson, *Baptists in Transition: Individualism and Christian Responsibility*, 142.
[197] Mounce, *Revelation*, 49.

understood as representing any myriad of different enemies of Christ, but never a literal beast-like creature from the black lagoon.

The early church does appear to lend some credence to a literal*ish* approach, as they certainly approached the Revelation in as literal of a way as any modern interpreters. This can be most easily recognized in their broad affirmation of chiliasm (a form of premillennialism).[198] However, in the ensuing centuries the expected kingdom on earth failed to arrive, and Greek thinking found its way into Christian hermeneutics. Slowly, approaches towards the book of Revelation (and other texts) became decreasingly literalistic and increasingly figurative, spiritualized, and allegorical. This can be recognized through the writings of Tyconius, whose approach greatly influenced the more famous Augustine of Hippo. Tyconius and Augustine did more to advance a spiritualized and allegorical approach to the Bible than most any others, such that they are said to have "interpreted nothing by the historical setting or events of the first century."[199]

Does this mean they were wrong? Certainly not. Does it mean that they made mistakes? Almost certainly. Decontextualizing the text before interpreting it is a disastrous approach. Wise though these men were, there must be some accommodation made for the original authorial intent as well as the original audience, and those two factors must be kept in mind when interpreting the text – even if it means accepting an interpretation that comes across as uncomfortable or difficult for us. It would be improper to say that the whole of the book of Revelation should be understood allegorically, spiritually, or figuratively. Even so, it would be equally improper to say that the whole of the book of Revelation should be understood literally. There is simply more nuance to it than to accept these all-encompassing frameworks. The Apostle John did not bind himself to speaking strictly literally or allegorically, and it does not appear at all to be the case that his original audience bound themselves to interpreting his message strictly literally or allegorically.

Ancient Interpretive Approach to the Structure of Revelation

Biblical interpreters would be greatly benefitted by reading the works of Nils Lund, an often-unheard-of Bible scholar who lectured and wrote on the topic of interpretation for over 30 years. He speaks of the importance of understanding that "in the New Testament we have not only a Greek but also a Hebrew environment and

---

[198] Justin Martyr, *Dialogue with Trypho*, 80-81.; Tertullian, *Against Marcion*, 3:25.; Eusebius, *Hist. Eccl.*, 3:39.; Irenaeus, *Against Heresies*, 5:30-36.

[199] Mounce, *The Book of Revelation*, 25.

background to take into account."[200] He explains that many New Testament students and scholars alike minimize the influence that the Hebrew culture and literary forms played on the New Testament because of an assumption that "the early Christian community [was] non-literary or perhaps even illiterate." But to the contrary, he notes that many Old Testament patterns and forms "deeply influenced Paul and other New Testament writers."[201]

One frequent literary approach in the Old Testament was the usage of what were called parallelisms. These ancient Hebrew parallelisms appear frequently throughout the whole of the Old Testament, whether in the books of the Law, the Prophets, or the Psalms. Lund brilliantly and briefly lays out four types of parallelisms which are used in the Old Testament, which might be understood in this manner:

Lundian Examples of Parallelism		
Type of Parallelism	**Description**	**Old Testament Example**
Synonymous	The central thought is repeated "with slight variations, and at times with increased emphasis."	Psalm 8:4
Antithetical	The central thought is contrasted against its inverse.	Proverbs 27:6-7
Synthetic	The central thought is repeated several times.	Psalm 1:1
Alternating	The central thought is repeated with interludes between each repetition.	Psalm 27:1
Fig. 2.1[202]		

What Lund concludes from this explanation of the use of parallelism is that when examining New Testament texts, readers ought to be aware of the atmosphere in which the texts were penned and in which they were read – which for most of the New Testament was a broadly Jewish setting. Because of this literary atmosphere, the

[200] Nils W. Lund, "The Presence of Chiasmus in the New Testament" *The Journal of* Religion 10:1 (Jan., 1930), 78.
[201] Ibid.
[202] Nils W. Lund, *Studies in the Book of Revelation*, 37-38.

individuals writing and reading the New Testament would have been familiar with this method of interpretation.

When examining the book of Revelation as a whole, one may think that they are entitled to approach it with little attention paid to this sort of cultural methodology, given that these methods are largely exemplified in *verses* rather than whole books, but the similarities between these Hebrew methods and the macrostructure of the book of Revelation have been recognized by many scholars, even those who disagree with Lund on meaningful points. For example, Kenneth Strand recognizes what he and Lund both refer to as a chiastic (parallelistic/recapitulative) structure in the Revelation, and although Strand disagrees with Lund on several points, he identifies eight sections in the text of Revelation through which this practice is manifested.[203] Lund would argue that there are at least two major reasons for believing that the book of Revelation should be interpreted in a manner aligned with the parallelistic (that is, recapitulative) approach: First, because "the whole mould [sic] of the book is based on patterns from the Old Testament"; and second, because "the ideas the author is conveying to his audience are those commonly accepted among first century Christians."[204]

This last statement is crucial. What Lund is saying is that it is proper to approach the book of Revelation just as John wrote it and just as a reader aware of the Jewish method of recapitulation would read it. And yet, at the same time, it is also proper to look for the commonly held conclusions that were drawn by first century Christians and view those as at least favored. Why? Because if anyone knew how John intended the book to be read, it was the audience to whom he originally wrote it. Thus, if all (or at a minimum, the majority) of John's readers agreed that certain texts were to be taken *figuratively* while others were to be taken *literally*; or if all (or the majority) of John's readers accepted certain events in the text as following after others rather than being separated in the recapitulative layout, then modern readers ought to follow their consensus. To put it briefly, they knew better than us what John meant when they read it because it was written by one of them, to them.

Defining Recapitulation

It may come as a surprise that someone so contrary to the pure-preterist interpretation of Revelation would be in favor of a recapitulative interpretation, as

---

203 Kenneth Strand, "The Eight Basic Visions in the Book of Revelation" *Andrews University Seminary Studies* 25 (1987): 107-121.

204 Lund, *Studies in the Book of Revelation*, 51.

recapitulation is often a trademark of preterists.[205] This is one unique aspect of this commentary, but hopefully it will not be unique for long: the approach herein is to be identified as *eclecticism*.[206] The four usual positions are preterism (conceiving of the Revelation as having been fulfilled entirely or largely in the first century), historicism (conceiving that the Revelation is fulfilled throughout church history), idealism (conceiving of Revelation as being fulfilled in largely spiritual ways), and futurism (conceiving of Revelation as being fulfilled mostly in the future). Eclecticism integrates aspects of each position. In eclecticism, the only position which is precluded is the early-date reliant version of pure-preterism – given the historical fact that the book was written after AD 70.[207] This provides quite a unique approach given the acceptance of recapitulation in Revelation.

To be clear from the outset, the position taken herein is that the book of Revelation finds its fulfillment throughout the church age. How is this not historicism? This contention is different in that it is argued that rather than the events described in Revelation occurring once and only once throughout history – leading to any number of theories as to when each event occurred – it is believed that many of the events described in Revelation occur in ways in *each generation*, with every generation of Christians being called to faithfully endure unto the end. Obviously, this necessitates a spiritual understanding of some aspects – an approach much more typical of an idealist. But the idealist, it is believed, overreaches by taking a spiritual fulfillment to too many things. What events in particular? Well, specifically, those events which have clearly not occurred yet – namely, the return of Christ, the millennial reign, the creation of a New Heaven and New Earth, and the eternal rest of the redeemed. Each of these things are yet to occur, and none of them may be taken as only being fulfilled spiritually. Therefore, there must be some sense in which the events told in the book will occur finally and most climactically prior to Christ's return.

Just as a woman in labor may experience contractions for many hours and days prior to the child actually being born, the experiences of Revelation have been ongoing

---

[205] Ekkehardt Muller, "Recapitulation in Revelation 4-11" *JATS* 9:1 (1998), 260.

[206] This term appears to have been coined by G.K. Beale and further elaborated by Jonathan Menn. See: Beale, *Revelation*, 48-49.; and especially Jonathan Menn, *Biblical Eschatology*, 195-196. It should also be noted that there have been historic premillennialists to see Revelation as recapitulatory. See J. Barton Payne, *Encyclopedia of Biblical Prophecy*, 596.

[207] Of course, Full-Preterism is also precluded, as it is heterodox. For more on the debate between these two views, see Jason L. Quintern and H. Michael Shultz Jr., *Revelation in Focus: Two Perspectives on Its Meaning and Timing*.

since the time of John.[208] However, that final "push" bringing the baby into the world is no less a contraction than those which went before it. In fact, it could be said to be the most painful, the most escalated of all. So also will be the tribulations and experiences of the Church. While each generation must face the hardship described in Revelation in their own respect, the final one prior to the return of Christ will experience these events in an escalated way, much more painfully than any which preceded them. This understanding will be found favorable to futurists, although they would be entirely contrary to the idea that the remainder of Revelation occurs throughout the church age, and certainly against the idea that it occurs in each generation in various ways. One can see, then, that the eclectic approach endorsed herein is partially compatible with each position, but not fully compatible with any single one of them.

This position is one that is much easier to understand upon recognition of recapitulations, as John attempts to describe to the people of God throughout history the various ways they might see their own story being told herein. For those who are generally unfamiliar with this terminology, take the word "recap" as your key to understanding what *recap*itulation is. When someone says that they believe Revelation is to be understood as a series of recapitulations, what they are saying is that the central storyline is at least at some point retold. This method is not a new one, as it goes back all the way to Victorinus of Pettau (d. 304 AD). He appears to be the first to propose a recapitulative method of interpreting Revelation (as well as the first to propose the "Nero Redivivus" idea).[209] He claimed that the seven bowls and seven trumpets were repetitious, saying, "the order of what is said is not to be looked at, for the Holy Spirit often returns to the present when He has traversed to the end of times and fills up what He neglected to say" before concluding succinctly, "order is not to be sought in the apocalypse; instead, we must follow the meaning of what is prophesied."[210]

Recapitulation as an interpretive method fell in popularity in the 14th century with the writings of Nicolas of Lyra, who largely coined what would now be identified as historicist interpretation.[211] There were a couple of German New Testament scholars in the mid-18th century who are noted as having "employed" the method, but they are very

---

[208] One might note that this is quite close to the Preterist view, with the distinguishing factor being that preterists claim the events took place in the time of John while this view holds that they took place then and also take place in each subsequent generation leading to a final culmination in the last day.
[209] Mounce, *The Book of Revelation*, 25.
[210] Johannes Havssleiter, ed., *Victorini Episcopi Petavionensis Opera*, 86. [From Victorinus, *Commentary on the Apocalypse*, 7:2. Author's translation]
[211] Mounce, *The Book of Revelation*, 25-26.

few and far between.[212] It seems to have come back into mainstream theorizing with William Lee in the late 1800's, and greatly increased in popularity after the publication of William Hendriksen's *More Than Conquerors* in 1940.[213]

Because of its widespread acceptance among critical scholars, the most popular alternative view – dubbed the "progression view" because of its conception of a chronological progression throughout Revelation – has largely been relegated as a position held only by futurists of a popular variety. However, many scholars even outside of the American scene have recently defended the progression position of interpretation in some of the most critical academic journals.[214] Those who hold to a "progressive" position on interpreting Revelation believe that it is in some sense "telescopic" or "dove-tailing."[215] Yet, perhaps as a surprise to some, many of those arguing for a progressive sequence still accept recapitulation in certain sections.[216]

Identifying and Defending the Style of Recapitulation Espoused Herein

Authors have long attempted to compose a universally agreeable standard around which recapitulations could be judged, without much fortune in doing so.[217] For example, R. Fowler White proposed a system in which recapitulations were to be recognized based on storylines which compose each section – that is, the general overview of each section would be the same. This position is favorable in some sense, as it maintains an element of simplicity that the lay-reader can certainly appreciate. After all, when reading through the Revelation, one must assume that the "beast" of Revelation 19 is the same beast as is mentioned in Revelation 13. Surely the False Prophet of Revelation 16 is the same as the False Prophet referenced in Revelation 20. The location and actions of these recurring characters definitely assist readers in understanding the chronology of events within the recapitulations. It is perhaps the case, though, that White went a step

---

[212] See Johan Albrecht Bengel, *Gnomon Novi Testamenti* (Tubingae, 1742). Referenced in Lund, "Presence of Chiasmus in the New Testament", 75.

[213] Robert L. Thomas, "The Structure of the Apocalypse: Recapitulation or Progression?" *The Masters Seminary Journal* 4:1 (Spring 1993), 47.

[214] For example, see Marko Jauhiainen, "Recapitulation and Chronological Progression in John's Apocalypse: Towards a New Perspective" *New Testament Studies* 49 (2003): 543-559. Published by Cambridge University Press.

[215] Thomas, "The Structure of the Apocalypse", 47.

[216] Ibid., 62.

[217] Time and space prevent the author from delving into the many proposals of various recapitulative divisions, but in short they can include anything from linguistic choices, the presence of doxologies, or any number of other factors which never seem to manifest any greater weight of logical reasoning than any others. For a helpful overview of some of the theories, see Elisabeth S. Fiorenza, "Composition and Structure of the Book of Revelation" *The Catholic Biblical Quarterly* 39:3 (July 1977), 361-362.

too far, saying that the "content of the visions" would ultimately be "the only relevant point."[218]

In contrast to White, Adela Collins slightly differs, offering a system in which the central key to identifying recapitulations would lie in the recognition of patterns and motifs rather than explicit characters or storylines.[219] Collins maintains that "each cycle of visions tells the story of the end in its own way," even going so far as to make the comparison that each "repetition is somewhat like that of a musical theme…"[220] This approach is also quite well-taken, as White's reliance on particular characters, events, or storylines leaves readers searching for figures and events which sometimes do not appear at all. If readers understand that each recapitulation is simply a retelling of the story with a different lens – or as Collins would put it – the playing of the same song on a different key or at a different volume, then the absence of certain indicators and markers is no large thing. And yet, this view does leave lacking what White's view maintained in the simplicity of being able to recognize key figures and events as corresponding to one another between recapitulations. If the themes and motifs are all that matter, then the specific content would seem to be almost completely subject to manipulation without consequence – and yet, many of the characters and events do seem to persist throughout the latter half of the book despite the clear shift of storylines.

As has already been noted, no system for identifying recapitulations has been universally accepted. As a result, much effort has been expended towards developing a system for this text in which they can be logically recognized and delimited. White's method of recognizing recapitulations through content repetition, as well as Collins' method of recognizing them through repetitious themes and motifs each serve well in positively identifying possible recapitulations, but in order to narrow down which possibilities are most likely to stand up to scrutiny, three additional metrics have been used. Though none of them constitute rules for positively identifying a recapitulation, they do provide a guide on the negative end for eliminating some from plausibility.

First, some recapitulations are recognizable because they initiate a new vision. New visions (in Revelation specifically) always carry two characteristics: a heavenly figure approaches John and he notes that he was "taken in the Spirit." This occurs in Revelation 1:10-11; 4:1-2; 17:1-3; and 21:9-10.[221] A second recognizable trait is sometimes seen

---

[218] R. Fowler White, "Making Sense of Rev 20:1-10? Harold Hoehner Versus Recapitulation" *Journal of the Evangelical Theological Society* 37:4 (December 1994), 540.
[219] As noted in Charles H. Giblin, "Recapitulation and the Literary Coherence of John's Apocalypse" *The Catholic Biblical Quarterly* 56 (1994), 82.
[220] Adela Y. Collins, *The Apocalypse,* New Testament Message: Biblical-Theological Commentary, 43.
[221] George Eldon Ladd, *A Commentary on the Revelation of John*, 221.

through linguistic indications within the text itself. This occurs, for example, in Revelation 15:1, when John inserts atypical language constituting a commentary of the ensuing sections. He introduces the plagues that follow by saying they are "the last, for with them the wrath of God is finished." This commentary on his own vision is rather uncharacteristic, and in the only other instances wherein he does something similar (15:7 and 16:1) the characters and events referenced are already known in the storyline. In 15:1, this commentary comes entirely anew with only John aware of what he is referencing, indicating that the storyline set to follow is not the same as what was previously written. Finally, a third metric is that of narrative indications. This is most easily described as the introduction of new settings, characters, or events that have nothing to do with those previous to them (a method just used conjunctively as a tool for confirming the uniqueness of the language in 15:1). Another example is that of Revelation 12:1-6, wherein new characters like the woman and the beast are introduced, as well as a new setting of the "wilderness" that has no place in the prior events. In summary, even if a section contains repetitious content, themes, or motifs as identified by White and Collins, but does not fit any of the three delimiting aspects, then it is unlikely to be a valid recapitulation.

This approach is seen as a variation from those taken before and is considered a great improvement on formulating a meaningful and defensible structure. While substantially different, the recapitulative divisions are similar in recognizable ways to the approach taken by J.P.M. Sweet in his 1979 commentary, *Revelation*.[222] Yet, the rationale for the division of these recapitulations is arguably much better justified. Kenneth Strand takes a similar approach when describing the events within each recapitulative subsection, claiming a "victorious-introduction scene… a basic prophetic description… an interlude… and the eschatological culmination."[223] However, his approach lacks a unifying macrostructure that brings the whole book into one comprehensive sum. Furthermore, one might compare this commentary's division structure to that of George E. Ladd's, whose commentary admirably attempted to divide the Revelation into four groups of seven, but did nothing to explain the omissions of whole sections of the book from that outline. Ladd evidently felt no conflict in labelling chapters 4, 12, 13, and 14 as "interludes which briefly interrupt the flow of the narrative and do not belong to the

[222] J.P.M. Sweet, *Revelation.*

[223] Kenneth Strand, "The Eight Basic Visions in the Book of Revelation" *Andrews University Seminary Studies* 25 (1987): 107-121.

four series of sevens" even though there was no other explanation for why they appeared where they did, or what purpose they served in being interjected into the text.[224]

Thus, the recognition of recapitulative sections in this commentary will be somewhere between the two approaches of White and Collins. Collins' emphasis on the overarching themes and motifs has been used to identify the eight sections of recapitulation, while White's attention to recurring characters and events has been applied to specify what aspects of recapitulation are taking place in each subsection. In applying these two approaches, delimiting them with my own three metrics, a new reflection has been made on the book, which is that it is not only recapitulative, but chiastic. For the first time (at least to the author's knowledge) this commentary will follow an outline for Revelation in which the recapitulations themselves form a chiastic structure across the entire book.

As one final point of clarification, let it be said forthrightly that chiastic scholars such as Nils Lund would likely reject the proposition that this commentary has anything equating to a chiasm in it. Lund, for example, required that a chiastic piece of literature have at its center "a turning point" which could also be called the "climax" upon which the entire story hinged.[225] This commentary does not have that. Rather, each recapitulation is said to tell the entire story from beginning to end, and therefore, the chiastic structure of the book is related to the macrostructure of the book as a whole, rather than the narrative within it. The author is nevertheless confident in the coining of the term "chiastic recapitulation" in describing this commentary, as Kenneth Strand argued against Lund that chiastic structures could be recognized based *both* on the basis of the macrostructure and also by the patterns manifested throughout each section. This commentary endeavors to manifest both.[226]

---

[224] George E. Ladd, *A Commentary on the Revelation of John*, 14.

[225] Nils W. Lund, *Studies in the Book of Revelation*, 42.

[226] Strand, "The Eight Basic Visions", 107-121.

The Chiastic Recapitulative Approach to Revelation

1a. **1:1-8** Prologue/Introduction

2a. **1:9-20** King Jesus Ruling in Heaven
3a. **2:1-3:22** God's Imperfect People

4a. **4:1-5:14** The Heavenly Preparation for the Tribulation
5a. **6:1-17** Overview of the Tribulation
6a. **7:1-17** PAUSE: The Church's Hope in the Tribulation
7a. **8:1** God Arrives on Earth

4b. **8:2-5** The Heavenly Preparation for Tribulation
5b. **8:6-9:21** Overview of the Tribulation
8a. **10:1-11** John Confirmed as the True Prophet
6b. **11:1-14** PAUSE: The Church's Hope in the Tribulation
7b. **11:15-19** God Arrives on Earth

4c. **12:1-6** The Heavenly Preparation for the Tribulation
5c. **12:7-13:10** Overview of the Tribulation
8b. **13:11-18** The Second Beast Condemned as the False Prophet
6c. **14:1-5** PAUSE: The Church's Hope in the Tribulation
7c. **14:6-20** God Arrives on Earth

4d. **15:1-8** The Heavenly Preparation for the Tribulation
5d. **16:1-18:24** Overview of the Tribulation
6d. **19:1-10** PAUSE: The Church's Hope in the Tribulation
7d. **19:11-21** God Arrives on Earth

2b. **20:1-15** King Jesus Ruling on Earth
3b. **21:1-22:5** God's Perfected People

1b. **22:6-21** Epilogue/Conclusion

Fig. 2.2

**Explanatory Note:* The use of the word "pause" in the place of what Strand and Ladd referred to as "interludes" is purely for the purpose of understandability. What have been referred to as interludes in the narrative are colloquially referred to as "pauses" in the story for the purpose of holding one's place while another narrative somewhat interrupts, importantly, before recommencing the previous narrative.

B. Approach to Scripture

As to the topic of what version of the Bible will be used, the issue deals less with a preference in translation choice, and more with a preference on textual basis. To avoid delving into an issue that is far too complicated to properly map out in a subsection such as this, let it be said as a point of introduction that some modern versions (such as the English Standard Version [ESV]) are based upon Greek texts which are different from other versions (such as the King James Version [KJV]). In this commentary, the Greek texts used to produce the ESV will be considered of much more value than that which was used to produce the KJV. It is this belief that will be explained in this section.

Erasmus and the Production of the Novum Instrumentum Omne

Desiderius Erasmus of Rotterdam was a Roman Catholic priest who lived from 1466-1536. He was a well-educated man, especially for his day, having mastered the Latin and Greek languages to such a degree that he was invited to teach Biblical languages at Cambridge in 1511, which he did until 1514 when he left England to return to mainland Europe so he could publish several important works. One of those works would be his 1516 edition of the Greek New Testament, which he entitled the "*Novum Instrumentum Omne*."[227] When composing his Greek New Testament, Erasmus consulted seven manuscripts:

Manuscripts Consulted by Erasmus		
Manuscript	**Containing**	**Date of Composition**
Codex 1*eap*	Whole New Testament except Revelation	12th Century
Codex 2*e*	The Gospels	12th Century
Codex 817	The Gospels	15th Century
Codex 2*ap*	Acts and the Epistles	12th Century (perhaps later)
Codex 4*ap*	Acts and the Epistles	15th Century
Codex 7*p*	The Pauline Epistles	11th Century
Codex 1*r*[228]	Revelation except for the last 6 verses (Rev. 22:16-21)	12th Century
Fig. 2.3[229]		

[227] William W. Combs, "Erasmus and the Textus Receptus" *Detroit Baptist Seminary Journal* 1:1 (Spring 1996), 37-38.

[228] While originally identified as "1*r*" on the basis of the historical development of the Greek New Testament beginning with Erasmus, this document is now identified frequently by the Gregory-Aland numbering system as "Miniscule 2814."

As can be seen, Erasmus relied on only one manuscript for his rendering of the book of Revelation, which had been borrowed from Jahannes Reuchlin – who in turn had borrowed it from the Dominicans. Importantly, Codex 1*r* (the manuscript now frequently known as 2814, and the only manuscript containing Revelation that Erasmus had access to), was not strictly a Greek edition of Revelation, but was rather a copy of a Greek commentary on Revelation written by Andreas of Caesarea.[230] Andreas penned the commentary sometime in the 7th century, meaning that the copy Erasmus possessed was penned several centuries after the original, with an unknown number of copies having been produced in that interim period. To add to the issues, the edition present at the time was centuries old, and consequently Erasmus required a new edition in order to use it for his purposes. Therefore, he commissioned a copyist (whose identity is lost to history) to produce another copy of this commentary for his use, upon completion of which he returned the 12th century copy to Reuchlin.[231]

For a couple centuries, the 12th century manuscript which Erasmus copied (sometimes called *Codex Reuchlini*) was lost. It was not until the mid-nineteenth century that Franz Delitzsch discovered it and publicized its contents.[232] That event has shaken the foundations of, at a minimum, the reliability of the book of Revelation in Erasmus' Greek New Testament. Delitzsch, upon his discovery of the original commentary, began to elaborate on the problems caused by that discovery, saying,

> If we look back at the comparison that has now been carried out between the Erasmian text and its source manuscript, not only has the unfortunate result emerged that Erasmus reproduced the text found very incorrectly, without re-collating it, as would have been his duty to correct, but also that many of the peculiar Erasmian readings which are based on misreading and negligent copying passed into the Stephaniana of 1550 and the Elzeviriana of 1624, and thus became parts of the Textus Receptus. The history of the New Testament text is a sad web of unscientificness, charlatanry and typographical nonsense. The criticism that began after 1650, which placed stricter demands on itself, is not yet finished with exposing and eliminating these falsifications consciously and unconsciously committed to the traditional text by earlier bungling.[233]

---

[229] Combs, "Erasmus and the Textus Receptus", 45.
[230] Combs, "Erasmus and the Textus Receptus", 46.
[231] Erika Rummel, *Erasmus' Annotations on the New Testament*, 38.
[232] Jan Krans, *Beyond What is Written: Erasmus and Beza as Conjectural Critics of the New Testament*, 54.
[233] Franz Delitzsch, *Handschriftliche Funde: Die Erasmischen Entstellungen des Textes der Apokalypse, Nachgewiesen aus dem verloren geglaubten Codex Reuchlins*, Book 1, 57. [*Author's translation*] This text is by

One may read this and wonder, what was Delitzsch's rationale for speaking so critically of Erasmus' translation? Upon review of the original manuscript, it became clear that even that manuscript had not been properly conveyed to Erasmus. When the copyist produced the fresh edition for Erasmus' use, he evidently misread it and introduced a number of errors into it before Erasmus ever laid a hand on it.[234] For example, notes William Combs, "in Revelation 17:4, Codex 1*r* and all other Greek manuscripts have the word α κάθαρτα ("impure"), but Erasmus' text reads α καθάρτητος, a word unknown in Greek literature. In a similar fashion, the words και παρέσται ("and is to come") in 17:8 were misread as καίπερ εστιν ("and yet is")." [235]

Beyond this, the final page of the commentary was missing, leaving the final six verses of Revelation missing. Erasmus was not secretive about how he addressed this problem, writing in his annotated edition "from our Latin we supplied the Greek."[236] This practice (which was not exclusive to his work in Revelation and which has never been corrected) was a major mistake. Combs, for simply one example, examines the Erasmian text and concludes that this practice alone "produced, by my count, twenty errors in his Greek NT which are still in [it] today."[237] To make matters worse, Erasmus writes in his annotated edition that he would frequently render the Greek not from the manuscripts before him, nor even from the Latin Vulgate, but from "other manuscripts he had seen in the course of his travels."[238] This appears to be his practice in Rev. 1:4 and 8:13.[239]

Thus, there are many reasons to believe that the edition of Revelation produced by Erasmus at the outset of the 16th century was not an accurate rendering of the Greek text that the church was given by the Apostle John. This conclusion has been repeatedly affirmed, but perhaps nowhere more strongly and clearly than by Combs who writes, "It is based on a few very late manuscripts, and in some cases has no Greek manuscript support whatever."[240]

There are some instances in which Erasmus cannot be held to blame, and thus the rationale for rejecting his rendering is not an attack on his character or even strictly an

---

far the most important book on the issue of Erasmus' failures in rendering Revelation, and it has yet to be translated into English. The full Codex Reuchlini is available in Book 2 of the text beginning on page 9.

234 Rummel, *Erasmus' Annotations*, 38.

235 Combs, "Erasmus and the Textus Receptus", 46.

236 Rummer, *Erasmus' Annotations*, 38, n.15. Originally in the Latin, "*ex nostris Latinis supplevimus Graeca.*"

237 Combs, "Erasmus and the Textus Receptus," 47.

238 Frederick H.A. Scrivener, *A Plain Introduction to the Criticism of the New Testament,* Vol. 2, 184.

239 Scrivener, *A Plain Introduction* Vol. 2, 184, n.1.

240 Combs, "Erasmus and the Textus Receptus", 53.

attack on his methods (though they certainly stand to be criticized). As noted, there were several obstacles which prevented Erasmus from making an accurate rendering of Revelation which were out of his control. He could not change the fact that there were no available Greek manuscripts of Revelation. He could not change that the only place to find it was in a commentary of relatively recent production, which was likely copied from its own original several times before getting to him. He could not change that the copyist made mistakes in copying the copy before delivering it to him.

Beyond all of this, there were other factors which Erasmus could not control that greatly disadvantaged him. For one example, in 1862 S.P. Tregelles examined the commentary Erasmus used, and noted that the "actual Scriptures were interspersed throughout the commentary" making it difficult to determine what was commentary on the Scripture and what was Scripture itself. Evidently, the only way that the Scriptures were demarcated was by the initial word, or sometimes even the initial letter, of the text being written in red ink rather than the standard black. The problem, then, is that when reading by candlelight it was understandably difficult to recognize the red ink as distinct from the black on such an old document.[241]

However, there is still a burden of guilt that resides on Erasmus for his insertions of terms and phrases into the Greek text that were derived either from the Latin Vulgate or some memory Erasmus himself had from a text he had seen at some point in his previous work. The chart that follows is compiled to show that Erasmus did not even render the Greek text that he produced from the Reuchlin text. That is not to say that his Greek rendering was necessarily incorrect, as several of the revisions that he made were closer to the original than the Reuchlin text. It is to say, though, as Tregelles notes, it appears that Erasmus took complete liberty in amending the Greek based on "what he believed to be the sacred text."[242]

---

[241] Delitzsch, *Hadschriftliche Funde,* Book 2, 2.

[242] Delitzsch, *Hadschriftliche Funde,* Book 2, 5.

Erasmian Departures from the Codex Reuchlini [243]		
Scripture	*Codex Reuchlini*	Erasmus' Rendering
Revelation 2:2	*PHRASE IS NOT PRESENT*	καὶ ἐπειράσω τοὺς φάσκοντας εἶναι ἀποστόλους καὶ
2:3	*PHRASE IS NOT PRESENT*	καὶ οὐ κέκμηκας
2:17	*PHRASE IS NOT PRESENT*	ὃ οὐδεὶς ἔγνω εἰ μὴ ὁ λαμβάνων
3:5	*PHRASE IS NOT PRESENT*	αὐτοῦ ἐκ τῆς βίβλου τῆς ζωῆς καὶ ἐξομολογήσομαι τὸ ὄνομα
5:14	*PHRASE IS NOT PRESENT*	εἴκοσιτέσσαρες
5:14	*PHRASE IS NOT PRESENT*	ζῶντι εἰς τοὺς αἰωνας τῶν αἰώνων[244]
6:1	*PHRASE IS NOT PRESENT*	καὶ βλέπε
6:3	*PHRASE IS NOT PRESENT*	καὶ βλέπε
6:5	*PHRASE IS NOT PRESENT*	καὶ βλέπε
6:7	*PHRASE IS NOT PRESENT*	καὶ βλέπε
6:11	*PHRASE IS NOT PRESENT*	ἑκάστοις στολαὶ λευκαὶ
7:17	*PHRASE IS NOT PRESENT*	καὶ ἐξαλείψει ὁ θεὸς πᾶν δάκρυον ἀπὸ τῶν ὀφθαλμῶν αὐτῶν[245]
13:4	*PHRASE IS NOT PRESENT*	καὶ προσεκύνησαν τὸ θηρίον λέγοντες τίς ὅμοιος τῷ θηρίῳ
13:5	*PHRASE IS NOT PRESENT*	καὶ ἐδόθη αὐτῷ στόμα λαλοῦν μεγάλα καὶ βλασφημίας
13:10	*PHRASE IS NOT PRESENT*	εἰς αἰχμαλωσίαν ὑπάγει
14:5	*PHRASE IS NOT PRESENT*	ἐνώπιον τοῦ θρόνου τοῦ θεοῦ
14:16	*PHRASE IS NOT PRESENT*	καθήμενος ἐπὶ τὴν νεφέλην τὸ δρέπανον αὐτοῦ
17:8	α κάθαρτα	α καθάρτητος
17:8	και παρέσται	καίπερ εστιν
20:10	*PHRASE IS NOT PRESENT*	εἰς τοὺς αἰῶνας τῶν αἰώνων
20:12	*PHRASE IS NOT PRESENT*	καὶ βιβλίον ἄλλο ἠνεῳχθη

243 This chart (which is not comprehensive) is largely a visual aid to summarize the conclusions of S.P. Tregelles in Delitzsch, *Hadschriftliche Funde,* Book 2; along with those of Combs in "Erasmus and the Textus Receptus", 46.

244 This phrase (as well as that added to 14:5) is neither in the Codex Reuchlini nor the Latin Vulgate.

245 Erasmus did not originally render this phrase in the text but returned to amend it after translating 21:4. Per Tregelles in Delitzsch, *Hadschriftliche Funde,* Book 2, 5.

20:14	*PHRASE IS NOT PRESENT*	οὗτος ἐστιν ὁ δεύτερός θάνατος
21:16	*PHRASE IS NOT PRESENT*	καὶ τὸ μῆκος αὐτῆς τοσοῦτόν ἐστίν ὅσον καὶ τὸ πλάτος
22:11	*PHRASE IS NOT PRESENT*	καὶ ὁ ῥυπῶν ῥυπωσάτω ἔτι καὶ ὁ δίκαιος δικαιωθήτω ἔτι καὶ ὁ ἅγιος ἁγιασθήτω ἔτι
22:16-21	*PASSAGE WAS MISSING*	Entire Passage
	Fig. 2.4	

Reworking Erasmus' Novum Instrumentum Omne into the Textus Receptus

Some have mistakenly believed that the Greek rendering produced by Desiderius Erasmus was the *Textus Receptus* (*TR*). While it is true that his Greek text was a primary ingredient in the *TR*, it would be incorrect to say they were equivalent to one another. This can be better understood by first grasping that Erasmus published five different editions of his Greek text, with several changes made across them. With regard to his rendering of the book of Revelation, Erasmus' first revision made no changes, as the Codex Cosendoucensis that he used to revise his text contained the entire New Testament – except Revelation. He evidently instructed proofreaders to correct the final six verses that he had supplied from the Latin, telling them to render the words as had been done in the recently published Aldine edition. The problem, as Krans puts it, was that "it seems Erasmus never realized that the text of the New Testament in the Aldine edition is derived from his own first edition."[246]

The third edition of his text saw some changes to Revelation as he used the Codex Montfortianus – but these revisions were of no greater quality than those made in his first edition, as he introduced errors that were once more his own mistake. For example, in Revelation 2:13, he erroneously asserted ἐμαῖς where the Greek read ἐν ταῖς.[247] His fourth edition was a recognizable improvement, as he utilized the Complutensian text to make corrections in 90 unique passages of Revelation.[248] This is remarkable, as there were 10 to 23 (depending on whose count one trusts) other places where he made revisions between the third and fourth editions in the entire Bible.[249] And yet, one is still left

[246] Krans, *Beyond What is Written*, 54, n.16.

[247] Frederick H.A. Scrivener, *A Plain Introduction to the Criticism of the New Testament*, Vol. 1, 200.

[248] Bruce M. Metzger and Bart D. Ehrman, *The Text of the New Testament: It's Transmission, Corruption, and Restoration* 4, 148.

[249] Tregelles agrees with Mills that there were only 10 other places of difference, while Scrivener says there were "106 or 113" total places with "90 being those from the Apocalypse." See Samuel P. Tregelles, *An Account of the Printed Text of the Greek New Testament*, 27.; and Scrivener, *A Plain Introduction*, 434.

somewhat unfulfilled by his work, as according to Tregelles, "more corrections *might* have been made; but Erasmus seems to have forgotten what all the places were which he had himself turned into Greek [from the Latin], ten years before, to supply the defects."[250] Thus, even his revisions of revisions in Revelation were flawed and incomplete.

Despite the fact that these errors were known almost immediately, most of them were (for whatever reason) treated as of little consequence – and never corrected. A man named Robert Estinne (more commonly known as Stephanus) began publishing editions of the Greek text in 1546 and went through four editions of his own by 1551.[251] His first two editions sought to find a middle-ground between the Erasmian texts and the Complutensian text, but by his third edition he recognizably relies on Erasmus more than any other source.[252]

Only a few years after Stephanus' fourth and final edition in 1551 (which notably was the first edition to mark verse divisions), Theodore de Beze (or Beza) began publishing his own Greek New Testaments in Geneva, going through ten editions between 1565 and 1611 (the final edition being published posthumously, with his final edition published while alive in 1604).[253] By 1588, however, it was clear that Beza was endeavoring to align his text with the fourth edition of Stephanus, as despite his greatly improved library of Greek manuscripts, his texts decreasingly variated from those of Stephanus who utilized none of those manuscripts.[254] Instead, Beza would maintain the rendering of Stephanus and place variant readings either in the margins or beneath the text. It has been noted that in many cases, Beza's notations of variants have shown what is now considered to be the proper term.[255]

Oddly enough, despite his evident hesitance to variate from the text produced by Stephanus, which itself was based off of the text produced by Erasmus, Beza took unfathomable liberty with the text by introducing some "conjectural emendations" in which he proposed a change to the text which had no manuscriptal evidence.[256] One such instance is found in Revelation 16:5, in which Beza read the text, "Righteous, O

---

[250] Tregelles, *An Account of the Printed Text*, 27.
[251] Metzger and Ehrman, *The Text of the New Testament*, 149.
[252] Ibid., 150. Metzger and Ehrman point out that Stephanus relied on Erasmus' 4th and 5th editions, which as shown above were improvements in regards to Revelation, but far from completely correct.
[253] Ibid., 151.
[254] Ibid., 151-152.
[255] White, *The King James Only Controversy*, 63.
[256] For a thorough treatment of this topic in both the Greek texts of Erasmus and Beza, see Jan Krans, *Beyond What is Written: Erasmus and Beza as Conjectural Critics of the New Testament*.

Lord, are you, who are and who were, the Holy One..." and chose to delete the final phrase and replace it, producing, "Righteous, O Lord, are you, who are and who were and who shall be..."[257] Interestingly, when the English translators rendering the King James Version in 1611 took up the Greek texts of Erasmus, Stephanus, and Beza, it was this phrase that made it into the English translation despite not being found in the *Textus Receptus* (see below). Evidently, there are no fewer than 9 instances in which Beza variated from Stephanus and Erasmus in his Greek rendering of the book of Revelation, and without spending unneeded space examining those variations, one can rightly imagine that some of those unique renderings made their way into texts supposedly based upon the *TR* despite his propositions being unfound therein.[258]

King James Diversion from the *Textus Receptus*		
Textus Receptus (Greek)	**Textus Receptus (English)**	**King James Version**
"καὶ ἤκουσα τοῦ ἀγγέλου τῶν ὑδάτων λέγοντος δίκαιος κύριε εἶ ὁ ὢν καὶ ὁ ἦν καὶ **ὁ ὅσιος** ὅτι ταῦτα ἔκρινας"	"And I heard the angel of the waters saying, 'Righteous, O Lord, art thou, who art and who wast and **the holy one**, that these things didst judge;"[259]	"And I heard the angel of the waters say, 'Thou art righteous, O Lord, which art, and wast, **and shalt be,** because thou hast judged thus."
Fig. 2.5		

As a conclusion to this subsection, let it be shown through a couple of graphs that the *Textus Receptus* makes a habit of not only deleting or omitting phrases that appear in the majority of the Greek manuscripts of Revelation, but it also makes a regular habit of imposing minority positions into the text – even when those "minority" positions have been historically shown to be entirely scribal errors caused by Erasmus, Stephanus, or Beza themselves, as in the case of Erasmus' misrendering of "tree" to "book" in Revelation 22:19, or in the case of Beza imposing "and shall come" upon Revelation 16:5. When writing a commentary on Revelation, it is (in the opinion of this author) irresponsible to use a text that clearly has so many mistakes or errors in it when superior texts exist. For this reason (among others) the English text used is the ESV, and the Greek text utilized is the NA-28 (the most recent edition as of the time of printing).

---

[257] Ibid.

[258] For the 9 variations between Stephanus and Beza in Revelation, as well as a list of 30 other places in which he variated from Stephanus throughout the New Testament, see Eduardus Reuss, *Bibliotheca Novi Testamenti* Graeci, 143-144.

[259] To avoid any bias, this rendering is taken directly from *The Interlinear Literal Translation of the Greek New Testament with the Authorized Version*, 653.

Instances of the Textus Receptus Omitting/Deleting the Text				
Ref.	ESV	Nestle-Aland 28	Textus Receptus	KJV
1:8[260]	"I am the Alpha and the Omega," says the Lord **God**…	Ἐγώ εἰμι τὸ ἄλφα καὶ τὸ ὦ, λέγει κύριος **ὁ θεός**,	ἐγώ εἰμι τὸ α καὶ τὸ ω ἀρχὴ καὶ τέλος, λέγει ὁ κύριος	I am Alpha and Omega, the beginning and the ending, saith the Lord…
6:1	the Lamb opened one of the **seven** seals…	τὸ ἀρνίον μίαν ἐκ τῶν **ἑπτὰ** σφραγίδων,	τὸ ἀρνίον μίαν ἐκ τῶν σφραγίδων	The Lamb opened one of the seals…
6:12	and the **full** moon became like blood,	καὶ ἡ σελήνη **ὅλη** ἐγένετο ὡς αἷμα	καὶ ἡ σελήνη ἐγένετο ὡς αἷμα	and the moon became like blood
8:7	These were thrown upon the earth. **And a third of the earth was burned up**, and a third of the trees were burned up…	καὶ ἐβλήθη εἰς τὴν γῆν, **καὶ τὸ τρίτον τῆς γῆς κατεκάη** καὶ τὸ τρίτον τῶν δένδρων	καὶ ἐβλήθη εἰς τὴν γῆν καὶ τὸ τρίτον τῶν δένδρων	They were cast upon the earth: and the third part of trees was burnt up…
14:1[261]	Who had **his name** and his Father's name written on their foreheads.	ἔχουσαι **τὸ ὄνομα αὐτοῦ** καὶ τὸ ὄνομα τοῦ Πατρὸς αὐτοῦ γεγραμμένον	ἔχουσαι τὸ ὄνομα τοῦ πατρὸς αὐτοῦ γεγραμμένον	Having his Father's name written in their foreheads.
Fig. 2.6				

[260] Metzger comments on this, saying, "If the longer text were original, no good reason can be found to account for the shorter text, whereas the presence of the longer expression in 21:6 obviously prompted some copyists to expand the text here." Bruce M. Metzger, *A Textual Commentary on the Greek New Testament* 3, 732.

[261] The error in this passage is easy to explain, as it is what is sometimes referred to as a *homoeoteleuton*, or a situation in which two phrases share a similar structure, and therefore are mistaken for one another. James White contends that "the repetition of the phrase 'his name' [τὸ ὄνομα] caused those few scribes to skip to the second occurrence, deleting the reference to the name of the Lamb." James White, *The King James Only Controversy*, 65-66. The same mistake was likely made in 8:7 due to the phrase "καὶ τὸ τρίτον" being repeated.

Instances of the Textus Receptus Taking Minority Positions				
Ref.	ESV	Nestle-Aland 28	Textus Receptus	KJV
1:6	And made us a kingdom, priests to his God…	καὶ ἐποίησεν ἡμᾶς βασιλείαν, ἱερεῖς τῷ θεῷ	καὶ ἐποίησεν ἡμᾶς **βασιλεῖς καὶ** ἱερεῖς τῷ θεῷ	And hath made us **kings and priests** unto God…
6:17[262]	The great day of their wrath has come…	ἡ μεγάλη τῆς ὀργῆς αὐτῶν,	ἡ μεγάλη τῆς ὀργῆς **αὐτοῦ**	The great day of **his** wrath is come;
8:13[263]	I heard an eagle…	ἤκουσα ἑνὸς ἀετοῦ	ἤκουσα ἑνὸς **ἀγγέλου**	I beheld, and heard an **angel**…
11:17[264]	Lord God Almighty, who is and who was, for you have…	κύριε ὁ θεὸς ὁ παντοκράτωρ, ὁ ὢν καὶ ὁ ἦν, ὅτι εἴληφας	κύριε ὁ θεὸς ὁ παντοκράτωρ ὁ ὢν καὶ ὁ ἦν **καὶ ὁ ἐρχόμενος** ὅτι εἴληφας	O Lord God Almighty, which art, and wast, **and art to come**; because thou hast
15:3[265]	O King of the nations!	ὁ βασιλεὺς τῶν ἐθνῶν·	ὁ βασιλεὺς τῶν **ἁγίων**	Thou King of the **saints.**

[262] J.K. Elliott explores the cause of this variant, which differs only in the tensing of the final word. Elliot notes that "αὐτοῦ [is] the easier reading as it avoids the ambiguity of the genitive plural and carries a reference to τῆς ὀργῆς τοῦ ἀρνίου in v. 16" but he also notes that David Aune differs in this interpretation, claiming that αὐτῶν presents no such ambiguity, as "αὐτῶν refers to the one on the throne and to the Lamb." James K. Elliott, "Revelations from the *Apparatus Criticus* of the Book of Revelation" *Union Seminary Quarterly Review* 63 (2012), 15.

[263] Metzger comments on this passage, saying, "The Textus Receptus… reads αγγελου. The substitution may have been accidental (a scribe misread ἀετοῦ as αγγελου) but more likely was deliberate, since the function ascribed to the eagle seems more appropriate to an angel (cf. 14.6)" He adds later, "had the Apocalyptist written αγγελου, αλλου would probably have taken the place of ἑνός; cf. 7.2; 8.3." Metzger, *A Textual Commentary*, 734.

[264] The TR includes the longer form of the tripartite expression found in 1:4, 8, and 4:8. Metzger notes that the shorter alternative has "superior external evidence and… best explains the origin of the other readings." Metzger, *A Textual Commentary*, 747. Elliot agrees that in this context "the coming of God has occurred or is occurring… and so [the third aspect of the phrase] demands omission." Elliott, "Revelations from the *Apparatus Criticus*", 16.

[265] Most scholars agree that the editors of the Textus Receptus introduced the word "αἰώνων" (eternal) due to a recollection of its appearance in 1 Timothy 1:17. When rendered in Latin, "αἰώνων" became *saeculorum*. When rendering the Latin back into Greek, *saeculorum* (the word for centuries or eternities) was often penned in shorthand as "sclorum" and could easily be mistaken for *sanctorum* (the word for saints) which was often written in shorthand as "sctorum." Only two Greek manuscripts support the inclusion of ἁγίων (296 and 2049), neither of which was available when the Textus Receptus was formed. Metzger, *A Textual Commentary*, 755-756. See also Elliot's comments, which display some skepticism, in Elliot, "Revelations from the *Apparatus Criticus*", 20-21.

20:9[266]	Fire came down from heaven and consumed them,	κατέβη πῦρ ἐκ τοῦ οὐρανοῦ καὶ κατέφαγεν αὐτούς.	κατέβη πῦρ **ἀπὸ τοῦ θεοῦ** ἐκ τοῦ οὐρανοῦ καὶ κατέφαγεν αὐτούς.	Fire came down **from God** out of heaven, and devoured them.
22:19[267]	In the tree of life	τοῦ ξύλου τῆς ζωῆς	**ἀπὸ βίβλου** τῆς ζωῆς	Of the **book** of life

Fig. 2.7

C. Approach to Eschatology

A few years ago, I was invited to speak at a conference on the eschatological position of Historic Premillennialism. I outlined in brief my understanding of the eschatological timeline with specific attention being paid to Revelation 19:11-20:10. During a panel discussion involving the speakers at the conference, the representative of the amillennialist view asked me if I was in line with men such as J. Webb Mealy and Eckhard Schnabel. I responded that I was most certainly not in line with J.W. Mealy and had little knowledge of the writings of Schnabel. Later, in an online Q&A session that followed the conference, I was asked if I was defending the position of New Creation Millennialism, rather than Historic Premillennialism. I responded that I was certainly not doing that – but that I was excited about a rumor I had heard which claimed that Thomas Schreiner was writing a commentary on Revelation from the New Creation Millennialist perspective.

The inquiries about my position have continued, with many returning to this question of whether or not I am truly a proponent of Historic Premillennialism, or if I am actually a New Creation Millennialist. With much more literature now in hand regarding the issue, I can now say with absolute conviction that what I am holding *is* Historic Premillennialism. The issue that I would like to provide clarity on is not whether I am a member of the New Creation Millennialist camp or not, but instead, whether the New Creation Millennialist camp is a separate position from Historic Premillennialism, or simply one position within that broader community.

---

[266] The weight of evidence is firmly in favor of the omission of God's name here, and Metzger theorizes that copyists introduced God's name here "in imitation of 21:2 and 10." Metzger, *A Textual Commentary,* 764-765.
[267] Elliot agrees with the majority of scholars in saying, "This change was due to a misreading of Latin via Erasmus." The Latin word for tree is "*ligno*" while the Latin word for book is "*libro.*" It is more important to recall that Erasmus' host text for Revelation lacked the final 6 verses, and therefore these verses were entirely back-translated from the Latin. Elliot points out, "[this interpretation] is without Greek support." There are no Greek manuscripts which support the phrase "book of life" in this verse. Elliot, "Revelations from the *Apparatus Criticus*", 22.

For an analogous example, one might note the widely recognized fact within the Dispensationalist framework that there is a broad majority which holds to a pretribulational rapture. And yet, within that same framework there are some who hold that the rapture occurs in the middle of the expected tribulation (such as Gleason Archer) as well as others who would hold that the rapture occurs at the end of the expected tribulation (such as Robert Gundry).[268] While the consequences of these distinctions produce differences in more than simply the chronology of the various positions, one would hardly accept the idea that they are each distinct eschatological frameworks. They would be rightly called "pretribulational dispensationalism", "midtribulational dispensationalism", and "posttribulational dispensationalism."[269]

Similarly, having examined the argument behind New Creation Millennialism, I do not believe it is appropriate at all to distinguish it as a unique eschatological framework apart from Historic Premillennialism. That is not to say that I entirely endorse what is currently being marketed as New Creation Millennialism, as I do not. It is to say that those aspects of my eschatological framework that align with those of the New Creation Millennialists do not in any way move me closer to them. Rather, having the historical testimony to claim that my views have always been known as Historic Premillennialism, the New Creation Millennialist position is shown to be one of many various positions within the broader Historic Premillennial camp.[270]

Historic Premillennialists as Identified in History

To begin to defend the claim that New Creation Millennialism (NCM) should be understood as one of the various positions under the umbrella of Historic Premillennialism (HP), let it first be noted that HP is known as such because it is the oldest form of Premillennialism deriving itself from the earliest church age, reaching even into the apostolic era. Polycarp, himself a disciple of the Apostle John, held to a form of premillennialism.[271] Papias, another disciple of John, was recognizably premillennial. Early Christian writings, such as the *Didache* seem to lend to a

---

[268] See Ben Chapman, ed., *Three Views on the Rapture*, and Robert H. Gundry, *The Church and the Tribulation: A Biblical Examination of Posttribulationism*.

[269] It should be noted that there are some within dispensationalism who do not fall neatly into any one of these positions, such as those who define themselves not as mid-tribulational, but as "pre-wrath." The ever-changing perspective on this issue is evidenced by the fact that in the second edition of *Three Views on the Rapture* (pub. 2010), midtribulational was replaced with "pre-wrath."

[270] At present, two camps within Historic Premillennialism dominate. Those following the teachings of George E. Ladd (sometimes called *Laddian Premillennialism*) and those differing from him on the future divine plan for national or ethnic Israel (sometimes called *Non-Laddian,* or more recently, *Irenaean Premillennialism*). For the latter, see Michael J. Svigel, *The Fathers on the Future* (Peabody, MA: Hendrickson Publishers, 2024).

[271] Polycarp, *The Epistle of Polycarp to the Philippians,* 5.

premillennial understanding of eschatology, as do other early authors such as Clement of Rome who was a disciple of the Apostle Paul.[272] Without making a very old argument, one must summarily say that if you study the eschatological frameworks of the early church fathers prior to Augustine (and even including Augustine in his early Christian life), one will find them to be in the majority, characteristically premillennial.

Some, particularly in recent years, have tried to undermine this argument by claiming that the early church fathers were not *premillennial*, but *chiliasts.* This distinction is rather difficult to define, even for those who are advocating it. In recent texts such as *The Rise and Fall of Dispensationalism* and others, authors have struggled to distinguish between chiliasm, Historic Premillennialism, "Old Premillennialism", "New Premillennialism", and "Dispensationalism."[273] This, in part, reflects the fact that in order for a group to be truly distinguished as a separate eschatological community, they should have major departures from other positions in aspects other than simple chronology.

Historically (even as recently as 100 years ago) many premillennialists used the term "chiliasts" to describe themselves and those who believed like them throughout history, despite having greatly differing understandings of the end times.[274] The unifying factor was a universal agreement on the concept of Christ's returning prior to his millennial reign. This identification, of course, predates the rise of dispensationalism, as during the 17th century, Robert Baillie, a Scottish theologian, bemoaned the fact that, "most of the chief divines here [that is, those penning the Westminster Confession of Faith], not only Independents, but others, such as Twisse, Marshall, Palmer, and many more, are express Chiliasts, i.e., believers in the Millennial Reign of Christ on earth."[275] Thus, it is clearly unhelpful to identify someone as distinct from Historic Premillennial by calling them "chiliasts."

Beyond this single identifier, there has been widespread diversity of thought within the Historic Premillennialist camp, with some notable guardrails. Distinctives of Dispensationalism such as the separation of Israel and the Church, multiple judgments at the end of the age for different people groups, a secret rapture, and the necessity of a literal approach to Scripture have never been widely held in the Historic Premillennialist camp. Sam Waldron, a committed amillennialist and President of Covenant Baptist

---

[272] As evidenced by the 16th article of *the Didache*. See also 1 Clement 23:5; 28:1; 50:3; or 2 Clement 5:5; 9:3; 11:4-7; 12:1; 14:1; 17:4-7.

[273] See H. Michael Shultz Jr., "Review of The Rise and Fall of Dispensationalism" *Ecclesia Militans* 1:1 (Winter 2023).

[274] Jesse Forrest Silver, *The Lord's Return*, 68.

[275] Andrew Bonar, *Redemption Drawing Nigh*, 25-26.

Theological Seminary, even went on record saying that dispensationalism is a departure from Historic Premillennialism, and even a rejection of it. He goes further, saying "Historic Premillennialism actually has more in common with Amillennialism and Postmillennialism than it does with Dispensationalism."[276] So, in short, when an amillennialist (or perhaps even a postmillennialist) reads an Historic Premillenial approach to prophecy, they should be thinking, "Okay, this is familiar... Yes, I'd agree... That's pretty close to what I'd say." This is because Historic Premillennialists stand at the headwaters of those two views and share much of the same historical development. The wide breadth of Historic Premillennialists leaves much breathing room, so much room that even New Creation Millennialists should still be considered as part of the camp.

To give a few examples of the breadth of thought still solidly within the Historic Premillennial camp, look first to William Twisse, one of the "chiliasts" referenced at the Westminster Assembly (he was actually the President of the assembly). He held that the thousand-year reign was "circumscribed within two resurrections, as it were the bounds."[277] This can hardly be understood to refer to any perspective other than premillennialism, and yet, he held that the redeemed would not spend eternity on the New Heavens and New Earth, but in Heaven with God. This is certainly a different position than that which is standard, but it presupposes that the millennium occurs on the New Heaven and New Earth – a position that many NCM are claiming is uniquely theirs, rather than belonging within the Historic Premillennial framework. Yet, if the premillennial system believed throughout history does not constitute "Historic Premillennialism" then what *does*? If the NCM advocates who seek to redefine the eschatological identifiers have their way, HP will become a position that is altogether impossible to rightly recognize or define.

It is no mischaracterization to say that the father and seniormost expert of NCM is J. Webb Mealy.[278] He independently published a book entitled *New Creation Millennialism* in 2019, in which he claimed to present not a "full-scale scholarly offering" but rather "an economical presentation of the main elements" of NCM.[279] In an attempt to help readers identify what distinguishes NCM from HP, he defines HP saying:

> (a) [Historic Premillennialism] reads Rev. 20:7-10 as picturing a rebellion of mortal people who have lived through the Parousia event, and/or their

---

[276] Sam Waldron, *MacArthur's Millennial Manifesto*, 124-125.

[277] William Twisse, *The Key of the* Revelation, 122.

[278] Mealy even refers to the position as "the view that I have given the name 'new creation millennialism.'" J. Webb Mealy, *New Creation Millennialism*, 9.

[279] Mealy, *New Creation Millennialism*, 10.

> progeny born during the millennium, (b) It reads Rev. 20:11-15 as a single judgment scene that is distinct from and occurs after the rebellion of 20:7-10, and (c) it reads Rev. 21:1-4, the new creation and the coming-to-earth of the New Jerusalem, as occurring after the judgment of Rev. 20:11-15.[280]

Elsewhere, he adds characteristics, saying that Historic Premillennialism:

> ...also sees the new creation spoken of in Rev. 21.1 as chronologically following the last judgment, so that the millennial kingdom is pictured as taking place in the context of the present creation, rather than in the context of the new creation described in Rev. 21.1-22.5... It assumes that John's intention was that his readers should picture considerable numbers of people who had not followed Christ during the career of the 'beast' (ch. 13) being spared at the parousia...It interprets these people as the 'subjects' who live under the millennial kingship of Christ and the saints. They are thus pictured as sharing the earth with Christ and the resurrected saints, yet living 'natural' (i.e. mortal) lives, and presumably multiplying during the millennial period. Thus the attack of Gog and Magog, which John says will happen at the end of the millennium (20.7-10), is interpreted on this view as a last rebellion by these non-resurrected peoples and/or their offspring.[281]

Mealy's definitions of HP represent what may be rightly understood as the majority position within the HP camp, that much is true. But to say that these are the defining characteristics of the position is to entirely disregard the fact that myriads of proponents of the position have defected from these characteristics without otherwise violating any of the key eschatological understandings in the camp.

For example, Mealy claims in both pieces that Historic Premillennialists view the new creation (here meaning the New Heaven and New Earth) as coming into being after the millennial reign. This is simply untrue. John Gill is a notable advocate of the view that the millennial reign is concurrent with the New Heaven and New Earth.[282] To accommodate this, Mealy writes an appendix to his *New Creation Millennialism* in which he claims that John Gill was not an Historic Premillennialist, but a New Creation Millennialist.[283] He pulls the same sleight of hand with Papias who is perhaps the earliest

---

[280] Mealy, *New Creation Millennialism*, 64.
[281] J. Webb Mealy, *After the Thousand Years: Resurrection and Judgment in Revelation 20*, 15-16.
[282] See Gill's Commentaries on Revelation 20-21.
[283] Mealy, *New Creation Millennialism*, 161-162.

Historic Premillennialist, showing that he at least subconsciously sees himself as the true exemplar of what has historically been called Historic Premillennialism.[284] But this conviction, that the millennium occurs on the New Heaven and New Earth, is the only aspect of Mealy's system that Gill or Papias might agree with. One can scarcely imagine what reaction would come from them if they knew someone was claiming that they held to the view that the new creation did not begin until the return of Christ (as Mealy claims).[285] Is, then, belief in the millennial reign's geographic location being that of the New Heaven and New Earth the lone mark of someone who is not a Historic Premillennialist, but a New Creation Millennialist?

Historic Premillennialists would certainly be surprised to find that to be the case. William Twisse would certainly be surprised to find that he was not in the same line as those earlier Historic Premillennialists (or chiliasts) with whom he was criticized.[286] Horatius Bonar argued that the New Heavens and the New Earth would be the setting of the millennial reign, and yet he believed that the unglorified would dwell in that same setting with the glorified.[287] This position seems to be distinct from both mainline HP and NCM as defined by Mealy. Ought we to create a new eschatological camp, Bonaristic Millennialism?

This title would serve little help, as Horatius' brother Andrew Bonar held to yet another eschatological position, in which those inhabitants of Christ's millennial kingdom are those who "are converted, sanctified, and saved…" and yet he also held that this group would be distinct from the Church, being instead the beneficiaries or perhaps even children of those members of the Church.[288] As odd as this system already appears, he also held that "there shall be some ungodly existing all along, during these thousand years."[289]

Thomas Goodwin agreed with Gill in his understanding that the millennial reign would occur in concurrence with the New Heavens and New Earth, as did Benjamin Keach.[290] And yet, Keach, Goodwin, and Gill would all disagree with the Bonar brothers in the idea that the unredeemed would inhabit the millennial kingdom. All of this is not even to introduce those figures such as William Sherwin who maintained such

---

[284] Mealy, *New Creation Millennialism*, 149-151.

[285] Mealy, *New Creation Millennialism*, 136.

[286] Twisse endorsed a view akin (or identical) to Gill's when he wrote the Preface to Joseph Mede, *The Key of Revelation*. For Mede's affirmation of this position see p. 87.

[287] Horatius Bonar, *Prophetical Landmarks*, 142.

[288] Bonar, *Redemption Drawing Nigh*, 125-126, 130.

[289] Bonar, *Redemption Drawing Nigh*, 328.

[290] Thomas Goodwin, *Exposition on the Book of Revelation*, 22.; Benjamin Keach, *A Golden Mine Opened*, 345.

complicated perspectives as to synonymize the millennial reign with the New Heavens and New Earth while also maintaining a commitment to the chronological nature of Revelation 19-21.[291] And time would fail to investigate the unique perspectives of men like Thomas Beverley, who held that both the righteous and wicked were resurrected at the beginning of the thousand years, with the wicked serving as the footstools for Christ's people for a thousand years, only to rise up and attempt an overthrowal in the end.[292]

All of this goes to show that it is entirely inappropriate for modern authors such as J. Webb Mealy to attempt to establish NCM as a unique position aside from HP. If Mealy wished to claim that he was departing from HP, he would have to do so by producing some position that is not yet represented within the HP community – which he has failed to do.

New Creation Millennialism Fails as an Alternative System Against Historic Premillennialism

In his recent commentary on Revelation, Thomas Schreiner writes that "no millennial view answers or can answer every question, but I suggest that the new-creation millennial view should be seriously considered."[293] This suggestion has been noted, and it is in response to this suggestion that the present section will be written. The previous section served to show that NCM is not distinct from HP but is rather a various view within that community. Now, it will be shown that while certain aspects of NCM are compelling, the *system* as a whole is not.

The most glaring failure of NCM, as has already been noted, is that many notable Historic Premillennialists like John Gill would grimace at the idea that the New Creation *begins* with the return of Christ, which is a central tenet of NCM as defined by Mealy.[294] Schreiner, regrettably, buys into this concept in his commentary, as he lists the very first feature of the NCM view as being that "the millennium is the first age of the new creation" and later, "the millennium is the first age of the new world that is coming."[295] This idea is, in this author's reckoning, poorly thought out. The Bible is abundantly clear

---

[291] William Sherwin, *The World to Come*, 37-38.

[292] Thomas Beverley, *An Appeal Most Humble Yet Most Earnestly by the Coming of Our Lord Jesus Christ*, 9. To understand the full complication of eschatological systems in the era, see Richard Baxter's engagement with Beverley's views in Richard Baxter, *The Glorious Kingdom of Christ, Described and Clearly Vindicated*, and Richard Baxter, *A Reply to Mr. Tho. Beverley's Answer to My Reasons Against His Doctrine of the Thousand Years Middle Kingdom and the Conversion of the Jews*.

[293] Thomas Schreiner, *Revelation* BECNT, 682.

[294] Mealy, *New Creation Millennialism,* 136.; Mealy explicitly says, "In the new creation (which follows upon the dissolution of the former heaven and earth at the Parousia), God's tabernacle will be among his people once and for all." Mealy, *After the Thousand Years*, 199. He later refers to the vision John has in Revelation 21 as "the inauguration of the new creation."

[295] Schreiner, *Revelation* BECNT, 677.

that the new creation worked by God began with the saving work of Christ – not with some renovation or recreation of a planet.

What further undermines the credibility of NCM as an alternative system is that even leading advocates of the NCM framework have departed from Mealy on this most central point. Take, for example, Eckhard Schnabel (who is identified by Schreiner as one of the two "significant advocates" of the view).[296] Mealy claims that Schnabel was "persuaded by the evidence presented in my monograph *After the Thousand Years*" and "follows my interpretation closely."[297] Schnabel, however, does not follow Mealy or Schreiner in believing that the new creation begins with the return of Christ. Instead, he speaks of the new creation as being "inaugurated by Jesus."[298] This directly contradicts what Mealy claims, as he twice refers to the vision John has in Revelation 21 as being "the inauguration of the new creation."[299]

Schnabel speaks similarly of the Kingdom of God and the new creation as both being "already/not-yet", existing in a spiritual sense at present but expected in a physical sense in the future.[300] And yet, rather than simply spiritualizing it to mean that it is experienced in Heaven by the redeemed who await its insertion into the earthly realm (as some, but not all, amillennialists conceive of the Kingdom of God), Schnabel speaks of the new creation as being something that is truly experienced at present (since the time of Christ) and which will come into full culmination in the future.[301]

At times, he refers to the new creation as becoming a reality to an individual at the time of their conversion, saying "the new birth of each believer *and the dawn of the new creation* change" their lives.[302] Thus, Schnabel holds, and explicitly defends, the position that the new creation does not begin with the return of Christ, but exists presently, as he says, "believers who have come to faith in Jesus are ἐν Χριστῷ and [are] thus a 'new creation.'"[303] Elsewhere, he specifies that while the term "new creation" does not exclusively refer to the believers in Christ, it can be used in various respects to refer to

---

[296] Schreiner, *Revelation* BECNT, 677.
[297] Mealy, *New Creation Millennialism*, 138.
[298] Eckhard Schnabel, *New Testament Theology*, 909. Indeed, Schnabel says the new creation is inaugurated by Jesus in every convert the moment they become a Christian (i.e., "the new birth").
[299] Mealy, *After the Thousand Years*, 205, 207.
[300] Schnabel, *New Testament Theology*, 651.
[301] Schnabel, *New Testament Theology*, 941
[302] Schnabel, *New Testament Theology*, 920. Earlier in the text (584), he claims that it is this "reality of the 'new creation' that prompts believers to live differently in the world, and states (464) that the new creation "protrudes into the present."
[303] Schnabel, *New Testament Theology*, 898.

those believers, the glorified community of believers, and the transformed universe.[304] In his writings, he refers to it as "both the refashioning of values and lifestyle that God initiates in conversion (2 Cor. 5:17) and also the future cosmic refashioning which will replace the 'present evil age.'"[305]

Rather than disconnecting this from his eschatology, Schnabel seems to be unavoidably clear that this "new creation" which occurs at salvation is connected to the new creation of the end times, as he writes, "the resurrection of Jesus Messiah signaled the beginning of the new creation which had been prophesied for the last days."[306] Further identifying this concept as similar to the HP understanding of the inaugurated Kingdom of God (as popularized by George Ladd), he claims that "the new creation has become a present reality through the ministry of Jesus." Importantly, after making this statement about the present reality of the new creation, he lists several Scriptures to the effect of that point, and concludes by saying, "Jesus Messiah, the Logos, the Son of God, the giver of life, has, through his life, death, resurrection, and exaltation, inaugurated the new age of eternal life, the new creation, whose full and permanent reality will be revealed in the future when Jesus returns."[307] Thus, his conception of the new creation is one which was inaugurated with Christ and moves forward progressively reaching its fullness in the *eschaton*. This is nothing short of tried-and-true, established Historic Premillennialism. George Ladd emphasized this point, saying, "The new earth of Revelation 21 is *the final term* in the revelation of how this redemption [of the created order as well as mankind] is to take place."[308] This is fundamentally different from the position of NCM, which seems to promote a conception of the new creation that is entirely yet to begin – and will only begin with the Second Advent.

For further explanation, Schnabel holds that despite living in the "present evil age" described by Paul in Galatians 1:4, the reality of the new creation enables the believers to leave that type of living behind, and instead live "for the new state of affairs inaugurated by the coming, the death, and the resurrection of Jesus Messiah, a state in which sinners who commit to faith in Jesus participate in the 'new creation.'"[309] Thus, the entire inter-Advent age (that is, the time between the resurrection of Christ and the return of Christ) is referred to by Schnabel as "the era of the promised 'new creation.'"[310]

---

[304] Schnabel, *New Testament Theology*, 596.
[305] Schnabel, *New Testament Theology*, 476.
[306] Schnabel, *New Testament Theology*, 855.
[307] Schnabel, *New Testament Theology*, 722.
[308] Ladd, *A Theology of the New Testament*, 682. Emphasis added.
[309] Schnabel, *New Testament Theology*, 571.
[310] Schnabel, *New Testament Theology*, 401.

Schreiner curiously holds to much the same thought, though evidently he, like Schnabel, has not realized that this disagrees with the NCM system. Schreiner notes in his commentary on Revelation, "the promise of end-time resurrection in the OT was not fulfilled and realized in Jesus… which means that the age to come had arrived, the new era was at hand, the eschaton had penetrated the present evil age."[311]

And yet, despite these great disagreements with the *system* of NCM as defined by Mealy, both Schreiner and Schnabel are identified as (and may self-identify as) leading figures of significance in advancing the system because they hold, as Historic Premillennialists have for centuries, that the millennial reign occurs concurrently with the New Heaven and New Earth.[312] That single factor proves determinative for the supposed distinction between Historic Premillennialists like George Ladd or the Bonar brothers and this supposedly new eschatological framework, New Creation Millennialism.

Before someone levels the accusation of making mountains out of molehills, let it be known that the issue of an inaugurated vs. yet to come new creation is not a small problem. New Creation Millennialism owes its very name to the idea that in this system the *new creation* begins with the *millennium*. If one holds, as Schnabel does, that the new creation is something that is presently experienced by Christians then the New Creation Millennialist *system* fails. This position is quite difficult to deny, given things like Paul's explicit statement of such in 2 Corinthians 5:17, or the implication of such a truth by Christ and the apostles elsewhere. For example, in Luke 23:43 "paradise" is said to be a place entered into by saints immediately after death, but in Revelation 22:1-5 it "belongs to the new creation."[313] It appears unavoidable that there is some overlap, or a sense of inaugurated participation in the new creation and our present era. One might wish to say that some of its eschatological elements are still valuable, but any elements that are presented in NCM which are of value have already been held by Historic Premillennialists for centuries. In short, to claim that NCM answers questions that Historic Premillennialism does not answer is to say one of two things by implication: either, the person does not know the broad beliefs held within the camp of Historic Premillennialists; or, the person does not understand the problems created by the answers produced by New Creation Millennialists.

One example of the many problems caused by NCM propositions, comes from the present explanation for *why* the wicked dead are resurrected at the end of the

---

311 Schreiner, *Revelation* BECNT, 84.
312 Schnabel, *New Testament Theology*, 859.
313 Koester, *Revelation*, 266.

millennium. Hundreds of years ago, John Gill wrote of the identification of Gog and Magog as the resurrected unredeemed.[314] That position, as has been shown, is one that has been around for a long time in the HP community. However, the rationale for *why* God raises the wicked dead only to defeat them in this final battle and then judge them (assuming one takes the ensuing judgment as chronologically following the millennium) has been a subject that most commentators either neglected to explain or intentionally omitted due to a lack of credible theory. J. Webb Mealy, however, seeks to answer this question. He says of those wicked dead raised at the end of the millennium:

> They have been raised for the purpose of evaluating them as to whether they will behave, upon their release from the prison of death, in a manner consistent with granting them unending life. They fail this final trial, and are condemned by their own actions to fiery destruction.[315]

In case the uncareful reader might have passed over what they just read, Mealy is contending for the idea that despite having died unconverted and without salvation, lost individuals will be given a second chance at salvation after the millennial reign. This is not a minor variation from standard Christian eschatology.

It must be hoped and prayed that Schreiner and Schnabel believe no such thing.[316] Schreiner is even careful to note in his commentary, "I don't espouse every feature of the position as it has been articulated by Mealy (such as his annihilationism)."[317] However, when he examines this passage in his recent commentary, he is quick to disagree with Mealy on his understanding of how this passage relates to Ezekiel, but says nothing to the effect of correcting or disagreeing with him on *why* they are raised. He claims that "Mealy is probably right" on the identity of those raised, and then remains silent on Mealy's elaboration of why they are raised.[318] This leaves one to wonder, why would such erudite scholars as Schnabel and Schreiner want their names attached to a system formulated by a man who neither believes in the orthodox doctrine of Hell, nor the orthodox doctrine of salvation – given that he believes individuals might be saved after dying unredeemed. That is a question I will leave to those men, if haply these words might fall under their eyes someday.

---

[314] See Gill's comments on Revelation 20:8.

[315] Mealy, *New Creation Millennialism*, 33.

[316] Indeed, since the time of Schreiner penning his most recent commentary on Revelation, Jim Hamilton has publicly stated that he is a New Creation Millennialist – despite holding to none of the distinctives of Mealy. I would desire for these men to maintain the historic premillennial moniker instead.

[317] Schreiner, *Revelation* BECNT, 677.

[318] Schreiner, *Revelation* BECNT, 695-696. While doubtful, it is possible Schreiner is not aware of Mealy's explanation.

Why Historic Premillennialism?

In answer to the question of why I believe the Historic Premillennial system of eschatology, my answer will be threefold. First, I believe the Historic Premillennial system because of its historic credibility. You will find no other system with roots in the very beginnings of Christianity, nor will you find any system with a greater heritage of Christian theologians stretching from the beginning of the Church age through the modern day. Second, I believe the Historic Premillennial system because of its expositional consistency. An Historic Premillennialist does not need to adapt his system of interpretation depending on what era of history or genre of text he is reading. And third, I believe Historic Premillennialism because of its exegetical certainty. When examining the most pertinent texts to the millennial debate, the system of Historic Premillennialism is the most able to remain in those texts and work with what is written without having to take abnormal or atypical approaches to the language or order thereof.

Looking first at this topic of historical credibility, one notes once more that the system is entitled "historic" premillennialism because it is the system that has been believed for the longest in Christian history. Scarcely anyone will argue against this point. Robert Franklin recently published a text entitled *Rediscovered Early Church Premillennialism*, in which he examines not *if* the early church was premillennial, but *in what ways* the early church was premillennial.[319] This position has been so thoroughly examined, confirmed, and defended, that certainly no further explanation of its validity is needed at this point in history.

What is little understood and appreciated, even at this advanced state of history, is the gravity of that reality. One author reflected on this fact and concluded,

> The early Church was solidly pre-millennial in faith. The doctrine found expression in apocalyptic literature. The Christian belief was founded upon the writings of the Old Testament prophets and the teachings of Jesus Christ. Later it was gathered from the inspired Epistles of the New Testament and confirmed by the Revelation to St. John on the Isle of Patmos."[320]

The premillennialism of the early Church was not simply inherited (as is that of many in the American South today). Instead, it was "founded upon the writings" of both the Old

[319] Robert Franklin, *Rediscovered Early Church Premillennialism*.

[320] Silver, *The Lord's Return*, 49.

and New Testaments. However, it was not their position *only* because of their understandings of the Bible. Papias and Polycarp, for example, were disciples of the Apostle John himself. Certainly, if anyone understood how the Revelation of St. John was supposed to be interpreted, it would be those to whom John taught it. Who would be better qualified to teach the Revelation as it should properly be taught than the Apostle John? Surely one would not be so blind as to believe that when John taught Polycarp and Papias how to understand the Revelation, he did so through any lens other than the premillennial lens – as evidenced by the fact that they both came away holding to this position. And if John taught his disciples to read the Revelation this way, is this not then the proper way to read it? True, John may have misunderstood his own vision – but that notwithstanding, at the very minimum, the premillennialist position he taught his disciples should at least be favored above the other perspectives and considered the default view.

And yet, it is not only the disciples of John who came away believing the premillennialist system. Clement of Rome, who is widely considered to have been a disciple of the Apostle Paul, writes in his letters to the church at Corinth of eschatological hope that one can only associate with a premillennialist schema.[321] Daniel Whitby, the father of modern postmillennialism, even mentions the universal acceptance of this view in the early church, writing, "It was received not only in the Eastern parts of the Church by Papias, Justin, Irenaeus, Nepos, Apollinaris, Methodius, but also in the West and South by Tertullian, Cyprian, Victorinus, Lactantius, and Severus, and if we may credit Gelasius Cyzicenus, by the first Nicene Council."[322] In this quote, Whitby presents an important detail, which is that at the Council of Nicaea (A.D. 325), it is widely noted that premillennialism was still the dominant position. Joseph Mede writes of this fact, recognizing "how powerful the chiliastical party yet was at the time of that Council."[323] Later in that comment, Mede even speculates that the Nicene Creed was framed in such a way as to be acceptable to premillennialists, because they had so much influence.

If Whitby knew what he was saying, it is likely he would have desired to take his comments on the historical case for "millennialism" back, as in his argument for a millennium – which in his day was intended to go against the amillennialist idea of currently inhabiting a spiritual millennium – he powerfully (and perhaps accidentally)

[321] 1 Clement 23:5-24:1, 28:1, and most powerfully 50:3 and 2 Clement 5:5, 9:3, 12:1, and most powerfully 17:4-7.

[322] Daniel Whitby, *A Treatise of Traditions* I, 79.

[323] Joseph Mede, *The Works*, 813.

supports the premillennial claim by noting that these who believed in a literal millennium to come "taught this doctrine, not as doctors only, but as witnesses of the tradition which they had received from Christ and his Apostles..."[324] Though Whitby seeks to support his thoughts on a real millennium, he inadvertently admits that premillennialism was inherited not only due to a certain interpretive method, but directly from the teachings of Christ and his Apostles.

Other early church fathers, living just after the time of the Apostles but well-within the time of the disciples of the Apostles, also testify to the overwhelming agreement in the early church that the premillennialist system was the correct one. Any layman could read the writings of Justin Martyr, Irenaeus, or Tertullian and understand that they were premillennial. In fact, the now-famous writing of Irenaeus, *Against Heresies*, was censored for centuries by the Catholic Church because he devoted five full chapters to defending the premillennial system.[325]

This ushers in the question: If premillennialism was the overwhelmingly accepted system of the early church, why did it die out? And the answer lies largely with Augustine of Hippo. Augustine was originally premillennial himself (by his own testimony).[326] However, he changed his position to what is now called amillennialism, and the rationale for this is seemingly (according to David R. Anderson), threefold:

First, he disdained the hedonistic festivals of the Donatists wherein they would grow drunk and sexually unrestrained. It is said that Augustine "associated this kind of behavior with the Jewish apocalyptic emphasis on grand feasts of celebration during the kingdom of the saints on earth." As a result, he rejected the eschatological thoughts of the Donatists and promoted inverse positions on earthly behavior, forwarding a position that "married men who indulged in sexual pleasure after procreation were guilty of venial sins."[327]

Second, he was unimpressed with the increasing anticipation among premillennialists regarding the year A.D. 500.[328] At that time, it was estimated by trusted sources that Christ had been born in the 5500th year since creation, and thus, the year 500

---

[324] Whitby, *A Treatise of Traditions*, 79.

[325] Irenaeus, *Against Heresies*, 5:31-36.

[326] Augustine, *City of God*, 20:7.

[327] David R. Anderson, "The Soteriological Impact of Augustine's Change from Premillennialism to Amillennialism: Part One" *Journal of the Grace Evangelical Society* (Spring 2002), 28.

[328] Anderson, "Soteriological Impact", 28.

would complete the six thousandth year, ushering in the seventh "day" – the expected millennial rest with Christ.[329]

Third, Augustine favored the allegorical and typological hermeneutic of interpretation, and used it "as a tool to do away with a literal, physical Millennium." By utilizing this method, says Anderson, Augustine "was able to turn numbers into symbols, to bind Satan in the sixth age of a thousand years rather than the seventh, and to have saints rule with Christ spiritually in the sixth age rather than the seventh."[330]

A year after the death of Augustine, it is widely claimed (and ferociously debated) that premillennialism was banned by the Catholic Church at the A.D. 431 Council of Ephesus.[331] Regardless of the debates surrounding that claim, it is undeniable that the Catholic Church *did* formally condemn premillennialism on 21 July 1944, when the Pope signed a decree reading, "the system of millenarianism cannot safely be taught."[332] This rejection of premillennialism is also enshrined in the Catholic Catechism, which reads "The Church has rejected even modified forms of this falsification of the kingdom to come under the name of millenarianism."[333] Thus, it is not outside the realm of possibilities that the Catholic Church had condemned premillennialism earlier in its history as well. Either way, the medieval Catholic devotion to Augustine would have almost required a shunning of premillennialism for the same reasons he personally gave.[334]

While some of Augustine's complaints against the contemporary premillennialists of his day may have been legitimate, it is easy to see that his only problem with the interpretive system itself was in its not coming from an allegorical approach – an approach readers should be aware has almost entirely been abandoned. His other

---

[329] Anderson, "Soteriological Impact", 29.

[330] Anderson, "Soteriological Impact", 29-30.

[331] Some of the sources supporting this claim (in order of most recent publication) are Andrew Bradstock, "Millenarianism in the Reformation and the English Revolution," in Stephen Hunt, ed., *Christian Millenarianism from the Early Church to Waco*, 77.; Eugene Weber, *Apocalypses: Prophecies, Cults, and Millennial Beliefs through the Ages* (Cambridge, MA: Harvard University Press, 1999), 147.; R.J. McKelvey, The Millennium and the Book of Revelation, 14.; Grant Underwood, *The Millenarian World of Early Mormonism*, 17.; William Alnor, *Soothsayers of the Second Advent*, 55.; Walter Price, *The Coming Antichrist*, 27.; Peter Toon, *Puritans, The Millennium and the Future of Israel: Puritan Eschatology 1600 to 1660*, 17.; André Feuillet, *The Apocalypse*, 119. All of these are cited by Francis Gumerlock as being incorrect in his "Millennialism and the Early Church Councils" *Fides et Historia* 36:2 (Fall 2004): 83-95.

[332] *Acta Apostolicae Sedis* 36:2:11 (Vatican): 212. Author's translation. Original Latin: "*systema Millenarismi mitigati tuto doceri non posase.*"

[333] Q. 676. In the Catholic Catechism. In this answer, it references DS 3839, which is the previously referenced decree.

[334] For the influence of Augustine on medieval theology, see Alister McGrath, *Iustitua Dei* 2, 24.

complaints, the hedonistic practices of some premillennialists and the ecstatic date-setting of others, do not typify historic premillennialism in the mainstream. Thus, each of his three reasons for disavowing the position are ultimately of no value at all. And yet, the Catholic Church's reliance on him led to a millennium of persecution for those who believed it.

While there are some noteworthy examples of premillennialists during the age of Catholic dominance, it was with the dawning of the Reformation that premillennialism truly reemerged, and that is appropriate as the Reformation brought with it what the early church had – access to the Scriptures and a disavowal of papal authority to decide what the proper interpretation of Scripture was. Cotton Mather would sum this situation up boldly, saying, "It sways something in me when I consider that the Chiliad [i.e., the millennial reign] was not denied until the antichrist began to reign."[335] Here, he refers to the antichrist in the typical Reformed manner, as most Reformers believed that the Pope of Rome was the antichrist. Thus, he implies (at least) that it was the work of the church at Rome, as service to antichrist, to remove the eschatological system of premillennialism.

Still, the Reformation era was not one of sweeping success for premillennialism, because while the Reformers took glee in reforming the soteriology of the Catholic Church, they were very hesitant to reform its eschatology. John Calvin, in fact, wrote a commentary on the entire New Testament – with the exception of the books of 2-3 John and Revelation. Despite his failure to spend due time examining and explaining what it was that he *did* believe about the Revelation, he was clear on his position towards premillennialism, calling it a "fiction too puerile to need or to deserve refutation."[336] While on the subject of Calvin, it is worth noting that one of the many crimes for which Michael Servetus was burned was for preaching a premillennialist-type coming kingdom.[337]

Other groups such as the Lutherans, Anglicans, and those who aligned with the Helvetic Confessions explicitly condemned premillennialism in their confessions.[338] In this era and those surrounding them, many premillennialists were killed for their beliefs

---

[335] Increase Mather, *The Mystery of Israel's Salvation*, xxxvii.

[336] John Calvin, *Institutes of the Christian Religion*, 3:25:5.

[337] Michael Servetus, *The Restoration of Christianity,* Marian Hillar and Christopher Hoffman, trans., (Lewiston, NY: Edwin Mellen Press, 2007).

[338] Augsburg Confession, 17.; Second Helvetic Confession, 11.; The 1553 edition of the "Forty-Two Articles" of the Anglican Church included Article 41 entitled "Heretics Called Millenarii" which said, "They that go about to renew the fable of heretics called Millenarii are repugnant to Holy Scripture, and cast themselves headlong into Jewish dotage."

such as John of Leiden (burned and stabbed, 1536), Hans Hut (burned, 1527), and John Matthys (drawn and quartered, 1534) to name a few. And yet, premillennialism continued to emerge and grow.

By the time of the Puritans, despite common misconceptions, premillennialism was a well-established position. In fact, in his doctoral dissertation, William Eamon comes to the shocking conclusion that "Puritan eschatology during the 17th century and in fact well into the 18th century, was characteristically pre-millennial."[339] Such great figures as John Bunyan, the beloved author of *Pilgrim's Progress*, and many others (see Fig. 2.7 below) would embrace premillennialism.

Interestingly, whenever a premillennialist enters the academic realm, it is often said that they have "brought academic credibility" to the position. For example, in the 1740's, J.A. Bengel (despite being Lutheran and therefore forbidden from believing it) presented a commentary on Revelation which defended the premillennialist view.[340] Reflecting on this, Charles Ryrie said that he "gave impetus to premillennialism in the scholarly world."[341] But this was scarcely forty years after Increase Mather (a premillennialist) served as President of Harvard. Similar claims have been made regarding George E. Ladd, but behind these repetitious statements that *premillennialism gained academic or scholarly credibility* is the idea that the default position of premillennialism is one of unacademic or unscholarly thought, an idea which is patently false.

In the modern era, historic premillennialists make up a great number of the most scholarly and academic theological thinkers one may care to know – and it has been this way for a long time. As a manner of concluding this point, simply look at a few of the names of those who have held to this view since the time of the Reformation:

---

339 William C. Eamon, "Kingdom and Church in New England; Puritan Eschatology John Cotton to Jonathan Edwards" (1970). The University of Montana: *Graduate Student Theses, Dissertations, & Professional Papers*. 136.; See also Thomas D. Ice, "Mathers, Richard, Increase, and Cotton" in *Dictionary of Premillennial Theology*, Mal Couch, ed., 250.

340 One need only read Bengel's commentary on Revelation 20:2 in his *Gnomon* to see his full commitment to the premillennial faith.

341 Charles C. Ryrie, *The Basis of the Premillennial Faith*, 31.

Noteworthy Historic Premillennialists Since the Reformation	
Name	**Known For**
William Twisse (1578-1646)	President of the Westminster Assembly.
Thomas Goodwin (1600-1680)	Puritan, Prolific Author, Member of the Westminster Assembly, President of Magdalen College – Oxford.
John Bunyan (1628-1688)	Puritan, Prolific Author, Famous for penning *The Pilgrim's Progress.*
Increase Mather (1639-1723)	Puritan, President – Harvard University.
Benjamin Keach (1640-1704)	Prolific Author, Pastor, Contributor to 1689 London Baptist Confession of Faith.
Cotton Mather (1663-1728)	Puritan, Historian, Prolific Author, Scientist.
Johann Albrecht Bengel (1687-1752)	Pietist, Greek Scholar, Textual Critic, Pastor.
John Gill (1697-1771)	Prolific Theologian, Pastor, Author, Linguistic Scholar, Polemicist.
Charles Wesley (1707-1788)	Prolific Hymnwriter, Poet, Pastor, Revivalist and Evangelist.
Augustus Toplady (1740-1778)	Prolific Author, Anglican Cleric, Hymnwriter.
E.B. Elliot (1793-1875)	Pastor, Author of *Horae Apocalypticae.*
Horatius Bonar (1808-1889)	Prolific Author, Pastor, Hymnwriter.
Andrew Bonar (1810-1892)	Author, Pastor, Revivalist, Theologian.
Henry Alford (1810-1871)	Greek Scholar, Textual Critic, Progenitor of "Alford's Law" of Biblical Interpretation.
Robert Murray McCheyne (1813-1843)	Evangelist, Hymnwriter, Pastor.
S.P. Tregelles (1813-1875)	Prolific Bible Scholar, Linguistic Expert, Hymnwriter.
J.C. Ryle (1816-1900)	Author, First Anglican Bishop of Liverpool.
Nathaniel West (1826-1906)	Pastor, Author.
Charles Spurgeon (1834-1892)	Prolific Speaker, Pastor, Author.
Theodor von Zahn (1838-1933)	Professor of Theology – University of Göttingen, Conservative Stalwart in German New Testament Scholarship, Major Proponent of *Heilgeschichte.*
Gordon Clark (1902-1985)	Leading Figure in Development of Presuppositional Apologetics.

George Eldon Ladd (1911-1982)	Professor of New Testament – Fuller Theological Seminary; Popularizer of "Inaugurated Eschatology."
Francis Schaeffer (1912-1984)	Prolific Author, Theologian, and Pastor.
Carl F.H. Henry (1913-2003)	Dean – Fuller Theological Seminary, Leader in the Evangelical Movement, Father of Presuppositional Apologetics.
Harold Lindsell (1913-1998)	Prolific Author, President of ETS, Leader in the Battle for Biblical Inerrancy.
J. Barton Payne (1922-1979)	Professor of Old Testament – Covenant Theological Seminary.
Jurgen Moltmann (1926 -	Prolific Author, Popularizer of "Social Trinitarianism", Professor of Systematic Theology – University of Tübingen.
Walter Martin (1928-1989)	Pastor, Author of *Kingdom of the Cults.*
John Warwick Montgomery (1931 -	Author, Christian Apologist,
Millard Erickson (1932 -	Prolific Author, Academic Dean – Bethel University.
James Montgomery Boice (1938-2000)	Prolific Author, Pastor, Lead figure in the Battle for Biblical Inerrancy.
John Piper (1946 -	Prolific Author, Pastor, Chancellor – Bethlehem College and Seminary.
D.A. Carson (1946 -	Prolific Author, Theologian, Research Professor of New Testament – Trinity Evangelical Divinity School.
Wayne Grudem (1948 -	Prolific Author, Professor of Theology and Biblical Studies – Phoenix Seminary.
Robert S. Rayburn (1950 -	Pastor, Popularizer of Covenant Successionism.
Randy Alcorn (1954 -	Prolific Author, Famous for Penning *Heaven.*
Bryan Chapell (1954 -	Pastor, President and Chancellor – Covenant Theological Seminary.
Craig Blomberg (1955 -	Author, Distinguished Professor Emeritus of the New Testament – Denver Seminary.
Al Mohler (1959 -	Prolific Author, President – Southern Baptist Theological Seminary (SBTS).

Hershael York (1960 -	Dean of Theology, SBTS.
Craig Keener (1960 -	Pastor, Professor of New Testament – Asbury Theological Seminary.
Reginald C. Kimbro (1962 -	President – Geneva Reformed Seminary.
Sung Wook Chung (1966 -	Author, International Educator, Professor of Christian Theology – Denver Seminary.
Michael Bird (1974 -	Author, Vice Principal and Distinguished Research Professor – Ridley College.
James Hamilton (1974 -	Pastor, Author, Professor of Biblical Theology – SBTS.
Fig. 2.8	

As the other two reasons for affirming Historic Premillennialism are purely based on personal interpretation, they will be somewhat brief. The second reason given was that of expositional consistency. Suffice it to say that in the author's experience, the Historic Premillennialist approach to the Bible as a whole has proven to be a tremendously enjoyable and understandable one. But, this is entirely subjective and is based purely on my experience – and therefore I will not try to defend this position against scrutiny. Readers may find that they better understand and recognize the amillennialist or postmillennialist view, and that is entirely out of anyone's control.

The third element leading me towards premillennialism, though, is a bit more objective. It is true that when examining the eschatological literature as a whole – meaning those texts in the Bible that seem to give direct insights regarding the end times – there is very little that seems to refer to the millennium directly.[342] Despite this, there is no necessity for something to be explained multiple times in the Bible in order for it to be true. Certainly, we would not take that approach when it came to a topic like Oedipal practices (having sexual relations with one's mother). Despite being forbidden only once in the Bible (Lev. 18:17) it is *rightly* assumed as unnegotiable that Oedipal practices are unacceptable. Thus, the frequency of a teaching plays no part in its validity.

Furthermore, it would be inappropriate to interpret passages in abnormal ways simply because one has no other mention of the figures or events occurring within that passage. The absence of a reference point would, instead, seem to lead readers to rely

[342] Although there is beyond ample literature explaining the premillennialist basis from the view of the Old Testament and elsewhere. For a brief examination of this, see Nathaniel West, *The Thousand Years in Both Testaments*. For a thorough and almost unfathomably detailed argument for the premillennial system, see the three-volume set, George N.H. Peters, *The Theocratic Kingdom*.

more directly on what *is* written. Therefore, when readers come to Revelation 19-20, it is absolutely essential that they approach it with the utmost care and respect for what is written, *because* it is the only place the millennium is explicitly addressed.

Those who come away from Revelation 19-20, having concluded that these chapters are not one continual story have almost unashamedly taken liberties with the text that they would not feel the liberty to take in any other place. Consider that the transitional phrase between chapters 19 and 20 is the Greek "Καὶ εἶδον" meaning "and I saw." It is used in 19:11; 19:17; 19:19; 20:1; 20:4; 20:11; and 20:12 strongly suggesting "a sequence" that is one continual event.[343] This is recognized by amillennialists, such as G.K. Beale, who wrote in his commentary on Revelation that when the phrase is used at the end of chapter 19, it "clearly indicate[s] sequence in historical time." Then, he says, "*the majority* of the 'and's in ch. 20 do indicate historical sequence..."[344] So, Beale recognizes that the last three times this phrase is used in chapter 19 it "clearly" shows historical sequence, and he affirms that *the majority of times* in chapter 20 it shows historical sequence. As this seems to lead unavoidably to the conclusion that chapter 20 (the millennium) follows chapter 19 (the return of Christ) he concludes that without delving outside of this passage, he cannot "solve the problem one way or another."[345] The reality is, there is no problem other than that which is created by believing anything other than premillennialism.

Furthermore, the narrative of Revelation 19 flows very naturally into Revelation 20. Even if one puts aside the linguistic case for continuity, it is obvious that from Chapters 12 and 13 forward, the forces of evil are revealed as the "unholy trinity" of the beast, the false prophet, and Satan himself. It is then no coincidence that Revelation 19 concludes with the defeat and incarceration of the beast and the false prophet (v. 20) and Revelation 20 opens with the defeat and incarceration of Satan himself. This sort of narrative continuity cannot be missed. Two members of the "unholy trinity" are addressed immediately before the final member is addressed in the same fashion, and there is no linguistic clue or note of there being a transition between scenes.

The reason that amillennialists like G.K. Beale and company have a "problem" to solve in this text is, if one follows the natural reading of the text, they will come to see that Revelation 19 and Revelation 20 are one continual story. This would be all the more clear if the text we read in the modern day were more like the text John wrote – without chapter and verse divisions. However, famed amillennialist Anthony Hoekema summed

---

[343] Robert Mounce, *The Book of Revelation* NICOT, 361.

[344] G.K. Beale, *The Book of Revelation* NIGTC, 975. Emphasis added.

[345] Beale, *The Book of Revelation,* 975. Emphasis added.

up precisely why that obvious conclusion must be adamantly denied by his camp when he wrote, "if what is presented in Revelation 20 must necessarily follow, in chronological order, what is described in chapter 19" … "we are then virtually compelled to believe that the thousand-year reign depicted in 20:4 must come after the return of Christ described in 19:11."[346] The problem for the amillennialist and postmillennialist is simply this: it does.

Conclusion

The approach that will be taken regarding the structure of Revelation has been explained. Not only will the author avoid convenient labelling within the preterist, historicist, futurist, or idealist approaches by taking the eclecticism approach (see footnote 206), but this commentary will also avoid the typical approach of premillennialists by addressing Revelation as a recapitulative book. Furthermore, those recapitulations – across the whole of the Revelation will be shown to have a chiastic element to them that lends some degree of intentional poetic beauty to John's apocalypse.

The approach that will be taken in regards to the Scriptural texts to be examined has been explained, as the author takes as his chosen translation the English Standard Version, not only for the sake of readability and convenience (although these reasons are nevertheless valuable) but more directly for the reasons of textual reliability when compared to texts based upon the *Textus Receptus*. Despite the great value of Erasmus' work, and the historical and traditional regard that ought to be given to the King James Version, it is simply believed that the ESV provides a more reliable text of Revelation.

And finally, the approach to eschatology has been explained in some detail. It is hoped that even if readers are not convinced by the arguments or historical background provided, they will at least understand why this author holds vigorously to the Historic Premillennialist position, as well as why (despite having some similarities in specific instances) he vigorously rejects any identification with the New Creation Millennialist movement.

[346] Anthony Hoekema, "Amillennialism" in Robert G. Clouse, *The Meaning of the Millennium*, 156.

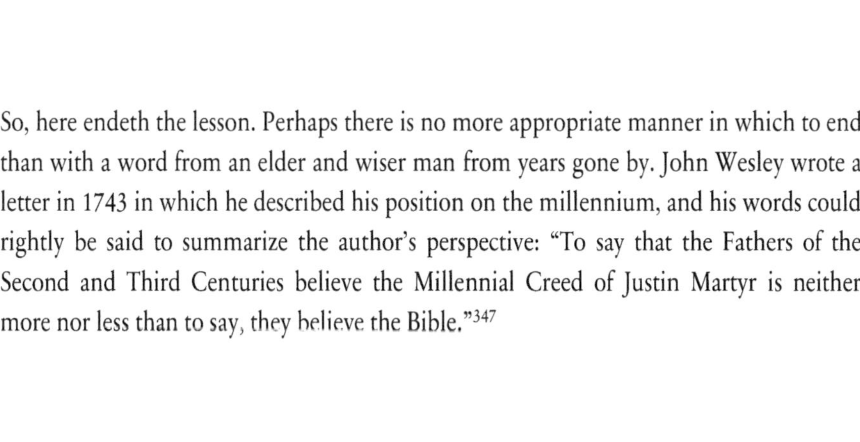

So, here endeth the lesson. Perhaps there is no more appropriate manner in which to end than with a word from an elder and wiser man from years gone by. John Wesley wrote a letter in 1743 in which he described his position on the millennium, and his words could rightly be said to summarize the author's perspective: "To say that the Fathers of the Second and Third Centuries believe the Millennial Creed of Justin Martyr is neither more nor less than to say, they believe the Bible."[347]

[347] "John Wesley to Dr. Conyers Middleton" (1749) in *Wesley's Works* (Vol. X): 29-30.

Part 2:
Introducing Tribulation

Disclaimer:

It will be important for readers who may be picking up the book at this point, having skipped the previous chapters, to know that "tribulation" as used in this book does not refer to a 7-year period just prior to the return of Christ. It is quite possible that a heightened sense of tribulation will occur just prior to the return of Christ (perhaps this is what Christ meant in using the term *Great Tribulation* in His Olivet Discourse), but to reserve the term "tribulation" for that late period would be counter to the position taken in this text.

Rather, in this text, "tribulation" refers both to that end-times era in which hardship will likely be more intense than ever before, as well as the entirety of the inter-advent era. That is to say, all Christians have lived in the era of *tribulation*. Thus, when the Apostle John wrote the Revelation to the churches of Asia Minor, they were enduring tribulation (as will be shown). And yet, all of John's admonitions for the churches of Asia Minor were still relevant and applicable to, say, the churches in Spain throughout the roughly 700 years of Muslim domination from the 700's through the 1400's. Further, John's admonitions for the churches of Asia Minor *are* still relevant and applicable to churches in America, or Africa, or Asia, or anywhere else today, and so long as the Lord prolongs His return, these admonitions will *always* be relevant and applicable. This is because each generation faces *tribulation*, although not every generation may be facing the *final* tribulation. Each generation faces its own *antichrists*, although not every generation is facing *The Antichrist*. So on and so forth – the point is hopefully made. The use of the term "tribulation" is intended for each and every generation of hardship, including that last era, but not exclusive to it.

Chapter 3:

(Revelation 1:1-8) Prologue and Introduction

(1:1-3) *The Blessing of the Saints*

(1:1-2)

> "The revelation of Jesus Christ, which God gave him to show to his servants the things that must soon take place. He made it known by sending his angel to his servant John, who bore witness to the word of God and to the testimony of Jesus Christ, even to all that he saw."
>
> "Ἀποκάλυψις Ἰησοῦ Χριστοῦ ἣν ἔδωκεν αὐτῷ ὁ θεὸς δεῖξαι τοῖς δούλοις αὐτοῦ ἃ δεῖ γενέσθαι ἐν τάχει, καὶ ἐσήμανεν ἀποστείλας διὰ τοῦ ἀγγέλου αὐτοῦ τῷ δούλῳ αὐτοῦ Ἰωάννῃ, "ὃς ἐμαρτύρησεν τὸν λόγον τοῦ θεοῦ καὶ τὴν μαρτυρίαν Ἰησοῦ Χριστοῦ ὅσα εἶδεν."

The Revelation opens with a statement about precisely what the book is and what purpose it is intended to accomplish. The Author is identified as **John** – that is, John the Apostle (see apostolicity). John may have introduced this book with his purpose with it borne in mind that his Gospel included a purpose statement somewhat toward the end (John 20:31). In his apocalypse, it appears that John wanted to give his readers his purpose at the beginning, rather than towards the end.

So, what is the book? It is first a **revelation,** that is, a *revealing* – coming from the Greek *Ἀποκάλυψις* (*apokalupsis*) which means "unveiling" – from which the book has traditionally taken its name. This book is, then, the revelation of, or *revealing* **of Jesus Christ.** Some have speculated over whether Jesus is described here as the one who is revealing something or if He is *Himself* the one being revealed. It is true that at times in the book, Jesus is depicted as the only one worthy to open the seals and begin the act of unveiling what is to come (5:5) and this truth should be of great encouragement, but it is more compelling to present Jesus as being the one who is revealed, given that this is often explicitly the case (14:14; 19:11).[348] There is no contradiction in holding that Jesus is both the revealer and the revealed.[349]

---

[348] This position is a minority position, but this author finds the exegetical case for its acceptance compelling. Generally, Christ is considered to be what is grammatically identified as the subjective genitive – that is, He is

It would be appropriate to assume from John's other writings that Jesus had been unveiled (or revealed) in His first advent, since He came in human flesh and dwelt amongst men (John 1:14). John is emphatic that anyone who denies this reality is denying something inherent to the Christian faith (2 John 1:7). And yet, it is nevertheless appropriate to understand that the first advent of Jesus Christ gave human beings a partial understanding of the person of Jesus Christ. Although He was at times gloriously displayed (such as on the Mount of Transfiguration, or through His various miracles), He was by-and-large displayed in a humble manner. The Bible is not shy about this, saying that He "emptied himself, by taking the form of a servant, being born in the likeness of men." (Phil. 2:7) Thus, it is true that the first advent showed us who Christ is, but at His Second Advent, a fuller display of His present glory will be revealed.[350]

It is worth noting the conveyance of this book. It is said that **God gave** this message to Jesus **to show His servants.**[351] John MacArthur poetically claims that this is "a reward for Christ's perfect submission and atonement" in which "the Father now presented to Him the great record of His future glory."[352] This author would amend that statement by pointing out that this is not simply a record of Christ's *future* glory, but of His *present* glory, which will be finally and in an unhindered fashion revealed in the last day. While we may read of it in this book and truly receive a right conveyance of His glory, in that day our faith shall be made sight, and that which we hoped for will finally be before us in the flesh. (1 Pet. 1:6-9; 1 John 3:2)

---

the subject that is carrying out the verb (i.e., He is revealing something). In most cases, the exegetical evidence for this is found not in the Greek but in the English renderings of the Greek, as the word "him" that immediately follows lacks a comma, indicating that this was a revelation that God gave to Christ in order to show others. (Thomas, *Revelation 1-7*, 61-62.) Assuming this is even worth considering, it still presents neither a positive case for the subjective sense, nor defeats the objective sense. The minority position (herein endorsed) is that Christ should rather be considered to be the objective genitive – that is, He is the object of the verb (i.e., He is that which is being revealed). This is the sense in which the phrase is used in 1 Cor. 1:7; 1 Pet. 1:7; and 1 Pet. 1:13. Even when it is debatable, as in Gal. 1:12, many scholars fray towards the objective sense when this phrase is used (Ladd, *Revelation*, 21). For further support of this view, see Philip E. Hughes, *Revelation*, 15. It is quite possible that John intentionally used this term to denote Christ as what is sometimes called a plenary genitive which is intentionally ambiguous and therefore permits both meanings. This, although never identified by this title, is the position taken in Keener, *NIV Application Commentary: Revelation*, 63, and Beale, *Revelation*, 183.

[349] This seems to be the reason many scholars, such as Mounce, take the subjective approach. They seem to believe Jesus cannot be the one revealing and being revealed – but is this not what He did through the entirety of His first Advent? Mounce, *Revelation*, 59.

[350] "The final 'coming' is the unveiling of what already is." Sweet, *Revelation*, 71.

[351] Counter to some theorists, the "servants" here are not only Christian prophets or apostles, but all Christians. Sweet, *Revelation*, 59.

[352] John MacArthur, *The MacArthur Bible Commentary*, 1992.

It is then said that **He made it known by sending His angel** which either refers to Jesus giving this message to an angel who was entrusted with conveying it to John, (although it could be argued that the angel does not become directly involved until chapter 17), or could be seen as an instance in which "angel" (*ἀγγέλου*) ought to be literally rendered as "messenger" in which case it would seem that "He" is still God the Father and the "angel" is Jesus Christ. Regardless of whether there is an angelic mediator or not, the message is said to come to John directly from God the Father. This displays Christ's willing submission to the Father (1 Cor. 15:28) in that He is willing to await direction from the Father before giving His revelation.

This detail may play some part in the interpretation of **soon take place**, as the vision is from the perspective of God rather than of man. However, two other interpretations seem plausible: (1) It is possible that the statement refers to the first three chapters (which arguably might refer to the churches of John's day alone), or (2) it is possible that the statement refers to the whole of the book of Revelation, with those events occurring throughout church history as well as in one culmination towards the end of time. Thus, one might take this phrase to refer to "soon" in a manner consistent with God's timing (wherein a day is a thousand years and a thousand years a single day; 2 Pet. 3:8), or to refer to "soon" in reference to John and his sense of timing, or to refer to "soon" in reference to all future readers who would endure their own version of these events in each generation leading up to that final generation.[353] This last possibility would seem to be the proper understanding, especially given that the exact same term (τάχει) is used in Romans 16:20 to refer to the Church's victory over Satan through the work of God.[354] While Satan has not been trampled underfoot by the Church completely, He is being defeated by the work of God who advances His kingdom in each generation through the existence and work of the Church and will ultimately and finally give us victory over Him in a climactic way when the end comes. Both senses are true.

---

[353] It is also worth noting that apocalyptic literature, such as Daniel 2:27-28 (which may serve as the point to which John refers with this phrase) and Ezekiel, authors always take an imminent view of eschatological events. It is in absolutely no way a defeater argument to hold that since the events described were said to have "soon" come to pass that the Revelation was proven false. The other possible interpretations show that not to be the case, but even if a purely futuristic interpretation is the only appropriate one, it is nevertheless the case that the apocalyptic genre of Revelation would provide one more explanation for this phrase. For more, see George Eldon Ladd, *Revelation*, 22.; and Robert Mounce, *The Book of Revelation*, 41, n.10. Mounce accuses those who hold to the association of this usage with that of 2 Peter 3:8 of involving John "in a verbal scam." Mounce, *Revelation*, 60.

[354] Beale also argues that this term is intended to be "a deliberate substitute" for the terminology used in Daniel 2:28. Beale, *Revelation*, 181.

This should give great hope to each and every generation, as regardless of what hardships they endure, or how closely or vaguely they mirror the signs in this book, they can know, as Mounce said, "history is not a haphazard sequence of unrelated events but a divinely decreed ordering of that which *must* take place."[355]

John's word choice in saying that the angel **made it known** to him foreshadows the nature of the Revelation itself. The word used (*ἐσήμανεν*) most frequently refers to the conveyance of a thought via visions, signs, metaphors, or symbols.[356] In fact, it is most regularly translated throughout the New Testament as the word "signifying." John, in identifying himself not as an apostle but as simply **his servant,** resembles the title of an Old Testament prophet (Jer. 29:19; 35:15) who so frequently received ecstatic and spiritual visions full of typological and unimaginable symbols.[357] It would appear, then, that John did not create his own symbols, but truly **bore witness… to all that he saw.**[358]

It is also interesting, in any case, that while it is Christ conveying to us the reality that we should look for the events described in this book (as it is the **testimony of Jesus Christ**), a pre-tribulation rapture never appears. One would expect it, but no such event is found in the text anywhere. The only "rapture" to be found is that which occurs at the Second Coming of Christ, as is noted also in the Olivet Discourse. It is, then, very odd that if there is such a pre-tribulation rapture, Jesus never mentions it at all in either of the instances wherein He speaks of the end times at great length. It appears that the next thing that Jesus wanted His people to expect was not a rapture, but the coming hardships described throughout Revelation (herein referred to tribulation – although not necessarily identically to that which is espoused in a Dispensationalist framework). Gundry would seem to rightly summarize the issue, saying,

> For the Church, *by far* the most important event shortly to take place is the pretribulational return of Christ if there be such. Yet, though John provides minute delineations of tribulational events and of the posttribulational advent and addresses and relates his book to churches, not a syllable depicts a pretibulational return of Christ.[359]

---

[355] Robert Mounce, *The Book of Revelation*, 41.
[356] Koester, *Revelation*, 211-212.
[357] Craig Keener, *The NIV Application Commentary: Revelation*, 64.
[358] Schreiner, through a much more thorough exploration of the Greek text, comes to this same conclusion. Thomas Schreiner, *Revelation* BECNT, 70.
[359] Robert Gundry, *The Church and the Tribulation*, 69. For a full defense of this thought see George Eldon Ladd, *The Blessed Hope*.

(1:3)

"Blessed is the one who reads aloud the words of this prophecy, and blessed are those who hear, and who keep what is written in it, for the time is near."

Μακάριος ὁ ἀναγινώσκων καὶ οἱ ἀκούοντες τοὺς λόγους τῆς προφητείας καὶ τηροῦντες τὰ ἐν αὐτῇ γεγραμμένα, ὁ γὰρ καιρὸς ἐγγύς."

The book is a **prophecy,** as a blessing is pronounced on those who **read aloud the words of this prophecy** (see verse 20). The nature of this book, being a prophecy, would require that at least some of the events held within John's Revelation would remain yet to be fulfilled at the time of his writing (see previous section on the dating of the book).

With consideration towards what this book is, it is sensical that **the one who reads**, **those who hear**, and **those who keep what is written** in it will be **blessed.**[360] This provides one of the first and foremost mistakes that many Christians make when reading and studying the book of Revelation. Many believe that the Revelation is a scary book that tells Christians about how awful things are going to be so that they can warn others and scare people into converting. And yet, John is clear that the point of the book is to be a blessing. That is, they are to be encouraged or considered favored by having received this book. This is not divorced from the reality that the events in it are intimidating, nor does it require the idea that the Church will be absent or that the world will be a much better place by then. In fact, each generation of readers and hearers are to understand that the events written in it are events they should expect to participate in and experience, as **the time is near** in which they will be fulfilled – near to every generation, and also near in terms of the timeline of God.

The beatitude here also provides a helpful solidification that this text is to be considered on par with other Scriptures, as the claim that those who hear and keep what is written will be blessed is almost certainly a reference to Luke 11:28, where Jesus says, "Blessed rather are those who hear the word of God and keep it." Thus, John seems to assert here that what is being written is to be considered **the word of God.**[361]

How could the Revelation be considered in this way? Consider again what the book truly is. It is a book intended to reveal to us who Jesus is. He is who and what is

---

[360] It will also prove helpful in future interpretations to note that the term "keep" here is the Greek *τηροῦντες*, which is the same root as what Christ promises to His Church in 3:10 when He says He will "keep" (*τηρήσω*) them from the hour that is coming. Rather than removing them, this word indicates a preservation through hardship – as it does here.

[361] See introductory section on the place of Revelation in the Canon.

being "revealed" in this revelation. Ought we not rejoice when reading about who Jesus is? Ought we not be encouraged? Any understanding of the book of Revelation, then, which leaves readers terrified or uninspired is certainly not the approach that was intended to be taken when reading it. To say it another way, if one leaves off reading the Revelation and is not encouraged or blessed, they have misunderstood it. Ladd would put it this way, "The Revelation was given not merely to impart information about the future, but to help God's people in the present…"[362] Matthew Henry would herald this sentiment centuries prior, saying, "this blessing [of verse 3] seems to be pronounced with a design to encourage us to study this book, and not be weary of looking into it…"[363]

(1:4-8) *The Doxology of the Lord*

(1:4)

> "John to the seven churches that are in Asia: Grace to you and peace from him who is and who was and who is to come, and from the seven spirits who are before his throne…"
>
> "Ἰωάννης ταῖς ἑπτὰ ἐκκλησίαις ταῖς ἐν τῇ Ἀσίᾳ· χάρις ὑμῖν καὶ εἰρήνη ἀπὸ ὁ ὢν καὶ ὁ ἦν καὶ ὁ ἐρχόμενος καὶ ἀπὸ τῶν ἑπτὰ πνευμάτων ἃ ἐνώπιον τοῦ θρόνου αὐτοῦ."

John introduces himself and his audience, which he here simply calls the **seven churches that are in Asia** but who will later be identified in verse 11 as the churches in the cities of Ephesus, Smyrna, Pergamos, Thyatira, Sardis, Philadelphia, and Laodicea. These churches were real, historical congregations in actual cities and towns of what we now call Asia Minor on the Eastern side of the Aegean Sea. Clearly, John wrote this letter to these churches directly – at least. It should be understood that the book is useful for the Church down throughout the ages, but it cannot be ignored that it was expected to have been beneficial to these seven churches in the time of John's life.

These seven churches were on a main road that formed an inverted horseshoe around the region of Asia Minor. While John certainly was aware of other churches in the region (such as Troas, Acts 20:5; Colossae; or Hieropolis, Col. 4:13), he sends these letters only to these churches and does not mention the others. While his rationale for this is not explained (aside from the fact that Jesus told him to do so), it should also be borne in mind that the lessons and admonitions taught to any single church were to be read and variously applied and followed by the other churches as well, as he concludes each insight with the phrase, "He who has an ear, let him hear what the Spirit says to the

---

[362] Ladd, *Revelation*, 23-24.

[363] Matthew Henry, *Matthew Henry's Commentary on the Whole Bible*, 1982.

churches…" It is always framed in the plural, such that every church was to read what Christ said to every other church as well as themselves.[364] Beyond this, Ladd claims that these seven churches were chosen to serve as "representative[s] of the church at large" and that while these letters were "addressed in particular to seven churches known to him, its message was also for the whole church in general."[365] This sentiment is incredibly valuable in rightly understanding and applying the Revelation, and was a thought that permeated the early church, as the Muratorian Fragment relays, "John also in the Apocalypse, though he writes to seven churches, nevertheless speaks to all."[366]

So, was this book written to the churches of Asia Minor in the late-first to early-second century? Yes. Are these admonitions valuable for churches outside of that orientation? Also, yes. And it should be remembered that while the Revelation is an apocalyptic piece of literature, it is also (at a minimum in its first three chapters) epistolary in nature. This is a crucial point in rightly applying the Revelation to everyday life. One would never assume that other canonical epistles only related to the original antecedents of the letter. Surely the teachings of the book of Romans apply to us as much as they did to the first-century church at Rome. Furthermore, one would scarcely believe that the teachings of the book of Galatians could not rightly be understood without a newspaper in hand. Still further, one would not dream of saying that a Christian would have no use of the letters to the church at Thessalonica, because they deal largely with end-times events and we are not (or perhaps even will not be) in those last days. No, the teachings of epistles directly applied to their original context, and also apply to Christians throughout Church History, including today, and will continue to apply through to the end when Christ does return. One makes a grave error if they read Revelation as something that *had* applicable meaning in the first century, or as something that *will only have* applicable meaning in the future. This book applies to all Christians throughout all time. (See comments on 2:28)

On the heels of this opening statement of purpose and pronouncement of blessing upon the saints who read, hear, and obey the words in this book, John turns and begins immediately to fully reveal to us who God is in words of praise. He begins with the statements **Grace to you and peace…** This is likely an amended greeting which integrated aspects of both Hebrew and Roman culture. The typical greeting for Romans

---

[364] It was not outside of the norm for Apostles to commend their intended recipients to give the letter to another group for their benefit, and also to read letters written to other groups for their own benefit. See Col. 4:16.

[365] Ladd, *Revelation*, 24.

[366] Hans Lietzmann, ed., *Das Muratorische Fragment und die Monarchianischen Prologue zu den Evangelien* 2, 58-62.

would have been "Hail" or "Welcome" (Greek, *χαῖρε*), but John uses a similar term, saying **grace** (Greek, *χάρις*). Similarly, the typical Jewish greeting was (and remains) the Hebrew term "Shalom" and this John translates over into the Greek (*εἰρήνη*) producing the English, **peace.** Thus, John combines Jewish and Gentile greetings to introduce his doxology, showing the expectation of unity in those two bodies while jointly praising God.

John begins by speaking of and describing **He who is and was and is to come...**[367] One may properly assume, based on what will follow in the first-person (v. 8) that this phrase is here intended to address God the Father. And what a leveling reality this is, that not only Christ will come, and not only the Holy Spirit will come, but the Father Himself is to come. His coming, like that of Christ, strikes fear in the unrepentant (Rev. 6:16) but for the people of God, what greater hope could there be than that our triune God will be with us?

He next describes **the seven Spirits who are before his throne.** This phrase has been somewhat mysterious to most interpreters, and it should not be assumed that this author has the perfect explanation for what or who precisely this depicts. However, there is good reason to believe that this refers to God the Holy Spirit. This sevenfold Spirit is referred to throughout the book of Revelation (1:4; 3:1; 4:5; 5:6). In Isaiah 11:2, the Holy Spirit of God is described as having diverse characteristics that could each be taken as depicting a respective Spirit – leading some to refer to this passage as describing the "sevenfold ministry of the Holy Spirit."[368] Still elsewhere the Holy Spirit is depicted in a sevenfold manner, such as in Zechariah 4:1-6 when He is depicted as the seven lampstands that give light to God's people. The description of someone in a sevenfold manner is closely associated with deity in Revelation, as Jesus is described in a sevenfold manner in 5:12, and the Father is also described in a sevenfold manner in 7:12. Therefore, it can be best and most safely assumed that this phrase depicts the Holy Spirit of God. One must be careful to maintain the unity of the Holy Spirit as a single person, but the diversity of His characteristics is a helpful explanation of this description.

---

[367] Beale mentions that John may have been using this formula as an apologetic against similar usages by pagans of his era who said such things of Zeus, Isis, and Osiris. Beale, *Revelation*, 188. However, the direct quotation of this phrase as coming from God in verse 8 seems to indicate that John used it because God used it of Himself.

[368] MacArthur, *The MacArthur Bible Commentary*, 1993. Contrary to the claim made by the editors of *The Moody Bible Commentary* that Isaiah 11:2 only gives six attributes, the Spirit is described here as being the Spirit (1) of the Lord; (2) of wisdom; (3) of understanding; (4) of counsel; (5) of might; (6) of knowledge; and (7) of fear of the Lord.

(1:5a)

> "And from Jesus Christ the faithful witness, the firstborn of the dead, and the ruler of kings on earth."
>
> "καὶ ἀπὸ Ἰησοῦ Χριστοῦ, ὁ μάρτυς, ὁ πιστός, ὁ πρωτότοκος τῶν νεκρῶν καὶ ὁ ἄρχων τῶν βασιλέων τῆς γῆς."

Finally, John describes **Jesus Christ, the faithful witness, the firstborn of the dead, the ruler kings on earth.** Here is the first of many descriptions of Jesus Christ in the Revelation. He is first called **the faithful witness**. Already this is the second time that John has used the word **witness,** though in verse 2 he used it in reference to himself. The Greek terms used (*μαρτυρίαν, μάρτυς*) both produce the transliterated term *martyr* – which does literally mean "witness."[369] In the book of Revelation, witnesses are always pictorial of God's people who are persecuted for their testimony of the truth. Thus, Christ here is shown to be the supreme (or **faithful**) witness who carried the truth of God and testified to that truth, ultimately dying as our exemplar of how to rightly live.

Having died faithfully, however, one is immediately reminded of the fact that Jesus is **the firstborn of the dead**, which asserts that although He died (and truly died at that), He also rose (and truly rose). Furthermore, one is meant to understand from this that it is not simply that Jesus Christ rose from the dead, but that He is only the first to do so.[370] And one must immediately ask the question, "Jesus is the first of *what group* to rise from the dead?" The answer must be that He is the first of all the witnesses. He is the first of all of those who will faithfully keep the testimony of God through suffering, persecution, and even martyrdom. This is certainly the conclusion that Paul came to when using this same term to describe Jesus elsewhere (Col. 1:18). Thus, if we die as He died, it is equally true that we will rise as He rose!

And for those who have not died, John affirms that Jesus is not simply someone whom you might have hope in once dead. Rather, He is **the ruler of kings on earth**, a term that further asserts the sovereignty and deity of Christ, as this is a descriptor throughout the Old Testament of God the Father (Ps. 89:27; Prov. 21:1; Dan. 2:21). With both the deity and sovereignty of Jesus Christ asserted, there ought to be nothing in all of God's creation that should discourage or frighten Christ's witnesses. If they live, they

---

[369] The exact same phrase is translated in Revelation 2:13 as "faithful witness" to describe Antipas who was martyred for the faith.

[370] Ladd holds that the priority of Christ's resurrection serves to affirm that "Jesus has been exalted to the position of firstborn son" with reference to Psalm 89:27. Ladd, *Revelation*, 25. This author is uncomfortable with that language, however, as it seems to imply that there was some time or sense in which Jesus was not in the position of firstborn son. Christ is the eternal Son of God, needing no "exaltation" to such a position.

have the confidence that Jesus Christ is ruling over their own rulers. If they are persecuted, they have an example in the person of Jesus Christ to be faithful to witness and testify to the truth, even if it brings us to the point of a martyr's death. And if we should be called on to die in such a way, those who endure such can be encouraged in that as they died like Christ, they shall also rise like He did.

This commendation of "grace and peace" in verses 4-5a should be recognized as fully what it is. This is nothing short of a statement of the triune God's greeting to His people. God the Father is first addressed, then God the Holy Spirit, and finally God the Son – each receiving due reverence.

(1:5b-6)

> "To him who loves us and has freed us from our sins by his blood and made us a kingdom, priests to his God and Father, to him be glory and dominion forever and ever. Amen."
>
> Τῷ ἀγαπῶντι ἡμᾶς καὶ λύσαντι ἡμᾶς ἐκ τῶν ἁμαρτιῶν ἡμῶν ἐν τῷ αἵματι αὐτοῦ, καὶ ἐποίησεν ἡμᾶς βασιλείαν, ἱερεῖς τῷ θεῷ καὶ πατρὶ αὐτοῦ, αὐτῷ ἡ δόξα καὶ τὸ κράτος εἰς τοὺς αἰῶνας [τῶν αἰώνων]· ἀμήν."

In light of this reality, John breaks into uncontrollable praise – an understandable reaction that some Christians in the modern age could stand to learn from. He writes, **to him who loves us and has freed us from our sins by his blood and made us a kingdom, priests to his God and Father, to him be glory and dominion forever and ever.** One is immediately confronted with the attitude and disposition in which John wrote the Revelation. It is very distinct from the attitude and disposition in which most modern Christians read it. Jesus is shown through the Revelation as being the one who **loves us** (*ἀγαπῶντι*) – in the present active participle form, which indicates that His love was present at the time of writing and continues to be present into the indefinite future so long as this book is read.[371] And in His great love for us, He **has freed us from our sins by His blood.**[372] This should serve as a great encouragement to those Christians engaging hardship, as despite their great difficulties, they might place their hope in the fact that Christ has stood in their place both physically and spiritually, and has freed

---

[371] Here is one of the first important distinctions between the TR and other Greek texts. While the TR renders this "loved" in the past tense (per the insertion of αγαπησαντι in place of ἀγαπῶντι), the Majority Byzantine and Alexandrian texts both show the word to be in the present tense.

[372] Oddly, the KJV renders the Greek term λύσαντι as "washed" despite that being unrecognizable as a possible rendering of that Greek term. Wesley J. Perschbacher, ed., *The New Analytical Greek Lexicon*, 261-262. The term for "wash" is used in Rev. 7:14 (ἔπλυναν) and 22:14 (πλύνοντες). Mounce theorizes that the error arose as a result of "in" being written in the TR rather than "by." Mounce, *Revelation*, 49.

them from that which is truly to be dreaded – He who can kill both soul and body in Hell. (Matt. 10:28)

His reference to Christ having **made us a kingdom, priests to his God and Father** is a direct reference to Exodus 19:5-6, which was a promise originally given to Israel but here delivered to the Church.[373] The assertion here is that the Church is a people who will reign with Christ (as members of His kingdom), and that they no longer stand in need of anyone to stand between them and God (as priests themselves). This was never actualized by Israel, as there was never a time when all of the Israelites ever ruled (only two tribes, Benjamin and Judah, were ever even represented on the throne of Israel), nor were they ever all priests (as only the Levites were priests). Isaiah 61:1-6 tells of this fulfillment coming to this world under the reign of the Messiah, and Christ explicitly claimed to have brought this to pass – although He importantly abstained from proclaiming its full culmination as having come (Luke 4:18-21). Thus, Christ's first coming initiated this truth for God's people (the Church) – who presently "live in the sphere of God's rule, a kingdom entered by faith in Jesus Christ." [374] Ladd commented on this verse and completely captured its meaning for the Church, saying,

> The Church is both a priesthood and a kingdom. The redeemed share the prerogative of their Great High Priest of entering into the very Holy of Holies and worshipping God. They are priests. The Church also shares the prerogative of their Lord and King. They are granted the right to rule with Christ. They are a kingdom, a nation of kings.[375]

And yet, there is still to come a greater manifestation of these truths. At Christ's second coming, God's people will finally experience this spiritual truth as physical reality. The early church understood this and expected to inherit the promises made to Israel as "their spiritual predecessors (1 Pet. 2:5, 9)."[376] Thus, the church needs no King but Christ, and each believer needs no priest to speak to God Himself.

Some have claimed that the final phrase, **to him be glory and dominion forever and ever** is directed at Jesus.[377] The Greek, however, seems to favor more that this phrase referred to God the Father, as "Jesus Christ" is in the genitive masculine singular (as is the pronoun "his" which precedes "God and Father." The words "God and Father" on the other hand are in the dative masculine singular, which is the case that the pronoun

---

[373] This phrase and its depiction will reappear in the Revelation, perhaps most notably in Revelation 5:9-10.

[374] MacArthur, *The MacArthur Bible Commentary*, 1993.

[375] Ladd, *The Gospel of the Kingdom*, 117.

[376] Mounce, *Revelation*, 50.

[377] William R. Newell, *The Book of the Revelation*, 13.

"him" is in when preceding glory and dominion. As a general rule, pronouns will match their intended antecedents in case. Recognizing this, nevertheless, does nothing to undermine the case for the divinity of Christ in John's Revelation.

(1:7)

> "Behold, he is coming with the clouds, and every eye will see him, even those who pierced him, and all tribes of the earth will wail on account of him. Even so. Amen."
>
> "Ἰδοὺ ἔρχεται μετὰ τῶν νεφελῶν, καὶ ὄψεται αὐτὸν πᾶς ὀφθαλμὸς καὶ οἵτινες αὐτὸν ἐξεκέντησαν, καὶ κόψονται ἐπ' αὐτὸν πᾶσαι αἱ φυλαὶ τῆς γῆς. ναί, ἀμήν."

Notice that John is not simply declaring praise for God, but victory in God. He goes on, **he is coming with the clouds, and every eye will see him, even those who pierced him, and all tribes of the earth will wail on account of him. Even so. Amen.** John anticipates a day in which the whole world will see, feel, and fully experience the presence of this great one who will ultimately be revealed, and even though they will wail and mourn on account of Him, so be it! His greatness must be known, either now or then. This is the only "coming" of Christ mentioned in Revelation, and it is a world-recognized, undeniable, public event in which He comes in glory and judgment.[378]

The idea of Christ **coming with the clouds** is something worth contemplation. Clearly, this refers to the promise of the coming Son of Man in Daniel 7:13, but what place do the clouds play specifically? Although it is most popularly accepted that Christ will literally appear to use the clouds as a form of transportation (as in Psalm 104:3), the term "with the clouds" would seem to designate some degree of independence from this interpretation, as opposed to the necessity of this interpretation if it said something like "on" or "in" the clouds (as in Isaiah 19:1).[379] It is also possible that this phrase imposes a sense of the presence of God (as in the cloud that filled the Tabernacle of Exodus 13:21 or the bright cloud that spoke from Heaven at Christ's baptism in Matthew 17:5). It is, admittedly, quite difficult to comprehend how it would be that **every eye will see him** given the curvature of the Earth if He came to any given location on literal clouds. And yet, it must be maintained that it was this manner of return that was promised in Acts 1:11. Perhaps both interpretations are correct.

The fact that **even those who pierced Him** will see Him only serves to further solidify the fact that **every eye will see Him.** The return of Christ is not some event of

---

[378] Gundry, *The Church and the Tribulation*, 69.; Mounce, *Revelation*, 51.
[379] Schreiner, *Revelation* BECNT, 88.

secrecy in which only His people will see Him. Rather, His return is a public event in which everyone, both believers and haters of God will see Him. In order that this phrase "those who pierced Him" could not be taken to refer strictly to Jews or Gentiles, it should be noted that in John 19:31-37, John refers to the Romans as those who pierced Him, and yet makes clear note that it was the Jews who requested that this be done. The original prophecy of this event in Zechariah 12:10 refers specifically to "the house of David." Thus, both the Gentiles and Jews are directly implicated in this phrase, **those who pierced Him**, alleviating it of any ethnic or racial connotations. This phrase, rather, refers to all unbelievers, both those who hate Christ, and those who generally disdain Him and His people.

Some see a connection between this and the promised salvation to the Jews in the last day (Romans 11:25-36). The ensuing **wailing on account of Him** seems to imply that there will be many of these individuals at His return who are entirely opposed to His coming. They regret that He has come, and desire more than anything else that He would not be coming (cf. Rev. 16:9, 11, 21).[380] And yet, while there is a possibility of their wailing implying fear or painful regret, it is also highly plausible that this is a double fulfillment of Zechariah 12:10. John notes in his Gospel (19:36-37) that Zechariah 12:10 was seemingly fulfilled at the crucifixion, but the resulting outpouring of "a spirit of grace and pleas for mercy" were not so obviously fulfilled. It could be, then, that the wailing at the return of Christ will mirror the wailing of those who cried out at the rededication of the foundation of the Temple (Ezra 3:13). Some wailed for joy and others in regret, "so that the people could not distinguish the sound of the joyful shout from the sound of the people's weeping..."

Thus, while there will undoubtedly be some who are wailing in fear or painful regret at the coming of Jesus Christ and others who are wailing in hope of being forgiven as a result of the outpouring of God's grace and mercy, John reflects on that reality and says, "**Even so. Amen.**" For the unredeemed, the coming of Christ will be an event of extreme regret, but for the people of God the coming of Christ will be an event of wonderous relief. Either way, all people will see Him, and some will receive judgment while others receive glory.

[380] Certainly, the event described here cannot be the destruction of Jerusalem in A.D. 70, as the Preterists sometimes hold. Those who wail are said to be of "all tribes of the earth," a phrase that does seem to be all-inclusive when used in Revelation (5:9; 7:9; 11:9; 13:7). See Schreiner, *Revelation* BECNT, 88-89, for a lengthier critique.

(1:8)

> "'I am the Alpha and the Omega,' says the Lord God, 'who is and who was and who is to come, the Almighty.'"
>
> "Ἐγώ εἰμι τὸ ἄλφα καὶ τὸ ὦ, λέγει κύριος ὁ θεός, ὁ ὢν καὶ ὁ ἦν καὶ ὁ ἐρχόμενος, ὁ παντοκράτωρ."

Once more before delving into the actual vision itself, John gives the readers a reminder of the greatness of God. He shows that the intent of the book is to reveal nothing more and nothing less than God's absolute sovereign reign and power and greatness over all things, from beginning to end.

The phrase **I am the Alpha and the Omega** refers to the Greek alphabet, and would form the equivalent of an English speaker saying, "I am A to Z." In the Hebraic tradition, the referencing of *Aleph* and *Tau* asserted the encapsulation of everything from the beginning to the end. This would mean that the speaker here is showing Himself to be entirely in control of all that is and was and ever shall be. Ladd takes this as the direct intention of the speaker, taking this phrase as a direct equivalent and confidently writes, "God is the absolute beginning and the end, and therefore Lord of all that happens in human history."[381]

There is some speculation over who is speaking in this verse. The content would seem to imply God the Father (see 1:4), but the context would seem to imply Jesus Christ. If it is the case that Jesus Christ said these last few phrases, there is certainly not a better argument to be made for Christ asserting His own divinity in the Bible. He will take the title "Alpha and Omega" for Himself in Rev. 22:13, but the following phrases leave no room for speculation. First, this figure is referred to as **the Lord God.** This Old Testament name is reserved exclusively for God, and goes all the way back to the Garden of Eden (Gen. 2:4ff). Then, He calls Himself He **who is, and was, and is to come**, which was just in verse 4 used to describe God the Father, and then finally takes on the term **the Almighty**, which is universally reserved for God. Thus, if this is Jesus Christ speaking, He is making abundantly clear that He is God. The majority opinion seems to be that the speaker is God the Father, but it must be admitted that the speaker is at least unclear – and given the infrequency with which God the Father speaks in Revelation (as only one

[381] Ladd, *Revelation*, 29.

other occasion is found; in Rev. 21:5ff), it is rational to hold the possibility that this is Jesus Christ speaking.[382]

[382] Mounce, *Revelation*, 51. For a lengthy investigation of the evidence for both positions, see Robert L. Thomas, *Revelation 1-7: An Exegetical Commentary*, 80.

Chapter 4:

(Revelation 1:9-20) King Jesus Ruling in Heaven

(vv. 9-20) *The Vision of the Seer*

(1:9)

"I, John, your brother and partner in the tribulation and the kingdom and the patient endurance that are in Jesus, was on the island called Patmos on account of the word of God and the testimony of Jesus."

"Ἐγὼ Ἰωάννης, ὁ ἀδελφὸς ὑμῶν καὶ συγκοινωνὸς ἐν τῇ θλίψει καὶ βασιλείᾳ καὶ ὑπομονῇ ἐν Ἰησοῦ, ἐγενόμην ἐν τῇ νήσῳ τῇ καλουμένῃ Πάτμῳ διὰ τὸν λόγον τοῦ θεοῦ καὶ τὴν μαρτυρίαν Ἰησοῦ."

John opens this section with a rather unexpected identification of himself. Rather than the typical introduction of Paul or Peter, who both were known to begin by saying, "Paul, an Apostle" (2 Cor. 1:1; Gal. 1:1; Eph. 1:1; Col. 1:1; 1 Tim. 1:1; 2 Tim. 1:1) or "Peter, an Apostle" (1 Pet. 1:1; 2 Pet. 1:1), in order to assert their authority and closeness to Christ, John begins by calling himself **your brother and partner in the tribulation and the kingdom and the patient endurance.** While the Apostolic authority of John should not be considered diminished, it is key to reflect on the fact that he asserted not his authority, but his brotherhood and partnership with both the saints in the churches around him, and, by implication, all the saints of all the ages.[383]

Further, it is worthwhile to reflect on the circumstance in which he claims to be our brother and partner. He says that he is our brother and partner **in the tribulation.** Reflecting back to verse 1 wherein Christ said that the events He would tell were to soon be fulfilled, it does appear that John held himself to be engaged in some degree of tribulation in his era.[384] The word rendered "tribulation" is the Greek *thlipsei* (θλίψει) which is from the same root that Jesus uses in His Olivet Discourse to discuss the hardships to come to His people in the last days. Thus, it is very possible that John

[383] It has also been noted that John was likely mirroring the practice of Daniel, who simply identified himself as "I, Daniel" (Dan. 8:15; 9:2; 10:2). His failing to identify himself as an apostle shows that, like Daniel, he anticipated that the intended audience would have no trouble understanding which John was writing. Newell, *Revelation*, 22.

[384] Beale seems to agree with this type of interpretation based on the terminology used in verse 1. Beale, *Revelation*, 181-182.

indicates here that the "tribulation" Jesus spoke of in that passage was one in which he considered himself presently engaged.[385] In this way, the preterist understanding of some aspects of the Olivet Discourse can be accepted, but certainly not all of them – and at the same time, if one expects a future fulfillment of the tribulation in a more intense manner, all of the elements found in the Olivet Discourse (prefigured in the destruction of Jerusalem in A.D. 70 or not) will be fulfilled in that final calamitous age. This will form what is sometimes called a *double fulfillment.*[386]

His comment about being a partner **in the kingdom and the patient endurance** certainly hearkens to the concept of Christians presently being a part of the kingdom of God in some sense. There is no room here for the idea that the kingdom that he claims to presently be a part of is in no way present, as he claims to already be a partner in it. Helpfully, he clarifies that the kingdom and patient endurance that he presently participates in **are in Jesus**. Thus, the promises of God are shown to truly find their fulfillment in Him. (2 Cor. 1:20) But here is a wonderful truth for all Christians to appreciate – John was equally aware of his participation in the kingdom, just as he was aware of his participation in the tribulation. He went through both, and patiently endured both just as we do and always will – until Christ returns. This sets the example of how to fulfill the commands of Jesus Christ and His Apostles, who both taught in various places "they that endure unto the end shall be saved" (Mt. 24:13) and "through many tribulations we must enter the Kingdom of God." (Acts 14:22)

Therefore, Christians can have a realistic expectation of what will come in the future, and how we are to behave in it. George Ladd, perhaps accidentally, addressed the primary criticism of this position when he said, "this conflict will last to the end of The Age. Final victory will be achieved only by the return of Christ. There is no room for an unqualified optimism." We must take a real look at what God has said will come, and along with John be "always ready to endure the tribulation as well as the kingdom and patience which are in Jesus."[387] Mounce notes that this is something that Christians

---

[385] While the author is sympathetic to this position, it is also the perspective of the author that there will be an increased degree of hardship in the end of days that will lead up to Christ's return. Thus, the "tribulation" is experienced across the entire inter-advent age, while the "great tribulation" will be experienced only in the end. Ladd commented on this, saying, "the Great Tribulation at the end will be only the intensification of what the Church has suffered throughout all history." Ladd, *Revelation*, 30. Gundry asserts that John, as "a member of the Church, grouped himself with the tribulational saints." Gundry, *The Church and the Tribulation*, 80. This is true of John and ourselves, whether we are persevering through tribulation, or *the* tribulation to come in the end.

[386] John Piper, *Come, Lord Jesus*, 106, 114, 186-187. Piper affirms Ladd's identification of this as "Prophetic Perspective."

[387] Ladd, *The Gospel of the Kingdom*, 137.

should expect to be their normal experience throughout life, "but it also extends to include that final period of intense affliction which precedes the establishment of the millennial kingdom."[388] Thus, whether in 100, 1000, or 10,000 AD, the promise of Christ remains true, "I have said these things to you, that in me you may have peace. In the world you will have tribulation. But take heart; I have overcome the world." (John 16:33) Because we have endured tribulation and have overcome many antichrists (1 John 2:18, 22; 4:3) for centuries, we can have faith and confidence that we will endure and overcome that final era of intense tribulation, as well as that final embodiment of Antichrist.[389]

The tensing of John's statement that he **was on the island called Patmos** indicates to us that at the time of his writing this he is no longer on the island.[390] Irenaeus claimed that John distributed Revelation after having returned to Ephesus, a thought which was seemingly affirmed by Eusebius, Jerome, and many other early authors both within and out of Asia.[391] Traditions have claimed that John returned to Ephesus after his imprisonment on Patmos, where he cared for Mary until she died and ultimately where he lived until he died. If true, this might explain why Ephesus is the first church on the list to receive a word from Christ. Robert Mounce rejects this theory, but also theorizes (based on variations in the *Textus Receptus*) that John added much of the introductory section after having completely written the rest of the book, indicating some degree of an editing process over time.[392]

Patmos was a small rocky island in the Aegean Sea to which we have reason to believe the Romans would send political rabble-rousers to avoid executing the leader of movements and creating a martyr around which they might rebel.[393] His crime is listed simply as being **on account of the word of God and the testimony of Jesus**, one can safely assume he was sent to Patmos by the Romans who wished to isolate him and his testimony without killing him, so as to avoid outraging the Christians who knew he was one of the few (perhaps only) remaining apostles.[394]

---

[388] Mounce, *Revelation*, 54.
[389] Gundry, *The Church and the Tribulation*, 49.
[390] Ladd, *Revelation*, 30.; Schreiner, *Revelation* BECNT, 97.; J. Ramsey Michaels, *Interpreting the Book of Revelation*, 15. For more on the date of John's exile and the cause of it, see Quintern and Shultz, *Revelation in Focus*, 89-90.
[391] Irenaeus, *Against Heresies*, 2:22:5; 3:3:4.; Eusebius, *History of the Church*, 3:20:10-11. F.J.A Hort, *The Apocalypse of St. John* I-III, xv-xix.
[392] Mounce, *Revelation*, 54-55, n.6; 39.
[393] Tacitus, *Annals*, 3:68; 4:30; 15:71.; Juvenal, *Satires*, 6:563-564. See Quintern and Shultz, *Revelation in Focus*, 89-90.
[394] Gregg, *Revelation: Four* Views, 86.

(1:10)

"I was in the Spirit on the Lord's day, and I heard behind me a loud voice like a trumpet..."

"ἐγενόμην ἐν πνεύματι ἐν τῇ κυριακῇ ἡμέρᾳ καὶ ἤκουσα ὀπίσω μου φωνὴν μεγάλην ὡς σάλπιγγος..."

Here, John gives us the first tell-tale sign that a new vision has begun, which is why this section is broken apart from that which preceded it (the introduction). The signs of a new vision are twofold (as previously noted). They are (1) John's statement of being **in the Spirit**, and (2) John being approached by some manner of a heavenly being, as here he claims to have **heard behind me a loud voice like a trumpet.**

His being **in the Spirit** should not be taken in the same sense in which Paul commends all Christians to constantly walk (Gal. 5:16) or in which Jesus told us we would walk (John 14:17) since it is said to have been the case for John in the past tense. He *was* in the Spirit in a way that he no longer is at the time of writing. Thus, the manner in which he was in the Spirit is better taken as referring to a trance of sorts in which a person was so overwhelmed by the Holy Spirit that they began seeing and experiencing the spiritual rather than the physical.[395] Paul reports that this happened to him (Acts 22:17) and a friend of his (2 Cor. 12:2), and Peter seems to have had a similar experience (Acts 10:10; 11:5).

It is worth noting that John uses the terminology of **the Lord's day.** Some have speculated that it ought to be rendered "I was taken by the Spirit to the Day of the Lord," but that rendering is not only grammatically and exegetically unlikely, but it also does not match the content which follows, as John reports much more than the day of the Lord.[396] Rather, the correct understanding is that John was taken in the Spirit on the Lord's Day, that is, on Sunday.[397] Perhaps it is speculative, but the author contends that it

---

[395] Ladd, *Revelation,* 31.

[396] Gundry, *The Church and the Tribulation*, 92-93.

[397] There is a very interesting theory established on the basis of first and second century manuscripts that contends that John used the adjective *κυριακῇ* (Lord's) as had Paul (1 Cor. 11:20), borrowing terminology from the Roman legal system in which they identified things as belonging to Caesar by denoting it with the adjective *κυριακός,* which they used to denote the term "Emperor's." Ancient scribal experts have noted that in the first century, specifically in Egypt and Asia Minor (where John was when he wrote Revelation), the phrase "Emperor's Day" was frequently used to speak of days designated as special to Caesar. Thus, John and Paul (as well as other early Christians) likely took this term in a form of defiance to show that the only Lord of the Christians was the Lord Jesus who rose on Sunday, which was hence, "The Lord's Day." Adolf Deissmann, *Light from the Ancient East,* Lionel Strachan, trans., 361-364. G.R. Beasley-Murray viewed this theory favorably, as does Robert Mounce. G.R. Beasley-Murray, *Revelation* NCBC, 64-65.; Mounce, *Revelation*, 56.

was likely John was praying or worshipping, maybe reciting scriptures or spiritual songs (as would have been his practice on Sundays when worshipping with other Christians) and it was in that context that the Holy Spirit overwhelmed him.[398]

He says that he **heard... a loud voice like a trumpet**. The voice of God is frequently described in this way throughout the Scriptures, with two prominent examples being that of Exodus 19:16 and another retelling of that same narrative in Hebrews 12. One will see this same connection made in Revelation 4:1.[399] Why this connection is made is up for speculation, but one plausible explanation is that the sound of a trumpet is unmistakable and undeniable.[400] It cannot be ignored. It is "loud and clear" in a sense. The consequences of this thought, that the voice of God is referred to as being trumpet-like, are interesting when considering passages like 1 Thessalonians 4:17. It could be that when Christ is set to come, rather than hearing a literal trumpet sound, the world will hear nothing less than the very voice of God telling Him to go, and telling His people to come to Himself.

(1:11)

> "...saying, "Write what you see in a book and send it to the seven churches, to Ephesus and to Smyrna and to Pergamum and to Thyatira and to Sardis and to Philadelphia and to Laodicea."
>
> "...λεγούσης· ὃ βλέπεις γράψον εἰς βιβλίον καὶ πέμψον ταῖς ἑπτὰ ἐκκλησίαις, εἰς Ἔφεσον καὶ εἰς Σμύρναν καὶ εἰς Πέργαμον καὶ εἰς Θυάτειρα καὶ εἰς Σάρδεις καὶ εἰς Φιλαδέλφειαν καὶ εἰς Λαοδίκειαν."

Once more, it is important to note that John is to **write** what he sees and **send it to the seven churches**, meaning that all seven churches are to receive the whole of what is written. The church at Ephesus, for example, would receive a copy of what is written, including the words of Christ to the church at Laodicea. Thus, while these letters were to individual churches, they are instructive for all of us regardless of where or when we are living.

The order in which the seven churches are listed, **Ephesus... Smyrna... Pergamum... Thyatira... Sardis... Philadelphia, and Laodicea**, is intentional. In

---

[398] The early church (even by the late-first century) had well-established the imperative to worship on the Lord's Day; see *The Didache*, 14.; also Ignatius, *Epistle to the Magnesians*, 9.; Acts 20:7; 1 Cor. 16:2.

[399] Ladd claims that both this voice and that referenced in 4:1 are the voices of angels – but for the reasons given this author disagrees. Angels are, indeed, much more frequently heard, but they are also identified when they speak (Rev. 5:2, 12; 7:2; 10:3; 14:15, 18; 19:17). Ladd, *Revelation,* 31.

[400] Mounce, *Revelation,* 56.

John's era, this would have been the order in which someone would arrive at each of the churches on a typical mail-route. The order, given by Christ, is intentional and instructive. Christ is sovereign over every detail of this world, including the very order in which people receive their mail. Without an obvious purpose for this order aside from the mail-route, and without any clear symbolism, it appears that Christ gave these churches in the order in which they appear as an exercise in simply manifesting His omniscience and sovereignty.[401] There may be some symbolism in the limitation of the churches at only seven. There were at least three other churches in the region (see comments on v. 4), so for some reason Christ chose these seven. The most prevalent theory is that these seven represent the full or complete Church, and therefore, while Christ addressed seven real, local gatherings, He also gave commendations to the whole body of Christ throughout the ages through them. There is another, perhaps simpler theory, which holds that these seven cities were not only connected via the mail route, but each represented "the distribution centers for the seven postal districts of west-central Asia Minor."[402]

It should be noted, even by Baptists, that some have inappropriately taken the directness of Christ's address as a defense of local church autonomy. One author even went so far as to say, "note that the book is to be sent to *each church individually.* There was then no 'synod,' 'convention,' 'conference,' or 'diocese' of Asia!"[403] This line of argument is, frankly, silly. It does nothing to consider the fact that at the time of John's receiving and writing this book, Christianity was fiercely persecuted to such a degree that to call it "illegal" is a major understatement. How could there be such organizational structures in such an era? One may even protest that there were, indeed, conferences and/or diocese, as evidenced by the Jerusalem Council.[404] Silly extrapolations like this are not only departures from the intended purpose of the text, they represent an intentional misconstruing of Christian ecclesial history.

---

[401] The historicist's sense of symbolism in these seven churches as reaching throughout the Church Age is very appealing, but lacks a "smoking gun" form of absolute proof (as far as the author has currently engaged).
[402] Mounce, *Revelation*, 56. This thought is proposed and thoroughly defended in the masterful and unparalleled, William Ramsay, *The Letters to the Seven Churches of Asia and Their Place in the Plan of the Apocalypse*, 185-196.
[403] Newell, *Revelation*, 25.
[404] This is not the position of this author, but the argument could be made, nonetheless.

(1:12)

> "Then I turned to see the voice that was speaking to me, and on turning I saw seven golden lampstands,"
>
> "Καὶ ἐπέστρεψα βλέπειν τὴν φωνὴν ἥτις ἐλάλει μετ' ἐμοῦ, καὶ ἐπιστρέψας εἶδον ἑπτὰ λυχνίας χρυσᾶς,"

John turns **to see the voice.**[405] It is interesting that he leaves up to speculation whether or not he recognized the voice. One could argue either way that John's turning to see the speaker constitutes reason for thinking he did or did not know them. It is hard to imagine that he would not have recognized the voice of Jesus Christ, but then again, several factors would lend to the idea that he would not recognize it – such as the description of a voice like a trumpet (or the resurrection passages wherein individuals did not even recognize Jesus who was present in front of them, such as John 20:15 and others).

Regardless of whom he expected to see when he turned, he was undoubtedly unprepared for what he did see. First, he **saw seven golden lampstands** (*λυχνίας;* stands for portable oil lamps).[406] This most likely is intended to depict the lamp which stood in the holy place in the Tabernacle.[407] Schreiner points out that this lamp in the tabernacle served as a forerunner of sorts for what would later be incorporated when the Temple was constructed (1 Kings. 7:48-49).[408] In both settings, these lamps were the only way you could see the throne of God atop the Ark of the Covenant (Exodus 25:31-37). This imagery is used in Zechariah 4:2 to depict Israel, but here in Revelation the imagery is used to depict who? Verse 20 supplies the answer. The lampstands depict the churches – the Israel of God.[409] So, here is the first instance in John's Revelation of the Church being depicted as the ultimate fulfillment of what Israel was in the Old Testament – the people of God.

When understanding this, the imagery is incredible. The lampstands are the only way to see God in His throne room, and in this passage, God says that His people are the

---

[405] The concept of *seeing* a voice that sounds like a trumpet is also an Old Testament reference (Ex. 20:18).
[406] Thomas, *Revelation 1-7*, 97. Quoting from William Henry Simcox, *The Revelation of St. John the Divine*, 47.
[407] Because of events in Jewish history well-beyond the purview of this treatise, modern menorah's have nine lamps rather than the original seven.
[408] Schreiner, *Revelation* BECNT, 100.
[409] Mounce also points out that the individualized lampstands in this picture hearken to Solomon's placing lamps before the inner sanctuary when the Temple was dedicated in 1 Kings 8:49. If that parallel holds true, it would seem that this is also an allusion to the fact that the Church has replaced the Temple (2 Cor. 6:16). Mounce, *Revelation*, 57. Newell echoes this thought. Newell, *Revelation*, 26.

lampstands. In this world, then, God's people are to show the world who God is and give them guidance on how to find Him.[410] In the Old Testament, that duty was placed on Israel, but in the New Testament, it rests on the Church (universal and locally assembled) who are to be the "light of the world." (Matt. 5:14).[411] Importantly, Christ will say later (Rev. 2:5) that those congregations who fail to shine the light of Christ will have their lampstand removed – some manner of an indication that Christ will anathemize them.

(1:13)

> "and in the midst of the lampstands one like a son of man, clothed with a long robe and with a golden sash around his chest."
>
> "καὶ ἐν μέσῳ τῶν λυχνιῶν ὅμοιον υἱὸν ἀνθρώπου ἐνδεδυμένον ποδήρη καὶ περιεζωσμένον πρὸς τοῖς μαστοῖς ζώνην χρυσᾶν."

Amongst those lampstands, John next says he saw **one like the son of man.** This, Christ's favorite moniker for himself, was one way in which He identified Himself as the eschatological figure of Daniel 7:13 who is given everlasting dominion, glory, an indestructible kingdom, and unending authority over all people, nations, and languages.[412] It was for claiming to be this figure that the Pharisees ended all speculation that Christ was (in their eyes) a blasphemer (Mark 14:62). The fact that this person, Christ, the eschatologically and eternally authoritative figure endowed with unquestionable power, is **in the midst of the lampstands** provides key insights into the fact that the Church (universal or locally assembled) holds no power in and of itself, but only operates with authority or power because of the presence, authority, and power of Christ within it – and yet, it is awesome that Christ endows the Church with this sort of gift, as He promised to always be "in the midst" of the locally assembled churches (Matt. 18:20). With this in mind, it is no great claim that the Church is chosen to bring others to God, as this was the supreme mission for which Christ was sent (1 John 4:9), and He accomplishes it by His working through local churches.

John then notices the clothing of Christ, which indicates something of His universal authority and power. He is said to be **clothed with a long robe.** This long robe (ἐνδεδυμένον ποδήρη) renders out literally to "robed to the feet." It is a phrase used only here in the New Testament, and seven times in the Greek Old Testament – all of which describe the clothing of the High Priest.[413] John, as someone who was intimately familiar

---

[410] Thomas, *Revelation 1-7*, 97.

[411] Ladd, *Revelation*, 32.

[412] Christ references this very passage in speaking of Himself in Mark 13:26.

[413] Mounce, *Revelation*, 58.

with the Jewish Temple practices (see John 18:15), would have known he was using the same term – and one must assume that it is intentionally used to depict the type of robe that the High Priest wore.[414] John was also the only disciple to mention the specific tunic that Christ wore as an undergarment (John 19:23). That tunic was the exact same piece of clothing that the High Priest was to wear under his robe (Ex. 28:32). So, while Christ was privately dressed in the garments of the High Priest in His life, John sees Him here, openly and publicly dressed to be recognizable as the High Priest among His people (Heb. 4:14-16).

Only after recognizing his distinct robe, John describes His wearing **a golden sash.** This sash has frequently been referenced as another aspect of the High Priestly garb (Exodus 39:29).[415] There is a problem with that assumption though, as the placement of the sash **around his chest** indicates that it is something other than the High Priest's sash. This *ζώνην* (usually, belt/waistband) is meant to be worn around the waist rather than the chest. Some commentators have sought to side-step this issue by claiming (without any support) that it was in fact to be worn "on the breast a little above the armpits."[416] This claim is entirely false. There are two passages that clarify where this belt was meant to be worn, Leviticus 16:4 and 8:7. In 16:4, it is recorded, "he shall tie the linen sash *around his waist...*" And in Leviticus 8:7 it says that indeed, when they put it on, "he put the coat on him and tied the sash *around his waist...*" Simply put, if Jesus is wearing this sash as another element of His High Priestly garb, He is wearing it wrong. That is not a small issue – as it was God's law that every element be worn precisely to His specifications. If Jesus is wearing this sash as an element of the High Priestly garb, and doing so wrongly, He is breaking the law of God.

Therefore, it must be (at least) entertained that this sash is intended to symbolize something else.[417] One notably neglected possibility of what this sash might have referred to is that of the sashes frequently worn by Romans of the day. A person was not even

---

[414] The robe of the High Priest is so easily recognizable that some have speculated that Paul's "thorn in the flesh" was blindness, with a primary form of support being the fact that he did not recognize the High Priest in Acts 23:5. Anyone who could not recognize the High Priest despite his unique clothing, they say, must have been nearly blind.

[415] This image is so frequently associated with High Priestly attire that it has been called "the critical verse par excellance" for determining "whether or not Revelation contains high priestly imagery for Jesus Christ." Ross E. Winkle, *Clothes Make the (One Like a Son of) Man: Dress Imagery in Revelation 1 as an Indicator of High Priestly Status* (Andrews University: PhD Dissertation, 2012), 10. It should be noted that there are at least three other possible meanings frequently applied to this symbol. Thomas, *Revelation 1-7*, 100.

[416] Thomas, *Revelation 1-7*, 100.

[417] See notes on 3:7.

allowed to wear such a sash if they were not a full Roman citizen.[418] There were essentially seven types of sashes (sometimes but not always called *togas* as togas frequently referred to the whole robe), each to be worn in a specific atmosphere by a certain person or official. In this depiction, one could argue that Christ is wearing a *toga praetexta*, which was "reserved for magistrates and high priests."[419] This would depict Christ as both a political and religious authority – but this would be somewhat problematic because the priesthood asserted by a *praetexta* was pagan. Instead, when it is considered that this is not simply a sash, but a **golden sash**, there is only one type of toga this can be: the *toga picta.* This toga was noted for its gold embroidery, and was easily recognized because it was so rarely worn.[420] Michael Dewar writes of the *toga picta* that "it was as rare a sight in the days of the Republic as the occasion for which it was reserved, the celebration of a triumph."[421]

It was considered such an honor to wear a *picta* that a proconsul of Rome was once reprimanded for wearing one because "he was inappropriately, and hubristically, overdressed."[422] For clarity, the *picta* was not to be worn by everyone in the triumph parade, but was reserved exclusively "for the triumphant generals."[423] In the lifetime of John, an ancient practice of the Roman senate sometimes awarding this sash to foreign kings to recognize their legitimacy was revived.[424]And still, despite its great infrequency and severe restriction of usage, the depiction of other kings or triumphant generals in such a glorious and praiseworthy fashion was too much for the Emperors of first-century Rome to swallow. As such, "victories and triumphs became the prerogative of the sovereign, and as the ideology of permanent imperial victory established itself, the *toga picta* came more and more to be associated with the person of the emperor."[425]

---

[418] J. Albert Harrill, "Coming of Age and Putting on Christ: The *Toga Virilis* Ceremony, Its Paraenesis, and Paul's Interpretation of Baptism in Galatians" *Novum Testamentum* 44 (2002): 255-266.

[419] Winkle, *Clothes Make the (One Like a Son of) Man*, 105, n.94.

[420] Michael Dewar, "Spinning the *Trabea*: Consular Robes and Propaganda in the Panegyrics of Claudian" in Jonathan Edmonson and Alison Keith, eds., *Roman Dress and the Fabrics of Roman Culture*, 219. Interestingly (given what is later said of Christ in verses 16 and 20) these togas also regularly incorporated stars into the design. Jonathan Edmondson, "Public Dress and Social Control in Late Republican and Early Imperial Rome" in *Roman Dress and the Fabrics of Roman* Culture, 29.

[421] Dewar, "Spinning the *Trabea*", 219.

[422] Jonathan Edmondson, "Public Dress and Social Control in Late Republican and Early Imperial Rome" in *Roman Dress and the Fabrics of Roman* Culture, 35.

[423] Michele George, "The 'Dark Side' of the Toga" in *Roman Dress and the Fabrics of Roman* Culture, 94.

[424] Tacitus, *Annals,* 4:26.

[425] Dewar, "Spinning the *Trabea*", 219.

Is this, then, the reference that Christ is conjuring in the mind of John by wearing this distinctive sash? The contention seems to hold a rather strong claim.[426] The depiction itself agrees with it, and the symbolism of the sash alone becomes deeply meaningful in a way that explains its specifically being noted (something other explanations do not explain). Christ is displayed as having authority over the priestly realm (wearing the garb of the High Priest), and the prophetic realm (as this garb could also be that of an Old Testament prophet; Zech. 3:4) but this sash shows His authority over the political realm (wearing the garb of a conquering general who is returning in triumph; a recognizably legitimate king). All three realms are present, and Christ does not seem to hesitate at all to integrate those realms, wearing the royal sash over His priestly and prophetic robe.[427] In this single verse, Christ is depicted as the victorious, conquering, triumphantly returning prophet, priest, and king. What is more, (as was implied in 1:7) He is again depicted as having authority over Jews (as High Priest) and Gentiles (as Roman conqueror). Jesus Christ is Prophet, Priest, and King, over all mankind.

(1:14)

"The hairs of his head were white, like white wool, like snow. His eyes were like a flame of fire,"

"ἡ δὲ κεφαλὴ αὐτοῦ καὶ αἱ τρίχες λευκαὶ ὡς ἔριον λευκὸν ὡς χιὼν καὶ οἱ ὀφθαλμοὶ αὐτοῦ ὡς φλὸξ πυρὸς"

Moving away from His clothing to His person directly, John says **the hairs of his head were white, like white wool, like snow**. There are many descriptions of Christ in the Revelation, many of which are largely (if not entirely) symbolic (such as His being described as a Lamb in 5:6). Here, one imagines that John is recalling the transfiguration of Christ, but he goes on to use greatly detailed language that is not used in any of the Gospel accounts of that event.[428] While it is wise to try to avoid explaining every single detail, there are some meaningful (and safe) assumptions to make based off of these descriptions. The white hair, for example, can safely be taken as seeking to indicate a few things. (1) It could be taken as a reference to (and assertion of) the divinity of Christ, as

---

[426] It is, however, admitted that this interpretation does not agree well with the usage of this phrase in Rev. 15:6.

[427] There is, then, no need to bicker over which depiction of Christ is intended – as does Koester, *Revelation*, 246.

[428] Matthew 17:1-8; Mark 9:2-8; Luke 9:28-36. Matthew notes that "his face shone like the sun, and his clothes became white as light." Mark makes mention of the "radiant, intensely white" clothes He was seen in. Luke simply accounts that "the appearance of his face was altered, and his clothing became dazzling white." Thus, white as a color of purity or divinity is maintained, but all the other details are entirely Johannine.

God Himself is described this way in Daniel 7:9.[429] (2) There are several instances in which the Bible refers to individuals with a "hoary head" (i.e., those with hair indicating their agedness) as being worthy of respect (Lev. 19:32). (3) Sometimes, hair that has lost its color (having gone white or gray) is referred to as a "crown of glory." (Prov. 16:31)[430] Thus, one could take this as being an assertion of Christ's being crowned with glory. Since God does not age, the description here is not at all intended to indicate the age of Christ. These three associations are much more likely to be the intended meanings.

Looking further in, John notices **his eyes were like a flame of fire.**[431] Some have taken this to mean that He has a piercing gaze that would intimidate, but it is more likely that it asserts His ability to see everything. Nothing is beyond His sight, and all that He sees, He sees completely and without reservation. This interpretation is drawn from the other instances in Revelation wherein this trait is mentioned. In Revelation 2:18-19, Christ's blazing eyes are tied to His knowing everything about those whom He sees. In Revelation 19:12, they again indicate His having knowledge that no other has.[432] This can also be taken as an allusion to the Old Testament depiction of heavenly beings, as an angelic figure whom Daniel sees is described in Daniel 10:6 as having "eyes like flaming torches."[433]

(1:15)

> "his feet were like burnished bronze, refined in a furnace, and his voice was like the roar of many waters."
>
> "καὶ οἱ πόδες αὐτοῦ ὅμοιοι χαλκολιβάνῳ ὡς ἐν καμίνῳ πεπυρωμένης καὶ ἡ φωνὴ αὐτοῦ ὡς φωνὴ ὑδάτων πολλῶν,"

Down below, **his feet were like burnished bronze, refined in a furnace.** Admittedly, the Greek term (χαλκολιβάνῳ) used to describe His feet here is a very unique term. It is only used twice in the Bible (here and Revelation 2:18, both in the exact same

---

[429] As Ladd, *Revelation*, 33.

[430] Mounce, *Revelation*, 58.

[431] There is no exegetical room for a distinction between the eyes as described here and as described in 19:12, as does Newell, *Revelation*, 27. The phrases are character-for-character identical, *ὀφθαλμοὶ ὡς φλὸξ πυρός*. "Eyes like blazing fire." Metzger asserts that the inclusion of *ὡς* in 19:12 is equal to any evidence to the contrary, and that it is therefore retained in the NA-28. Metzger, *Textual Commentary*, 763.

[432] Ladd, *Revelation*, 33.

[433] Schreiner, *Revelation* BECNT, 104.; Thomas, *Revelation 1-7*, 101.; Sweet, *Revelation*, 72. Schreiner notes this connection, but doubts that it was intended here as it undermines the previous allusion which asserts the divinity of Christ. Sweet sees no such conflict. For a thorough discussion, see Keener, *NIV Application Revelation*, 110.

way) and is unfound in any extrabiblical Greek literature.[434] It refers to a variety of metals, some of which are most pure when white and others of which maintain a deep tint even at perfect purity.[435] Thus, it is impossible to deduce a certain color from this description. What can be safely understood is that whatever type of metal it was, the metal is made of valuable and strong components such as bronze, brass, or even gold. It may seem to be a little-nuanced thought, but this description of Christ's feet may serve to indicate that He is firmly grounded, unmovable, stable, strong, and solid.

Clarifying that it was indeed this figure who was speaking, John describes **his voice** as **like the roar of many waters,** using the exact terminology used to describe the voice of God in Ezekiel 43:2. One might wish to say that His voice is then loud and drowns out (excuse the pun) all other sounds, and that is probably somewhat true.[436] The same phrase is used in Revelation 19:6 to describe the sound of all the redeemed singing in Heaven, so it is likely that John heard this sound as a pleasant, perhaps even soothing sound. But one can easily understand how the sound of many waters could be calming to one person and anxiety provoking to another. Someone who can swim might sit beside a waterfall and hear its crashing sound with great delight, while someone who cannot swim might hear that same waterfall with great trepidation and fear. In the same way, a Christian might hear Christ's voice and find it wonderful and delightful, while the unregenerate might hear it and cry out to the mountains and rocks, "fall on us and hide us from the face of him who is seated on the throne." (Rev. 6:16)

(1:16)

> "In his right hand he held seven stars, from his mouth came a sharp two-edged sword, and his face was like the sun shining in full strength."
>
> "καὶ ἔχων ἐν τῇ δεξιᾷ χειρὶ αὐτοῦ ἀστέρας ἑπτὰ καὶ ἐκ τοῦ στόματος αὐτοῦ ῥομφαία δίστομος ὀξεῖα ἐκπορευομένη καὶ ἡ ὄψις αὐτοῦ ὡς ὁ ἥλιος φαίνει ἐν τῇ δυνάμει αὐτοῦ."

Though He stands regally enough, He also has **in His right hand… seven stars.** These stars will be discussed at length in verse 20.[437] In quite terrifying and magnificent

---

[434] Mounce, *Revelation*, 59.
[435] Perschbacher, *The New Analytical Greek Lexicon*, 435.
[436] Ladd simply passes over this detail, assuming the description simply denotes mightiness. Ladd, *Revelation*, 33.
[437] it should be noted that some scholars theorize that John is here flouting the Roman Emperor (as they say he had in v. 10 with his usage of *κυριακῇ* when discussing the Lord's Day; see note 395). Domitian had his son deified and coins were struck depicting his son playing with stars. Sweet, *Revelation*, 71. Schreiner's description that "Domitian... minted a coin in honor of his son on which Domitian holds seven stars to signify

fashion, John describes a **sharp two-edged sword** coming **from his mouth**.[438] It does not take much imagination or Biblical knowledge to put together that this (almost certainly) represents the Word of God (cf., Ephesians 6:17 and Hebrews 4:12). But one might still be left wondering what precisely is meant by saying God's Word is a "sharp two-edged sword." It is true that God's Word cuts everyone. To those who hear God's Word and repent, it is the most precious "cutting" tool, which culls us and prunes us and trims us of all which would keep us from God. But, to those who hear God's Word and reject it, it is the most painful "cutting" tool, condemning and damning them, leaving them with no excuse in the end. Thus, whether cutting to salvation or damnation, God's Word cuts.

It is, after all, by the Word of God that Christ will destroy the nations in that final eschatological conflict most frequently referred to as the Battle of Armageddon (Rev. 19:5). And yet, God's Word is not only capable of destroying. It was by His Word that God created everything (both the verbal, literal "word" of Genesis 1, and the person of the *Logos* who is identified as the creator in John 1).[439] Beyond even this, the Word is used as a threat and a promise. His Word is a lamp unto our feet and a light to our path (Psalm 119:105), but if we refuse to obey His word, He promises that this same Word will be what He uses to destroy us if we do not repent (Rev. 2:16). Ladd summarizes the point perfectly, saying, "He shall speak, and it shall be done."[440]

Drawing back outward, John describes **his face** as if it was **the sun shining in full strength**.[441] Throughout the Bible, this sort of terminology is used to refer to righteousness pure and undefiled. In Daniel 12:3, it is said to be the type of glory that the righteous redeemed will have when raised.[442] However, while this would not be an inappropriate reference to make in understanding John's description, this seems to be a more direct reference to something that John witnesses previously. In Matthew 17:1-2,

---

his rule over the world" appears to indicate that Domitian rather than his son appeared on the coin, which is incorrect. If, on the other hand, Schreiner means that Domitian simply "held" (as in, he believed) the stars to signify his (that is, his son's) rule, then the verbiage could certainly have been better chosen. Schreiner, *Revelation* BECNT, 106. Domitian did not appear on the coin, but rather, the figure of a small child appears on the coin "juggling" seven stars.

[438] One has difficulty ignoring an allusion here to Isaiah 11:4.

[439] See also Colossians 1.

[440] Ladd, *Revelation*, 33.

[441] Mounce interestingly points out that the word rendered "face" (*ὄψις*) can be taken to mean both "face" in the sense of the front of one's head, as well as "face" in the sense of the entire front of an object, as one might say "facing me." Thus, the glorious radiance of Christ here may be taken as describing not only the front of his head but as the entirety of his body (as in the transfiguration). Mounce, *Revelation*, 60.

[442] Matthew 13:43 echoes this sentiment.

John, Peter, and James saw Jesus transfigured with a "face that shined like the Sun." John is once again seeing Christ in His true righteous and unleashed form.

(1:17a)

> "When I saw him, I fell at his feet as though dead. But he laid his right hand on me, saying…"
>
> "Καὶ ὅτε εἶδον αὐτόν, ἔπεσα πρὸς τοὺς πόδας αὐτοῦ ὡς νεκρός, καὶ ἔθηκεν τὴν δεξιὰν αὐτοῦ ἐπ' ἐμὲ λέγων·"

In response to seeing Him this way, John says that he **fell at his feet as though dead.** Several different thoughts could be formed in light of this reaction on the part of John. First, there must be some attention paid to the purity that is required to see God (Heb. 12:14). Evidently, even John – despite being a living apostle who had walked with Jesus and performed miracles, who had been entrusted with the responsibility of caring for Christ's mother and who had been preserved alive when all of his fellow apostles had been martyred – was still not holy enough to behold Him. No unglorified person could possibly behold the unleashed glory of Christ and maintain any sense of composure. Some speculate that John falls down in an act of worship, rather than weakness.[443] While this is possible, it seems more likely that John simply cannot compose himself in the sight of the glorious Christ. In other instances wherein John falls down to worship (Rev. 19:10; 22:9), he specifies that it was for this purpose that he fell. Here, in contrast, he does not say he fell down to worship, but rather that he fell at Christ's feet **as though dead**. This strongly suggests an incapacity to do otherwise.

Secondly, one must recognize John's reliance on Old Testament passages of like fashion to describe his own experience. For instance, when reading Daniel 10:8-10, one will find a strikingly similar course of events. A vision comes on a man while alone, he hears a voice before seeing the speaker, he retains no strength and falls on his face, and a hand touches and restores him.[444] May we one day experience what Daniel and John did. When John says **he laid his right hand on me**, we must dream that one day we too will

---

[443] Schreiner, *Revelation* BECNT, 108.

[444] Schreiner (along with Aune and Osborne) believes this gesture endows John with some level of authority – along the lines of laying hands on someone during an ordination. This seems a stretch too far, as that is not the intended result in the parallel event of Daniel 10, and the idea that John would need a special authority to convey the vision he is about to receive would seemingly undermine his apostolic authority in the first place. Schreiner, *Revelation* BECNT, 108. The position taken here is more in line with that of Henry, *Matthew Henry's Commentary*, 1983.

fall at the feet of Christ and have His holy, nail-scarred hands lift us from our humility.[445] And may we also hear Him say…

(1:17b-18)

> "Fear not, I am the first and the last, and the living one. I died, and behold I am alive forevermore, and I have the keys of Death and Hades."
>
> "μὴ φοβοῦ· ἐγώ εἰμι ὁ πρῶτος καὶ ὁ ἔσχατος καὶ ὁ ζῶν, καὶ ἐγενόμην νεκρὸς καὶ ἰδοὺ ζῶν εἰμι εἰς τοὺς αἰῶνας τῶν αἰώνων καὶ ἔχω τὰς κλεῖς τοῦ θανάτου καὶ τοῦ ᾅδου.

Every aspect of this phrase would have rung in the ears of John as Christ said it, reminding him of all the times that Jesus said them when they walked together during His ministry. His first words, **fear not**, would have no doubt brought John back to that awesome moment wherein he, Peter, and James went up on the mountain and saw Christ transfigured.[446] They fell in terror in that moment as well (Matt. 17:6), "but Jesus came and touched them, saying, 'Rise, and have no fear.'" (Matt. 17:7) It is possible that it may have taken John back to that awful night rowing against the wind on the sea of Galilee. When morning came and Christ came walking on the water, it was these words that He first said to them to calm them in their panic (Matt. 14:27).

As Christ goes on, **I am** would have undoubtedly taken the seer back to the countless instances in which Christ used this phrase (ἐγώ εἰμι) to introduce Himself. He had said, "I am he [the Messiah]" (John 4:26), "I am the bread of life" (6:35), "I am the living bread" (6:51), "I am the light of the world" (8:12), "I am the door" (10:7), "I am the good shepherd" (10:11), "I am the Son of God" (10:36), "I am the resurrection and the life" (11:25), "I am the way, the truth, and the life" (14:6), "I am the true vine" (15:1), or perhaps most importantly, when Christ allowed the name to stand alone when asserting His own identity as God – "before Abraham was, I am." (8:58)

And yet, Christ identifies Himself in a new way that John had never heard Him say before, saying **I am the first and the last.** This clause was nothing short of an absolute assertion of divinity on the part of Jesus Christ. Being "the beginning and the end" is an attribution of God alone (Isaiah 44:6; 18:12). Thus, in this one phrase, Christ reminds John of all the things He said of Himself when living as a man, and also affirms His complete deity in the past, present, and future.

---

[445] One may also see here the lack of a unified picture in these highly-symbolic descriptions, as Jesus is previously described as having the stars in His right hand, while here it is said that He lays His right hand on John. Mounce, *Revelation*, 60-61.

[446] Mounce, *Revelation*, 61.

As all of this floods John's mind with memories of years long-gone-by, it can hardly be denied that John's heart would throb as he also remembered how all of this ended. All of the "I am" statements that Christ gave, and all of the times that He told His disciples not to fear – all of it found its end at a hill called Golgotha, where Jesus suffered and died on a cross. John, after all, was the only disciple who was at the cross with Christ. What, in that moment, could John have needed to hear? Nothing less than precisely what Jesus says. Christ speaks into the hurting heart of John (and millions of His people who will read these words in years to come), saying I am **the living one. I died, and behold I am alive forevermore.**[447]

These words simply must have floored John. The Greek phrase rendered "the living one" is *καὶ ὁ ζῶν*. The word, *ζῶν* is a verb that literally means "to live." In a sense, it is as if Jesus says to John "I am what it is to live." Rather than simply saying "I am alive" (although this is an accurate rendering), Jesus says something deeper – something more in line with the idea that He *is* life. Just as God is said to *be* love (1 John 4:8, 16) rather than just *loving*, and He is said to *be* Spirit (John 4:24) rather than only *spiritual*, and He is said to *be* light rather than only *illuminating* (1 John 1:5) – notably all in John's writings – here Jesus is shown to be more than simply alive. He *is* life. And though John had watched Him die, He was now so full of life that He will live forevermore.

Beyond simply holding His own life in perpetuity, Jesus assures John that He has **the keys of Death and Hades.**[448] The Jewish mind conceived of a single intermediary state between the time of death and the end of time, frequently identified by the word *Hades*. The New Testament reveals a deeper understanding of how the intermediary state (between death and resurrection) works, but Christ maintains the usage of this word to show that He has the power to release His people from the power of both death and the place of the dead. His power (as asserted by His usage of the image of "having keys" to something; i.e., the ability to open and close it at will with perfect authority to do so) is most obviously manifested in the fact that He has freed Himself from it. This power, as He has just shown, is not temporal but is permanent. Having said that He will never die again, but is instead **alive forevermore**, He promises to John (and therefore all of those who read or hear this book) that He has the power to do the same for them.

---

[447] Newell makes the interesting observation that this term rendered *alive* "is used in the New Testament only of those in the body." He extends this to mean that not only is Christ asserting His being alive, but specifically, His being alive in His risen body – emphasizing His humanity alongside His deity in the previous phrase "I am the first and the last." Newell, *Revelation*, 29.

[448] As with "the Lord's Day" and the terminology of Christ's holding the stars, this may be another jab at false religions. Mounce mentions how the Jewish literature depicted God alone as holding these keys (referencing the Jerusalem Targum), and both he and Schreiner make mention of the Greek myth of Hecate, a goddess, holding the keys to Hades. Mounce, *Revelation*, 61.; Schreiner, *Revelation* BECNT, 110-111.

Excurses: "Keys"

Roman Catholics draw heavily from Matthew 16:17-19 for the establishment of the Papacy. In this passage, Jesus pronounces a blessing on Peter, and says that He will give to Peter "the keys of the kingdom of heaven, and whatever you bind on earth shall be bound in heaven, and whatever you loose on earth shall be loosed in heaven." And yet, in Revelation 1, Jesus claims to maintain the keys to Death and Hades. What, then, did He give Peter?

First of all, one must recognize that Peter was only given this blessing *first* – not solely. In Matthew 18:18-19, Jesus gives this same blessing to all the rest of the disciples. So, what precisely was He giving them? Jesus called them the "keys of the kingdom of heaven." Does this mean that Peter and the disciples had the authority to grant or forbid salvation to someone? Well, not exactly. In Luke 11:52, Jesus pronounces woe on the Jewish religious leaders because "you have taken away the key of knowledge. You did not enter yourselves, and you hindered those who were entering." This "key of knowledge" that He referred to is the proper understanding of God's Word. Having obscured the meaning of God's Word, they had taken away the key that would grant multitudes entrance into the Kingdom of God – and Christ says they did not even use it to enter into His Kingdom themselves.

When Peter professes, in Matthew 16, the truth about who Jesus is, he manifests that he has properly understood God's Word, and more than that, has believed it, and more than that, has publicly professed it in the presence of others. Thus, Christ says to Peter, "I give you the keys of the kingdom" – the keys that formerly belonged to the Jewish leaders and priests responsible with reading and explaining God's Word (Nehemiah 8:7-8). Having rejected God's Word (both inscripturated and incarnate), they had forfeited their place as the people who would open the gates of the kingdom of God to allow the nations to come in. But Christ says to Peter here that He is going to use Peter to build His Church.[449]

This directly explains why Christ first said He was giving the keys to Peter, as Peter was the first to proclaim the Gospel at Pentecost in Acts 2 where he preached to the Jews, and later at Cornelius' house in Acts 10, where he preached to the Gentiles. It is very sensical, then, that Peter would be the first identified as having "the keys to the

[449] Ladd, *The Gospel of the Kingdom*, 111-114.

kingdom." After him, of course, the others would likewise preach the Word of God, which is the conduit through which God gives faith (Rom. 10:17). Therefore, Peter was given the keys when he properly understood, believed, and preached the Word of God. Then the other disciples were given it in due season. And today, Christians in the Church are keyholders themselves, opening the gates of Heaven to all to whom they preach the Gospel, and essentially closing the gates (as the Pharisees did) to all to whom they refuse to preach the Gospel. This directly correlates with Christ's later statements regarding the authority of the Church in the circumstances of Church discipline (Matt. 18:15-20).

What, then, of the binding? This apostolic authority to bind or loose is often misunderstood as well. It is clear that the apostles were entrusted by Christ with the ability to bind new teachings and instructions on God's people, as they formed the foundation of the Church in those early years. (Eph. 2:20) They bound new things by declaring unlawful things which previously were lawful, such as necessitating circumcision (Gal. 5:1-2) or practicing certain holidays and festivals (Gal. 4:9-10). In contrast, they also loosed old things by declaring lawful that which previously was unlawful, such as dealing with Gentiles (Acts 10, Gal. 2), or eating unclean foods (Acts 9). They most clearly manifested this authority by writing Scriptures that they recognized as on par with the Old Testament (2 Pet. 3:16). And yet, they clearly maintained that they had no authority over the conveyance of salvation (Acts 10:26), nor does anyone else – including Abraham (Luke 16:26).

These keys in Revelation 1:18, in contrast, are not identified as the "keys to the kingdom" but rather as "the keys of Death and Hades." This, coming from an entirely different context, does assert both contextually and explicitly that Christ is claiming to have authority over the eternal state, both in His possessing the power to physically maintain someone's life by liberating their body from the consequences of *Death*, and in His possessing the spiritual power to release someone's soul from the intermediate place of the dead, *Hades*.

Jesus releases Death's sting and He raises individuals from the grave. He is the one who assigns eternal rewards and punishments. And He is the only one who can rightly place anyone in either place of eternal existence – Heaven or Hell. No Pope, Priest, Pastor, or Parishioner has anything approaching the authority of Jesus Christ, as He alone holds the keys to Death and Hell, and He will not be loaning them out or relinquishing them to anyone.

Fig. 4.1

Jesus has, then, given John a threefold comfort. He can have comfort because Jesus is **the first and the last**. All things live and move and have their being in Him. (Acts 17:28). Secondly, he can have comfort because Christ **died** but is now **alive forevermore.** Yes, John watched him die on that cross many years prior, but he (and we) need to be reminded that His death on the cross, while real, was the only death He will ever die (Rom. 6:9) – and He ever lives to make intercession for us. (Heb. 7:25) Finally, John could take comfort in the fact that Christ has **the keys of Death and Hades**, securing for him that not only does Christ rule and reign over his present life as the one who died and lives forever, but Christ also will rule and reign in the life to come. No matter where we go, there is no place where Christ is not king. As the psalmist penned thousands of years ago, "If I ascend to heaven, you are there! If I make my bed in Sheol, you are there!" (Ps. 139:8)[450]

(1:19)

> "Write therefore the things that you have seen, those that are and those that are to take place after this."
>
> "γράψον οὖν ἃ εἶδες καὶ ἃ εἰσὶν καὶ ἃ μέλλει γενέσθαι μετὰ ταῦτα."

Christ seems to prompt John to **write**, and He is sure to clarify what He is to write. This is the first instance in which this author must depart notably from the translation rendered in the ESV, as some of the words inserted bear a consequence on the meaning of the text that is not so obvious in the Greek. The original phraseology, would read:

---

[450] This reference helpfully introduces the fact that Hades is a Greek translation of the Hebrew term *Sheol.* They are taken to be the same place, and although progressive revelation assists readers in mapping a better position of this place of the dead, it is not to be taken as some third realm between Heaven and Hell. Old Testament saints anticipated going there (Gen. 37:35) and it is also said that some there do not thank God (Ps. 6:5) clearly asserting the presence of those who are not saints. This place, then, should not be taken as some mythical third realm in the likeness of a purgatory, "Abraham's Bosom" or otherwise. It is simply a word that means "the grave" or the place of the dead – including both Heaven and Hell.

Proposed Translation of Rev. 1:19	
Greek	English
γράψον	Write
οὖν	therefore
ἃ	what
εἶδες	you saw
καὶ	and
ἃ	what
εἰσὶν	**they signify[451]**
καὶ	and
ἃ	what
μέλλει	will
γενέσθαι	happen
μετὰ	after
ταῦτα	this.
Fig. 4.2	

The key distinction (emboldened) is the translation of *εἰσὶν* as "they signify" which is more helpful in deducing the intended meaning than the rendering "they are" although the real change comes in rendering *καὶ ἃ εἰσὶν* as "what they are" rather than "those that are."[452] Certainly the word *εἰσὶν* literally translates to "to be" which would render over in English as "are" and no argument is being made against that at all. It would be sufficient to translate the verse literally as "Write therefore the things that you have seen, what they are, and what shall take place after this." However, it is helpful and permissible to render *εἰσὶν* as "signify" because words simultaneously have denotations and connotations. The denotation of *εἰσὶν* is inarguably "are." But to tell what things *are* is in many contexts nothing less than to describe what they signify. To illustrate, imagine a child brought an adult several papers with a series of unintelligible scribbles on them and proudly presented them as a collective masterpiece to be marveled at. The adult might say, "Oh, very nice! I like these drawings. Tell me what they are!" The child might respond, "they're drawings!" To which the adult would say, "Yes, but what *are* they?" What the adult means to say is, "what do these scribblings *signify*? What is the meaning,

---

451 Thayer defends this rendering, saying of this word's various usages that its meaning is "often *to denote, signify, import*" and notes its meaning as being "this signifies, when interpreted" on several Biblical occasions. Joseph H. Thayer, *Thayer's Greek-English Lexicon of the New Testament*, 176.

452 Moses Stuart, *A Commentary on the Apocalypse,* Vol. II, 54.

or the thought represented by these drawings?" This is the connotation of the question both in the case of the adult in the illustration and of Christ when He says, "write therefore the things that you have seen, what *they are*, and what is to take place after this." It is not so much a statement of chronology, as explicative force.

While linguistic experts such as Thayer and Vincent maintain that this is a valid translation of the word, one can determine that this is the most likely intention of the word by examining the word's usage in the immediate context of Revelation 1 as well as in the broad context of Revelation as a whole.[453] In the immediate context, one will notice that in the very next verse the term is used twice, and both times it is more appropriately understood as the term "signify" than "are." He says that the "seven stars that you saw in my right hand... *εἰσὶν* the angels." Perhaps one might make the argument that John actually saw an angel and mistook it for a star, but surely readers understand without any explanation that the Apostle John did not see a church (whether a body of believers or a building with a steeple) and misidentify it as a lampstand. He indeed saw a lampstand, but Christ tells him that the seven lampstands "*εἰσὶν* the seven churches"; that is, they signify them. It would be silly to say that the lampstands *are* the seven churches without grasping the representative nature of that statement.

For the broader context within Revelation, John describes seven torches of fire in 4:5, saying they "*εἰσὶν* the seven spirits of God." Again, the Spirit of God is not bodily a torch of fire – but the torch is rather a sign representing Him. Again, in 5:6, it is said that the Lamb has "seven horns with seven eyes which *εἰσὶν* the seven spirits of God" – again a representative understanding is the only sensical approach. In 5:8, the twenty-four elders hold golden bowls full of "incenses which *εἰσὶν* the prayers of the saints" – a usage which is obviously representative. In 17:9 the seven heads of the beast "*εἰσὶν* seven mountains," but in the very next verse it is said that they "*εἰσὶν* also seven kings." In 17:12, the ten horns of the beast "*εἰσὶν* ten kings." In 17:15, the waters "*εἰσὶν* peoples and multitudes and nations and languages." Without any doubt, not a single instance here would be better translated as "are" than "signify."[454]

A more consistent rendering of Revelation 1:19 then, based on the immediate and broader contexts, would be "Write, therefore, the things you saw, and what they signify, and the things that are going to happen afterward." Exegetically, this rendering makes verse 20 much clearer as a transitional verse between chapters 1 and 2. Verse 20 uses the same terminology, calling to mind the things John "saw" (*εἶδες*) just as Jesus calls him to

---

[453] Thayer, *Thayer's Greek-English Lexicon,* 176.; Marvin R. Vincent, *Word Studies in the New Testament* 2, 433.
[454] Thomas, *Revelation 1-7,* 114-115. Thomas rejects this interpretation, but his reason for doing so is unconvincing.

write of the things he saw (εἶδες) in verse 19. His repeating the term "which are" or "which signify" (ἃ εἰσὶν) is also indicative of this connection between verses 19-20.[455] What is more, the fact that John would be tasked with explaining what these signs signify would be in line with the manner in which this Revelation was conveyed to him, as in 1:1 he said God "made it known," using a term (ἐσήμανεν) which most frequently refers to the conveyance of a thought through signs – and which is frequently translated throughout the New Testament as "signify."[456]

What this would mean is that the command given in this verse is threefold but only relates to two objects or time frames: John is commissioned to write **what he has seen**, and then write the meaning and purpose of each thing he has seen, and then write what **will take place after this.**[457] He does so by penning this first vision of the Son of Man along with the stars and lampstands, and then begins detailing the meaning of what he has seen immediately in verse 20. Then, come chapters 2-3, wherein John continues explaining the purpose of Christ's being depicted as walking among those lampstands and holding their stars in His hand. Each of the letters to the seven churches carries a reference to the original depiction of Christ – which was not a coincidence, but a specific duty with which John was charged, as he was expected to explain the meaning of the original vision he saw of Christ and how it pertained to God's people.

After this initial vision has concluded, John begins a new vision in 4:1 which initiates those things **which will take place after this**.[458] At this point, John makes very little effort to explain what the signs mean, as he was not commissioned to tell what the signs in this latter vision represented. With the first portion (those things which he had seen) he was commissioned to explain what the signs signify. In this latter portion (those which will take place) he is not commissioned (or obviously able) to explain the signs. There is no clear chronological break in these terms such as would indicate a division of

---

[455] J. Ramsey Michaels, *Interpreting the Book of Revelation*, 101-102.
[456] Koester, *Revelation*, 211-212.
[457] While mentioned by Mounce, this position is not the twofold contention that he finally supports. This author finds his contention to be exegetically weaker than the position herein contended. As he rightly mentions, the position contended here was a very popular position in the nineteenth century writings of Moses Stuart and in passing by Joseph Seiss, *The Apocalypse,* Vol. I, 105; as well as earlier writings such as Campegius Vitringa's *Anakrisis Apocalypsios Joannis Apostoli*, 56-58. It has some recent support as found in Alfred Plummer, "The Revelation of St. John the Divine" in *The Pulpit Commentary* Vol. 22, 8, who wrote "It is possible that... 'the things which are,' refers to the realities symbolized" and, while not explicitly laid out the same way, is practically identical to that position endorsed in Jurgen Roloff, *Revelation: A Continental Commentary*, 38.
[458] A very helpful and thorough exploration of the various approaches to this verse is given in G.K. Beale, *The Book of Revelation* NIGTC, 152-170.

dispensations or ages.[459] John is simply called to explicitly identify the meaning of the signs he saw in this first vision, without being told to do so for the rest.

It should be borne in mind that some events under the category of "to take place after" (that is, in the future) are predicated on events which have already occurred in John's past and therefore necessitate the detailing of previous events. For instance, the birth of Jesus, His being persecuted by Satan, and His ascending into Heaven are all events that occurred in John's past – and yet they are mentioned in Revelation 12:2-5 (a section under the category of "to take place after"). This does not discount the reality that those events occurring as a result of it are still to occur in John's future. It does, however, discount the idea that there are separate dispensations envisioned here. The commission given here simply teaches John how to write his book. It does not at all divide up God's interactions with mankind. The birth, persecution, and ascension of Christ as depicted in Revelation 12 walks the reader directly into the Church engaging tribulation – tribulation which will occur throughout the entire inter-advent age, and which will escalate just before the Second Advent. There is no recognizable break in dispensation, either in 12:2-5 or 1:19.[460]

In short, this verse tells of what John is expected to write about each thing that he sees. Regarding the first vision (1:9-3:22) he is to explain the signs and their purposes. Thereafter, when explaining the things which are to come, he is not expected to interpret the signs unless the explanation is an aspect of the vision itself (ex., Rev. 7:13-14; 17:7). Verse 19, while providing some element of instruction regarding what to expect in the book, does not provide any overarching insight about the application of each section to a specific era in history. Every part of the Revelation of St. John is applicable to every generation of Christians. Chapters 1-3 are helpfully explained, and the remainder is subject to interpretation. For some reason, God has chosen (in His sovereignty) to leave some aspects of this latter portion unclear. At one point, John even intended to write an explanation of what he heard, and God told him not to (Rev. 10:4). There are evidently some mysteries that God is content to explain beforehand (1:20); some that He was content to reveal and explain to John about the future (Rev. 17:7); and some which He desires to explain or reveal to us Himself at His coming (Rev. 10:7).

---

[459] Gundry, *The Church and the Tribulation,* 64-66, 78.

[460] While this author disagrees with some of the conclusions that he draws, this difficulty is helpfully explained in Schreiner, *Revelation* BECNT, 111-112.

(1:20)

"As for the mystery of the seven stars that you saw in my right hand, and the seven golden lampstands, the seven stars are the angels of the seven churches, and the seven lampstands are the seven churches."

"τὸ μυστήριον τῶν ἑπτὰ ἀστέρων οὓς εἶδες ἐπὶ τῆς δεξιᾶς μου καὶ τὰς ἑπτὰ λυχνίας τὰς χρυσᾶς· οἱ ἑπτὰ ἀστέρες ἄγγελοι τῶν ἑπτὰ ἐκκλησιῶν εισιν καὶ αἱ λυχνίαι αἱ ἑπτὰ ἑπτὰ ἐκκλησίαι εἰσίν."

In His explanation, Christ says that **the seven stars are the angels of the seven churches.** There is nothing approaching a consensus on what precisely that means. There appear to be three possible meanings. First, and perhaps most obvious, is the understanding that these "angels" are literally that – heavenly beings – who are evidently assigned to the churches for what we must assume is some form of guardianship or overwatch.[461] This explanation, however, creates some questions that are hard to answer. Why would John be commissioned to write letters to angels? Each letter in chapters 2-3 begins "to the angel of... write..." Certainly God could have simply conveyed what He wanted to say to the angels without using a human intermediary. One might even argue (based on 1:1) that the vision was given to John by an angel. So, God the Father gave this message to Jesus, who gave it to and angel, who gave it to John – to give to an angel? That seems obtusely complicated. Furthermore, why did angels need to hear these things? The ensuing letters are largely littered with corrections and rebukes. The angels surely had done no wrong.

A second explanation is that the churches themselves are represented in Heaven by spiritual conglomerates of their character (sometimes called "prevailing spirits"), and that these single soul-like representatives are referred to as "angels."[462] The idea would be that when God sees a locally assembled church, He sees it as a single operating body of believers, and that body has a soulishness that is composed of both good and evil, much like a single person is. This would result in this soulishness, then, being what God is commending, exhorting, condemning, and rebuking in these letters. While this view is commonly held, it appears very complicated and would not be obvious to most any reader unless they were already taught to hold such a view. It has already been noted that

[461] Schreiner, *Revelation* BECNT, 105, 113-114.

[462] Mounce, *Revelation*, 66. Mounce seems to draw this idea from a brief comment made by Robbins, or a possible position explained by Brownlee, but Mounce recognizes that Brownlee himself later gave up the position in exchange for the position that "angel" means the bishop or pastor of each church. See R.F. Robbins, *The Revelation of Jesus Christ*,53.; and W.H. Brownlee, "The Priestly Character of the Church in the Apocalypse" *New Testament Studies* 5 (1958), 224-225.

this symbolism is particularly complex, as Jesus notes by using the term "a mystery," but His explanation is nothing equating to this position – something He surely would have given hints towards had it been the proper understanding. As complex as this explanation is, it would require some weighty support that is hitherto unsupplied.

A final explanation, which is that favored by the author, is that the word "angel" ought to be understood in its direct sense, meaning "messenger." The context of the Greek word *ἄγγελοι* is a major factor in interpreting the word. Schreiner rejects this explanation, saying, "we have no instance in the NT or in Revelation where the word ἄγγελος (*angelos*) refers to a pastor, overseer, elder, or any human leader."[463] This is, however, factually incorrect.[464] In Matthew 11:10, Jesus describes John the Baptist as God's "messenger" (Gr., *ἄγγελόν; angelon*). Mark uses this same term to describe John the Baptist in Mark 1:2. One might argue, "those references were quotations from an Old Testament passage." This makes no difference in the usage of the word angel to describe a Godly man. One may still object, "certainly John was a unique case." Perhaps. But were his disciples also unique? In Luke 7:24, the disciples of John the Baptist are identified as *ἀγγέλων* (literally, angels). Luke even refers to the disciples of Jesus as *ἀγγέλους* in Luke 9:52. In reference to the spies who went in and hid with Rahab, James calls them *ἀγγέλους* (angels) in James 2:25. Thus, whether coming from the pen of Matthew, Mark, Luke, or James, this word definitely *is* used in the Bible to refer to human beings, leaders or otherwise. It is perhaps most compelling to note that Jesus Himself used the word this way.

In this context, it would appear most likely that this "angel" or "messenger" would be the pastor (or perhaps because it is plural, elders) of each church to whom it is addressed.[465] Thus, the pastor (or elders) were commissioned to read aloud (1:3) the letter they received from John in the presence of their congregations, and their congregations were to hear and keep what was written in it (and as will be seen in Rev. 22:18-19, they were to be careful to maintain it exactly as it was when they received it).[466]

This makes more sense than the first explanation, because nowhere else in the Bible do we have anything equating to an assertion that churches have guardian angels.

---

[463] Schreiner, *Revelation* BECNT, 113.

[464] Thomas is quick to point out that the word "is used of both human envoys and spirit beings…" Thomas, *Revelation 1-7*, 127.

[465] This notably is the view taken by the likes of John Gill, Matthew Henry, and more recently, John MacArthur.

[466] Mounce, *Revelation*, 43. Both Newell and Seiss maintain that the direct communication of Jesus with the pastor/elder of each church serves the argument of local church autonomy. Seiss argues, "there was just one angel for one church, not one angel for the seven churches; and so each angel was simply the pastor in charge of his particular Church." Seiss, *The Apocalypse*, 111. See comments on 1:11.

One might argue that individuals have guardian angels (Matt. 18:10), or even that whole nations have guardian angels (Dan. 10:13) – although neither of these positions would be particularly strong. Nevertheless, those arguments could be Scripturally made. But the argument for churches having guardian angels? That simply doesn't exist. As for the second explanation, to be frank, it requires a very complex understanding of the text, and is based on almost no Biblical foundation whatsoever. The third explanation, though, carries with it both the exegetical evidence and logical understandability that lends to its credibility, as well as some historical precedence, as Tertullian would record that in the early church, an official position in many churches was that of "reader."[467] John opened the book with a blessing on those who "read aloud" the words written herein. Perhaps these were precisely those of whom he spoke.

The consequences of this position are massive. This would indicate to us that not only is Jesus living and moving amongst **the lampstands** which **are the churches** (for more commentary on them see 1:11), but that He personally holds the elders and pastors of His churches in His own hands. While it is true that Christ holds all believers in His hands (John 10:28), it is also true that there is a Biblical precedent for believing that Christ makes some distinctions between the laity and the clergy. For example, the clergy are told to expect a stricter judgment (James 3:1). Is it, then, any great stretch to see here a corresponding comfort to that harrowing warning in James 3:1? If the clergy must live under the weight of knowing they will receive a much stricter judgment, let them also receive the relieving comfort of knowing that they are in some sense held in the hands of Christ in a way that is not said of everyone.

Conclusion

Chapter 1 only introduces the first vision which spans from 1:9-3:22, but it valuably frames the other chapters by giving the signs that John is expected to explain. This is why it is important to understand the nature of the terms *εἶδες* and *ἃ εἰσὶν*, as they link 1:19-20 with 2:1ff. In keeping with the metric by which one may recognize breaks in Revelation, it is proper to look for a new vision, linguistic indications, or narrative indications of a break in the story. The new vision does not begin until 4:1, the linguistic indications (as shown through the terms previously mentioned) indicate continuity between 1:19-20 and 2:1ff, and the narrative is consistent with Christ identifying the seven churches and their seven angels in 1:11, 20, and throughout chapters 2-3. With those indicators all pointing towards continuity, one is best served to examine Revelation 1:9-3:22 as one section.

---

[467] Tertullian, *Prescription Against Heretics*, 41.

What purpose does this section serve? It seems that Christ intends this section to serve explanatory and instructional purposes. First, Christ gives this section such that the Church may understand Christ and His perfection in holiness, power, divinity, and humanity, as well as its place in Christ's sight and care, its responsibility to obedience, and its call to purity before the Lord. Second, this section is incredibly practical and seeks to give general standards to which Christians can seek to conform themselves when engaging the future events set to occur in the remaining chapters of the book.[468]

---

[468] Thomas, *Revelation 1-7*, 125.

Chapter 5:

(Revelation 2:1-3:22) God's Imperfect People

Introducing the Seven Churches

While the various interpretive approaches of Revelation play a part from the outset, the distinctions between the preterist, historicist, futurist, and idealists become very clear at the beginning of the second chapter. The preterist emphasizes the directness of the letters to the churches, which were (they are correct to point out) literal churches in existence in the time of John's writing. From this they reason that some, or the bulk of, or in some cases all of the prophetic events in Revelation were fulfilled in the lifetime of those individuals in the churches to whom the letter is initially addressed in these chapters. The historicist emphasizes the recognition of traits found in these churches, which seem to have been prevalent in the Church at certain points in church history. From this they reason that some, or the bulk, of the prophetic events in Revelation were fulfilled throughout the Church Age. The futurist emphasizes the dramatic shift in nature between the epistolary genre of these opening chapters and those apocalyptic chapters which follow it. From this they reason that some, or the bulk of, or in some cases all of the prophetic events in Revelation are yet to be fulfilled in the future. The idealist emphasizes the spiritual continuity between the churches in these chapters and the Church throughout history. From this, they reason that some, or the bulk of, or in some cases all of the prophetic events in Revelation are to be fulfilled in a spiritual rather than literal manner.

The approach of this commentary is dubbed eclecticism, due to its integration of the most valuable and reasonable elements of each of these views without full alignment with any one of them. While the term "eclecticism" might be new, the position is not.[469] For example, 100 years ago, Henry W. Frost wrote a book entitled *Matthew Twenty-Four and the Revelation* in which he wrote of the letters to the seven churches:

> These letters are to be regarded as presenting three different views; first, the historic, the seven portraying actually, seven Asiatic churches which had existed in apostolic times, and thus representatively, the whole church of the apostolic period; second, the prophetic, the seven portraying the

[469] Quintern and Shultz, *Revelation in Focus,* 29-32.

> church as it will be found in the seven year period of the Antichrist, in Asia and elsewhere; and third, the progressive, the seven portraying the course of the church in both of the above periods, from the beginning to the end.[470]

This understanding of the letters to the churches is that endorsed herein.[471] There was indeed a direct purpose for which these letters were written, which would have been understood and applied in the era of John. There is also truth to the idea that these churches depict the Church throughout the inter-advent age, giving descriptions and corrective prescriptions throughout. And still more, there is also truth to the concept that these churches describe the Church in the last day – the successes of it in some areas and the hardship of it in others. Wholistically, these churches were, are, and shall be the reflection of Christ on His people. Thus, the preterist, historicist, futurist, and idealist each have some degree of correctness – whilst erring in their exclusivity of the other positions. These letters were not *only* for the early church, nor *only* for the future church, nor respectively *only* for certain periods of time in church history, nor will they *only* find their fulfillment spiritually – truth is found in each, but not exclusively in any.

[470] Henry W. Frost, *Matthew Twenty-Four and the Revelation*, 141.

[471] With a notable diversion on the necessity of a seven-year tribulation period, which is not espoused.

(2:1-7) *Ephesus: The Loveless Church*

(2:1)

> "To the angel of the church in Ephesus write: 'The words of him who holds the seven stars in his right hand, who walks among the seven golden lampstands."
>
> "Τῷ ἀγγέλῳ τῆς ἐν Ἐφέσῳ ἐκκλησίας γράψον· Τάδε λέγει ὁ κρατῶν τοὺς ἑπτὰ ἀστέρας ἐν τῇ δεξιᾷ αὐτοῦ, ὁ περιπατῶν ἐν μέσῳ τῶν ἑπτὰ λυχνιῶν τῶν χρυσῶν·"

Christ begins telling John to **write** to **the angel of the church in Ephesus**.[472] It has already been noted that this was likely the city that John returned to having been released from his captivity on Patmos after Domitian died.[473] Thus, it was likely that this was the first church which would have received the letters. Whether that was the case by design or simply by divine foreknowledge is not clear, but in either case, it is at least convenient that Christ's first letter is addressed to the church which would naturally first receive John's writings.

If one accepts the proposition that "angel" here means pastor/elder, then it becomes even more natural that John would write to them first, as he was likely familiar with the churches, their individual struggles, and possibly even their specific pastor(s).[474] The pastoral team of Ephesus in the first century was, in a word, unparalleled. Of course, the Apostle Paul could be considered the "founding pastor" or church planter, having evidently planted it on his second missionary journey (Acts 18:19-21), initially leaving them under the care of Aquila and Priscilla, with Apollos coming soon after and several others who followed him of similarly incredible repute. Timothy is noted as being an early pastor at Ephesus (1 Tim. 1:3). When Timothy was called away to the assistance of Paul, he was replaced by Tychicus (2 Tim. 4:9-12) who is said to have been a "beloved brother and faithful minister in the Lord" known to "encourage" their hearts. (Eph. 6:21-22) It is broadly believed that the Apostle John himself served the church for some time, living there both before and after his exile, and until his death.[475] According to early history, in the years after John's death, Onesimus (the subject of Paul's letter to

[472] As mentioned in the notes on 1:9, although called to write what he saw at the time of receiving the vision, it is possible that John penned these visions sometime later with specific attention to literary strategy, form, and word choice. J. Ramsey Michaels, *Interpreting the Book of Revelation*, 15-16.
[473] Eusebius, *Ecclesiastical History*, 3:18:1; 3:20:10-11.
[474] Sweet, *Revelation*, 77.
[475] Irenaeus, *Against Heresies,* 3:3:4. This testimony, while written by Irenaeus who lived a generation after John, is said to have been told to him by Polycarp (a disciple of the Apostle John). Thus, it would seem to be a highly reliable claim, having come from someone who was an eye-witness to the events.

Philemon) became the pastor there.[476] For these reasons and others, commentators have confidently declared the church at Ephesus as "the most important church" in Asia.[477]

Regarding the city itself, **Ephesus** was a massive city at the time of John's writing. It was a port city which sat at the convergence of several major trade routes, so commerce and travel through Ephesus made the city swell to a population of about 250,000.[478] Travelers would walk or ride into the city on a brick avenue that was thirty-five feet wide and flanked by stone columns, leading to the center of the city. At its center was a major stadium, a thriving marketplace, and a theatre equipped to seat 25,000 people, which had at some times even hosted the Olympic and gladiatorial games.[479]

With all of this, one might imagine that the citizens were materialists, but they were *very* religious. In the city, there was a temple dedicated to the imperial cult (that is, temples dedicated to the worship of deceased and deified Roman Caesars), as well as a Jewish synagogue, temples to Apollo and Athena, a sanctuary dedicated to Zeus, along with various public dedications to Aphrodite, Hecate, Isis, Sarapis, and other ancient gods. The presence of an imperial temple impressed the Romans so much that they granted the city self-government (although they maintained a Roman Governor there to settle major disputes). By far, though, the most important monument, building, or site in the city was the Temple of Artemis (sometimes called Diana in Latin). It was four times the size of the Greek Parthenon, standing 425 feet long, 220 feet wide, and 65 feet high, having taken 120 years to build. The central architect overseeing its construction (Chersiphron) is said to have been "driven to such a state of anxiety and desperation as to contemplate suicide." He is said to have had a dream in which Diana comforted him and even intervened to secure its construction, leading locals to believe that the temple itself, constructed of marble overlaid with gold and jewels, was a work of the gods.[480] Unsurprisingly, it was considered one of the seven marvels of the ancient world. Along with the presence of such religiously pluralistic architecture was the regular occurrence of religious festivals to these various gods, with some of the largest honoring Demeter, Isis, Artemis, and Dionysus. These festivals involved plays, athletic competitions, musical performances, parades, banquets, and sometimes the donning of costumes by the general public.[481]

---

[476] Ignatius, *Epistle to the Ephesians*, 1.

[477] Ladd, *Revelation*, 37.

[478] Mounce and Schreiner claim it was the convergence of three trade routes, while MacArthur claims it was four.

[479] Koester, *Revelation*, 260; Sweet, *Revelation*, 79.

[480] Pliny the Elder, *Natural History*, 21:14.

[481] Koester, *Revelation*, 259.

One can imagine, then, that although the leadership of the church at Ephesus was second to none, the religious atmosphere there was far from Christian. In Acts 19:13-19, one gains an insight into the regular religious ongoings of the city, when the seven sons of Sceva attempt to use superstition and magic to perform exorcisms without any real idea of what they are doing.

This sort of religious confusion in Ephesus caused even the most sincere Christians to make mistakes. Having left Priscilla and Aquila in Ephesus (Acts 18:18-21), Paul returned to find that a young man named Apollos had come preaching an incomplete Gospel – despite his best efforts. (Acts 18:24-19:7) This was perhaps the catalyst for their seriousness about understanding and protecting correct doctrine (see Rev. 2:2,6) although it is also known that Paul commended Timothy to guard right doctrine there as well (1 Tim. 1:3). They likely had to have this sort of seriousness about orthodoxy, because when orthopraxy became their norm, they immediately engaged organized opposition due to the toll that their stance took on the idolatry market in the city (Acts 19:24-41).

Knowing all of this about the church and their circumstances, Christ begins by having John explain to them and remind them of his being **him who holds the seven stars in his right hand.** As Paul had left under persecution, only to die at the hands of the Romans; As Apollos had attempted to rightly teach them but had in his own insufficiency left them incomplete; As Timothy was very young (something they evidently felt unsure of; 1 Tim. 4:12-16); As John was exiled, then very aged and infirm, then dead; As Onesimus was a former runaway slave (whose background likely haunted him) – they had every imaginable human reason to wonder if the leadership of their church was proper. Each man had either come under such fierce opposition or had major "red flags" which would keep most modern pastor search committees from extending the call. Christ reminds them in this moment that their pastor is held in His hand.[482] He is guiding their leader through persecution, and His Spirit is guiding their leader into all truth (John 16:13).

Of interest to the linguist is the fact that the word rendered **holds** is a different Greek term here than was used in 1:16. In 1:16 the word used was *ἔχων*, which typically asserts possession without any real comment on the manner thereof. A modern English equivalent would be the word "have." One might have said in 1:16, "he *has* the seven stars." But here in 2:1, the Greek term used is *κρατῶν*, which is a much more aggressive

[482] It is almost required that each reader go and read Matthew Henry's comments on this verse to hear the beautiful consequences he provides as a result of this reality.

word for possession. It is a word meaning something closer to "ruling" or "exercising power over."[483] One could take from it that rather than simply reminding them that He has possession of their leaders, He could also be reminding them that He has complete control over who their leader is, what they teach, and whether anything undesirable would ever befall them (i.e., martyrdom, arrest, beating, etc.).

Not only were they to find encouragement in that, but the congregation itself was to know that Christ **walks among the seven golden lampstands**. He is not only sovereignly guarding and guiding their leaders, but He is also sovereignly guarding and guiding *them*. The church itself is to know that Christ is living and moving amongst them, ever bringing unity and liberty to them (John 17:21; 2 Cor. 3:17). In another sense, the fact that He **walks among** them, rather than simply being "in the midst" of them as He appeared in 1:13, appears to be a reference to the manner in which the High Priest would tend the lampstands in the Old Testament Temple.[484] In much the same way that the High Priest had walked among the lampstands, keeping their light shining and well-tended, Christ walks among the churches, keeping their light shining and well-tended.

(2:2)

> "'I know your works, your toil and your patient endurance, and how you cannot bear with those who are evil, but have tested those who call themselves apostles and are not, and found them to be false."
>
> "οἶδα τὰ ἔργα σου καὶ τὸν κόπον καὶ τὴν ὑπομονήν σου καὶ ὅτι οὐ δύνῃ βαστάσαι κακούς, καὶ ἐπείρασας τοὺς λέγοντας ἑαυτοὺς ἀποστόλους καὶ οὐκ εἰσὶν καὶ εὗρες αὐτοὺς ψευδεῖς,"

However, moving away from this initial explanation of who He is and what encouragement they ought to take from His person, Christ reminds them also through John, **"I know your works."** He is the one who has eyes of fire which see and consume everything which goes before them – nothing is hidden from Him. He is the one who is "directly cognizant of every detail about every assembly of His on earth."[485] Rather than the standard word typically used for knowledge (γινώσκω; ginosko) which denotes a knowledge which progresses, increases, solidifies, or grows, the word that is used here

---

[483] Thayer's gives the root κράτος as simply meaning "majesty". E.A. Sophocles, *Greek Lexicon of the Roman and Byzantine Periods*, 689. Perschbacher, more helpfully, notes that the root might mean in this instance, "power, sway, dominion." Wesley J. Pershcbacher, *The New Analytical Greek Lexicon*, 247.

[484] Thomas, *Revelation 1-7*, 132. Mounce sees here a reference to Leviticus 26:12 wherein God promises to personally walk amongst His people and be their God as they are His people. Perhaps this is a temporary spiritual fulfillment which serves as a shadow of the later literal fulfillment found in chapters 21-22.

[485] Newell, *Revelation*, 37.

(and which is always used in Revelation of Christ's knowledge) for **know** is the word *oida* (*οἶδα*), which is said by Thomas to be a word which "reflects full or complete knowledge" and "depicts absolute clearness of mental vision, which photographs all facts of life as they pass."[486]

What Christ reflects on in their works is quite remarkable. First, he notes their **toil.** Christ is aware of their active work in laboring for His glory against the tide of public opinion in their local area. He has not forgotten their toil; it has not gone unnoticed. We would be benefitted by knowing that Christ does not ignore or forget the labor and work we have put in. And in addition to this, he is also aware of their **patient endurance.** While toiling asserts something of actively engaging in work, patient endurance seems to be an ever-ongoing passive activity that one would have to determine in their minds to maintain.[487] While enduring hardships, even without active labor to reflect on, Christ was still watching with great interest. This also should tell us something of great value: God knows both the things we *do* for Him and the things that we have *done* to us for Him – and He forgets neither.

Of the former, their active **toil**, Christ notes one particular act they have done of which He is proud: **you cannot bear with those who are evil, but have tested those who call themselves apostles and are not, and found them to be false.** Modern Christians would do well to notice that Christ is praising this church for calling out false teaching and refusing to tolerate it at all. He seems to love that they guard and protect their church by fencing doctrine. These **false apostles** were evidently itinerant preachers who went from town to town claiming to be apostles, preaching false doctrines.[488] The Ephesians had been led astray before (Acts 18-19) but now wouldn't let these false teachers be a part of their church.[489] It would have been a bit easier for the Ephesians to identify who was truly an apostle and who was not, given their leadership, but Christ nevertheless commends them for it.

This should serve as a stark commendation from Christ against simply allowing anyone and everyone to teach, preach, or serve in the local church. The Church is for everyone, but not everyone is for the church. Those identified here as **those who are evil** are certainly individuals who profess to be Christians but do "not live up to proper

---

[486] Thomas, *Revelation 1-7*, 133.

[487] Koester, *Revelation*, 261.

[488] Paul addressed individuals such as these (although the specific individuals were certainly not the same) in 2 Cor. 11:13-15, calling them servants of Satan.

[489] Schreiner points out that the testing and rejection of these false-apostles seems to have been something the Ephesians accomplished in the past, while their engagement with the Nicolaitans (v. 6) is a present battle. Schreiner, *Revelation* BECNT, 123.

standards."[490] Newell comments that in this instance, "ministerial courtesy had no place" going on later to conclude regarding false teachers, "we are not to suffer them to preach and teach in our assemblies."[491] Perhaps he doesn't go far enough, as it should be noted that in both the case of these false-apostles and the subsequently mentioned Nicolaitans (see notes on v. 6) the biggest thorn in their side was not the pluralistic false religions of Ephesus, but those groups which claimed to be Christian. Koester succinctly sums it up, "the principal conflict is with different Christian groups, not with outsiders."[492]

(2:3)

"I know you are enduring patiently and bearing up for my name's sake, and you have not grown weary."

"καὶ ὑπομονὴν ἔχεις καὶ ἐβάστασας διὰ τὸ ὄνομά μου καὶ οὐ κεκοπίακες."

Addressing the latter of their works, their passive works of **enduring patiently**, Christ knows that they are **bearing** this **up for** His **name's sake**. There is something poetic here, as Christ has in the previous verse commended them for their refusing to "bear" false teachers, while here He praises them for "bearing" the hardships they endure. It is also a clear reference to what Christ promised would come in Matthew 10:22 and 24:9.

This verse forms the end of one long sentence in the Greek which began in verse 1, and when read as one long statement, readers can truly see how encouraging, aware, and caring Christ is about this church. He knows what they are going through, whether actively or passively. He seems to be proud or impressed with the fidelity to truth and their endurance, having **not grown weary**.

Elsewhere in His Word, God promises to deliver what He has promised to those who have such endurance (Heb. 10:36), and through Paul's writing to the Galatians called His people to "not grow weary of doing good, for in due season we will reap, if we do not give up." (Gal. 6:9) These thoughts likely came to mind as the readers and listeners heard these commendations from Christ for their patient endurance and persistence in doing good. One can scarcely imagine being praised by Christ in these ways. What an uplifting moment this must have been – and what an encouragement it should be for us. Christ knows our active works and our passive works, our faithful works and our patient endurance of hardship. Of our active works, He has promised to

---

[490] Thomas, *Revelation 1-7*, 135.
[491] Newell, *Revelation*, 37.
[492] Koester, *Revelation*, 262.

reward someone for even giving a cup of cold water (Matt. 10:42). He promises to bless those who do good.

And further, He promises to reward those who do not give up. He says that the one "who endures to the end will be saved." (Matt. 24:13) Christ does not forget our works or our endurance. He sees us – and He remembers.

(2:4)

"But I have this against you, that you have abandoned the love you had at first."

"ἀλλ' ἔχω κατὰ σοῦ ὅτι τὴν ἀγάπην σου τὴν πρώτην ἀφῆκες."

For all that Christ commends, He points out one flaw that He takes very seriously, which is that they have **abandoned the love** they **had at first.**[493] It is incredible that their lack of love is what Christ would rebuke in them and command them to correct, given that He has just praised them for their commitment to true doctrine and in verse 6 He is going to further praise them for what they hate. This shows a great complexity in Christ regarding the issues of loving and hating.

It appears that Christ is rebuking them for **abandoning the love** that is commanded – and typical – of a Christian. This would seem to be the meaning of His saying that they once had this love. It could be understood as any or all four aspects of the love that Christians are called to display: (1) Love for God; Matthew 22:37-38. (2) Love for neighbor; Matthew 22:39. (3) Love for other Christians; John 13:35. (4) Love for enemies; Matthew 5:44. If any (or all) of these aspects of Christian love were missing, Christ would be right to say they had abandoned the love they had at first, that is, upon their conversion. These four aspects of love are produced by the work of the Holy Spirit within a believer.

It appears most likely that what occurred was the elevation of love for good doctrine and teaching over love for neighbors, enemies, and even other Christians. This is a valuable lesson – loving the Word of God and loving the teachings of God is not the same as loving God. Many make that mistake and end up in the same situation as the Pharisees did in Christ's day. To love God's Word to such a degree that it causes you to fail to love those whom God has called you to love is to fail to truly understand and apply

[493] The phraseology here, "love you had at first" is preferential over "first love" as the latter implies that the love was first in a line of love for different objects, while the former implies a love that was had in the beginning of a long period of time. Linguistically, either is possible, but verse 5 seems to commend the former interpretation as Christ calls them to return to the works they did at first, showing that the usage of this word regards order, not object.

God's Word in the first place. Ladd put it helpfully, saying, "doctrinal purity and loyalty can never be a substitute for love."[494] To be more direct in the context of the church at Ephesus, one might say that Christ praises them for keeping lost people out of their podiums but condemns them for running lost people out of their pews.

Christ calls His people to strictly guard the truth of the Gospel against antinomians, but also comes down hard on legalists who would formulate a *Gestapo* to go about searching for any hint of a mistake in doctrine or teaching so as to throw someone out. One might even consider them as having manifested the truth of Christ's promise that whenever false prophets arise, "the love of many will grow cold."[495] (Matthew 24:11-12) Uncomfortably, it is not the lawless or apostate who lose love when the false prophets arise, but Christ's people themselves. Christians today must heed this warning.

(2:5)

> "Remember therefore from where you have fallen; repent, and do the works you did at first. If not, I will come to you and remove your lampstand from its place, unless you repent."
>
> "μνημόνευε οὖν πόθεν πέπτωκας καὶ μετανόησον καὶ τὰ πρῶτα ἔργα ποίησον· εἰ δὲ μή, ἔρχομαί σοι καὶ κινήσω τὴν λυχνίαν σου ἐκ τοῦ τόπου αὐτῆς, ἐὰν μὴ μετανοήσῃς."

The punishment for the kind of legalism mentioned in verse 4 is severe. Christ describes them as having **fallen.** Whereas previously He praises them for "bearing up" and "enduring", words which certainly attest to their strength, solidarity, and durability, now he describes them with a term that portrays them as weak, insecure, and vulnerable. Their lack of love has actively harmed them and Christ says that if they do not **repent, and do the works** they had previously done (that is, to return to properly loving and faithfully upholding the truth of Christ), then Christ **will come** and **remove** their **lampstand from its place.**[496] This refers back to verse 1, wherein the characteristic of

---

[494] Ladd, *Revelation*, 39.

[495] This connection helpfully derived from Sweet, *Revelation*, 79.

[496] Beale and Koester take lengths to explain that this "coming" is not the same as that final Parousia of Christ in which He will "come" for the whole world. Rather, this "coming" seems to be intended directly towards the Ephesians – and by extension, all churches who are like them. Beale, *Revelation*, 231-233.; Koester, *Revelation*, 270. See comments on 3:3. It should be noted, for the sake of those Preterists who insist that this must have referred to the destruction of Jerusalem in AD 70 that if this threat related to the destruction of Jerusalem, a congregation in Ephesus would have gleaned nothing from the threat. After all, a group of Gentile believers in Asia Minor would not be harmed by Christ executing judgment on Jerusalem. The "coming" here is, then, neither the Parousia nor AD 70.

Christ which John is to mention (and explain through this message) is Christ's being the one who walks among the seven golden lampstands and hold their stars in His hand.

What is meant by **remove your lampstand**? The image, which hearkened to the manner in which the High Priest tended the lamps in the Temple by which the seat of God could be seen, is likely intended to remind Christians that lest Christ continually tend and build His church, the light that shows the world who God is will go out. The church has been entrusted with being this light (Matt. 5:14), and if it fails to show people who God is through its lighting the world as the lamps lit the Temple in the Old Testament, then it is useless. Thus, as Christ tends the church at Ephesus here, He so tends all churches and believers – just as He said He would (John 15:2). But the removal of the lampstand remains a curious and ominous threat. Would it mean the extinguishing of the church? In a sense, yes and no.[497]

Ancient commentators were quick to point out the language rendered "remove" (κινήσω) indicates not extinguishing or elimination, but displacement. Caesarius of Arles, writing in the 6th Century, noted that "he says that this lampstand is to be moved, not taken away."[498] If that is the correct way to read it, then rather than Christ threatening to extinguish the testimony of the church, it would seem that He threatens to either take the wicked people out of their midst (purging them) or to take the righteous individuals out of their midst (bereaving them). In both cases, the guilty party would be unable to continue fooling others into believing that they are Christ's representatives for long. In the case of the church at Ephesus directly, it appears that in the 11th Century (over a millennium after their warning), their lampstand was removed, as the church at Ephesus disappeared and has never revived. In the 14th Century the city was formally surrendered to the Muslim Turks and has been Islamic dominated ever since.[499] So, did Christ extinguish their light? Yes, but only by moving that which was valuable elsewhere, and leaving the dross behind – the remnant of which remains to this day.

One should take with great solemnity the gravity of Christ's words of rebuke. The Ephesian church had rightly stood firm for doctrinal fidelity, and had endured hardship faithfully, but in doing so had lost the love that is to typify Christians.[500] This cannot be stated more clearly – Christ would prefer a church to close and to have its light carried

---

[497] For further explanation of this position, see Koester, *Revelation*, 270. Ladd interprets this phrase as implying the absolute elimination of the church. Ladd, *Revelation*, 40. It has even been said that this elimination view is validated by the fact that "there is today no church in Ephesus. The place itself is a ruin." William Hendrickson, *More than Conquerors*, 69. This author is unconvinced.
[498] William Weinrich, ed., *Ancient Christian Commentary of Scripture: New Testament XII, Revelation*, 21.
[499] J. Barton Payne, *Encyclopedia of Biblical Prophecy*, 604.
[500] Koester, *Revelation*, 262.

on by someone else than to have a church operating under faithful endurance with doctrinal fidelity, yet without love. Though Revelation is largely intended to call Christians to endure hardship faithfully, it is not coincidental that the first letter to the churches given by Christ in this book is a call to not only endure faithfully, but to do so without sacrificing love.[501]

(2:6)

"Yet this you have: you hate the works of the Nicolaitans, which I also hate."

"ἀλλὰ τοῦτο ἔχεις, ὅτι μισεῖς τὰ ἔργα τῶν Νικολαϊτῶν ἃ κἀγὼ μισῶ."

In a manner that He will repeat with each church, Christ completes what is sometimes colloquially called a "criticism sandwich." In these situations, praise is followed by criticism, and then a final praise is given to conclude the review. Christ has praised them for their good works in toiling, enduring, and testing. They were then critiqued for their lack of love, and now finally, He is going to praise them once more – interestingly enough for their hatred. He says of them that they **hate the works of the Nicolaitans, which I also hate.**

Who are these **Nicolaitans**? There is not much consensus, but there is a very old tradition which seems quite believable. In Acts 6:3-5, several men are called upon to serve the early church in Jerusalem.[502] One of those individuals selected was a man named Nicolas. Tradition holds that, being one of those selected by the Apostles, Nicolas held some sway in this early church community, and unfortunately fell under the influence of a heretic named Cerinthus.[503] Cerinthus taught what is now referred to as Gnosticism, and evidently Nicolas began teaching and advocating for it himself with no small amount of success due to his position.[504]

The origin of these **Nicolaitans** is not nearly as clear to deduce as their teachings. It seems quite obvious that their teachings were in line with Gnosticism, which taught that personal spiritual knowledge was of the utmost importance, superseding any other

---

[501] Sweet, *Revelation*, 80.

[502] This has frequently been identified as the first selection/ordination of deacons.

[503] Irenaeus, *Against Heresies*, 1:26:1-3. This contention holds the most historical support, being attested to by Irenaeus, Tertullian, Hippolytus, Dorotheus of Tyre, Jerome, Augustine, Eusebius, and more. Thomas, *Revelation 1-7*, 148.

[504] Hippolytus, *Refutation of All Heresies*, 7:24. Clement of Alexandria claims that the teachings of Nicolaus were "perverted" by his followers, alleviating him of responsibility for this heretical cult bearing his name. See Clement of Alexandria, *Stromata*, 2:20, 3:4.

authority such as scripture, the leaders of the church, or traditions handed down.[505] There are some teachings which dominated their practice, but it is not clear which of those teachings is in mind here. The whole system seems to be the object of Christ's hatred here. One can see, when looking to verses 14-15, that the practices which followed from their beliefs were abhorrent, leading them to eat food sacrificed to idols (forbidden in Acts 15:29) as well as to shamelessly commit sexual immoralities (such as indulging in Roman orgies believed to please gods of fertility).

What of this word **hate**? Some would prefer to believe that Christ does not have hatred in Him. However, there is simply no room for such an idea here, as the word used (*μισῶ; misō*) is a possible ancestor of the English term, *misery*. It is a word that strongly asserts disgust, detest, or hatred. One might wish to say that Christ's hatred is in some sense different from human hatred, but this verse also leaves no room for that as He seems to align His hatred with the exact nature of theirs, saying, **you hate... I also hate.** Robert Thomas helpfully notes that "this was no mere disapproval. It is hatred in the absolute sense... It matches the hatred of the Lord Himself..."[506] This doctrine, that God (and naturally, Christ) has hatred is a concept much neglected over the course of the last half century, but it is an exceedingly Biblical doctrine. There are things (and people; Ps. 5:5) God hates. Sweet points out, "love does not preclude hating..."[507] True love, in fact, necessitates hatred. A love for babies necessitates a hatred for abortion. A love of safety necessitates a hatred of endangerment. Here, the Ephesians are shown to have (negatively) abandoned their love for what is good, but they have (positively) not abandoned their hatred for evil.[508]

So, what is it in this context that God (and the Ephesian church) is said to hate? In brief, it is the **works of the Nicolaitans**, which would include their false-teaching and all results thereof. They taught people that each person could find their own truth (as personal spiritual illumination was the central goal); they taught that one ought to discard the authority of the scriptures, the religious leaders, the apostles, prophets, disciples, pastors, and all previous leaders who came before them; and they taught that one should disregard any rules which have been handed down through tradition,

---

[505] Irenaeus, *Against Heresies*, 3:11:1. Koester is skeptical of the association of the Nicolaitans with gnostics, but based on what is known of them in this passage as well as the early historical testimony borne of them, this association seems perfectly reasonable to maintain. Koester, *Revelation*, 264. Walvoord, along with Lange (116), considers the Nicolaitans as "forerunners of the clerical hierarchy superimposed upon the laity and robbing them of spiritual freedom" an evident jab at non-congregational church governing systems. Walvoord, *Revelation*, 58.

[506] Thomas, *Revelation 1-7*, 147.

[507] Sweet, *Revelation*, 82.

[508] Thomas, *Revelation 1-7*, 147.

choosing rather to do what makes you happy, enjoying your body however you like – specifically when it comes to sexual expression – eating whatever you like, and refusing to allow anyone to make you feel as though any of this separated you from God. Sound familiar? This is the dominant thought of the 21st Century, and of this sort of teaching Christ says, "I'm glad your church hates it, because I hate it too." It must be noted, however, that it is **the works** which are hated, rather than the **Nicolaitans** themselves. It has already been stated that Christ calls the Ephesian church (and all of His churches) to love others, even if that involves hating what they do.[509]

(2:7)

> "He who has an ear, let him hear what the Spirit says to the churches. To the one who conquers I will grant to eat of the tree of life, which is in the paradise of God.'"
>
> "Ὁ ἔχων οὖς ἀκουσάτω τί τὸ πνεῦμα λέγει ταῖς ἐκκλησίαις. Τῷ νικῶντι δώσω αὐτῷ φαγεῖν ἐκ τοῦ ξύλου τῆς ζωῆς, ὅ ἐστιν ἐν τῷ παραδείσῳ τοῦ θεοῦ."

Interestingly, it is **the Spirit** who is said to here give a word to the churches, although it is clear that the words themselves are proceeding from the mouth of Christ the Son. This is an example of how God in Trinity operates. Christ says something, but although it comes from His mouth it is said to be a word coming from the Spirit. They speak together in unison and total agreement.[510]

His words go to all who have **an ear** to hear. This is a phrase regularly used by Jesus (Matt. 11:15; Mark 7:16; Luke 8:8) and generally calls individuals to pay special attention to what is said. In John's writings, however, the phrase is conspicuously missing. In fact, it never occurs in anything he wrote until here. The only time that John records Jesus in like fashion is in John 10:27-28, wherein He says "my sheep hear my voice, and I know them, and they follow me. I give them eternal life, and they will never perish, and no one will snatch them out of my hand." It would be logical, then, to assume that when John refers to the one **who has an ear**, he refers to those who are Christ's sheep (that is, the elect). This means that not only was this letter to the Ephesian church intended to be read by the other six churches as well, but by all churches throughout all time – as it was a letter directly to the elect of the church of Ephesus, and

---

[509] While difficult to explain in short, the doctrine of the hatred of God is one worth investigating. This author holds it as a Biblical teaching that God loves and hates individuals and actions, sometimes doing both simultaneously.

[510] Koester would say, "the Spirit can be distinguished from Jesus yet does not work independently of Jesus." Koester, *Revelation*, 265.

indirectly to the elect of all ages.[511] Christ seems to assert that these have a God-given blessing to hear and understand His Word while others ignore it (Matt. 13:10-15; Is. 6:8-10).

In line with this anticipated audience, Christ next refers to **the one who conquers**. One must then ask, "conquers what?" Conquering suggests conflict and warfare, and in this context it appears that the conflict is of a spiritual nature rather than a physical.[512] Each aspect of this letter to the Ephesian church has either praised or condemned them for their affections and ability to endure hardship. There has been no mention of any physical capabilities – good or bad. Thus, this spiritual warfare is one that Christ calls His churches to prevail in – and this is a theme which will recur throughout the Revelation. Though the Church is constantly afflicted, tried, persecuted, and even martyred, they are called "those who conquered the beast" in the end (Rev. 15:2).

This concept is one worth emphasizing: Revelation, though a story of Christ and His people warring against the seemingly overwhelming powers of evil, is nevertheless the story of their victory over these forces. However, contrary to the hopes of many starry-eyed optimists, "the victory is not a physical or worldly one; it is a victory analogous to the victory won by Christ Himself, even though it involved his death on the cross."[513] It would appear that though Christ calls His people to be victorious, He has no intention of this being done through any form of physical conquering or even through an overwhelming of the opposing forces in this life. Even if His people die in the attempt, they are said to be conquerors – asserting that the result as judged in this world is of absolutely no consequence in how God (the ultimate judge) presents the victor.[514] George Ladd would summarize it this way,

---

[511] This expands upon a thought forwarded by Thomas, who taught, "The use of the plural *tais ekklesiais* indicates the universal character of the invitation each time it occurs in these two chapters (cf. Mark 13:37; Rev. 2:23) (Lee; Charles). By means of this call the message to a single congregation is extended to all the churches of Asia and through them, as representatives, to the church throughout the world (Swete; Beasley-Murray)." Thomas, *Revelation 1-7*, 150.

[512] Koester helpfully describes three areas in which the verb *nikan* (here formulated as *νικῶντι*) would be used. Koester, *Revelation*, 265. It is also noteworthy that some (as Walvoord) theorize the Nicolaitans as being a group named for their conquering the people (as Nikolaus means "conqueror of the people") and consequently hold that Christ is juxtaposing the conquering done by His people (spiritual) over against the conquering done by the world (physical). Sweet, *Revelation*, 83.

[513] Ladd, *Revelation*, 40.

[514] The teaching that God determines what victory is rather than our perception is an ancient one, as Tertullian wrote a letter encouraging Christians not to flee from persecution, but to endure it. He wrote, "Who sets the terms of any contest if not the one who provides the crown and the prizes? You will find the terms of this contest decreed in the Apocalypse, where he proclaims the rewards of victory, especially for those who really come through persecution victorious, and in their victorious struggle have fought not merely against flesh and blood but against the spirits of wickedness. Obviously, then, the superintendent of the games and the one

> Their very martyrdom was their victory, for they conquered every satanic effort to turn their loyalty and devotion away from Christ and remained true. The conqueror, then, is the victim of persecution whose death is not loss but is in reality his victory.[515]

Those who conquer, then, are not necessarily those who appear to win in this world. Christ, for example, is called the Lion of the Tribe of Judah who "has conquered." (Rev. 5:5) And yet, how did Christ conquer? By being a "faithful witness" (martyr). (Rev. 1:5) He testified of God's truth even in the face of death, and when death came, He was faithful to death. That is how Christians are expected to conquer and arise as conquerors.

The promise that the Spirit (through Christ) gives to **the one who conquers is to eat of the tree of life which is in the paradise of God.**[516] As in the Garden of Eden, eating of the tree of life represents everlasting life, and therefore, eternal salvation and security (cf. 22:1-2). Does this, then, mean that only those who are martyred will receive salvation? Are we led into an Islamic-like form of security wherein we can only gain assurance of salvation through dying for the cause of our God? Ladd, again, answers quite helpfully in this regard, saying,

> Every disciple of Jesus must be in principle a martyr and be ready to lay down his life for his faith. The revelation pictures a life and death struggle between Christ and Antichrist for the hearts of man; and the conqueror is he who is unswervingly loyal to his Lord even though it costs him his life.[517]

So, the answer to that question is, again, yes and no. Must we be individuals who lay down our lives for the sake of Christ? Yes. But what does it mean to lay down our lives? It is the seeking *first* the kingdom of God and His righteousness such that all the rest of our lives would be added to us as God sees fit. (Matthew 6:33) Does this include literal martyrdom in the fashion of Stephen, Paul, Peter, and Christ? Yes, absolutely. But for those who do not die a martyr's death, it is equally true that they will be held to this standard – did you give your entire life to Christ to do with what He pleased? John elsewhere describes what it is to conquer, saying it is no less or more than to simply

---

who sets the prize is the one who decides who is the winner of the contest. The essence, then, of a persecution is the glory of God, whether he approves or condemns, raises up or casts down." Tertullian, *On Flight During Persecution*, 1:5.

[515] Ladd, *Revelation*, 41.

[516] Koester has a very interesting section on the possible cultural references in this phraseology, as Ephesus was home to a shrine to Artemis which began as a tree, as well as a sacred area designated as "paradise." Koester, *Revelation*, 265-266.

[517] Ladd, *Revelation*, 41.

"believe that Jesus is the Son of God."[518] So, to those who conquer (that is, those who faithfully believe unto the end, regardless of what may come), He will **grant to eat of the tree of life.**

This final term, **the paradise of God**, clearly refers to nothing and nowhere short of the eternal abode of God – the New Jerusalem.[519] This is the place to which Christ went when He left this world (Luke 23:43). It is the place that Paul's friend was caught up to, which we must synonymize with Heaven (2 Cor. 12:4). And by extension of the presence of the tree of life there, it is the place which God's people will inhabit for all eternity along with Him (Revelation 22:2). This latter reference gives us an insight into the reality that God's abode, correctly identified as Heaven and enjoyed by the redeemed dead at present, is one of the many elements of the New Creation which is enjoyed in-part now, but which will be more thoroughly and fully enjoyed in the eternal state when we shall ever be with the Lord.

This final verse, then, could be paraphrased: To all of God's people who have a God-given blessing to be able to hear His Words and obey them, the Spirit within you calls you to give your life over wholly to God, and in exchange, He will give you eternal life in His presence forever. Did the Ephesians heed this call? History indicates they did. In the early second-century (very soon after John's writing the Revelation) Ignatius wrote an epistle to the church at Ephesus in which he commends them for their "unanimity and harmonious love."[520] It seems they not only listened, but heeded the words of Jesus Christ. But what of us? How are future generations of churches to heed the words given to the Ephesian church? We are to always be testing and sifting the teachings put before us, as false teachings will certainly come, and yet, we are to do so with nothing but love for God, neighbor, brother, and enemy.

---

[518] 1 John 5:5. This thought helpfully pointed out in John Walvoord, *Revelation*, 44.

[519] Payne, *Encyclopedia of Biblical Prophecy*, 604.

[520] Ignatius, *The Epistles of Ignatius to the Ephesians,* 4:1. In this letter, Ignatius uses the term "love" (ἀγάπη or some close variant) at least 11 times. See Michael W. Thomas, *The Apostolic Fathers* 3rd Ed., 182-201.

(2:8-11) *Smyrna: The Suffering Church*

(2:8)

> "And to the angel of the church in Smyrna write: 'The words of the first and the last, who died and came to life."
>
> "Καὶ τῷ ἀγγέλῳ τῆς ἐν Σμύρνῃ ἐκκλησίας γράψον· Τάδε λέγει ὁ πρῶτος καὶ ὁ ἔσχατος, ὃς ἐγένετο νεκρὸς καὶ ἔζησεν·"

Introducing His second letter, Christ addresses it **to the angel of the church in Smyrna.**[521] Second in terms of population (trailing only Ephesus) with roughly 200,000 inhabitants, **Smyrna** itself was also a major seaport on the East coast of the Aegean Sea.[522] Historically, the city had benefitted from this strategic location as well as its being an early ally of the city of Rome long before Rome became the major empire it is now remembered as. Because of this longstanding alliance, the Imperial cult was at least as strong, if not stronger, in Smyrna than it was anywhere else in the world.[523] Thus, the religious allegiance of the citizens of Smyrna was expected to be unwavering and unquestionable. It is then somewhat surprising that the church at Smyrna existed from the time of John forward, and with no small degree of success and development, as evidenced by Ignatius' letter to them which recognized their Bishop, deacons, and elders.[524]

Culturally, the city could boast of having been the birthplace of Homer who wrote the Iliad and Odyssey. Smyrna was home to a 20,000-seat public theatre (the largest in Asia) in no small part because of this cultural tie to the early playwright.[525] They also maintained a massive stadium and a reputable library (something of rarity in the ancient world) and some records indicate that there was once a reputable medical school there.[526]

Into this city flowing with religious idolatry and cultural entertainment came **the words of the first and the last, who died and came to life.** Jesus, again, uses this term **the first and the last** to describe Himself, which was used in the Old Testament to

---

[521] R.C.H. Lenski looks to the mixed usage of singular and plural pronouns in this letter and sees confirmation that the "angel" represents the pastor, as in verse 10 alone, Christ seems to address a single person (the angel) by using a singular pronoun and then gives commendations to the church at large with the use of a plural pronoun. R.C.H. Lenski, *The Interpretation of St. John's Revelation*, 99.

[522] Mounce, Revelation, 73. Today, the city is called Izmir and is the third largest city in Turkey with a massive 3-million-person population, illustrating its fantastic location. Clyde Fant and Mitchell Reddish, *A Guide to Biblical Sites in Greece and Turkey*, 318.

[523] Tacitus, *Annals*, 4:56.

[524] Ignatius, *Epistle to the Smyrnaeans,* 8, 12.

[525] Mounce, *Revelation*, 73.

[526] Strabo, *Geography*, 12:8:20.

describe God (Is. 44:6; 48:12), before reaching back once more to explain the significance of at least one characteristic John saw of Christ in chapter one.[527] Jesus follows His claim to deity with a reference to His eternality and supremacy over death, being the one **who died and came to life.**[528] Why might the Christian citizens of Smyrna need to be particularly mindful of Christ's power and authority over death?

(2:9)

> "'I know your tribulation and your poverty (but you are rich) and the slander of those who say that they are Jews and are not, but are a synagogue of Satan."
>
> "οἶδά σου τὴν θλῖψιν καὶ τὴν πτωχείαν, ἀλλὰ πλούσιος εἶ, καὶ τὴν βλασφημίαν ἐκ τῶν λεγόντων Ἰουδαίους εἶναι ἑαυτοὺς καὶ οὐκ εἰσὶν ἀλλὰ συναγωγὴ τοῦ σατανᾶ."

It seems that Christ reminds the people of Smyrna of His power and authority over death because they are suffering **tribulation and... poverty.** These first two hardships, tribulation and poverty, are causally connected. This is already the second time that a Christian is noted as enduring **tribulation** (1:9), but in the earliest instance it was John who identified with other Christians as enduring it. In this instance, Jesus Himself acknowledges the tribulation (θλῖψιν, perhaps better rendered *affliction*) of His people. The tribulation experienced at Smyrna would come close to the heart of the Apostle John, though long after his own death. One of his disciples, Polycarp, would become Bishop of Smyrna, and after several years in that position would be martyred in the city in a gruesome manner. The church at Smyrna wrote a letter in the aftermath detailing his being bound, taken to the stadium in Smyrna, immolated, and finally stabbed to death due to the fire failing to consume him.[529] What is even worse is that he is said to have been the twelfth Christian martyred in Smyrna, testifying to a lengthy history of this kind of tragedy.[530] With this sort of tribulation in mind, it is significant that Jesus is not unaware of His people's suffering or afflictions. He is not ignorant of the ways they are mistreated, nor is He unsure of who is responsible for their hardship (per the following statements in the verse). This is a great cause for encouragement.

---

[527] Mounce, Revelation, 74. Schreiner sees in this statement a reminder to the church at Smyrna that Christ is in complete control of all things, from beginning to end, including their suffering, such that they may know that "the persecution of the believers doesn't signify that the world is spinning out of the Son of Man's control." Schreiner, *Revelation* BECNT, 133.

[528] Notation should be made of the fact that this, the first time the term "came to life" (ἔζησεν) is used, it refers to a literal, bodily resurrection – and no less of an important one than that of Jesus Christ Himself. See notes on 20:4.

[529] *Martyrdom of Polycarp*, 15-16.

[530] Thomas, *Revelation 1-7*, 160.

Being causally connected, the Christians of Smyrna are in **poverty** because of their enduring tribulation. This experience of poverty would have been emphasized by the fact that Smyrna, like Ephesus, was a thriving and wealthy city.[531] Relative poverty, that is, poverty in the presence of those who are not suffering from it, is often one key factor in identifying areas prone to theft and robbery. The Smyrnaens are described as experiencing a particularly humiliating form of poverty, as the usual Greek word for poverty (*penia*, πενίᾱ) is not used. The word chosen by Christ is *ptocheian* (*πτωχείαν*) which denotes having "nothing at all."[532] It should not, then, be overlooked that although the Christians in Smyrna were oppressed and impoverished, they are not guilty of any criminal activity, or even mistreatment of neighbors and government figures. In their situation, it is remarkable that they are not the church which forgot to love.

The reason for their poverty despite living in a city with many opportunities for financial success was likely their refusal to participate in the cultural, religious, and social practices of the non-christian citizens of the city.[533] In the early church, it was not uncommon for churches to be regularly plundered for their refusal to participate in practices expected of them, and those who persecuted them were infrequently (if ever) prosecuted.[534]

Despite their poverty, Christ tells them that they **are rich**. Just as Christ called the Ephesian church to "conquer" despite this carrying no earthly connotations, He further asserts the priority of the spiritual over the physical by telling these impoverished individuals that they are indeed wealthy. This is nothing short of a confirmation of their participation in what Christ Himself exemplified and promised His people (2 Cor. 8:9), and the lifestyle to which He called His disciples in Matthew 6:19-24. Jesus' concept of wealth was innately spiritual, as He conceived of His kingdom as being "not of this world."[535] (John 18:36) In accordance with this, He promised those who endured persecution for leaving behind the hopes of attaining wealth in this world a greater wealth in the end (Mark 10:29-30). Paul reflected that this was also true of himself and his companions in 2 Cor. 6:10, saying one could rightly describe their situation as "having nothing, and yet possessing everything."

---

[531] One can reflect on the wealth of Ephesus from the Biblical account of Paul's experiencing riots as a result of his interrupting the idolatrous silversmith trade in Acts 19. One may safely imagine a market of similar size and traffic would have existed in Smyrna, along with many other financially successful endeavors.
[532] Thomas, *Revelation 1-7*, 163.
[533] Schreiner, *Revelation* BECNT, 134.
[534] For a scriptural example of this, see Hebrews 10:34.
[535] Support for this is also found in Schreiner, *Revelation* BECNT, 134, who says they were "poor materially but spiritually rich, rich in the things that truly count in life."

Beyond the tribulation and poverty, they are said to be enduring **slander.**[536] While slander might sound like a small thing when compared with poverty or outright persecution, the types of things being said of these individuals were especially heinous. Schreiner writes that while Jesus is "fully aware of what their Jewish opponents are saying... we wish that we had the same knowledge..."[537] This desire to know what the slander was is echoed by Ladd.[538] Fortunately, many of the early records which presently exist maintain rumors that were spread about Christians in the first few centuries, many of these rumors being spread by Jews. Bart Wagemakers gives a few examples of the types of slanderous things spread about early Christians in his 2010 essay, "Incest, Infanticide, and Cannibalism."[539]

Wagemakers recounts several early documents which tell of Christians engaging in incest.[540] Early authors, such as Theophilus of Antioch make mention of this specific rumor, saying that "senseless men... allege that the wives of us all are held in common and made promiscuous use of; and that we even commit incest with our own sisters."[541] The author of the early-2nd century *Epistle to Diognetus*, when asked to describe Christians to someone who had no experience with them, felt the need to write, "They marry like everyone else, and have children, but they do not destroy their children. They share their food but not their wives."[542]

Despite this and other attempts to clarify the Christian position on marriage, the rumor pervaded well-into the Patristic era. Justin Martyr references this rumor and elaborates on the frequent assumption that Christians make a habit of "upsetting the lamp" or "extinguishing the lights."[543] While these terms mean little to us, they would have been stabbing and deeply offensive accusations in the day, as they showed someone's familiarity with a popular rumor about Christian church services. The third-century author, Minucius Felix, writes this rumor in no less detail than one can expect would be given on a street corner or around a table:

---

[536] Ladd helpfully points out that while the Greek word used is blasphemian (βλασφημίαν), it is inappropriate in this context to translate it as "blasphemy" since it refers not to "blasphemy of the name of God but slanderous accusations against men." Ladd, *Revelation*, 43. This is conspired by Thomas, *Revelation 1-7*, 164.

[537] Schreiner, *Revelation* BECNT, 135.

[538] Ladd, *Revelation*, 43.

[539] Bart Wagemakers, "Incest, Infanticide, and Cannibalism: Anti-Christian Imputations in the Roman Empire" *Greece & Rome* 57:2 (October 2010): 337-354.

[540] Wagemakers, "Incest, Infanticide, and Cannibalism", 338-339.

[541] Theophilus of Antioch, *To Autolycus*, 3:4.

[542] *Letter to Diognetus*, 5:6-7. While this author translates some of the Greek terms differently than Dr. Holmes, it is appreciated that he translates *κοίτην* as "wives" rather than the literal translation, "marriage bed." Wives is certainly the original authorial intent. Holmes, *Apostolic Fathers*, 702-703.

[543] Justin Martyr, *First Apology*, 26; *Dialogue with Trypho*, 10.

> On a solemn day they [the Christians] assemble at the feast, with all their children, sisters, mothers, people of every sex and of every age. There, after much feasting, when the fellowship has grown warm, and the fervour (sic) of incestuous lust has grown hot with drunkenness, a dog that has been tied to the chandelier is provoked, by throwing a small piece of offal beyond the length of a line by which he is bound, to rush and spring; and thus the conscious light being overturned and extinguished in the shameless darkness, the connections of abominable lust involve them in the uncertainty of fate. Although not all in fact, yet in consciousness all are alike incestuous, since by the desire of all of them everything is sought for which can happen in the act of each individual.[544]

Unfortunately, Minucius' telling of the rumor was not the most vivid. The rumor sometimes took forms which were only more grotesque, as it is recounted a century later by Epiphanius of Salamis that many believe the following to be a standard Christian celebration of the Eucharist:

> They start feasting right away—and they set the table with lavish provisions for eating meat and drinking wine even if they are poor. But then, after a drinking bout and, let us say, stuffing their overstuffed veins, they get hot for each other next. And the husband will move away from his wife and tell her—speaking to his own wife! — 'Get up, perform the Agape with the brother.' And when the wretched couple has made love—and I am truly ashamed to mention the vile things they do, for as the holy apostle says, 'It is a shame even to speak' of what goes on among them. Still, I should not be ashamed to say what they are not ashamed to do, to arouse horror by every means in those who hear what obscenities they are prepared to perform. For after having made love with the passion of fornication in addition, to lift their blasphemy up to heaven, the woman and man receive the man's emission on their own hands. And they stand with their eyes raised heavenward but the filth on their hands and pray, if you please— the ones they call Stratiotics and Gnostics—and offer that stuff on their hands to the true Father of all, and say, 'We offer thee this gift, the body of Christ.' And then they eat it partaking of their own dirt, and say, 'This is the body of Christ; and this is the Pascha, because of which our bodies suffer and are compelled to acknowledge the passion of Christ.' And so with the woman's emission when she happens to be having

[544] Minucius Felix, *Octavius*, 9.

> her period—they likewise take the unclean menstrual blood they gather from her, and eat it in common. And 'This,' they say, 'is the blood of Christ.'[545]

This disgusting rumor circulated for several centuries, and clearly only grew more and more depraved with each passing generation.[546]

Wagemakers also points out several instances in which Christians were rumored to kill unwanted children. The *Epistle to Diognetus* addressed this alongside the claim of their sharing wives, but even earlier Christians had explicitly forbidden this practice. In the very early 2nd-Century, it was written in one of the first Christian manuals of standard behavior, *The Didache*, "You shall not abort a child nor, again, commit infanticide. You must not withhold your hand from your son or your daughter, but from their youth you shall teach them the fear of God."[547] Despite this straightforward instruction not to harm children, the rumor spread that Christians not only harmed them, but did heinous acts to and with them. Epiphanius recounts the rumor:

> They extract the fetus at the stage which is appropriate for their enterprise, take this aborted infant, and cut it up in a trough with a pestle. And they mix honey, pepper, and certain other perfumes and spices with it to keep from getting sick, and then all the revellers (sic) in this herd of swine and dogs assemble, and each eats a piece of the child with his fingers.[548]

This rumor leads into the third major slander said of Christians, which was that they not only killed babies, but that they ate them.[549] Cannibalism was a frequently retorted rumor against Christians, largely because of poor efforts to understand the language of the Lord's Supper. So frequent was this misunderstanding of "eating the body of the Son" that Christian services were commonly called "Thyestean feasts." Theyestes was a Greek mythological figure who committed adultery with his brother's wife. When his brother discovered this, he held a feast, and served Thyestes his three sons, whom he had killed and butchered.[550] This name for Christian services was so common that

---

545 Einar Thomassen and Johannes van Oort, eds., Frank Williams, trans., *The Panarion of Epiphanius of* Salamis, 93-94. Quotation from 26:4:3-8.

546 Origen also gives the details of this rumor in the early 3rd century, though with fewer details. Origen, *Contra Censum*, 6:27.

547 *The Didache*, 19:5. As translated in Holmes, *Apostolic Fathers*, 435-437.

548 Thomassen and Oort, *Panarion*, 94-95. Quoting from 26:5:5.

549 Both Origen and Tertullian engage these rumors. Origen, *Contra Celsum*, 6:27; Tertullian, *First Apology*, 7:1, 8:3, 8:7.

550 Wagemakers, "Incest, Infanticide, and Cannibalism", 340.

Athenagoras acknowledges the title in his *Plea for the Christians.*[551] Read once more from Minucius' account of how a young person is initiated into the Christian community:

> Now the story about the initiation of young novices is as much to be detested as it is well known. An infant covered over with meal, that it may deceive the unwary, is placed before him who is to be stained with their rites: this infant is slain by the young pupil, who has been urged on as if to harmless blows on the surface of the meal, with dark and secret wounds. Thirstily — O horror! — they lick up its blood; eagerly they divide its limbs. By this victim they are pledged together; with this consciousness of wickedness they are covenanted to mutual silence.[552]

These and other slanderous rumors pervade early Christian history.[553] It is no stretch to say that early documentation largely testifies to the fact that these rumors found their origin in Jewish mouths.[554] If the historical narrative testifies to it, Jesus validates it in this verse by stating outright that **those who say** such things at least claimed to be Jews. In the city of Smyrna specifically, it was the Jewish population which contributed to the martyrdom of the Christian Bishop of the city, Polycarp, and refused to allow the Christians to take possession of his remains afterwards.[555] This antagonism between Jews and Christians might have been little understood by outsiders, but with Christianity being a somewhat new religion, and having for their leaders a group of Jews who proclaimed the kingdom of Jesus who Himself was a Jew, it was considered wise to take the Jewish testimony of this new "sect" of Judaism as reliable. After all, who would better be able to tell of the errors in this new "cult" of Jesus?

The fact that Jesus refers to these individuals as **those who say that they are Jews and are not** shows that He is in full agreement with the Apostle Paul about the terminology of "Jew" and "Israel." In Romans 2:28-29, for instance, Paul introduces a distinction between those who claim the ethnicity and physicality of being Jews and those who are actually Jews. Clearly, in the mind of Paul (and evidently in the mind of Jesus and therefore God) simply being an ethnic descendant of Israel (or Abraham per Gal. 3:7) is not synonymous with being what God considers a "Jew" or a member of

---

[551] Athenagoras, *A Plea for the Christians*, 3.

[552] Minucius Felix, *Octavius*, 9.

[553] Barclay lists six "ever-recurring slanders" which were levelled at Christians in this era: Cannibalism, sexual immorality, destroying families, atheism, political disloyalty and anarchism, and pyromania. William Barclay, *The Revelation of John* Vol. 1, 98.

[554] Origen, *Contra Celsum*, 6:27. This is also confirmed by Justin Martyr, Tertullian, and Ignatius, alongside others. See Mounce, *Revelation*, 75, n.12.

[555] *Martyrdom of Polycarp*, 18.

"Israel."[556] Although these individuals may have been ethnically children of Israel, they are not considered by Jesus to be truly Jewish, because as Paul would say, "no one is a Jew who is merely one outwardly… but a Jew is one inwardly."[557] (Rom. 2:28-29)

Who then are truly "Jews" in the eyes of Jesus (and therefore in reality)? While it is a statement which will draw the daggers from many, it is true to say that when God looks for "Jews" in the time after the resurrection of Jesus Christ, He looks to Christians. Noone has yet said it more clearly than Thomas Schreiner, who wrote,

> It follows, then, that believers in Christ, his disciples, are true Jews. Paul argues that those who have received the Spirit are true Jews and the true circumcision. True Jewishness is a spiritual reality, and Paul identifies believers in Jesus Christ as the true Israel.[558]

As if the declaration that these individuals are not truly Jews although they claim to be would not be enough, Jesus clarifies what these people really are. He says they **are a synagogue of Satan**. While some may take this as a remark that ought to be quietly read over with some discomfort due to the ease it would provide for antisemites to portray Jews as instruments of Satan, two important considerations should also be carried forward emphatically: First, John (who wrote these words) was himself ethnically Jewish, as was Christ who said them. There is therefore no room for the idea that this is permissive towards hatred of ethnic Jews. Second, one should notice that in the following verse Jesus alludes to the jailers and policing authorities in Smyrna (who most certainly were Romans; i.e., Gentiles) as "the devil." Christ's use of these terms, identifying the enemies of His people as Satan-led or embodying the devilish, shows readers and hearers that the individuals standing against God's people are not truly the enemy. Rather, Satan is.[559]

Instead of seeing the Jews or the persecuting government forces as the enemy, Christ leads His people to see through this surface-level conflict and understand that "we do not wrestle against flesh and blood, but against the rulers, against the authorities, against the cosmic powers over this present darkness, against the spiritual forces of evil in the heavenly places." (Eph. 6:12) Let it be proclaimed for generations to come: the enemy of God and His people is not Islam or the Muslims who believe it; our enemy is not Judaism or Jews, nor any other religious system or its adherents; our enemy is not any

---

[556] Ladd, *Revelation*, 43.
[557] Schreiner, *Revelation* BECNT, 136.
[558] Schreiner, *Revelation* BECNT, 136.
[559] Mounce, *Revelation*, 76.

government system, communist, socialist, capitalist, liberal, conservative; our enemy is not white or black, American, European, African, or Asian; our true enemy is Satan and all sin which he utilizes for his purposes.

Not to be too soft on those outside of God's kingdom, though, it must be maintained that there is no such thing as any other god than Yahweh, the God of the Old and New Testaments, the Trinitarian God who has revealed Himself as the Father, the Son, and the Holy Spirit. Any worship offered to any deity, falsely-so-called, is nothing short of worship of Satan and demons. This is true of all who offer worship to Allah, Brahma, Vishnu, Shiva, Amaterasu Okimaki, Lao Tsu, all other false-gods, and for that matter all false-conceptions of Yahweh which deny His true being including His character or His trinity, such as is worshipped by modalistic pseudochristians or Jews. While Jews once worshipped the one true God, it is correct to say that they have rejected the Son and accordingly the Father also (1 John 2:23), and are therefore "no longer a synagogue of the Lord but in reality a synagogue of Satan."[560] Little has changed since Jesus stood before them Himself and proclaimed that they were not the children of God, but rather were the children of the devil (John 8:31-47).

(2:10)

> "Do not fear what you are about to suffer. Behold, the devil is about to throw some of you into prison, that you may be tested, and for ten days you will have tribulation. Be faithful unto death, and I will give you the crown of life."
>
> "μηδὲν φοβοῦ ἃ μέλλεις πάσχειν. ἰδοὺ μέλλει βάλλειν ὁ διάβολος ἐξ ὑμῶν εἰς φυλακὴν ἵνα πειρασθῆτε καὶ ἕξετε θλῖψιν ἡμερῶν δέκα. γίνου πιστὸς ἄχρι θανάτου, καὶ δώσω σοι τὸν στέφανον τῆς ζωῆς."

The phrasing of **do not fear** (μηδὲν φοβοῦ) leans towards the possibility that Christ was commending them to "stop being afraid."[561] This helps interpreters understand what Jesus is actually commending them to do. Rather than admonishing them not to have any sense of dread or nervousness (for no one truly has any control over these feelings), it seems that Jesus is commanding them to stop allowing their fear to influence their actions. In a sense, one might more easily understand it as a positive command rather than a negative command. Rather than saying, "do not fear" modern interpreters could perhaps better understand it as "be brave." Bravery, after all, is

---

[560] Ladd, *Revelation*, 44. This firmness is equally proclaimed in A.T. Robertson, *Word Pictures in the New Testament* VI, 302, who states unequivocally, "These are Jews in name only, not spiritual Jews... serving the devil instead of the Lord."

[561] Mounce, *Revelation*, 76, n. 16.; Thomas, *Revelation 1-7*, 166.

continued virtuous action in the face of fear. The fact that he calls them, then, to not fear **what** they **are about to suffer** shows that they are being called to persevere in their Christian ethics and action while undergoing imprisonment, as **the devil** is **about to throw** them **into prison** to **be tested.** Some have helpfully pointed out that this does not refer to their being tested (or *tried*) by the government or policing forces, but rather it refers to their undergoing a "trial of faith." When understood in this way, one can see that their testing could be considered a test from God as much as from Satan.[562]

While it is important to maintain that Satan is the cause and source of their being tested, it is not inappropriate to imagine that God would allow this test for the purpose of fortifying their faith and/or advancing the Christian faith by their faithful endurance and testimony.[563] This seems to be a clear conclusion to draw from other instances in which the temptation or testing of God's people occurs, such as the account of Job or the 40 days Jesus spent in the wilderness. All of this also points out that God does not keep His people *from* suffering, but keeps them *through* suffering, as in this verse He outright tells them **you are about to suffer**, and He does not change it. Let it never be said that God would never allow His people to go through tribulation. Instead, Christians must know that God permits His people to endure tribulation for their good and for His glory.

Christ says that they are to have tribulation **for ten days.** The great difficulty in rightly understanding what these **ten days** represent is in maintaining what John must have meant to the church at Smyrna in the late-first century, while also maintaining some sense of meaning in this phrase for the Church universal throughout the ages. Most frequently, interpreters (even those most inclined to a literal interpretation) take the phrase to be entirely symbolic, depicting a "round number" meaning that the Smyrnaens would be persecuted for a short or "brief" period of time, specifically under the Romans.[564] One can see the appeal of the idea, but to envision the suffering of the Christian church (even in Smyrna alone) under the Romans as having occurred for a *short* period of time that could be likened to ten days is hard to swallow. Even if one accepts that this pertains strictly to persecution by Rome, the Roman persecution of Christianity would continue for another 200 years![565] This would leave the Christians in

---

[562] Lenski, *The Interpretation of St. John's Revelation*, 99.

[563] It is important to note that the word "test" (Gr., πειρασθῆτε) comes from the same root as "tempted" (πειραζόμενος) in James 1:13. Thus, James' statement that no one should say they are tested/tempted by God should be borne in mind when understanding who is responsible for this test of the church at Smyrna.

[564] Payne, *Encyclopedia of Biblical Prophecy*, 605.; Ladd, *Revelation*, 44.; MacArthur, *MacArthur Bible Commentary*, 1997.; Barclay, *Revelation of John*, 96.; Koester, *Revelation*, 277.

[565] There is an interesting view that holds the "ten days" as referring to ten periods of time in which Christians will be persecuted by the Romans, but this entirely relies on the early dating of the book of Revelation, as it begins the list with Nero. Thomas, *Revelation 1-7*, 169.

Smyrna a century after receiving John's letter greatly confused as they continued to suffer the ravages of the Roman Empire.

Of a saner persuasion is Robert Thomas, who holds that the most preferable interpretation is that "the ten days are literal and refer to an unknown persecution within a definite period of time during the generation to which this message was addressed."[566] One can easily see why this position would be preferred – it is rather straight forward. One might complain against it that the point of including it in Scripture then becomes somewhat difficult to understand; that without any knowledge of how to apply this to Christians throughout the ages, and without any knowledge of how it was to apply to the Christians at Smyrna, this text then becomes impossible to apply to anyone. But this is not true, as one can see that this interpretative approach is not unique. To be sure, there are instances in the Bible wherein authors give specific cultural or circumstantial addresses, such as when Paul says to the church at Corinth that they ought to "greet one another with a holy kiss." (2 Cor. 13:12) It is the case that although Christians may not literally kiss one another in all cultures across all time periods, this text is not impossible to apply. The general concept of peacefully and lovingly welcoming one another upon gathering is applicable to all. So, we have both an original application to that text for the Corinthians and a separate albeit textually and conceptually deduced application for modern Christians.

So, the interpretative principle of understanding a cultural or circumstantial commendation as time-bound and nevertheless conceptually (or perhaps *spiritually*) applicable to all Christians across all time is one that interpreters are familiar and comfortable with. How, then, is one to take this **ten day** statement? If one accepts Thomas' contention that this referred to a ten-day persecution that is no longer maintained in history, then a conceptual or spiritual application for modern Christians is likely merited while maintaining the literal application for the Smyrnaens. What conceptual or spiritual applications might modern Christians take from this? The ancient writer Primasius provides a very helpful approach when he likens the ten literal days of suffering that the Smyrnaens endured to the ten literal commandments that Moses brought down from Mt. Sinai.[567] Jesus certainly believed that each of the ten commandments in the Decalogue were literally meant to be followed (see Mark 10:19), but He also felt entirely at liberty to summarize them (along with all the other laws) down in two central premises for Christians to apply throughout the ages (Matt. 22:37-40). In the same way, while the ten days of suffering were literal days of suffering for the

[566] Thomas, *Revelation 1-7*, 170.

[567] Primasius, *Commentary on the Apocalypse*, 2:10.

Christians of Smyrna, Primasius surmises that the application for later Christians is to see "the course of the present life [as] signified by the ten days."[568]

Just as the church at Smyrna was to steel itself and prepare for a period of affliction, the Church throughout the ages should steel itself for its own periods of affliction which will persist over the centuries. Regardless of what afflictions and persecutions may come, Christians are to see in the church at Smyrna an example of those who although facing severe suffering pressed on to the end.[569] Christians may also see in the promise of Christ a guarantee that one day the suffering *will* end. He has determined only to allow His people to be persecuted for a definite period of time – the end of which He will bring to pass, and that with great power and swiftness.

It is important to maintain, though, that while Christ secures that an end will come to this period of suffering, it is nevertheless unavoidable that they **will have tribulation** for these ten days. The Christian life will be fraught with that which Christ promised His disciples in Matthew 24:4-14. He called them to endure faithfully through that period because "the end is not yet." (Matthew 24:6) So, as the Christians in Smyrna found out, and as every generation of Christians will find, tribulation is not solely an end-times event saved for that final generation of people. Every generation will go through their own tribulation, leading to what Christ terms the "Great Tribulation" which will occur just prior to His return (Matthew 24:21). Is it then fair to say that we are in what Christ called "tribulation?" Absolutely. And yet, we endure faithfully, knowing that as we grow closer to the return of Christ, the need for strong and faithful Christians will only increase as Satan sees the day approaching. As Robert Gundry put it,

> The facts that the Church has been destined to tribulations in general (1 Thess. 3:3) and that throughout this age the church has been opposed by and has suffered from antichrists (1 John 2:18, 22; 4:3) constitute presumptive evidence that the Church will endure *the* tribulation and withstand *the* Antichrist.[570]

Once again, Christ calls His people to **be faithful unto death**. As was the case in verse 7, this is truly a call to those who may face martyrdom, but it is also applicable to those Christians who may never stand at the tip of a sword or the end of a gun. It is a call

---

[568] Translation by William Weinrich, ed., *Ancient Christian Commentary XII: Revelation*, 26.

[569] A.T. Robertson sees the Greek phraseology as also retaining the possible meaning of "within ten days" so as to make Christ's words to them not a statement about the longevity or brevity of the impending suffering, but more of a statement of the imminence of the suffering. This may well be. Robertson, *Word Pictures in the New Testament VI*, 302.

[570] Gundry, *The Church and the Tribulation*, 49.

to all of God's people to lay down their lives for the cause of Christ, whether that means setting aside personal desires and dreams by sacrificing time and money or whether it means laying aside a future altogether, all Christians are called to be faithful until they die – however soon or distant that may be.

To those who do this (which will be all true Christians), Christ **will give… the crown of life.** While this is almost an exact reiteration of what James says in James 1:12, John is able to pen an even more glorious realization which is that Jesus Christ Himself will be the one to personally convey this crown on His people. This duty is not delegated to an angel, but appears to be very personal, and at the very least, this secures for each and every believer that they will have individual and personal relationships with Christ of a deeply intimate nature the moment they arrive in the presence of God.

It is crucial, at the same time, to note the type of **crown** that Christ is said to convey. The typical image of a crown conjures thoughts of royalty, but the Greek word for that type of "crown" is *diadema* (διάδημα). It is a word that John was certainly aware of and familiar with, given that he uses it three times in Revelation (Rev. 12:3; 13:1; 19:12). Yet, in this verse John uses the Greek word *stephanon* (στέφανον) which would more properly depict a laurel wreath such as that given to Olympic athletes (something the people of Smyrna would have been well-aware of since they had frequently hosted the games). Gloriously, this is the exact word that is used every time the Gospel authors describe the crown of thorns which was placed on Christ's head (Matthew 27:29; Mark 15:17; John 19:2).

With this association, it is hard to imagine that Christ would literally place a crown like that which He wore during His Passion on us. On the other hand, it is absolutely sensical to believe that this is a symbolic statement meant to assert to us that Christ will convey on us the salvation and rewards which He merited by going to that cross, which is precisely what each of the promises at the end of the letters is meant to bring to mind – that Christ will personally and undoubtedly deliver salvation to His people.[571] Thus, just like the *stephanon*-type crown, the value is not found in the crown itself, but in the meaning of the crown.[572] The crown symbolizes a victory that the person wearing it has won, and that victory in the case of the Christian is victory over death and Hell – a victory which was truly won by Christ (who first wore the crown) but which is conveyed to us by Him.

---

[571] Thomas, *Revelation 1-7*, 173.
[572] Mounce, *Revelation*, 76.

(2:11)

"He who has an ear, let him hear what the Spirit says to the churches. The one who conquers will not be hurt by the second death.'"

"Ὁ ἔχων οὖς ἀκουσάτω τί τὸ πνεῦμα λέγει ταῖς ἐκκλησίαις. Ὁ νικῶν οὐ μὴ ἀδικηθῇ ἐκ τοῦ θανάτου τοῦ δευτέρου."

Christ's conclusory words, **he who has an ear, let him hear what the Spirit says,** will be echoed across each of the seven letters (2:7; 2:11; 2:17; 2:29; 3:6; 3:13; 3:22) and always asserts that the words given in this particular commendation are directly addressed to God's people (see notes on v.7).[573]

Continuing His standard method of teaching His people about His reward for **the one who conquers,** Jesus uses the language here of such a person **not** being **hurt by the second death.** This is the first mention of the "second death" in John's Revelation, and the concept will not reappear until chapter 20. However, in chapters 20 and 21 it features prominently, being mentioned three times (20:6; 20:14; 21:8) and is (fortunately for the reader) directly defined as being an eternal habitation of the lake burning with fire and brimstone.

The terming of this punishment as "the second death" ought not be interpreted as delivering unredeemed souls into some deathly blackness in the likeness of the annihilationist dream. Thomas Watson powerfully and properly described those who endure the second death as "always dying – but never dead."[574] The ancient author Lactantius wrote of it, saying, "we thus define the second death: death is the suffering of eternal pain; or thus: death is the condemnation of souls for their desserts to eternal punishments."[575] It is therefore crucial that Christ says to these who **conquer** (another allusion to faithful endurance even to death) that they **will not be hurt by the second death** – which is nothing short of saying they will not experience that punishment due to sinners because of their wickedness (Rev. 21:8). In fact, the Greek used could be taken as more assertive and firmer than the ESV renders. The Greek terms *οὐ μὴ* literally mean "no" and "not" producing a strong double negative. One Greek expert claimed that "it is the strongest negative assertion about the future of which the Greek language is capable."[576] If Jesus had framed His statement as a question, it would be fair to word it, "Will the conquerors be harmed by the second death? No! Absolutely not!" It is

---

[573] This phrase will appear once more in Revelation 13:9 and asserts there this same addressal.
[574] Thomas Watson, *A Body of Practical Divinity*, 46.
[575] Lactantius, *Divine Institutes,* 2:13.
[576] Thomas, *Revelation 1-7*, 174.

somewhat difficult to convey this, but in an effort to recognize this emphasis, the NIV renders it "will not be hurt *at all* by the second death." The LSB renders it "will *never* be hurt by the second death" which rendering the CSB also favors.

The clarity of the statement leaves no doubt whatsoever – the people of God will not in any way at all suffer any of the consequences of God's condemnation and wrath. What a surge of encouragement and comfort the Christian should feel, as surely the people of Smyrna felt, that regardless of what pains are endured in the coming about of the first death, there is certainty that there will be absolutely no pain in the eternal state for those who endure faithfully. No sword will pierce, nor will any cancer seethe, nor will any depression burden, forever and ever. Christ began this letter by reminding them that He was the one who was dead and now lives, and having passed through the veil of darkness He now stands triumphantly as Lord of death and the place of the dead, holding the keys to both (1:18), proclaiming deliverance to those of His followers who may pass through this same veil very soon.[577]

In this letter to the church at Smyrna, Christ begins by asserting His preeminence over all that could ever come upon His people. He then warns them of the suffering that is certain to come through persecution and tribulation in their life, and concludes by promising them that nothing at all in the punishment due to the wicked will ever hurt them. May all Christians of all eras hear these words and take heart – our suffering will not last forever. "The Lord will not cast off forever, but, though he cause grief, he will have compassion according to the abundance of his steadfast love." (Lam. 3:31-32)

---

[577] Mounce, *Revelation*, 74.

(2:12-17) *Pergamum: The Worldly Church*

(2:12)

> "And to the angel of the church in Pergamum write: 'The words of him who has the sharp two-edged sword."
>
> "Καὶ τῷ ἀγγέλῳ τῆς ἐν Περγάμῳ ἐκκλησίας γράψον· Τάδε λέγει ὁ ἔχων τὴν ῥομφαίαν τὴν δίστομον τὴν ὀξεῖαν·"

The Lord once again begins addressing the **angel of the church**, which has special emphasis in the case of the church at Pergamum. The church at Pergamum, as will be shown, had a problem that required the execution of church discipline. Although Christ addresses each of these letters to the "angel" of the church (which has been argued to represent the pastor(s) of the churches; see comments on 1:20), it is particularly instructive that when a church stood in need of proper church discipline but failed in general to carry it out, Christ expected the pastor to take the responsibility to lead the church in that practice even if it went against their desires.[578]

The **church at Pergamum** (or sometimes *Pergamos* or *Pergamus*) was one of the younger congregations in Asia minor, only having been established in the mid-80's.[579] It was planted in the midst of a city which served as the political capital of Asia for over 250 years.[580] For Americans, one might consider the city of Ephesus as New York while Pergamum would be Washington, D.C. While it was not the largest city or even the wealthiest city, it was a greatly powerful city politically speaking. Pergamum was prominently known for two things. First, being a political capital in the era of Roman domination, it was known to have unrelenting emphasis on Emperor worship. In fact, it held an even lengthier history of Emperor worship than Smyrna, boasting of the oldest Imperial temple in the East.[581] Some have, consequently, said Pergamum was a political capital and a spiritual capital of Asia.[582] Because of its unshakable loyalty to Emperor and Rome, the city's government was granted such extensive freedom to operate that Rome bestowed on them "the right of the sword."[583] This endowed them with the power to execute people without formal approval by a Roman governor, a privilege they carried

---

[578] Koester, *Revelation*, 282.
[579] Schreiner, *Revelation* BECNT, 142.; Koester, *Revelation*, 286.
[580] Thomas, *Revelation 1-7*, 179.
[581] Thomas, *Revelation 1-7*, 179.
[582] Sweet, *Revelation*, 87.
[583] Justinian, *The Digest of Justinian*, Charles H. Monro, trans., 1:2:1. "Imperium is where an officer is in possession of the power of the sword for the purpose of punishing."; Koester, *Revelation*, 286.; Mounce, *Revelation*, 79.

out with frequency on those who refused emperor worship (which they deemed "high treason").[584]

The second thing Pergamum was known for as a city was its healing capacities through a combination of religious and medical practices. It would later become the birthplace of one of the most famous medical professionals of the time, Galen. Galen would become a personal friend of Emperor Marcus Aurelius, and would serve as the personal physician to his son and future Emperor, Commodus.[585] The city also housed what is rightly identified as one of the world's oldest medical schools with hundreds of apprentice doctors studying there year-round.[586] To accommodate these students, Pergamum constructed the second largest library in the world at its time, which boasted over 200,000 volumes.[587] The erudite reputation of the city extended back generations, as paper itself was created in Pergamum when papyrus from Egypt became scarce. The word "parchment" literally comes from the Greek name "Pergamum."[588]

One must understand, then, the atmosphere in which the church at Pergamum existed. Their city was one of fierce loyalty to paganism and the worship of a false-god, and the government of that city (which was intrinsically tied to this paganism) wielded unchecked power over the citizens, including the ability to execute dissidents at will. Beyond this, the culture was one of great pride and pomp. Not only was the idea of denying paganism politically inappropriate, but it was also likely considered anti-intellectual. In a city with a thriving medical school and a massive library, both full of individuals who affirmed pagan worship, to reject paganism would be to reject the advice of doctors, lawyers, teachers, and the most educated leaders of the day. As a result, those who failed to practice these pagan religions would have been considered not only unpatriotic or disloyal, but unintelligent, uneducated, uninformed, and unacademic. Some Christians (both in the present time and in those to come) will surely find this to be like looking in a mirror.

It is to these Christians that the omniscient One sends **the words of him who has the sharp two-edged sword.** As the point of this first section is the explanation of what has been seen (see comments on 1:19), Christ continues to reference those elements of His own appearance that John beheld, showing how those characteristics impact the

---

[584] Ladd, *Revelation*, 45.

[585] Richard Walzer, *Galen on Jews and Christians*, 9.

[586] For a wonderfully thorough and interactive exploration of the Asklepieion of Pergamon, make use of C.G. Williamson, "Heroes in the Asklepieion of Pergamon" via the University of Groningen. https://storymaps.arcgis.com/stories/2ec37fc9dff24ccf8ccf693b4a3f680c

[587] Koester, *Revelation,* 282.; Thomas, *Revelation 1-7*, 180.

[588] Everett Ferguson, *Backgrounds of Early Christianity*, 92.

churches. In this instance, the church at Pergamum is meant to understand that Christ's Word is a sharp and two-edged sword (1:16).[589] Why would they need to know this detail specifically?

There appear to be two primary reasons why the church at Pergamum needed to remember the sword-like quality of Christ's Word. First, as regards those outside of the church, they stood in need of reminding that Christ ultimately held the sword, not the government. Although the government of Pergamum had what they were told was "unchecked" authority over life and death, ultimately Christ is the one who holds such truly unchecked authority. In fact, He holds all authority over life and death, such that the government could never take the life of someone whom Christ has decided they are not to harm.[590] In this sense, the sword-like quality of the Word of Christ would serve as a great comfort to the church at Pergamum, as it should to all Christians everywhere.

Yet, there is a second reason why the church at Pergamum needed to recall the sharp two-edgedness of Christ's sword-like Word, and it is much more direct. The fact that Christ's Word cuts both-ways asserts that it will divide His people from those who despise His Word. When God's people hear His Word, they are "cut" by it in that it convicts them and causes them to repent, bowing in submission to God and seeking greater reconciliation to Him by greater conformation to it. When the enemies of Christ hear His word, they are also convicted by it, but they reject it, and often stiffen their necks in opposition to Him. They become so offended by His assertions of authority and His statements of their wrongdoing that they become more actively antagonistic to His purposes. Thus, as the Puritans were fond of saying, "the same Sun which melts the wax, hardens the clay."[591] The church at Pergamum needed to be clear about who they were. Evidently, as will be seen, they were much like the pagans around them.

[589] The Greek term John uses for sword (ῥομφαίαν) is also indicative of the symbolic nature of this "sword" since the usual word for sword is μάχαιρα (Rom. 13:4) and is sometimes used by John in instances wherein a literal sword would make more sense (Rev. 6:4;13:10;13:14). Sweet, *Revelation*, 88. J.A.D. Weima points out that the word ῥομφαίαν was occasionally used in secular sources to refer to a sword carried by soldiers, but Sweet notes that this was "very rare." J.A.D. Weima, *The Sermons to the Seven Churches of Revelation: A Commentary and Guide*, 93.

[590] The most prominent examples of this are found in the book of Daniel, specifically in 3:16-28 and 6:1-24.

[591] Though much older, this saying is attested in Charles H. Spurgeon, "The Lesson of the Almond Tree" *Metropolitan Tabernacle Pulpit* Vol. 46 (7 April 1881).

(2:13)

"'I know where you dwell, where Satan's throne is. Yet you hold fast my name, and you did not deny my faith even in the days of Antipas my faithful witness, who was killed among you, where Satan dwells."

"οἶδα ποῦ κατοικεῖς, ὅπου ὁ θρόνος τοῦ σατανᾶ, καὶ κρατεῖς τὸ ὄνομά μου καὶ οὐκ ἠρνήσω τὴν πίστιν μου καὶ ἐν ταῖς ἡμέραις Ἀντιπᾶς ὁ μάρτυς μου ὁ πιστός μου, ὃς ἀπεκτάνθη παρ' ὑμῖν, ὅπου ὁ σατανᾶς κατοικεῖ."

Curious as it may sound, Jesus begins speaking to the people of Pergamum by reminding them that he knows **where you dwell.** The word "dwell" identifies the place where they permanently reside.[592] This should give us great comfort, as we are reminded that regardless of where we are at any given moment, God is aware of our situation. Not only is He maintaining watch over us, but this watch extends even when we are in deeply evil and God-forsaken places, as Christ later refers to them as living **where Satan dwells.**

There is much speculation over the exact reference that Christ is making when He refers to the dwelling place of the Pegameans as being **where Satan's throne is.**[593] It would seem that this deals with both the political and spiritual allegiance of the city.[594] Politically, they were loyal to the Emperor with religious zeal, even to the point of offering religious worship and sacrifice to him. It has been said that worship of the emperor as divine "had been made the touchstone of civic loyalty under Domitian."[595] In every way except the physical, the people of Pergamum had sought to move the literal throne of the emperor of Rome into their city, and some have even said that Pergamum prefigured Constantinople in this way, serving as an Eastern "throne" for Roman and Satanic activity opposite the Western "throne" in the city of Rome.[596]

More compelling, however, is the likelihood that Christ refers to the city's medical professionals idolizing the false-god of healing, Asclepius.[597] An ancient geographer, Pausanias, described the temple of Asclepius, which held a 20-foot-tall ivory

---

[592] William Barclay, *The Revelation of John* I, 112.

[593] Early commentators speculated that "those persons are the throne of Satan whom he owns in wickedness." Tyconius, *Commentary on the Apocalypse*, 2:13. Quoted in Weinrich, ed., *Ancient Christian Commentary on Scripture* XII, 30.

[594] Ladd, *Revelation*, 46. Exegetically, the phrase "Satan's throne" (θρόνος τοῦ σατανᾶ) implies that "Satan controls and gives power to his throne." Thomas, *Revelation 1-7*, 182. Therefore, this throne might be one that is influenced by Satan, rather than being some manner of spiritual headquarters for Satan himself. Satanic by proxy if you will.

[595] Hampton J. Keathley III, *Studies in Revelation*, 63.

[596] Mounce, *Revelation*, 79.

[597] Sweet, *Revelation*, 87.

and gold statue of him "seated on a throne, grasping a staff, while holding his other hand over the head of the serpent."[598] As mentioned in the notes to verse 9, there is no "middle-ground" when it comes to the worship of deities or divine beings. One is either worshipping the one true God, or they are worshipping the Satanic and demonic. In the case of the people of Pergamum, their city god, Asclepius (sometimes *Asklepios*), was attributed with being a god of healing powers, which further encouraged the students at the medical school in town and therefore became integrated into "the heart of everything," but Christians understand that if there was any legitimacy to the spirituality surrounding Asclepius, it was not divine, but demonic.[599]

Early Christians saw Asclepius as a pagan attempt to take the healing powers of Jesus and attribute them to a made-up god of their own.[600] He was said to have given sight to the blind and to have made the lame able to walk. Justin Martyr points this out in his *First Apology*.[601] Later, in his *Dialogue with Trypho*, he writes of Asclepius, "When [Satan] brings forward Aescalapius (sic) as the raiser of the dead and the healer of all diseases, may I not say that in this matter likewise he has imitated the prophecies of Christ?"[602] Sometimes, Asclepius was even referred to by the title "Asclepius Soter" which literally translates out to "Asclepius [the] Savior."[603] Twentieth century German scholars often speculated that John's emphasis throughout his writings on the healing power of Jesus as well as His destruction of the Satanic are evidences that John himself was attempting to emphasize Christ's supremacy over Asclepius, and although this thought fell in popularity in the late portion of the century, it has recently been redefended.[604] The symbol of Asclepius, which was emblazoned on all that associated with him, was a serpent for several reasons. One reason was that each deity had an animal which it was

[598] Pausaniua, *Description of Greece*, 2:27:2. Quoted from *Pausanias' Description of Greece with an English Translation in Four Volumes,* W.H.S. Jones, trans.

[599] Jan Den Boeft, "Christ and Asklepios" *Euphrosyne* 25 (1997), 337. Importantly (for those interested in the dating of the book of Revelation), Sweet notes that "the cult of Asclepius only blossomed at the end of Domitian's reign." Sweet, *Revelation*, 87, n.5. This is affirmed by Boeft, "Christ and Asklepios", 339.

[600] See Clement of Alexandria, *Exhortation to the Heathen*, 4.; Athenagoras, *A Plea for the Christians*, 18,30.; Origen, *Contra Celsus,* 3:22-25, 42.

[601] Justin Martyr, *First Apology*, 22.

[602] Justin Martyr, *Dialogue with Trypho*, 69.

[603] Publius Aelius Aristides, *Orations,* 42:4. Quoted in *P. Aelius Aristides: The Complete Works* I, Charles A. Behr, trans., 425. See also J.B. Ward-Perkins, *Roman Imperial Architecture*, 277, 284.

[604] Karl H. Rengstorf, *Die Anfänge der Auseinandersetzung zwischen Christusglaube und Asklepiosfrömmigkeit* 30.; Erich Boehringer, *Altertümer von Pergamon* 8, 19-20. This thought, while rejected by Boeft outright, has been subsequently supported in such works as Robin Thompson, "Healing at the Pool of Bethesda: A Challenge to Asclepius?" *Bulletin for Biblical Research* 27:1 (2017): 65-84.

generally associated with anyway. Dionysus, for example, was sometimes referred to simply as "the bull."[605]

This shared symbolism caused great conflict with those of a Judeo-Christian culture, wherein the serpent was not a symbol of healing but the central symbol for evil, including Satan himself. Therefore, with Asclepius being the city god, taxes were collected for the funding of the practice of his worship, and Christians had moral qualms about giving money to pagan worship, especially when it was directly depicted by the very symbol for Satan. The pagans saw it as contributing to the public health, while Christians saw it as giving money directly to Satan. Evidently, God was sympathetic to their position, as Christ identifies this as the **throne** of **Satan** – a place where he has absolute rule and power. This was perhaps only undergirded by the strong connection that the city had with Rome and the Emperor cult, showing a complete dedication to paganism.

It was also true that they associated Asclepius with snakes since they often used serpents and venom in their medical practices. This symbol remains a staple in modern medical communities, as hospitals, ambulances, and even the World Health Organization are recognized by a symbol depicting a snake twisted around a staff – a symbol which undoubtedly derives from the massive statue of Asclepius in Pergamum previously described by Pausanias. The Hippocratic Oath, taken by medical professionals to this day, originally read, "I swear in the name of Apollo, Asclepius, Hugieia, and Panakeia, that I will do nothing harmful to the patient…"[606] It is clear, though, by the removal of the names of these ancient false-gods that to associate modern medical practices with those performed in this era is quite a reach. The line between medical and mystical was then quite transparent, as sick individuals would beg Asclepius' favor by feeding a snake, and then spend the night in a temple filled with roaming nonvenomous snakes.[607] It was considered a promise of a cure if one of the snakes touched you at any point in the night, as Asclepius, it was said, incarnated as a snake.[608]

Beyond the worship and commitment to Satan was the fact that those who did such things wielded the power to execute anyone who refused. In light of this, the Christians in Pergamum are commended by Christ, who says, **you hold fast my name, and you did not deny my faith even in the days of Antipas my faithful witness, who**

---

[605] Thomas, *Revelation 1-7*, 179.

[606] Farnell, *Greek Hero Cults*, 269.

[607] Thomas, *Revelation 1-7*, 179.

[608] William Barclay, *Letters to the Seven Churches*, 43.; Lewis R. Farnell, *Greek Hero Cults and Ideas of* Immortality, 240.

was killed among you, where Satan dwells. The reality of martyrdom was not only something they had heard of or even witnessed, it was something that had occurred in their own congregation. History tells us that Antipas was the pastor (or bishop) of the church at Pergamum, with some indicating that he was only the second pastor of the church, following Gaius whom John knew personally (3 John 1).[609] Once again, John's personal relationship with the churches of Asia minor shines through, as this detail must have passed through his hand with great care and love, remembering the men who previously led this church.

It is worthy of mentioning, although perhaps only in passing, that once again Christ uses an emphatic term for "hold" when He describes how they **hold fast my name.** Rather than the standard word for possession that He has used previously (ἔχω; 1:16), He uses the word κρατεῖς (from the root κρατέω as in 2:14) which asserts a strong hold of firm commitment and grip. This guides readers and listeners to understand that their faith is not a passive or loosely held one, but a firm commitment – as evidenced by the fact that they **did not deny** the faith **even in the days of Antipas.**

Antipas was **killed among** his people, there in Pergamum **where Satan dwells.**[610] It is not all that clear whether he is called a **faithful witness** *because* he was martyred (the Greek word *martyr* being identical in the Greek with the modern word *witness* as reflected in the KJV) or whether he was martyred *because* he was a faithful witness. Koester argues that "death [is] the culmination of witness" which would seem to combine the concepts, forming a synthesis in which a person is a *witness* until they produce their final *witness* by becoming a *martyr*.[611] Christ identifies Himself by this same title earlier in 1:5, and certainly both are true of Him. In any case, this sets a precedent which is worth maintaining throughout the book of Revelation, which is that the word "witness" seems to represent those members of God's people who are persecuted for their faithfulness to God's Word and will.

The martyrdom of Antipas occurred in AD 92, and was marked by particular heinousness.[612] He was killed in a torture devise now known as the "Brazen Bull" wherein a person was locked inside a life-sized bull made of bronze, which would then

609 Otto F.A. Mainardus, "The Christian Remains of the Seven Churches of the Apocalypse" *The Biblical Archaeologist* 37:3 (September 1974), 76.

610 This precise phrasing is used by Tertullian in one of the only extra-biblical references to Antipas. Tertullian, *Scorpiace*, 12.

611 Koester, *Revelation*, 287.

612 Godefridus Henschenius and Daniel Papebrochius, *Acta Sanctorum der Bollandisten*, April 2.

have a fire kindled beneath the stomach.[613] The engineer who built the bull had also installed a series of musical pipes which led to the mouth and nose of the bull from within. As a result, the screams and wails of the person being roasted alive came out of the bull as sounds very similar to the groaning of a bull.[614] Due to the nature of this execution, the bones of those executed would remain within after their demise. Because of the manner of their death, their bones would be very smooth and shiny, causing many of the executioners to harvest the bones and make decorative jewelry out of them for resale. Numerous Christians are said to have endured this death, Antipas included.[615]

(2:14-15)

> "But I have a few things against you: you have some there who hold the teaching of Balaam, who taught Balak to put a stumbling block before the sons of Israel, so that they might eat food sacrificed to idols and practice sexual immorality. So also you have some who hold the teaching of the Nicolaitans."
>
> "ἀλλ' ἔχω κατὰ σοῦ ὀλίγα ὅτι ἔχεις ἐκεῖ κρατοῦντας τὴν διδαχὴν Βαλαάμ, ὃς ἐδίδασκεν τῷ Βαλὰκ βαλεῖν σκάνδαλον ἐνώπιον τῶν υἱῶν Ἰσραὴλ φαγεῖν εἰδωλόθυτα καὶ πορνεῦσαι. οὕτως ἔχεις καὶ σὺ κρατοῦντας τὴν διδαχὴν [τῶν] Νικολαΐτῶν ὁμοίως."

If they were encouraged by the commendations from Christ, they must have been equally terrified by the fact that He said He had **a few things against** them. To the church in Ephesus He had said he had one thing against them. To the church in Smyrna, nothing was said in critique. Here, Christ has a list of complaints. The first is that they **have some... who hold the teaching of Balaam.** Again, the use of different terms for possession is instructive. Christ says that he "has" (ἔχω) a few things against them, first being that they "have" (ἔχεις) some who *hold* (κρατοῦντας) the teaching of Balaam. This last word differs from the previous two in root, coming instead from the same root as that used in Christ's previous commendation to them. In the exact same way that the

---

[613] Georgius Cedrenus, *Corpus Scriptorum Historiae* Byzantinae, 566. "Bos aereus Pegamo fuit allatus. Caminus fuit, in qua ustus est Antipas sanctus martyr." Cedrenus (often *Kedrenos*) was a 12th Century historian who recorded here what was also reported by Symeon Metaphrastes in the 10th Century, who carried forward the words of Andreas of Caesarea in the 6th Century, who had read the first-hand record of the martyrdom of Antipas handed down since the time of Tertullian in the 2nd Century. While the recorded martyrdom Andreas read is no longer extant, there is no reason to believe that his report, or Symeon's, or Cedrenus' were in any way incorrect. Once more, the only reason for recent denials of the legitimacy of this account is because it also records that this martyrdom occurred in the year AD 92 under Emperor Domitian. Once more, advocates for an early date of Revelation are required to deny centuries of established history to maintain their position – so they do.

[614] Mark Donnelly and Daniel Diehl, *The Big Book of Pain: Torture and Punishment Through History*, 56.

[615] Victoria Gerhold, "The Legend of Euphratas" *Dumbarton Oaks Papers* 74 (2020), 86.

church leadership seemed to "hold" to Christ's name, there were some in their churches who (with equal commitment and fortitude) **"hold"** to the teaching of Balaam. This will only grow worse in the verse 15, as there are still others who **hold** (same Greek root) to **the teaching of the Nicolaitans.**[616]

What is meant by **the teaching of Balaam**? He specifically notes that Balaam **taught Balak to put a stumbling block before the sons of Israel.** This refers to an Old Testament event in Numbers 25:1-5 (summarized in Num. 31:16) wherein Balaam (a pagan seer) convinced Midianite women to intermarry with Israelite men, which in turn led to the Israelite men allowing the Midianites to keep their false religion. The plan succeeded, and God's people (having compromised on God's Word) ultimately did not fulfill His command and were repeatedly led astray from God's path. Consequently, Balaam became a name for all who would promote compromise with false-religions or sinful practices for the sake of peace. Robert Thomas goes so far as to identify Balaam as "the father of religious syncretism."[617] Ladd (and Mounce after him) calls Balaam "a prototype of those who promote compromise with paganism…" or "a prototype of all corrupt teachers who betrayed believers into fatal compromise with worldly ideologies.[618] The Apostle Peter refers to those like him as being those whose loyalty can be bought (2 Pet. 2:15).[619]

Hence, when Christ says that there are some who **hold to the teaching of Balaam**, He clarifies in what way they are compromising with the world for the sake of peace by saying they have done so in order that **they might eat food sacrificed to idols and practice sexual immorality.** While there are many possible applications of this practice, the most easily recognized was that of the Imperial cult.[620] The regular practice upon arrival at the temple was to make a sacrifice which would then be consumed by the worshippers, who would then be given the opportunity to sleep with temple prostitutes who were expected to improve the fertility of the worshippers. Evidently, members of the church at Pergamum had so compromised with their surrounding culture that some had

---

[616] Thomas, *Revelation 1-7*, 189.

[617] Thomas, *Revelation 1-7*, 190. Thomas summarizes the error of Balaam as the teaching that God's people should "relax their principles the way Balaam did" when he used his prophetic gift for sinful purposes to benefit Balak.

[618] Ladd, *Revelation*, 47.; Mounce, *Revelation*, 81.

[619] See also Jude 11.

[620] The Greek term for "sacrificed to idols" (εἰδωλόθυτα) was a Christian neologism used to pejoratively refer to the sacrifices made by Roman worshippers. The Romans referred to their sacrifices as *theothyta* (*sacrificed to gods*) but the Christians referred to these same sacrifices as *eidōlothyta* (*sacrificed to idols*) indicating that the Roman "gods" were not gods, but only idols. Koester, *Revelation*, 288.

affirmed or even begun participating in the pagan sacrifices and sexual practices of their worship.[621]

It is possible that one might have argued, "The idols are fake and the Lord knows my heart, that my worship here is purely for social purposes. I know there is nothing legitimate here, nor any God but the Lord, and as long as I maintain that truth, this practice is nothing." But God asserts quite the inverse here. He reprimands this on an actional basis first. He is offended that they would **eat food sacrificed to idols and practice sexual immorality** regardless of the supposed "intentions of their heart" or any proposed sufficient causes for it. In this is an important first lesson, which is that Christians are not allowed to compromise on the truth of the Gospel (even feigningly) for the sake of living at peace with the world. This is, notably, the inverse to Islam, which has a law known as *Taqiyya*, permitting adherents to both directly deny their faith when they feel endangered and behave in ways that are intended to mislead onlookers into thinking they are not Muslim when they feel it would be "prudential."[622] Christians, as shown in this instance, do not get to deny the name of Christ or engage in pagan practices because it is "prudential" for them to do so.[623]

But God is not finished reprimanding them. He does not stop at simply reprimanding them for their actions, but goes on to reprimand them for the beliefs which undergirded them, calling them out for having **some who hold the teaching of the Nicolaitans.** As previously mentioned, this **hold** they have is one of firm commitment. The teaching of the Nicolaitans (discussed in the notes on 2:6) could be summed up quickly as this: Individuals can (and should) find the truth that works for them, and therefore, each person should seek out what works best for them regardless of scriptural, apostolic, or traditional teachings. So, while some might have held to the teachings of Christ while practicing the pagan traditions of the Roman Imperial cult, others evidently did the inverse, believing in some other form of worship (or god) while feigning allegiance to Christ by maintaining a presence in the church at Pergamum. It is also possible that a third group existed which participated in pagan worship, not because they believed in it, but because their friends and family members did.

---

[621] It is also possible this alludes to spiritual unfaithfulness – a theme frequently referred to by sexual reference in Revelation. The children of Israel were referred to as "whoring with the daughters of Moab" in their spiritual unfaithfulness in the time of Balaam (Num. 25:1-3). See Sweet, *Revelation*, 89; or Thomas, *Revelation 1-7*, 192.

[622] Etan Kohlberg, "Taqiyya in Shi'i Theology and Religion," in *Secrecy and Concealment: Studies in the History of Mediterranean and Near Eastern Religions*, ed. Hans G. Kippenberg and Guy G. Stroumsa, 345-346.

[623] Paul addressed this very error in 1 Corinthians 10:21, and perhaps engaged the same problem (eating and drinking as part of pagan sacrifices and then taking part in Christian worship; 1 Cor. 7:7-13). Ladd, *Revelation*, 47.

This sort of behavior is very familiar to modern Christians, as many of us have friends and family members who are not Christians, and this sometimes leads to us not living up to our Christian commitments to make them feel more comfortable. Other times, we have friends and family who claim to be Christians, but who live in unrelenting and unrepentant sin, and oftentimes we turn a blind eye, not telling them of the sinfulness of their life and practice for one reason or another. The Christians at Pergamum were no different than those who accept practicing homosexuals into their churches, or those who ignore the heterosexual couple clearly living in sin together. They adapted their religion to the culture so as to maintain social currency. Some participated in the sin with their friends and family members, while others simply consented to it behind the guise of some idea that what is true for them may not be true for others. They accepted multiple types of heretics in their ranks.[624] How does Christ address such a people?

(2:16)

> "Therefore repent. If not, I will come to you soon and war against them with the sword of my mouth."
>
> "μετανόησον οὖν· εἰ δὲ μή, ἔρχομαί σοι ταχὺ καὶ πολεμήσω μετ' αὐτῶν ἐν τῇ ῥομφαίᾳ τοῦ στόματός μου."

Christ calls this people to **repent.**[625] He does not tell them that there is some room for this if they will simply refine their practices. He calls them to absolutely repent. There seems to be some degree of acknowledgement that they may not want to do so because of the cost of repenting, so Christ produces a cost which will be paid **if** they do **not** repent: **I will come to you soon and war against them with the sword of my mouth.** The sword which Christ emphasized in the first verse to this church is recalled, and rather than serving as a source of encouragement, it serves here as a threat. What more harrowing threat could there be than to have Christ say that His Word, which serves as a lamp unto our feet and a light unto our path, could be turned against us as the weapon with which He brings war on us? He even emphasizes the immediacy with which He expects them to repent by saying He will **come to you *soon.***[626] Christ does not wait for us to finish our sinful business before expecting us to act in accordance with His

---

[624] Thomas, *Revelation 1-7*, 188.

[625] The form of this word "repent" (μετανόησον; singular) indicates that the repentance expected is not of the several groups individually but is expected of the whole church collectively. The leaders must repent of their failure to execute church discipline just as those idolaters, sexual deviants, and heretics must repent of their errors. Sweet, *Revelation*, 90.

[626] See notes on 2:5 regarding the "coming" Jesus refers to in these passages.

command. There is no room for "one last time" with Christ. He calls His people to repent immediately.

It should be noted, however, that Christ says if the church does not repent, He will come to "you" and **war against *them*.** What is being said here pertains directly to church discipline.[627] The leaders at the church at Pergamum were commended for firmly holding to the name of Christ, even through persecution, but for one reason or another, they had not done their job maintaining the purity of their congregations (quite the inverse of the Ephesian church). One might imagine that they had not performed church discipline on those worshipping in pagan ways or living in sexual promiscuity because they loved them. They suffered from precisely the inverse issue as the church at Ephesus, who had cast out false teachers but forgotten love.[628] So, Christ reminds these Christians that if they will not discipline those living sinfully among their church (which is a means of grace intended to restore a Christian to right relationship with God through punishment) then Christ will come and **war against** those living in sin in their congregation.

It is the love of the Christians at Pergamum which is to motivate them to execute church discipline on their friends and loved ones, because in so doing, they would deliver them from the wrath of Christ which would quickly come if they did not repent. The Christians, then, were called not to be tolerant for the sake of love, but to be direct with those living in sin amongst them for the sake of love. And how loving Christ is in this moment! Hypocrites and heretics alike will be forgiven by Christ if they will only repent![629]

It is true that the wicked were expected not to go on living in sin while carrying the name of Christ, but to repent of their sin for the sake of the name of Christ. Christ calls all men to do what is difficult, in love, because of love, for the sake of God who loves us but will not by any means clear the guilty (Exodus 34:7). Simultaneously, God, in His great love, stretches out His hands all day long to a disobedient and contrary people. If we will but turn from our wicked ways and return to the Lord, our God will abundantly pardon.

---

[627] Mounce puts it directly, "Only a portion of the church has fallen prey to the pernicious doctrine of the Balaamites, but all are guilty of not taking action against their presence." Mounce, *Revelation*, 82. See also Thomas, *Revelation 1-7*, 192.

[628] Mounce, *Revelation*, 82.

[629] Koester, *Revelation*, 289.

(2:17)

> "He who has an ear, let him hear what the Spirit says to the churches. To the one who conquers I will give some of the hidden manna, and I will give him a white stone, with a new name written on the stone that no one knows except the one who receives it.'"

> "Ὁ ἔχων οὖς ἀκουσάτω τί τὸ πνεῦμα λέγει ταῖς ἐκκλησίαις. Τῷ νικῶντι δώσω αὐτῷ τοῦ μάννα τοῦ κεκρυμμένου καὶ δώσω αὐτῷ ψῆφον λευκήν, καὶ ἐπὶ τὴν ψῆφον ὄνομα καινὸν γεγραμμένον ὃ οὐδεὶς οἶδεν εἰ μὴ ὁ λαμβάνων."

Christ again calls to those who have **an ear**, calling them to **hear what the Spirit says to the churches.**[630] With this call comes a promise, like the promises which conclude the other letters, which is in essence a promise of eternal life. He assures **the one who conquers** that He will be given **some of the hidden manna.** The usage of this image is particularly interesting, given the previous mention of Balaam. In the time of Balaam, the Israelites were dependent on manna for life. Elsewhere in John's writings (John 6:48-51), Christ had identified Himself as the "true bread from heaven." (John 6:32) In short, Jesus identified Himself as the substance that the shadow of the manna in the Old Testament had depicted.[631] So, here, Christ (in a masterfully poetic way) has referred to the Old Testament instance in which the Israelites (who relied on manna for life) had been led astray by Balaam, and then He promises that if they will **conquer** (that is, to maintain faithful perseverance through to the end) He will **give** them **some of the hidden manna** (which is Himself). Altogether, Christ might well have simply given them an ultimatum: Choose, Balaam or Me.

He then gives another reference, saying **I will give him a white stone, with a new name written on the stone that no one knows except the one who receives it.** There has been no small amount of speculation over what precisely this refers to, but the most likely case is that for what was known as a *tesserae*.[632] A *tesserae* was a small token which indicated that someone was a member of a certain tribe or group – often granting special rights, entitlements, or admission to restricted areas.[633]

Rubina Raja, an expert on *tesserae*, writes that in the era of John's writing and well-beyond it,

---

[630] See notes on 2:7.

[631] This interpretation is widely accepted and has been since ancient times. See Andrew of Caesarea, *Commentary on the Apocalypse*, 2:17.

[632] Mounce, *Revelation*, 83. Also Sweet, *Revelation*, 90. Sweet simply refers to this stone as a "ticket of admission."

[633] William Smith, *Dictionary of Greek and Roman Antiquity*, 550.

> The *tesserae* functioned as entrance tickets to religious banquets, which were hosted by priests, both as individuals and as groups, which is clear from the inscriptions that often state names of priests or groups of priests and the deity to whom they dedicated the banquet.[634]

When given, the giver would say something along the lines of, "Henceforth, you and anyone with whom you share this tile will be welcomed in my home."[635] Christ, then, offers to those who **conquer** to invite them into His banquet, which carries with it irrevocable access to His own home as well. In Revelation 19:9, it is proclaimed, "Blessed are those who are *invited* to the marriage supper of the Lamb." If this is the reference that Christ is making, it is nothing short of a promise of one's being blessed by God with salvation and participation in the marriage supper of the Lamb.

This also sheds beautiful light on the meaning of the **new name written on the stone that no one knows except the one who receives it.** The Greek word rendered "new" (καινὸν) does not necessarily assert that the thing did not previously exist. Rather, it asserts new in the sense of quality – one might use the word "fresh" or "untarnished." It does not seem that Christ will give us new names, such that "Jonathan" will now be "Isaac."[636] Instead, it seems that Christ will give us a new name which carries with it none of the baggage that our present name carries. All of the sins and faults, mistakes and failures that we have committed which are tied to our names for the length of our lives will not be remembered in eternity because rather than having our identity in ourselves, our identity will be entirely wrapped up in the person and work of Christ. In John's era, it was the name of the priest or the god to be worshipped which was written on the *tesserae*. On the stone that Christ promises to give His people, there is only one name. The name of the High Priest who Himself is the God to be worshipped – Jesus Christ.

This is why He can say that **no one knows** this new name **except the one who receives it.** Individuals do not understand the glory of the name of Jesus Christ until they have personally received it. Christ promises to write His own name on His redeemed people (Rev. 3:12). Of course, this is true of those who have conquered, but is it not also true of those of us who have **received** Christ that we presently walk in the newness of life (Rom. 6:4)? This *new* name is a name without any sin, baggage, debt, or guilt. It is *new* in the sense that we shall be *new* (Philippians 3:21) and in the sense that

---

[634] Rubina Raja, "In and Out of Contexts: Explaining Religious Complexity through the Banqueting Tesserae from Palmyra" *Religion in the Roman Empire* 2:3 (2016), 347.
[635] Bruce Herman, "Making and Breaking: Art, Hospitality, and Eucharist" *Boisi Center for Religion and American Public Life* (2016), 3.
[636] Although there are Scriptures that might lend to this idea as well, such as Isaiah 62:2 and 65:15.

the Heavens and Earth shall be *new* in the *New Age*. But J.P.M. Sweet perfectly sums it up, saying, "New (*kainos*) means new in quality, belonging to the New Age, which for the Christian is already here (cf. 2 Cor. 5:17)."[637] As will be shown in Rev. 14:1, the people of God, alive in this world, bear the name and mark of Jesus Christ right now. They will maintain that name into the eternal state, only to find it even more meaningful, more satisfying, and more rewarding than ever before. What was partially experienced in this world in the "new name" by which God called us when He asserted ownership over us (Is. 43:1) in our presently experienced "new creation" will be fully experienced in the culminated "new creation" in the end when our faith is made sight.

The citizens of Pergamum might have recalled something very close to home in this statement. Centuries before, Zoroastrians from Babylon had fled West seeking refuge in times of strife and had found solace in Pergamum. Their high priest was recognized under the name "Pontifex Maximus" or "the Supreme Bridge-Builder." He was assumed to be the one who bridged mortals and the spiritual realm.[638] Naturally, when the city surrendered fully to Roman rule and religiously embraced Emperor worship, they carried this title forward as it was then a title also held by the highest ranking Roman priest – and would later be assumed by the Emperor himself.[639] Thus, this concept of names carrying religious weight for generation after generation was one that the people of Pergamum were deeply familiar with in their pagan atmosphere. The setting aside of such names and titles in exchange for a new name of the true Pontifex Maximus would, for them, carry with it all the religious weight and beauty, absent the pagan heritage.[640] Let us praise God that there is not a man born of woman, save Christ alone, who can bear the name Pontifex Maximus, and yet, Christ bears this name, and because of His bridging the gap between ourselves and God, He has promised to write a new, untarnished name on all of His people – indeed, His own new name (cf. 3:12; 19:12).

What, then, is the ultimate lesson for the modern church as gleaned from the church at Pergamum? Do not compromise for the sake of safety or comfort. Whether it means losing friends or family members, leaving behind cultural ties and traditions which have been maintained for generations, or losing our very lives, God's people simply cannot compromise on His commands, lest we forfeit our invitation to the wedding feast, our new name, and our receiving the bread of life – Jesus Christ.

---

[637] Sweet, *Revelation*, 91. Mounce almost exactly copies this statement, although without citation. Mounce, *Revelation*, 83.

[638] Keathley III, *Studies in Revelation*, 63.

[639] Gary Forsythe, *A Critical History of Early Rome: From Prehistory to the First Punic War*, 136.

[640] It must not go unsaid that this title is still carried forward by pagans worshipping a man as a god today. May they quit their error and see Jesus Christ as the only bridge (pontifex) between God and man.

(2:18-29) *Thyatira: The False-Teaching Church*

(2:18)

"And to the angel of the church in Thyatira write: 'The words of the Son of God, who has eyes like a flame of fire, and whose feet are like burnished bronze."

"Καὶ τῷ ἀγγέλῳ τῆς ἐν Θυατείροις ἐκκλησίας γράψον· Τάδε λέγει ὁ υἱὸς τοῦ θεοῦ, ὁ ἔχων τοὺς ὀφθαλμοὺς αὐτοῦ ὡς φλόγα πυρὸς καὶ οἱ πόδες αὐτοῦ ὅμοιοι χαλκολιβάνῳ·"

The letter to the church of Thyatira is one of the most pertinent letters for modern readers to hear and apply.[641] It addresses several issues which are highly contemplated and debated, and from the outset the letter assumes that it is **the angel of the church** (that is, the pastor of each local congregation; see comments on 1:20) who will help guide his people through these complicated issues. Pastors of the modern day must learn from those who have tragically failed and refuse to forfeit their place as arbiters of truth in eras of confusion.[642]

The city of **Thyatira** is widely considered to be the least prominent city to have received a letter from Christ.[643] Unlike those which preceded and followed it, Thyatira served as the capital of nothing, it had no major temple to which pilgrimages would be made, it had no major architectural spectacles, no major port, and was home to no major industry. It was fortunate to have Roman help in reconstruction following an earthquake in AD 25.[644] In response they constructed a series of dedications to Augustus as a son of the gods, which likely contributed to their later receiving favor from Vespasian and Domitian in the form of road maintenance.[645] The primary occupation of those living in the city was trading (especially slave trading), a job which depended not on individuals settling in the city, but on people passing through the city with different needs and interests all the time. There was no manufacturing hub, as nothing was created in the

---

[641] Some historicists have argued that this church represents the era of the Catholic Church in full power, but that would seem much more aligned with the previous church. See notes on 2:17. Newell, *Revelation*, 53. Others, especially in the early church, found meaning in the name "Thyatira" (*for sacrifice*). Weinrich, *ACCS* XII, 34.

[642] Weinrich, *ACCS* XII, 35. Quoting Caesarius of Arles, *Exposition of the Apocalypse* 2:20:2. Caesarius believes the central thought taken from this letter is that Christ desires for "the leaders of the churches... to impose the severity of ecclesiastical discipline upon the extravagant and the fornicator and those who do whatever other kind of evil."

[643] Ladd, *Revelation*, 49.

[644] Seutonius, *The Lives of the Twelve Caesars*, 126.

[645] Koester, *Revelation*, 295.

city. It was purely a city of receiving and trading.[646] As such, it was a city which could easily have been overlooked or forgotten.

However, Christ did not forget the Christian church at **Thyatira**. In fact, to this congregation living in an almost forgotten or unremarkable city, Jesus sent the longest letter of all.[647] This manifests a valuable lesson, which is that Jesus Christ does not value His churches (or the individuals who make up these congregations) on the basis of their size, income, location, potential, or history. A church plant in the rural backwoods of West Virginia or Montana is just as valuable as a megachurch in downtown Atlanta or Los Angeles. The Christians only freshly walking in the Christian faith are of equal concern to Christ as the 70-year veteran of the faith. The Christian languishing in poverty on the streets of Visakhapatnam are just as important as the wealthy Christian awakening each morning to automatically opening curtains in a suite in Paris.

In fact, Christ reminds them that these are **the words of the Son of God, who has eyes like a flame of fire.** Although they may have felt that they were unimportant or forgotten, generally overlooked by anyone of prestige, Jesus wants them to know that they are seen by the **Son of God**. This title was popularly applied to Augustus in Thyatira (and by the time of this letter had been applied to Tiberius, Titus, and Domitian), so Christ uses their familiarity with the prestige of this title illegitimately applied to those who would usurp God's glory to assert His own legitimate glory which He will later say is given to Him by God (2:27).[648] Having established that He is truly the most prestigious man to ever live, He reminds them that He is intimately aware of their situation, having eyes which "discern all things."[649] He recalls the attribute of Himself first mentioned in 1:14, to remind them that He sees everything, including their humble estate. [650] Soon, He will show them that He is not only aware of the details of their humility, but also of the details of their sin – a terrifying reality for all to be mindful of.

He also calls their attention to an attribute of Himself which speaks not to His knowledge of their holiness (or lack thereof), but which speaks to His own holiness and solidarity. He reminds them that He has **feet... like burnished bronze.** Interestingly, this is strikingly similar to the description made of the heavenly being whom Daniel saw (Dan. 10:6) and may even be paired with His naming Himself the "Son of God" in an effort to call to mind the furnace scene of Daniel 3 – given that this is the only time in

[646] The only Biblical figure from Thyatira is Lydia who converts under the preaching of Paul at Philippi (Acts 16:14), and her trade shows the usual practice of citizens of this city, as she "sold purple cloth."
[647] Colin J. Hemer, *The Letters to the Seven Churches of Asia in their Local Setting*, 106.
[648] Koester, *Revelation*, 298.
[649] Weinrich, *ACCS* XII, 34. Quoting Apringius of Beja, *Tractate on the Apocalpyse*, 2:18.
[650] Mounce, *Revelation*, 85.

the Revelation that Jesus is explicitly called the "Son of God."[651] This Christ from whom they receive a letter is one who does not change. If ever there has been a person who was reliable; if ever there has been a person who was dependable to stay the same, it is Jesus Christ (Heb. 13:8). Each of these attributes, Christ's omniscience and immutability, will come into play as He speaks to the Christians of Thyatira.

(2:19)

> "'I know your works, your love and faith and service and patient endurance, and that your latter works exceed the first."
>
> "οἶδά σου τὰ ἔργα καὶ τὴν ἀγάπην καὶ τὴν πίστιν καὶ τὴν διακονίαν καὶ τὴν ὑπομονήν σου, καὶ τὰ ἔργα σου τὰ ἔσχατα πλείονα τῶν πρώτων."

The pertinence of His having such omniscience is immediately brought to light as He opens with the truth that He **knows their works**. Though their daily lives may have seemed to them and to others around them as of little ultimate value, Jesus was as aware and familiar with their works as He was with anyone else's. In detailing their works, He appears to lay out a series of cause-and-effects which their works manifested. The **love** seems to have fortified their **faith**, and their **faith** served to fortify their commitment to **service**, and their commitment to **service** served to fortify their **patient endurance.** It is quite difficult to give up on a cause when someone else's well-being depends on you. For the people of Thyatira, their endurance was the result of the fact that they served others; and this service proceeded from their shared faith; and this shared faith was a product of love for one another and for God. This is a template of a healthy church (1 John 4:20; James 2:14-20).

Beyond the good works that Christ knows them to do, He even commends them for the fact **that your latter works exceed the first**. One could take this statement two ways: successively or sequentially. It could be that Christ means by this statement that the latter work *listed* (patient endurance) is greater than the first work (love), but while Christ repeats over and over the value of patient endurance it does seem odd that He would commend them for something that He criticized the Ephesians church for (faithful endurance at the expense of love). Thus, it would appear that the sequential understanding is more likely, meaning that Christ commends them for the fact that at present they are more loving, more faithful, more service oriented, more patient in enduring hardship than they were when they first began as a church.[652] Every pastor

---

[651] Sweet, *Revelation*, 93.

[652] Koester, *Revelation*, 298. Koester boldly translates it, "the works you have done most recently."

should shutter at this commendation. Are our churches more loving, faithful, service oriented, and patiently enduring hardship than when they began?

(2:20)

> "But I have this against you, that you tolerate that woman Jezebel, who calls herself a prophetess and is teaching and seducing my servants to practice sexual immorality and to eat food sacrificed to idols."
>
> "ἀλλ' ἔχω κατὰ σοῦ ὅτι ἀφεῖς τὴν γυναῖκα Ἰεζάβελ, ἡ λέγουσα ἑαυτὴν προφῆτιν καὶ διδάσκει καὶ πλανᾷ τοὺς ἐμοὺς δούλους πορνεῦσαι καὶ φαγεῖν εἰδωλόθυτα."

And yet, as Christ has in previous cases, He begins unfolding the meat of His "criticism sandwich" which has praise on either end of the critique. In the case of the church at Thyatira, He had **this against you, that you tolerate that woman Jezebel**. The trend developing in these letters is hard to miss. The church at Ephesus was commended for refusing to tolerate false teachers, the church at Pergamum was reprimanded for tolerating false teachers, and now the church at Thyatira is reprimanded for tolerating false teachers. While there are different things to praise about churches, Christ seems to have a consistent and careful eye on the pulpit. He has said nothing thus far about the amount of money a church brings in, or how many converts they make – but He has repeatedly addressed who they are putting up in front of His people to speak. Churches of the modern day should take heed – Christ will hold us accountable for who we allow to get up and speak in His churches. Ladd even notes that the people of Thyatira "recognized the presence of the false prophetess; they recognized also the evil character of her teaching, but they tolerantly refused to deal with her."[653] It would seem that the *avoid* aspect is the key step in Romans 16:17, but the Christians of Thyatira were content to simply "watch."

In their specific case, they tolerated a **woman** Christ identifies with the name **Jezebel**, who **called herself a prophetess**. It is highly unlikely that the woman in question was actually named "Jezebel" as this name was already a name of infamy in the time of the first century.[654] Jezebel had assumed the authority of her equally wicked husband Ahab, then-king of Israel nearly 1000 years prior to John's writing Revelation. One of the first things she did was remove all of the prophets of God (1 Kings 18:4, 13) so that she could control the religious teaching of the Israelites herself. Even after God's

---

[653] Ladd, *Revelation*, 51.

[654] Andrew of Caesarea theorized that the "Jezebel" referred to here was indeed not even a person, but a heresy figuratively so-called. Andrew of Caesarea, *Commentary on the Apocalypse,* Eugenia Scarvelis Constantinou, trans., 70.

manifesting His power over her, she only further vowed to kill the last of those who would stand in defiance of her in the name of God (1 Kings 19:3-8). She manifested this same degree of outlandish defiance of any authority other than her own in her marriage, as she tongue-lashed her husband as a weak man before circumventing him, murdering their neighbor, and taking whatever she wanted (1 Kings 21:1-16). Her final end was death by being thrown out a window, later to be eaten by wild dogs (2 Kings 9:30-37). Because of all this, her legacy was cemented as one of infamy (see 2 Kings 9:22).

Obviously, no parent would name their daughter after such a monstrous woman any more than a modern parent would name their son "Hitler." The attribution of this name to the woman in the church at Thyatira, then, appears to be a move by Christ towards labelling her character. It seems that the church at Thyatira had been allowing a woman to stand and prophesy to them, as she **calls herself a prophetess.** Notice, nobody ordained her; God did not call her; she rests strictly on her own testimony as a prophetess without any other confirmation – "***she calls herself.***" This is a trademark introduction to a false-teacher: They rarely have anyone who tells them that they ought to be teaching, and rarely will they be able to justify their supposed calling from the Word of God.

What is meant by the fact that she **calls herself a prophetess**? In general, prophesying in the New Testament refers to two acts: foretelling and forthtelling.[655] The first is future-prediction, which is what most people think of when they hear "prophet." It was a very serious thing to claim, as the punishment for being a false-prophet was death (Deut. 18:20). The second form of prophecy is preaching the Word of God as already known. In truth, it would not be incorrect to call preachers and pastors "prophets" or to say that they have the gift of "prophecy" given that they stand and exposit the Word of God as delivered down through the ages. In regards to this woman, Jezebel, it is not altogether clear which form of prophecy she was practicing, but in either case, she was being permitted to stand before the church and declare what she claimed to be the Word of God.

The problem with this woman is twofold in that she [1] **calls herself a prophetess** and [2] **is teaching and seducing my servants to practice sexual immorality and to eat food sacrificed to idols.** Not only is this woman usurping authority that is not hers to have by standing and proclaiming herself as a prophetess (when she truly was not), but she is going further in teaching false and sinful things.[656]

---

[655] Ladd contends for a third category of prophecy which operated before the widespread availability of the Canon of Scripture, but it is hard to defend his position without first assuming it. Ladd, *Revelation*, 51.

[656] Koester points out that there is some reason for maintaining the place of female prophetesses in the early church according to Luke 2:36; Acts 21:9; and 1 Cor. 11:5, while also recognizing the other restrictions on

The church at Thyatira is to address both of these errors, first *that* she is teaching, and second, *what* she is teaching.[657] The correction for their error would follow that order, as they would first remove her from teaching or leading, and then they would correct all of her false teachings.

How she came to be such a successful teacher in the church in the first place derives most likely from the situation of those living in the city. As previously mentioned, the primary occupation in the city was trading, and as a result, most of those in the city were aligned with one another in guilds (somewhat like modern unions with marked differences). These guilds would hold meetings not unlike modern conventions.[658] At these conventions, they would have meals based around food which had been sacrificed to the city god, Apollo Tyrimnos.[659] This city god was claimed to have merged with the latest Caesar, both of whom would then be considered the son of Zeus. As referenced in the notes on 2:14, the Imperial cult regularly offered temple prostitutes who were to serve the worshippers as a part of the service.

It appears that this Jezebel figure was, by her preaching, convincing individuals within the church that they could maintain their business associations with others in the guilds, even going to and participating in these "conventions" or festivals which included eating idolatrous food and participating in sexual perversions while holding to the Christian faith.[660] If she was pretending to be a fortune-teller, she might have claimed to have received a special revelation from God to the effect that such behavior was permissible. This seems to be the most likely case, as one can reflect on such things occurring even into the modern day. Many charlatans appear on the scene claiming to have some "special word from the Lord" that usually circumvents, amends, or annuls what has previously been said by God in His written Word.

---

women's teaching roles as noted in 1 Cor. 14:34 and 1 Tim. 2:12. Ultimately he concludes, "Revelation challenges Jezebel's teaching because of its content, not because of her gender." Koester, *Revelation*, 299. Sweet, in contrast, sees the prevalence of female prophetesses as a product of the proto-montanist movement and even attributes it as being one of the contributing factors towards the Pastoral Epistle's "regulation of the conduct of women and their support for the regular ministry of elders and deacons." Sweet, *Revelation*, 94, n.1. Regardless of her gender, claiming to be a prophet when not called of God to be such is a heinous sin. See Jer. 23:19-21.

[657] Mounce speculates that this Jezebel figure may never have formally spoken in the church gathering, but this seems highly unlikely given that she is referred to as both prophesying and teaching – both exercises clearly related to the practice of the church gathered in the New Testament.

[658] Ladd, *Revelation*, 50.

[659] Koester, *Revelation*, 296.

[660] Mounce, *Revelation*, 86-87.

(2:21)

"I gave her time to repent, but she refuses to repent of her sexual immorality."

"καὶ ἔδωκα αὐτῇ χρόνον ἵνα μετανοήσῃ, καὶ οὐ θέλει μετανοῆσαι ἐκ τῆς πορνείας αὐτῆς."

Christ responds to this woman in much the same way that He responds to all who claim to have a fresh and new Word from the Lord separate from His written word: **I gave her time to repent.**[661] It is purely to the praise of God that He shows such grace to the undeserving as to give time for repentance even to those who stand in His congregations, falsely claiming to speak on His behalf (see, for contrast, Jeremiah 23:19-21), telling His people to do what He has explicitly told them not to do. How merciful is this Christ? One is tempted to say unendingly merciful, but that is not quite right. The **time** He has given her **to repent** seems to have expired, as He says **she refuses to repent**. What a terrifying reality to reckon, that Christ's offered opportunity to repent has an expiration date.

The situation in the church at Thyatira is becoming more and more clear. It seems that the pastor of the church preaches a true Gospel. After all, the church is not condemned for unwaveringly following Jezebel, they are condemned for tolerating her. As she attended and occasionally spoke to the church, she was also given the opportunity to hear the preached Word of God, which called her to repent, but she refused. Christ regularly uses this language of **sexual immorality** to refer to those who have spiritually strayed from the faithful path of following God.[662] He will use this language later in Revelation, both in the positive and negative sense, to refer to those who are faithful and unfaithful.

(2:22-23)

"Behold, I will throw her onto a sickbed, and those who commit adultery with her I will throw into great tribulation, unless they repent of her works, and I will strike her children dead. And all the churches will know that I am he who searches mind and heart, and I will give to each of you according to your works."

"ἰδοὺ βάλλω αὐτὴν εἰς κλίνην καὶ τοὺς μοιχεύοντας μετ' αὐτῆς εἰς θλῖψιν μεγάλην, ἐὰν μὴ μετανοήσωσιν ἐκ τῶν ἔργων αὐτῆς, καὶ τὰ τέκνα αὐτῆς ἀποκτενῶ ἐν θανάτῳ. καὶ γνώσονται πᾶσαι αἱ ἐκκλησίαι ὅτι ἐγώ εἰμι ὁ ἐραυνῶν νεφροὺς καὶ καρδίας, καὶ δώσω ὑμῖν ἑκάστῳ κατὰ τὰ ἔργα ὑμῶν."

---

[661] Sweet uniquely proposes that the "time" she was given is alluded to in 3 John 10. Sweet, *Revelation*, 95.
[662] Andrew of Caesarea, *Commentary on the Apocalypse*, 70. Also see footnote 617.

Christ's response to this woman who has gone on in "sexual perversion" is to **throw her into a sickbed.**[663] There is something deeply poetic about this response, as Christ seems to say something along the lines of "if you will not get out of the whore's bed, I will throw you into the hospital bed." Of course, this is all analogistic for her doctrinal infidelity in leading Christ's people astray, but the punishment for her spiritual malpractice at least appears to be physical in nature.[664] There are two possible approaches to this, however. The first interpretation would lead readers to assume that Christ would literally strike this woman with some manner of physical malady (as He has at times done; Numbers 12:1-15).[665] The other approach would be much more symbolic, holding that Christ is going to make the fruit of all her work poisonous such that everyone who partook of her teaching would not be blessed by it, but cursed by it.

This latter approach seems to be the more likely case given the fact that Christ also says He is going to **throw into great tribulation** all **those who commit adultery with her** and even **strike her children dead.** Those who partook of her fallacious ministry and led others astray by multiplying her teaching would equally be thrown into a whirlwind of **great tribulation.** This phrase, which in the Greek is the same as what Christ used in Matthew 24:21 to describe that final era of hardship coming on the world (θλῖψιν μεγάλην) may refer simply to a tribulation which will be massive in both size and intensity.[666] The reason for this becomes one of the primary purposes for which Christ allows His people to endure tribulation – tribulation purges the church of false believers. In eras of persecution, the Christian church has become smaller but holier; fewer but purer. While these followers of Jezebel would undoubtedly be purged out of the church

---

[663] These Greek terms are rich with meaning. The term for "throw" (βάλλω) is a word with a future and present activity; as a man on his way to the gallows might answer the question "what are you doing right now" by saying, "I am being executed." The action is future, but its carrying-out is so immediate that it is termed in the present. Of even greater interest is the fact that Jesus says He will not (βάλλω) any new thing on His people in verse 24. This detail was gleaned from Schreiner, *Revelation* BECNT, 167. Beyond this, while the Greek word κλίνην does literally mean "bed" the connotation in which it was used denoted something akin to the modern phrase "bedridden." There was another related word (κλίνικός) that referred to a physician who attended bedridden individuals. Therefore, in this case it is appropriate to take this term as implying something of a "sickbed." E.A. Sophocles, *Greek Lexicon*, 669.

[664] Koester, *Revelation*, 299-300.

[665] This approach, given the words that follow, seems to lead readers to believe that this Jezebel figure was not only telling parishioners that they could partake in the idolatrous and perhaps sexually promiscuous practices of the pagan religions around them, but that she also partook of them, acting as a temple prostitute in some ways herself. Perhaps, then, the sickness Christ threatens her with is a severe STD which poisons all her lovers.

[666] Although Sweet, without further explanation, claims this "suggests the tribulation of the last days." It is hard to imagine how this could be, given the almost 2000 years of history which has passed – unless one assumes some alternative history in which Christ returned to end the world simply because these individuals refused to repent. Certainly, that is incorrect. Sweet, *Revelation*, 95.

at Thyatira in a time of hardship, the true believers would remain and persevere unto the end. This is at least partially the point of allowing His people to endure such hardship. As all Christians will endure tribulation, even "great tribulation," they can know that Christ is with them. For these wicked and adulterous false-believers, they will endure **great tribulation** alone, and will ultimately reveal their false-profession to avoid the most severe hardships. This will not serve them, however, as the tribulation is not ultimately being sent and overseen by the oppressors, but by God Himself. Thus, even if they seek to appease their wicked oppressors, they will still see God **strike** their **children dead.**

It should be noted that the only way **those who commit adultery with her** might be spared from enduring this **great tribulation** is if they **repent of her works**. Repentance, of course, would signify two things: First, that they had ears to hear what Christ was saying; and second, that God had granted them repentance (2 Tim. 2:25). Each of these would be some fruit of true salvation, which is an interesting reflection – that someone might truly be involved in false-teaching, or may be truly deceived into following a false-teacher, and yet have genuine faith in God and legitimate Christian salvation. Still, the proof of this is repentance, and not simply repentance, but repentance **of her works.** Everything she has done, said, written, and taught must be disavowed. One might also notice that Christ is no longer offering such an opportunity to her. Only her followers and co-laborers are now offered the opportunity to avoid punishment by repentance.[667] Indeed, Christ gave her time to repent, but she refused (v. 21). Now, the time for her repentance is over.

Those individuals referred to as **her children** almost certainly are those who had been converted to whatever religion she professed under her teaching.[668] While the language is uncomfortable to most Protestants who eschew any such usage of "father" and "child" type language because of the Catholic connotations related to the priesthood, it is true that the Apostle Paul referred to those converted under his ministry as his children (1 Cor. 4:14), specifically Timothy (1 Cor. 4:17; 1 Tim. 1:2; 1:18; 2 Tim. 1:2),

---

[667] Mounce and Sweet seem to attempt to alleviate blame away from her co-laborers, but Christ does not seem to have any such level of special favor on them as opposed to Jezebel or her children. Mounce, *Revelation*, 88.; Sweet, *Revelation*, 95. The severity of the consequence is not to be taken as a sign of favor or the lack thereof, as Jezebel herself receives the most lenient (sickness), her co-laborers a more severe (distress), and her children the most severe (death). Koester even notes that the word rendered death can elsewhere in Revelation be taken as meaning "plague or sickness." Koester, *Revelation*, 300. Certainly, Kiddle most properly understands the point here, saying, "John was not concerned with degrees of punishment: the fact that he wished to press home was that disaster hung over them, a sudden and complete punishment which repentance alone could avert." Martin Kiddle, *The Revelation of St. John*, 41.

[668] Ladd, *Revelation*, 52.; Mounce, *Revelation*, 88. Mounce is wise to note that the "second generation of heretics" endorsing and forwarding her teachings are not the antecedents of this term, but rather, those converted by her.

although he was also careful to warn against taking this practice too far (1 Cor. 3:4). Nevertheless, in this instance, the reference to the **children** of Jezebel undoubtedly refers to those converted to this false religion she teaches, and it is their supposed spiritual life which Christ says He will **strike... dead.**[669] He will make clear to them, by the destruction of all of her works and the apostasy of all of her co-laborers that she was a false prophetess, a false teacher, a pseudo-spiritual leader, and all of those who were won over to her teaching will have their spiritual hopes (which were wrapped up in her) die within them.[670]

The result of all of this is that **all the churches will know that I am he who searches mind and heart**. This phrase, and the universality of it, should be cause for real fear and trembling among all of those who lead churches. Christ, in His ministry, warned everyone that "nothing is hidden that will not be made manifest, nor is anything secret that will not be known and come to light." (Luke 8:17) And God in the Old Testament said to Samuel, that He "sees not as man sees: man looks on the outward appearance, but the LORD looks on the heart." (1 Samuel 16:7) Evidently in Thyatira (and elsewhere given the phrase **all the churches**) those leading in the church must have thought that God was only privy to what was done in the church house, or perhaps only what they asked Him to see and bless. But God does not stay at the church, nor does God give us privacy in our own homes. There is nowhere that His eye does not see, nor any threshold that His foot does not cross. When those professing Christians took part in the idolatrous and sexually immoral practices of the Imperial cult, God was present. And each time a modern-day pastor commits those same practices, God is present. How often have we seen a man or woman of esteem, a person of supposedly great faith and piety, revealed to be nothing short of a sexual deviant, financial crook, or a tyrannous monster? His Word holds true, in the end, **all the churches will know that I am he who searches mind and heart.**

What is perhaps the only thing more terrifying than the reality that God will reveal the most heinous secrets of the mind and hearts of man is that He also promises to **give to each of you according to your works.** This phrase and that which precedes are unmistakable references to Jeremiah 17:10, in which God called for Judah's repentance just prior to His bringing judgment on them for their unfaithfulness.[671] They did not repent, and judgment came. In the direct context, it appears that this promise pertains to

---

[669] Schreiner, *Revelation* BECNT, 165.

[670] Weinrich, *ACCS* XII, 36. "The words 'I will kill' do not refer to that death that is visible, but to spiritual death." Quoting from Tyconius, *Commentary on the Apocalypse*, 2:23.

[671] Mounce, *Revelation*, 89.; Koester, *Revelation*, 300.

those involved in the wickedness of Jezebel (given the following change in address in verse 24), such that these wicked followers and co-laborers of Jezebel will "get what they deserve."[672] They may not believe that God will do what He says, but if they would simply remember the last group of people who heard these words and whether or not God kept His Word, they would probably have responded differently.

On a broader scale, Christ promises to do this for all people. The final judgment of mankind will involve the reckoning of all works by all individuals, good or evil (Dan. 12:2). This is how the Bible always frames it, as Christ will "gather his wheat into the barn, but the chaff he will burn with unquenchable fire" (Matt. 3:12) or as Paul says, "each one [will] receive what is due for what he has done in the body, whether good or evil." (2 Cor. 5:10) For the Christian, however, this must not strike fear or trembling, as all punishment due to us for all the evil we ever committed was poured out on Christ on the cross, such that we now stand with absolutely no condemnation in the sight of God (Rom. 8:1). There will be nothing dispensed but rewards, including rewards for even the most trivial of acts (Matt. 10:42). For the non-Christian, however, it is an altogether different story. There will be nothing redeeming or rewarding for them at this judgment, as even their most righteous deeds are polluted with sin (Is. 64:6). No reward whatsoever can be expected for them, and what is worse, is that every single evil thing they ever did will be called forward for punishment, even the most trivial passing word (Matt. 12:36). So, for the Christian and non-Christian alike, we must all hear these words and do what the followers of Jezebel evidently failed to do – believe that they will truly come to pass again.

(2:24)

> "But to the rest of you in Thyatira, who do not hold this teaching, who have not learned what some call the deep things of Satan, to you I say, I do not lay on you any other burden."
>
> "ὑμῖν δὲ λέγω τοῖς λοιποῖς τοῖς ἐν Θυατείροις, ὅσοι οὐκ ἔχουσιν τὴν διδαχὴν ταύτην, οἵτινες οὐκ ἔγνωσαν τὰ βαθέα τοῦ σατανᾶ ὡς λέγουσιν· οὐ βάλλω ἐφ' ὑμᾶς ἄλλο βάρος,"

Having spent much time speaking of this grave error and addressing those who have committed it, contributed to it, and fallen prey to it, Christ now turns to **the rest of you in Thyatira, who do not hold this teaching.** This must have been a major moment of relief for many sitting in the church at Thyatira as this letter was read. One can only

---

[672] This theme will reappear explicitly in Revelation 16:6.

imagine their fear in hearing how thoroughly Christ knew of the situation in their church, but as He concludes, He reminds them that He is also thoroughly aware that there are some in this congregation **who do not hold this teaching**. He has not forgotten or overlooked them, nor will He ever forget or overlook even the small contingency of faithful believers in a wicked situation. Just as He did when the real Jezebel walked the Earth, God remembered His remnant (1 Kings 19:18), and He will always maintain a remnant of His people in times of darkness and wickedness (Rom. 11:2-5).

They are also identified as those **who have not learned what some call the deep things of Satan**. It is quite possible that there were many who referred to these teachings as "the deep things" which one might only have revealed to them by a prophet or prophetess. Paul utilized a similar phrase when referring to aspects of God bordering on incomprehensible to human beings (1 Cor. 2:10). These types of things are likely what Jezebel claimed to be teaching.[673] Christ corrects this misnomer by saying that what she teaches are the **deep things *of Satan***.[674] If this is so, Jezebel and her co-laborers were forerunners in marketing their teachings as some deeper knowledge that Christians were not all privy to, but which one could have revealed to them either by reaching a "higher plane" of spirituality or by hearing the revelation given to those who had already reached it. This is a common concept taught by quacks and crooks in the modern day, and it seems to have been prevalent in the early church with the rise of cults like the Gnostics – whose very name asserts this thought.

To those persevering in the truth under such fallacious teachings, Christ says that He does **not lay on you any other burden**. How loving, caring, thoughtful, and considerate is Christ that He considers our perseverance as sufficient for us. When false teachers have infiltrated the church at Thyatira, Christ does not lambast the faithful believers, but instead calls them to simply refuse to tolerate this false teaching. While He certainly has the right to reprimand the faithful believers for allowing the Jezebel situation to get to the point that it is in, He does no such thing. He calls them (in so many words) to "cast out the slave woman and her son" (Gal. 4:30) such that their church might be purified. He does not expect them to go tit-for-tat in an ongoing debate

---

[673] A.T. Robertson, *Word Pictures in the New Testament* VI, 310-311.

[674] Lilje, like Robertson, Mounce, Hemer, Sweet, and others, associates Jezebel with the Gnostics who "boasted that they had a special gift of the Spirit by means of which they could fathom the 'depths of God.' The seer here confronts them harshly with a sarcastic reversal of their main slogan. They think that they have had a profound insight into the Spirit of God; but... at the most, all that they have done is to gain an insight into 'the depths of Satan.'" Hanns Lilje, *The Last Book of the Bible,* Olive Wyon, trans., 86. Schreiner thoroughly disagrees and disputes this position, but ignores the points which undermine his own position as given in Koester. Schreiner, *Revelation* BECNT, 167.; Koester, *Revelation*, 301.

with her, attempting to rectify this relationship and maintain her so as to not lose her.[675] He does not encourage them to feel any regret for what has occurred. Christ simply calls them to act where they are and refuses to **lay on** them **any other burden.** This is truly the Spirit of Christ. One might call to mind the story of the woman with the alabaster box. When she acted in a way that made little sense to the disciples and others around, Christ defended her with the words, "she has done what she could." (Mark 14:8) In truth, this is all Christ does expect of us – to do what we can. He does not lay on us any other burden than this: do what you can.[676]

(2:25)

"Only hold fast what you have until I come."

"πλὴν ὃ ἔχετε κρατήσατε ἄχρι[ς] οὗ ἂν ἥξω."

And to those who **hold fast** (again, a firm and unrelenting grasp; see 2:13-14) to His truth, He commends them to go on holding to **what you have** and not let go **until I come.** Modern Christians could stand to meditate on this whole situation: A person arose claiming to have a "new word" from the Lord, some deeper knowledge than what had previously been revealed. Christ responded by absolutely castigating this person, along with those who worked alongside them, and calling all who believed in this new teaching to repent of it. Then, Christ called those who disbelieved to continue believing what they already did **until** He returns. Does the church, then, need direct revelation from God? Does the church need a "fresh word" from the Lord? Do we need prophets or prophetesses to give us a word from God for us? Christ says no.

The Lord Himself, in the Word of the Lord, tells His people in His churches that we are to **hold fast to what** we **have until** He **comes.** The very word used to render **hold fast** (κρατήσατε) has been said to be "a common metaphor to describe strict adherence to a tradition or teaching..."[677] This may be called by some "traditionalism," but Christ instills the principle that for His Church there are no new instructions; no new reports; no new words; no new revelations. We have no need or use for them. Rather, the Word of God as given in the 66 books of the Holy Bible are the only revelation from God needed or permitted and must be held to firmly and without the

---

[675] Andrew of Caesarea, *Commentary on the Apocalypse*, 70-71.

[676] This tenderness is recognized in the distinction of translation regarding the word βάλλω. When referring to Jezebel, it is said that Christ will (βάλλω) her – and is rendered as "throw." But when referring to the Church it is said that He will not (βάλλω) any new thing on us – rendered as "lay." Even if both terms were rendered identically, the thought would convey that Christ is willing to be aggressive with His enemies but is gentle and tender with His own people.

[677] Thomas, *Revelation 1-7*, 230.

slightest release until He returns. A major lesson of the church at Thyatira is that religious accommodation is associated with Jezebel, not Jesus.[678]

Of a more personal nature, it is noticeable in this short and simple verse that Christ's encouragement to His people is that He will come. He has laid on us no other burden than to **hold fast** to what we have been entrusted with. Naturally, Christians are to not only "hold" what Christ has given us, but also entrust it to other "faithful men, who will be able to teach others also." (2 Tim. 2:2) But while this is our standing order from the Lord, our ever-constant point of confidence and optimism is found not in some promise of our own deliverance from hardship, nor in some supposed promise of unrelenting success on our part. No, the optimism to be found in the Revelation of St. John is found in this, "In this world you will have trouble. But take heart! I have overcome the world." (John 16:33) Despite the seemingly unrelenting outpouring of Satanic hardship and tribulation that Christians endure, the blessed hope of our people is the return of our King who is sovereign, faithful, and victorious. [679]

(2:26-28)

> "The one who conquers and who keeps my works until the end, to him I will give authority over the nations, and he will rule them with a rod of iron, as when earthen pots are broken in pieces, even as I myself have received authority from my Father. And I will give him the morning star."
>
> "Καὶ ὁ νικῶν καὶ ὁ τηρῶν ἄχρι τέλους τὰ ἔργα μου, δώσω αὐτῷ ἐξουσίαν ἐπὶ τῶν ἐθνῶν καὶ ποιμανεῖ αὐτοὺς ἐν ῥάβδῳ σιδηρᾷ ὡς τὰ σκεύη τὰ κεραμικὰ συντρίβεται, ὡς κἀγὼ εἴληφα παρὰ τοῦ πατρός μου, καὶ δώσω αὐτῷ τὸν ἀστέρα τὸν πρωϊνόν."

Returning to the same language that He uses for each of the previous churches, Christ refers to those individuals who persevere through tribulation and hardship faithfully as **the one who conquers and who keeps my works until the end**. It would be wise of readers to notice that in verses 25-26, Jesus refers to the time in which He will come as **the end**. He uses clearly repetitious phraseology, "until I come" with "until the end" to assert their identification.[680] Even a headstrong Dispensationalist like William Newell (perhaps unthinkingly) recognizes this, as he says that the coming of Christ pictured in verse 25 is no other than "the sure and imminent personal coming again"

---

[678] Koester, *Revelation*, 306.

[679] For brief comments on the optimism/pessimism of Revelation, see Mounce, *Revelation*, 7.

[680] The Greek, like the English, uses the same word for "until" – *achri* (ἄχρι) such that Robertson feels comfort in simply quoting the Greek as proof of the union of these two events. A.T. Robertson, *Word Pictures* VI, 312. "Unto the end (achri telous). That is, *achri hou an hexo* above."

even arguing in most direct terms that "the Lord's return, and not the recovery of the Church to her first estate, much less the conversion of the world, is the *only object of hope*."[681] Regardless of one's convictions regarding the nature of the millennium, there is simply no room for any time period between Jesus' return for His people and **the end.**[682]

One should further notice a caveat added by Christ in this address that does not appear in the others. Rather than simply referring to them as **the one who conquers** (as 2:7, 11, 17; 3:5, 12, 21) He adds on **and keeps my works until the end.** One might think that this is adding another requirement onto His expectations, but this would be contrary to what He said immediately preceding this statement in verse 24. Rather, what Christ has done is given the church a useful juxtaposition. In verse 22, Christ called those following and working for the advancement of the teaching of Jezebel to "repent of *her works*."[683] Here, Christ calls those who follow and work for the advancement of His teaching to **keep my works until the end.** Everything that Jezebel had taught and done was to be disavowed, supplanted, and destroyed, but everything that Christ has taught and done is to be solidified, held to, and maintained forever.

To those who do this, which is nothing short of maintaining faithful belief and commitment to Christ until the end, He promises to **give authority over the nations**. This is an eschatological hope that extends back far into the Old Testament. In fact, Christ uses the precise language used in many Old Testament prophesies of this event when He says the one to whom He gives this authority **will rule them with a rod of iron, as when earthen pots are broken in pieces**. These terms come from all over the Old Testament, specifically Psalm 2:9, Isaiah 30:14, and Jeremiah 19:11. These terms speak of an era in which the Kingdom of God will be established by and through the smashing destruction of the present evil powers. While the inauguration of Christ's reign was seen at Calvary, and is experienced in the soul of every believer, it will only be fully realized when the whole of the wicked powers opposing Him are entirely displaced. What is groundbreaking (forgive the pun) is that Christ says that this authority (which has always been attributed to the Messiah) will be given by Him to His people.

In keeping with the purpose of this first vision, this detail that He will **give authority over the nations** to His people has explanatory value, as it elaborates on what John first saw in Rev. 1:6. Not only will He reign, but His people (the Kingdom, priests)

---

[681] Newell, *Revelation*, 60. Emphasis maintained.

[682] Gundry, *The Church and the Tribulation*, 140-141.

[683] Schreiner points out that this is an instance of Revelation's high Christology, as anyone claiming that others should keep their works must be divine. Schreiner, *Revelation* BECNT, 168.

will rule alongside Him.[684] Elsewhere in John's Revelation, as he outlines the future to come, one will see that this event indeed will come, wherein Christ rules the nations with a rod of iron (Rev. 12:5; 19:15), but at His first coming (as pictured in 12:5) it is envisioned as a future event, and at His Second coming (picture in 19:15) it is *still* envisioned as a future event. This means that the era in which Christ – and His people with Him – rule the nations with a rod of iron follows both His first and second advents.[685] It is then sensible to take this rule as occurring in what is commonly referred to as the Millennial Reign (pictured in Rev. 20).

It may still seem somewhat odd, though, that Christ claims that He will not rule the world alone, but will share that rule with **the one who conquers and who keeps my works until the end**. However, it ought not be any oddity to those familiar with Christ's promises for His people. In Luke 19:11-27, Christ speaks in a parable about what will occur at His return, when "having received the kingdom" He will say to His servants "you shall have authority over ten cities" and to others "you are to be over five cities."[686] Christ concludes the parable by saying, "but as for these enemies of mine, who did not want me to reign over them, bring them here and slaughter them before me." The fulfillment of this prophetic parable is reiterated later in Revelation 5:10 as well, with clarity that it will occur "on the earth." Schreiner directly sums up the purpose of this when he succinctly writes, "the rule of believers over all things restores the original commission of Adam and Eve in the garden and fits the notion that believers are a kingdom."[687]

This understanding of the "goodness and severity" of Christ's coming reign with His people appears to resolve the seeming difficulty many have with interpreting the verb ποιμανεῖ.[688] The Hebrew referent in Psalm 2:9 (תְּרֹעֵם) means "break" or "shatter" but when it was translated into the Septuagint it became ποιμανεῖ which generally means "shepherd."[689] How, then, should this be rendered? This author certainly believes the translators of the ESV have found a perfectly fitting word that captures both contexts fairly in rendering the term "rule." As a Shepherd guides and guards the sheep, so Christ

---

[684] Ladd, *Revelation*, 53.

[685] Schreiner, *Revelation* BECNT, 169. "The authority promised here is probably exclusively future, referring to a rule that will be granted when Jesus returns." Sweet entirely misses this point and proposes that this "authority" refers to martyrdom – a point hard to grasp. Sweet, *Revelation*, 96.

[686] Andrew of Caesarea makes a similar association but does not press it nearly as far as here. Andrew of Caesarea, *Commentary on the Apocalypse*, 71. Christ made similar promises to His disciples elsewhere, including Matthew 5:5 and 19:28. Paul seems to imply something along this same line of thought in 1 Cor. 6:2.

[687] Schreiner, *Revelation* BECNT, 169.

[688] For information on this discussion, see Hemer, *The Letters to the Seven Churches*, 124-125.

[689] Mounce, *Revelation*, 90.

will do that for His people and so they will do with those placed under their authority (see above, Luke 19:11-27).[690] But regarding those who oppose Christ and His people, it is equally fair to say they will be "ruled" with aggression, being **broken in pieces** as depicted in Jeremiah 18:1-11.[691] After all, one can scarcely avoid the obvious fulfillment of this, as depicted in Revelation 19:21. This imagery would have been directly clear to the people of Thyatira, who were known to have many potters in their city.[692]

This authority is only Christ's to give, just as He Himself **received authority from my Father**. This serves as a reminder that there is (economically at least) a submission of the Son to the Father in authority, which will pervade into the reign of Christ. Paul said nothing less in 1 Corinthians 15:28, saying that when Christ has assumed this reign of all things under Himself, He will then recognize His own submission to the Father. This provides a valuable insight into how Christ's people can reign *with* Him whilst maintaining submission *to* Him. The Son **received authority from** His **Father**, and although reigning with absolute authority, still recognizes the source of that authority as in some sense worthy of submission. Similarly, Christ promises to **give authority** to His people, who although reigning with absolute authority (hence the **rod of iron**) will maintain a constant recognition of the source of that authority as in a real sense worthy of submission.

The final gift (as if there was need of more) which Christ promises to give to His people is **the morning star.** Much like the "hidden manna" or the "crown of life" or the "tree of life", this gift symbolically represents eternal life. Furthermore, just as Christ identified Himself as the "true manna" He is identified elsewhere in Revelation as being the "morning star" (Rev. 22:16).[693] Perhaps more directly in regards to this church would be the fact that the false-prophet Balaam had foreseen the coming of this "star… out of Jacob" who would also be "a scepter… out of Israel" which would "crush the forehead of Moab and break down all the sons of Sheth." (Num. 24:17) The rod, the star, and the powerful reign would all be very familiar to the believers at Thyatira, as the true believers

---

690 A similar connection is also made in Andrew of Caesarea, *Commentary on the Apocalypse*, 71.

691 Both positions are presented without seeming contradiction in both Sweet, *Revelation*, 96.; and Koester, *Revelation*, 302.

692 Hemer, *The Letters to the Seven Churches*, 125. Mounce is quick to point out that Hemer denies the idea of ποιμανεῖ meaning anything akin to smashing or destruction, but that is because Hemer sets the interpretations up as an either-or. If choosing whether Christ will act as destroyer or shepherd, indeed, interpreters will be forced to hold that He will act as shepherd. But when bearing in mind that He will act as Shepherd to some and destroyer to others, both interpretations fit perfectly in line with the context. Mounce, *Revelation*, 90, n.34.

693 Ladd finds this concept hard to follow, but I consider it appealing and legitimate. Ladd, *Revelation*, 54.

had likely spent much time studying the Old Testament in reference to false-prophets in their work to address Jezebel.

Understanding the meaning and application of the phrase **morning star** also helps readers understand a central principle towards interpreting Revelation 1-3 in general. Some commentators have at various points in their commentaries simply folded and admitted defeat by saying that something written must have had contemporary meaning to those Christians in the churches originally receiving the letters, which has been lost to time. Such astute scholars as Robert Thomas do this. In his first volume on Revelation, when he commentates on the "ten days" of tribulation the people of Smyrna would experience (2:10), he concludes that the ten days "are literal and refer to an unknown persecution..."[694] Rather than entertain anything relatively spiritualistic or symbolic, he accepts that God had John write down something in the Holy Scriptures which would never be understood by any generation of Christians except that first one. Colin Hemer does something similar when discussing this verse, Revelation 2:28. Of the meaning of **morning star**, he says, "the precise point of this promise is lost..."[695] This is a tragedy. To conclude this, genuinely believe it, and teach it to others is to vastly overemphasize the epistolary nature of Revelation over against its apocalyptic nature.[696] Yes, this section was written in an epistolary way to seven literal churches in real history – and yet, it is also equally apocalyptic in nature, dictating God's instructions for His people not only in the first century, but across and throughout the entire inter-advent age. To say the meaning of these terms was lost after that first generation is to render certain passages of God's Word meaningless for almost 2000 years now.

These believers at Thyatira were expected to turn false-believers and those led astray by Jezebel and others towards the truth of Christ. The fulfillment of what Balaam predicted did nothing to validate the false-prophetess in their midst. And still, Christ references another Old Testament passage with His promise, that "those who turn many to righteousness" will shine "like the stars forever and ever." (Daniel 12:3) If they did what Christ called them to do, as simple as it was, they would receive that glory which belongs to Christ Himself in both form (shining like a star) and honorific duty (ruling the nations). This is how Christ spoke to those under false-teachers: He referred to the Scriptures as delivered down through the ages to be their guide and constant hope. Similarly, just as this same promise applied to the church at Thyatira in the first-century, Christians of the twenty-first century must apply this same concept. By turning false-

---

[694] Thomas, *Revelation 1-7*, 170.

[695] Hemer, *The Letters to the Seven Churches*, 126.

[696] See comments on 1:4.

believers and those led astray by the modern Jezebels and co-laborers of our day (and all those to follow), we may turn many to righteousness and in return receive both an intimate closeness with Christ Himself, and at His commissioning, the very glory that belongs to Him.[697] The meaning was direct to the people of Thyatira, and it is to us as well.

(2:29)

"He who has an ear, let him hear what the Spirit says to the churches.'"

"Ὁ ἔχων οὖς ἀκουσάτω τί τὸ πνεῦμα λέγει ταῖς ἐκκλησίαις."

Again, Christ completes this letter by addressing it to **he who has an ear**, asking those who understand to **hear what the Spirit says to the churches.** One must imagine that there would have been many sitting in the church at Thyatira hearing this letter and knowing precisely what Christ was telling them to do. If they had access to it, they might have recalled the words of Paul given to the church at Corinth, "Go out from their midst, and be separate from them… touch no unclean thing; then I will welcome you and I will be a father to you, and you shall be sons and daughters to me." (2 Cor. 6:17-18) But in this instance, they were not called to leave the church for the sake of purity, they were called to stay in it and purify it from within. Others, sitting in this church at the time, must have heard these words with great offense – Jezebel specifically.

The church at Thyatira should serve as an example that proclamation and maintenance of the truth, along with faithfulness to Christ and His Word, is always the right thing to do, regardless of how far-gone a church might seem. Each and every pastor stepping into a church as a shepherd must understand that a primary duty (as there was no other burden laid on the Christians of Thyatira) is to proclaim truth, guard the pulpit and the lectern, and do what must be done to eradicate false-teaching from that congregation.

---

[697] Schreiner, *Revelation* BECNT, 171.

(3:1-6) *Sardis: The Dead Church*

(3:1)

> "And to the angel of the church in Sardis write: 'The words of him who has the seven spirits of God and the seven stars. 'I know your works. You have the reputation of being alive, but you are dead."
>
> "Καὶ τῷ ἀγγέλῳ τῆς ἐν Σάρδεσιν ἐκκλησίας γράψον· Τάδε λέγει ὁ ἔχων τὰ ἑπτὰ πνεύματα τοῦ θεοῦ καὶ τοὺς ἑπτὰ ἀστέρας· οἶδά σου τὰ ἔργα ὅτι ὄνομα ἔχεις ὅτι ζῇς, καὶ νεκρὸς εἶ."

While other churches are given a "criticism sandwich" in which Christ begins with a commendation of their good, then notes their failures, and finishes with another commendation (Ephesus, Thyatira) and still other churches receive nothing but commendation (Smyrna, Philadelphia), **the church in Sardis** stands alongside Laodicea as the two churches who receive no real commendation. It appears they are doing nearly nothing right. Why they had fallen into this state is up for speculation, but by the time they receive this letter they are certainly in a sorry state.

Sardis itself was a city whose glory had gone with the wind.[698] Although the city experienced some degree of material prosperity even in John's era, its sparce population rendered it mediocre in comparison to its former place on the world stage.[699] Sardis had once stood as a major power on the worldwide stage, but in the wake of various military failures, its glory was reduced to something of a bygone era. The city only continued to fall apart into the Christian era, as in AD 17 they were devastated by a catastrophic earthquake. Pliny said it was the "greatest earthquake in human memory" and that twelve cities were destroyed entirely in one night (Sardis and Philadelphia among them).[700] Tacitus spoke of the event, saying

> Twelve important cities of Asia collapsed in an earthquake, the time being night, so that the havoc was the less foreseen and the more devastating. Even the usual resource in these catastrophes, a rush to open ground, was unavailing, as the fugitives were swallowed up in yawning chasms. Accounts are given of huge mountains sinking, of former plains seen heaved aloft, of fires flashing out amid

---

[698] Ladd speaks to this degradation in some length. Ladd, *Revelation*, 55. In the modern era the city of Sart occupies the historical location of Sardis. Thomas, *Revelation 1-7*, 242.
[699] Sweet, *Revelation*, 98.
[700] Pliny, *Natural History*, 2:86:200.

the ruin. As the disaster fell heaviest on the Sardians, it brought them the largest measure of sympathy...[701]

After this major earthquake, despite charity from Rome to rebuild, Sardis was rendered relatively insignificant and never fully recovered.[702] This may have contributed to the general sense of complacency one might recognize in Christ's reflection of the church there.[703] The city was situated atop Mount Tmolus, a mountain plateau with 1500-foot rock walls leading up to it on all sides except the south, making the city a natural citadel of impregnable magnitude.[704]

To the credit of this natural defensive position, the city was never conquered by a frontal attack in its lengthy history. However, in 549 BC, Cyrus the Great sieged the city, and having reached a stalemate chose to deploy a climber to scale up a crevice in the rock wall. This climber scaled the walls, infiltrated the city, and opened the gates from within. Herodotus writes of the event, saying that a Persian man named Hyroeades mounted the fortress "where no guard was stationed, since no one feared that it could be taken by an attack made there." He concludes the section by saying, "and thus Sardis was taken and all the city sacked."[705] Centuries later in about 200 BC, having regained some prestige for themselves, Antiochus the Great sieged the city again.[706] Again, reaching a stalemate, he deployed 15 men to make a similar ascent up the walls, which was once again successful because, as Polybius writes, "he had discovered the remissness of the guard" and again later "he knew for a certainty that the wall was not guarded and was usually deserted."[707] They again opened the gates from within the city and the city again fell into the hands of their enemies. The question on both occasions was, "Where were the guards?"

Because of this repeated failure to maintain discipline and attention in a time of the most severe need, Sardis developed the reputation and legacy of being lazy, inattentive, and difficult to motivate. Had they simply maintained awareness, they would have been immovable and impregnable, but instead they fell on several occasions to their own lack of regard. It is to the Christians in this city, citizens who would have been aware of this reputation about themselves, that Christ writes the letter.

---

[701] Tacitus, *Annals*, 2:47:1-2.

[702] Hemer, *Letters to the Seven Churches*, 30, 129.

[703] Koester, *Revelation*, 309-312.

[704] Mounce, *Revelation*, 91-92.

[705] Herodotus, *Histories*, 1:84:2, 5.

[706] Dates vary for this conflict, with some as early as 216 BC and others as late as 195 BC.

[707] Polybius, *Histories*, 7:15:6-9.

Christ addresses His **words** as being from He **who has the seven spirits of God and the seven stars.** As He has done in each of the letters, Christ calls their attention to the attributes described of Him in chapter 1. Here, He begins by calling their attention to the fact that He has the **seven spirits of God.**[708] As discussed in the notes on 1:4, it is most reasonable to conclude that this expression refers to the Holy Spirit, as such a sevenfold term is used of the Holy Spirit in passages such as Zechariah 4 and Isaiah 11.[709] As for the **seven stars**, these were explicitly said to have referred to the "angels of the seven churches" (1:20) which were identified herein as most probably being the pastors of those churches.

When Christ describes Himself in each letter, the attribute He brings to mind always has some pertinence to the church addressed. Here, the church at Sardis would be wise to remember that Christ has the Holy Spirit (the seven spirits of God) and the pastor of the church (the seven stars) at His disposal, because He tells them at present, **I know your works. You have the reputation of being alive, but you are dead.** First of all, unlike others who might be fooled into believing their reputation, Christ knows their works. Schreiner interestingly points out that this church likely received honor on the basis of its good name and reputation, and it is possible that "other churches looked up the church of Sardis."[710] Mounce draws the association between them and "nominally Christian" churches of the modern era, and ancient commentators associated them with those who "are Christians in name only."[711]

The Greek term used for "life" (ζῆς) does not describe outward physical life (as would βίος) but rather describes inward spiritual life.[712] Unfortunately for them, Jesus knows the truth about their state, which is that they are **dead.** The importance of the Holy Spirit, then, comes to light. The Holy Spirit of God Himself gives life (John 6:63; 2 Cor. 3:6). If the church at Sardis is to arise from the dead, they will only do so at the work of God the Holy Spirit.[713] Modern churches and Christians would do well to remember that regardless of whether or not other people think we have spiritual life, Jesus knows the truth – and He is not fooled.

---

[708] Schreiner and Thomas see here some connection with the doctrine later known to Christian history as the *Filioque* Controversy. Schreiner, *Revelation* BECNT, 176.; Thomas, *Revelation 1-7*, 244.

[709] It should be noted that the Father (Rev. 7:12) and the Son (Rev. 5:12) also receive a sevenfold description in the Revelation as well.

[710] Schreiner, *Revelation* BECNT, 176.

[711] Mounce, *Revelation*, 93.; Apringius of Beja, *Tractate on the Apocalypse*, 3:2.; Victorinus of Petovium, *Commentary on the Apocalypse*, 3:1.

[712] Thomas, *Revelation 1-7*, 247.

[713] Ladd, *Revelation*, 55.

Furthermore, the pastor of the church (represented by the seven stars/angels) must know that Christ is the one who holds them in His hand, as God the Son also has the ability to give them life (1 Cor. 15:45). If the church at Sardis is to arise from the dead, the pastors must lead the congregation to rely on God in Trinity: Father, Son, and Holy Spirit.[714] It is only through recognition and admission of their state as **dead** rather than **alive** as is rumored that they will turn to God in faith and receive true life.

(3:2-3a)

> "Wake up, and strengthen what remains and is about to die, for I have not found your works complete in the sight of my God. Remember, then, what you received and heard. Keep it, and repent."
>
> "γίνου γρηγορῶν καὶ στήρισον τὰ λοιπὰ ἃ ἔμελλον ἀποθανεῖν, οὐ γὰρ εὕρηκά σου τὰ ἔργα πεπληρωμένα ἐνώπιον τοῦ θεοῦ μου. μνημόνευε οὖν πῶς εἴληφας καὶ ἤκουσας καὶ τήρει καὶ μετανόησον."

Christ gives the church at Sardis five commands to correct their course, all of which seem to build in terms of importance with the first being the most rudimentary and the last being the most crucially valuable.[715]

1. He calls out to them, **wake up**! Historically, Sardis had been thrice devastated while asleep. Twice during war, they had been infiltrated by enemies who sacked their city because of their lack of awareness. Then, in AD 17, an earthquake had come in the night to the peril of many citizens and the destruction of their livelihood. To the Christians in the city, Christ says, **wake up**. Their church was in danger and like the guards of the city in years gone by, or the citizens the night the horrific earthquake came, it appeared at this moment that the Christians were asleep, resting on their reputation to keep them safe. In fact, the Greek terms used (γίνου γρηγορῶν) are in such a casing that would permit them to be rendered more literally as "be awake."[716] The latter word is used by Jesus three times in the Olivet Discourse when teaching His people to watch for His coming (Matt. 24:42, 43; 25:13). It is not simply a call for them to rise from sleeping, but rather, not to sleep. In the Olivet Discourse, it refers to Christ's people not being taken unaware by things they should have expected to occur, and the sentiment is similar here. In fact, a common denotation of the Greek term is "alertness in prayer."[717] The

[714] Bede, *Explanation of the Apocalypse*, 3:1.
[715] Mounce, *Revelation*, 93.
[716] Ladd, *Revelation*, 56.
[717] Gundry, *The Church and the Tribulation*, 32.

Christians in Sardis are to be aware so they can engage what they should be expecting to come.

2. Once awake (or watching), they are to **strengthen what remains and is about to die.** In keeping with the analogy of the church as the city citadel preparing to be invaded, one could say that Christ calls them to fortify the walls. The church stood in need of fortification because Christ had examined them and reflected that He had **not found** their **works complete in the sight of my God.**[718] It sadly appears that the church at Sardis had allowed almost all of their work to come to naught, with only a remnant of **what remains** (λοιπὰ) continuing alive, and even that was **about to die.** They have not only allowed themselves to become defenseless but have also neglected the purity of themselves within. While the Ephesian church was commended for maintaining a proper relationship with the enemies outside (eschewing false teachers, etc.) but were reprimanded for neglecting love within, the people of Sardis have nothing to commend. They fail in engaging those outside of the church, and fail to rightly maintain themselves within. They are called to **strengthen** what remains, before it too dies.
3. Having strengthened what remains alive in their church, they are to **remember, then, what** they **received and heard.** Building upon the previous steps of coming to an awareness of their own failures and need for fortification, and saving that which is about to die which they should maintain, they are to then return to that which they have allowed to die and restore it to life. Unlike the Sardians around them, they were to rebuild what had been lost – not allowing it to disappear into rubble never to be resurrected. It seems reasonable (at least on linguistic grounds) to conclude that this entails a return to the Gospel, given Paul's words in 1 Corinthians 15:3-4.[719] Simply put, they must return to the Word of the Lord which they had previously **received and heard.**
4. Having returned to the Word of the Lord, they are to **keep it.** It is not enough to simply preach and teach the Word of God in a church – it must be applied and maintained. In fact, the term rendered "keep" is going to reappear frequently after this point in Revelation. It has been used only once to this point (2:26) but will reappear in 3:8, 10 (twice); 12:17; 14:12; 16:15; 22:7; and 22:9. Every time this word is used, it is in the context of maintaining faithfulness to Christ despite

[718] Sweet points out that Christ's usage of **my God** "expresses Christ's special relationship with God in judging the church..." Sweet, *Revelation*, 99.

[719] The Greek terms used for "receive," both here (εἴληφας) and in 1 Cor. 15:3 (παρέλαβον), each share the same root (λαμβάνω). While far from the most frequent connotation, there is a precedent for this root to be used when referring to the manner in which Christians receive the Word of the Lord (1 Cor. 11:23; Gal. 1:12) or the way that non-christians refuse the Word of the Lord (John 1:11).

opposition. To be "kept" in the book of Revelation always means something along the lines of "protected", "guarded" or "maintained" in time of hardship. It should be noticed that the church at Sardis is the only church which has no mention of persecution at all. This should not surprise anyone, as they have failed to keep the central tenets of the Christian faith and have allowed almost all of their Christian testimony and work to die. There is no need to persecute them! But if they become aware of their failures, strengthen what remains, and begin once more to return to and maintain a faithfulness to Christ, immediately persecution is sure to come – against which they will need to persevere and maintain the truth of the Gospel as they failed to do in the past.

5. Finally, Christ calls them to **repent.** It would seem obvious that this would be called for, though perhaps a bit out of order. One might even think that the first four commands were a description of repentance. However, the nuance of the word "repent" (μετανόησον) might be lost on modern Christians who are deeply focused on outward actions as the fruit of repentance.[720] While action is certainly a sign of repentance, it is not necessarily all that repentance is. Judas, for example, behaved in a repentant manner by returning the money for which he betrayed Christ (Matt. 27:3) and yet was certainly no Christian bearing fruit of repentance (John 17:12). Repentance, while manifested by action and behavior, is more closely associated with a change in mindset, disposition, or conviction. John the Baptist, for example, assumed that repentance within a person would produce actions in accordance with that inward change (Matt. 3:8). Therefore, when Christ calls the church at Sardis to do all these previous actions, there is a possibility that they may have done all of these things without surrendering their heart, soul, mind, and strength to Christ.

So, Christ calls them to do five things, each becoming more important than the last. First, recognize the failures and sins they are committing, and **wake up.** Second, and even more importantly, **strengthen what remains and is about to die.** Third, and even more importantly, **remember, then, what you received and heard.** Having returned to the truth of God's Word, fourth, and even more importantly, they were to **keep it.** Rather than allowing it to fade once more, they were to persevere despite the coming persecution. Fifth and finally, and most importantly, they were to **repent.** Without repentance, all of it would simply be works fit for destruction.

[720] Μετανόησον holds a connotation of change of heart, as contrasted with μεταμέλομαι which simply means to feel regret. Thomas, *Revelation*, 1-7.

(3:3b)

> "If you will not wake up, I will come like a thief, and you will not know at what hour I will come against you."
>
> "ἐὰν οὖν μὴ γρηγορήσῃς, ἥξω ὡς κλέπτης, καὶ οὐ μὴ γνῷς ποίαν ὥραν ἥξω ἐπὶ σέ."

Given their proclivity towards failing to do what is needed, Christ warns them that **if you will not wake up, I will come**. The fourth command He gave them (to keep His Word) seemed to indicate that if they did what He called them to do, they would begin experiencing hardship and persecution which they would be expected to persevere through. At present, they experienced no persecution because of their lack of Christian commitment. Certainly, it must have occurred to them that Christ was calling them to a much more difficult lifestyle, and their initial reaction likely would have been to refuse. So, Christ reminds them that the choice is not "persecution or ease." Rather, the choice He presents them with is "wrath at the hand of the world or wrath at the hand of Almighty God." He had presented His disciples with a similar ultimatum in Matthew 10:28. If they will not follow His commands, He **will come**, and the manner in which He says He will come would have been very familiar to the people of Sardis.

Readers should be attentive to the fact that Jesus is not threatening to come to them, as if the second coming or some other personal visitation is in view.[721] Certainly the faithfulness or lack thereof in a small congregation in 1st Century Asia-Minor was not the determining factor on the timing of the Second Coming of Jesus, and the idea that Jesus would pay a personal visit to a church to correct some error in their midst seems Scripturally foreign as well. The threat Jesus gave, rather, was that if they did not take up faithful living then **I will come like a thief.**[722] That is, they would be unprepared to meet Him, whether that consisted of their going to Him in death or His coming to them in the Second Coming.[723] It is not the timing of His coming, but their complete unpreparedness for that event that is threatened, as Jesus says **and you will not know what hour I will come against you.**

Unpreparedness for the coming of Christ is a trait of those who are not redeemed. In fact, this very term is used to describe how Christ's people will *not* feel at His coming

---

[721] These two options are the only positions considered in Schreiner, *Revelation* BECNT, 179.

[722] Sweet, *Revelation*, 99.

[723] This interpretation is represented early in the Christian tradition. Andrew of Caesarea writes, "Neither the death of an individual nor the common consummation [resurrection at the Second Coming] is known to anyone. To those who are prepared, either will be the cessation of toil; however, to those who are unprepared, like a 'thief' he will bring on spiritual death." Andrew of Caesarea, *Commentary on the Apocalypse*, 3:3.

(1 Thess. 5:4). So, this threat from Christ seems to be precisely the inverse of His promises to all of those who persevere or endure unto the end. If they endure, He will reward them with eternal life – which is not a shock because it was their having received eternal life itself which endowed them with the capacity to endure. Similarly, those who fail to endure will receive a shock when He comes because He will **come against** them to punish their unfaithfulness – which was a manifestation of the fact that they did not have eternal life within them anyway. To the Sardians, this threat would have been especially understandable, as they had thrice been taken by surprise to great loss. In their location, there was no excuse for being surprised. It was not the coming of an invader that harmed them – it was their lack of preparation. For those at the Second Coming of Jesus, as well, it is not His Coming that will be the problem, it is being unprepared.

(3:4)

> "Yet you have still a few names in Sardis, people who have not soiled their garments, and they will walk with me in white, for they are worthy."
>
> "ἀλλ' ἔχεις ὀλίγα ὀνόματα ἐν Σάρδεσιν ἃ οὐκ ἐμόλυναν τὰ ἱμάτια αὐτῶν, καὶ περιπατήσουσιν μετ' ἐμοῦ ἐν λευκοῖς, ὅτι ἄξιοί εἰσιν."

Despite not having any commendation to give the church, Christ does mention that there are **still a few names in Sardis** of those individuals **who have not soiled their garments**. It should first be noted that the implication here is that there was once a time in which all of those in the church at Sardis had clean garments. The cleanness of those who have **not soiled their garments** is strictly a work of maintenance. Those who no longer have "clean garments" have allowed their garments to become soiled.

Excurses: "Clean Garments"

What is meant by "clean garments" in the book of Revelation? This term is always connected with those who are righteous (Rev. 3:4, 5, 18; 4:4; 16:15; 19:13, 16). The connection is so closely made that it would be easy to believe that the garments represent salvation itself. There could be some Biblical case made for such an assumption based on such verses as Isaiah 61:10, "I will greatly rejoice in the Lord; my soul shall exult in my God, for he has clothed me with *the garments of salvation*; he has covered me with the robe of righteousness, as a bridegroom decks himself like a priest with a beautiful headdress, and as a bride adorns herself with her jewels."

However, it appears more consistent to hold that the garments spoken of throughout Revelation refer to the righteous *works* of those referred to rather than their salvation. Although a different Greek term, Revelation 19:8 refers to the clothing being worn by the saints to be "the righteous deeds of the saints." This concept is one that reaches back well-into the Old Testament, as in Psalm 132:9, "Let your priests be clothed with righteousness, and let your saints shout for joy."

And yet, there is something more that should be discussed in reference to God's interest in the "garments" of His people. In Matthew 22:1-14, Jesus tells a parable of a wedding feast to which many people are invited. The original recipients of invitations simply refuse to come, prompting the king hosting the wedding to tell his servants to go out and compel others to come as his guests. Curiously, having filled the wedding hall with "all whom they found, both bad and good," the king comes and sees a man who is not wearing a wedding garment. Finding the man with no good excuse for being inappropriately dressed, the king calls the attendants to "bind him hand and foot and cast him into outer darkness. In that place there will be weeping and gnashing of teeth.'" What is one to make of this parable, with the continued use of "garments" as referenced throughout John's Revelation?

While righteous deeds (Rev. 19:8) are not meritorious of salvation, they are the product of salvation, and will necessarily follow it such that if anyone makes a profession of faith in Jesus Christ whilst bearing no fruit, they will be easily identified as not belonging in the wedding hall. Thus, when the king throws the poorly-dressed man out of the wedding, he is not doing so out of some bitter classism, but out of respect for those who rightly recognized the honor of being brought into the wedding feast, and who acted in accordance with that recognition by dressing in wedding garments. To drop the allegory, God will not allow those who make a profession of faith to come into His Kingdom if their lives bore no fruit of truly having been converted. This is not because of some expectation of meritorious works on our part in order to gain admission, but because the lack of righteous works displays the lack of inward change that would have necessarily come if we had been filled with the Holy Spirit.

Fig. 5.1

In the case of the church at Sardis, Christ says that there were many in that church who had allowed their garments to become **soiled**. That is, while they once bore the fruit of salvation, they now manifested that their previous testimony was phony. And yet, there were "a few names" on their church roll of people who had **not soiled their garments** – whose lives continued to testify to the fact that they knew God and were truly His people.

To those individuals Christ promises that **they will walk with me in white, for they are worthy.** Obviously, the whiteness of the garment they will walk with Christ in is referent to the purity that He gives eternally (Rev. 7:14), glorifying all of those who come into His eternal kingdom.[724] It is this second phrase that is curious, as He gives this to them because **they are worthy**. Why? They are only worthy because they are in Christ. Their perseverance through hardship is the proof of the legitimacy of their salvation. It is not efficacious in any way, as if it *made* them worthy, but it is illustrative of the fact that **they are worthy**.[725] All of those in Christ have Him alone as all our righteousness (1 Cor. 1:30).[726] These individuals in the church at Sardis who had persevered through hardship, who had **not soiled their garments**, were those who made clear that they were Christians – and Christians, because of the imputed active and inactive obedience of Jesus Christ on their behalf, are worthy to walk with Him in white.[727] And what a glorious thing – that we will one day **walk** with Jesus Christ. Schreiner concludes that this can mean nothing short of having "fellowship with Christ, living with him and enjoying Him…."[728] As the hymn has said for nearly two hundred years:

When He shall come with trumpet sound
O may I then in Him be found;
Dressed in His righteousness alone,
Faultless to stand before the throne!

On Christ the solid Rock I stand!
All other ground is sinking sand!
All other ground is sinking sand!

---

[724] Ladd is quick to point out that the bestowal of these white garments is "in the Messianic Kingdom when those who have remained faithful in a pagan and corrupt society will experience the consummation of fellowship with the Lord." Ladd, *Revelation,* 57. Sweet notes that this may also refer to the victory won by them, as in the case of Roman triumphs wherein white robes were frequent. Sweet, *Revelation*, 100.
[725] Thomas, *Revelation*, 257-258.
[726] Newell, *Revelation*, 66.
[727] For a succinct but able defense of the imputation of both the active and inactive obedience of Christ, see John Piper, *Counted Righteous In Christ*.
[728] Schreiner, *Revelation* BECNT, 180.

(3:5)

"The one who conquers will be clothed thus in white garments, and I will never blot his name out of the book of life. I will confess his name before my Father and before his angels."

"Ὁ νικῶν οὕτως περιβαλεῖται ἐν ἱματίοις λευκοῖς καὶ οὐ μὴ ἐξαλείψω τὸ ὄνομα αὐτοῦ ἐκ τῆς βίβλου τῆς ζωῆς καὶ ὁμολογήσω τὸ ὄνομα αὐτοῦ ἐνώπιον τοῦ πατρός μου καὶ ἐνώπιον τῶν ἀγγέλων αὐτοῦ."

To this one who **will be clothed thus in white garments**, that is, the one who does not soil their garments but keeps His Word and commandments by living faithfully even in times of persecution, which is what it means to **conquer**, Christ further promises to **never blot his name out of the book of life** but rather to **confess his name before my Father and before his angels.**

This, the first mention of the **book of life**, introduces a major figure in the Revelation. This book will reappear explicitly in 13:8, 17:8, 20:15, and 21:27 as the book in which are written the names of all of those who are redeemed. While it appears elsewhere in the Bible (Philippians 4:3) it features prominently in Revelation. It is said that the book was written "from the foundation of the world." It seems evident, then, that the book is no longer being added to, but this specific promise from Christ that He will **never blot his name out of the book of life** raises the question of whether names can be removed from the book. It is certainly not a necessary conclusion that they can be, given that all Christ promises is that He *won't* remove names, but it is fair to say that it is a reasonable question to ask – for why would Christ promise not to do something if it could not be done?

A deeper study of this book gives several details about it that help in answering this question. Philippians 4:3 says the names of those written therein are the names of those who labor for the advancement of the name and Kingdom of God. Revelation 3:5 affirms that Christ will not remove the names of those who persevere from the book. Rev. 13:8 says those not written in the book will worship the Antichrist. Rev. 17:8 says it was written before the world began. Rev. 20:12 says all who ever lived will be judged based (at least in part) by what is written therein. Rev. 20:15 says that all who are not found written in it will go to Hell. Finally, Rev. 21:27 says those who are written in it will live with Christ on the New Heaven and New Earth. So, in short, this book is the book of all those who ever have been or ever will be redeemed by Jesus Christ to live eternally with Him – and to be excluded from this record is to be destined for Hell.

Those who take from this passage some implication that names might be removed from the book of life often reference Old Testament passages such as Exodus 32:32-33 or Psalm 69:28.[729] In Ex. 32, there is reference made to individuals being "blotted out of" a book. It is never called the "book of life" but that is sometimes assumed. However, when God carries out the "blotting out" of those from this book, He ends their lives, implying that in this instance, being removed from the book at hand refers simply to dying. Ladd likens this to a "civic registry" which lists "the names of living citizens."[730] Colin Hemer, in his historical text exploring the seven churches, concludes that this is the most likely way the original audience would have understood both this reference and the others in Revelation 21 and elsewhere.[731] This makes more sense when considering it alongside Psalm 69:28, in which reference is made to some being "blotted out of the book of the living." Rather than referring to someone being removed from the "book of life" they are said to be removed from the list of those living – i.e., they are to die. It is likely that the Sardians would have been particularly aware of this sort of record, as their city historically held the royal archives of the Seleucids, which contained the census information for the whole Empire.[732]

The lone other instance in which any inclination towards the idea that names might be removed from the book of life comes from a textual error found in the *Textus Receptus* in Revelation 22:19. As has already been somewhat explained in the section addressing the approach to Scripture (see Figs. 2:4 and 2:7), the final few verses of Revelation (22:16-21) were entirely missing from the Erasmian sources, meaning that Erasmus composed these verses himself in a manner that produced an error in 22:19 where the Latin word *ligno* (tree) was mistaken for the Latin word *libro* (book). Clearly, this is an issue not to be addressed by adapting one's theology, but by understanding the error in the *Textus Receptus.*

This promise of Christ, that He will **never blot** the **name** of those who are faithful to Him **out of the book of life** but will rather **confess** their **name before my Father and before his angels** is meant to inspire confidence and courage in those believers who maintained faithfulness in Sardis. The entire point of it was that they would hear of their solidarity in the hand of Christ, and of the surety of their being

---

[729] Hemer notes that these passages and others (such as Isaiah 4:3) depict "a register of actual Israelite citizens [which] served as a model for allusion to a citizen-roll of the Heavenly Kingdom." Hemer, *Letters to the Seven Churches,* 148.

[730] Ladd, *Revelation*, 57-58. Thomas also lends some credence to this interpretation despite never endorsing it himself. Thomas, *Revelation 1-7*, 262.

[731] Hemer, *Letters to the Seven Churches*, 52, 148. "The idea of a citizen-register was equally familiar in the Greek world."

[732] Edwyn R. Bevan, *The House of Seleucus* Vol. 1, 151.

confessed as righteous before the Father (cf. Matthew 10:32) and boldly continue to live faithfully. It would be to act in great violence on this text (and the entirety of the remaining Scriptures addressing the subject) to take this verse as implying anything close to a possibility of losing one's salvation. Of much greater faithfulness to the text would be to emphasize the repeated usage on Christ's part of the Greek word ὄνομα.[733] It is first used in verse 1 to refer to the "reputation" they have – literally the "name" they have. He uses the word again in verse 4 to refer to those "few names" who have not soiled their garments. In verse 5 He says that He will not **blot out** the **name** of those who are faithful, and finally says that instead He will confess their **name**. The contrast is clear. For those who care only for the "name" they have amongst others, their name will die with them (Prov. 11:7) by the work of Christ's judgment upon them. But for those who care for their faithfulness to Christ above their reputation in the world, their "name" will be known by Christ, eternally written, and confessed by Him before His Father (Matt. 10:32).

(3:6)

"He who has an ear, let him hear what the Spirit says to the churches.'"

"Ὁ ἔχων οὖς ἀκουσάτω τί τὸ πνεῦμα λέγει ταῖς ἐκκλησίαις."

As with all the other letters, this message was not exclusively for the church at Sardis, although it was directly addressed to them with particular attention paid to their circumstance and need. This message was also to be read and understood (and in some sense applied) by each of the other six churches, as well as all the other churches of our Lord down through the ages. This was not simply what one pastor of one church was to hear, understand, and apply. This is addressed to anyone **who has an ear**, because it is not simply what was said to the Christians in Sardis, it is **what the Spirit says to the churches.**

[733] While reference to this is made in by Sweet, great credit must go to Schreiner for making this point so clear. Sweet, *Revelation*, 99.; Schreiner, *Revelation* BECNT, 176.

(3:7-13) *Philadelphia: The Living Church*

(3:7)

> "And to the angel of the church in Philadelphia write: 'The words of the holy one, the true one, who has the key of David, who opens and no one will shut, who shuts and no one opens."
>
> "Καὶ τῷ ἀγγέλῳ τῆς ἐν Φιλαδελφείᾳ ἐκκλησίας γράψον· Τάδε λέγει ὁ ἅγιος, ὁ ἀληθινός, ὁ ἔχων τὴν κλεῖν Δαυίδ, ὁ ἀνοίγων καὶ οὐδεὶς κλείσει καὶ κλείων καὶ οὐδεὶς ἀνοίγει·"

The sixth letter is addressed **to the angel of the church in Philadelphia**. The people of **Philadelphia** were few in number, as the city had lost much of its population in the massive earthquake of AD 17 (see notes on 3:1). The city was one of the worst hit by this earthquake, and received tax relief and government funding to rebuild. Tiberius was so involved with the rebuilding of the city that he decided to rename it after himself, calling it Neocaesarea.[734] In the aftermath of the earthquake, many fled the area because of fear of future reoccurences. This sets an interesting precedent for the people of Philadelphia, who though few in number, have stayed where they are through hardship. Analogically, the church of Philadelphia appears to be those who through persecution and hardship of their own have remained faithful and true to God.

As each church receives some manner of explanation of the description of Jesus as seen in Revelation 1, it is fitting that the Philadelphians receive an emphatic reminder that He is **the holy one, the true one.** Christ's holiness was repeatedly seen through His having "a long robe" like that of the High Priest and having hair which was "white like wool, like snow." His status as truth embodied (though clearly testified to in John's Gospel; John 14:6) was seen in His having eyes "like a flame of fire" through which no falsehood could remain.

It is also true that these words **the holy one, the true one** are Biblically reserved for God. In Isaiah 40:25 and 1 John 2:20, to give a couple examples, God is called "the Holy One." While the term is also applied to Jesus (Mark 1:24; Luke 4:34; John 6:69), the words together clearly assert deity to Christ (cf. Rev. 6:10).

Of particular interest, however, is the added note that He **has the key of David**. While the initial view of Christ portrayed Him as indeed having keys in His hands, those keys were said to be the "keys of Death and Hell." Here, the specific nature of the key is

---

[734] Ashcraft, *Broadman*, 272.

somewhat more specific. In 1:18 He used the language of having the keys of Death and Hell to portray to His readers that He had complete authority, not only over their lives, but also over everything that followed life. There was no place to which they would go after death in which Christ would not be the ultimate authority.

Here in 3:7, however, Christ gives an even greater comfort to His people by recalling an Old Testament story. The term **key of David** recalls the story of King Hezekiah in Isaiah 22:15-25. God called King Hezekiah to give something referred to in Isaiah 22:22 as "the key of the house of David" to a servant named Eliakim. With this key, Eliakim was to have authority to admit or deny anyone entry into the King's house. In that story, the exact words used of Eliakim's authority in Isa. 22:22 were that "he shall open and none shall shut; and he shall shut and none shall open." Thus, when Christ says He is the one **who opens and no one will shut, who shuts and no one opens**, He is calling us to see in Him the ultimate fulfillment of what Eliakim was in his own day. This also stands as an explanatory note of John's first description of Jesus, as the person bearing the key in Isaiah 22 is described as also being clothed "with your robe" and having "your sash on him" with the authority of the King Himself. The parallels between this person's adornment and duty and those of Christ as described in Revelation 1:13 are unmistakable.

Jesus claims to be the fulfillment of this one who holds the **key of David**, and in so doing, He is claiming the right to grant entrance to the Davidic king of Israel's home. Since there was no Davidic King in the era, Christ's original readers and listeners would have understood that He was claiming to be the one who has authority to open and close the doors to the Kingdom of Heaven. As the King of Israel – not the ethnic, national people but the more encompassing spiritual people of God (Rom. 9:6) – Jesus has the authority to admit or refuse anyone entrance into the home of the true Davidic King. The home of the Davidic King no longer existed on earth. For years, Herod claimed to be the king of Israel, but the Jews did not accept him, considering him a usurper instituted by Rome because he was not of the line of David. It would have, then, been readily apparent to those reading this in the aftermath of the fall of Jerusalem that Jesus was claiming to be able to grant admission "to David's house – the messianic kingdom" of which they had long awaited the restoration.[735] To all outward appearances, any hope of David's kingdom being restored was lost with the destruction of Jerusalem in AD 70, but Jesus asserts here that the Kingdom of Israel was not gone. Rather, it had become a spiritual reality yet to be physically realized. God's Kingdom exists spiritually in and through His people, Christ alone grants or denies admission to that Kingdom, and Christ

---

[735] Ladd, *Revelation*, 59.

alone will bring that kingdom to physical reality when He returns to live and rule amongst His people as the true Davidic King over all Israel – Jew and Gentile alike.[736]

(3:8)

> "'I know your works. Behold, I have set before you an open door, which no one is able to shut. I know that you have but little power, and yet you have kept my word and have not denied my name."
>
> "οἶδά σου τὰ ἔργα, ἰδοὺ δέδωκα ἐνώπιόν σου θύραν ἠνεῳγμένην, ἣν οὐδεὶς δύναται κλεῖσαι αὐτήν, ὅτι μικρὰν ἔχεις δύναμιν καὶ ἐτήρησάς μου τὸν λόγον καὶ οὐκ ἠρνήσω τὸ ὄνομά μου."

Following this great revelation, that Christ is the one who grants or refuses admission into the house of the King of Israel (that is, Christ Himself), He reminds the church at Philadelphia that He also knows their **works.** While this is cause for trepidation in most any person, and especially among those in the churches receiving these letters, the church at Philadelphia receives no criticism. Christ instead tells them – in the wake of reminding them that He holds the keys to God's Kingdom – that He has **set before you an open door**, which in keeping with His previous statement **no one is able to shut.**[737] This admission into God's Kingdom carries with it a clear implication of salvation. Christ promises to these individuals that He has opened the door to the Kingdom for them, and no one can shut it.[738]

While this is a massive promise to the people of Philadelphia, one might wonder why Christ gives such words of encouragement and comfort to them specifically. This is perhaps answered by the fact that they are said to **have but little power, and yet… have kept my word and have not denied my name.** Recalling once again the context of the city of Philadelphia, one would be wise to remember that the city had undergone great turmoil through the earthquake of AD 17, and as a result had most of its population scatter in fear of continued calamities. The church appears to embody the spiritual truth that this physically represented, which is that when hardship comes most individuals will scatter in fear – but Christ recognizes that although these individuals **have but little**

---

[736] Several commentators, such as Mounce and Schreiner, see here a contrast to the practice of the Jews in the day which was to excommunicate any Jews who believed Jesus was the Messiah (John 9:22). Mounce, *Revelation*, 100.

[737] Schreiner points out that this may also be a direct assertion of Christ's deity, as such power is asserted of God in Job 12:14. Schreiner, *Revelation* BECNT, 187.

[738] Mounce, *Revelation*, 101. "No matter if the door to the synagogue has been closed, the door into the messianic kingdom remains open."

power they are remembered and were to be encouraged and comforted because through the hardship they **have kept my word and have not denied my name.**

While this directly applied to the Philadelphia church, which was small by most any standard and exercised little power over their community and world, it is also true of all Christians throughout the Christian age, and of that final Christian generation which will see the end. Christians have always been, are now, and will until the end be in the minority in this world, exercising comparatively **little power.** Even today, when most estimates hold the "Christian" faith to number at almost two and half billion (2,500,000,000) adherents (rendering it the most widely attested religion in the world), that includes individuals of faiths which deny the true Christian doctrines of salvation by grace alone through faith alone in Christ alone on the authority of Scripture alone for the glory of God alone. If one were to figure-out those groups, it would quickly become apparent that even those professing true Christianity number roughly three quarters of a billion (750,000,000) individuals, and amongst those it is likely that more than half cannot be taken as giving a credible profession of faith. Truly Christian individuals in this world represent, then, what is probably the smallest of the five major world religions – and this at the conclusion of the most successful generation of worldwide Christian evangelization in human history. It must be remembered in generations to come wherein this façade of Christian domination is broken that those Christians who faithfully persevere through hardship can know that the door to the Kingdom stands open to them and none can shut it to deny them.

(3:9)

> "Behold, I will make those of the synagogue of Satan who say that they are Jews and are not, but lie—behold, I will make them come and bow down before your feet, and they will learn that I have loved you."
>
> "ἰδοὺ διδῶ ἐκ τῆς συναγωγῆς τοῦ σατανᾶ τῶν λεγόντων ἑαυτοὺς Ἰουδαίους εἶναι, καὶ οὐκ εἰσὶν ἀλλὰ ψεύδονται. ἰδοὺ ποιήσω αὐτοὺς ἵνα ἥξουσιν καὶ προσκυνήσουσιν ἐνώπιον τῶν ποδῶν σου καὶ γνῶσιν ὅτι ἐγὼ ἠγάπησά σε."

Importantly, the hope of those who persevere is not *only* in the eternal reward reserved for them, but is also found in a promise of overcoming those evil and hateful individuals who despise and wickedly use them. Case and point, Christ promises that He **will make those of the synagogue of Satan, who say that they are Jews and are not, but lie** to **come and bow down before your feet** and **learn that I have loved you.** These are the same words Christ used in 2:9 to refer to those ethnically Jewish individuals who do not represent true Israel (see notes on 2:9).[739] Just as He does in 3:7, Christ reemphasizes that despite the continued presence of those ethnic Jews in the diaspora following the destruction of Jerusalem, God's relationship to His people of "Israel" and its members the true "Jews" has not changed whatsoever. What has changed is the identity of Israel and the Jews, as "rejection of their Messiah has led to the denial of the true spiritual Judaism of the Jewish people."[740] Those who are ethnically children of Israel are no longer Israel, but are instead those **who say they are Jews** now, and **are not, but lie.** In this era, they represented the central persecuting force of Christians across the world, as they spread dangerously slanderous lies about Christians in those early years (see again notes on 2:9). Ladd points out that this may even be a further elaboration of Christ's possession of the key of David, having taken it away from the Jews who once had the ability to bring others into the Kingdom (Matt. 23:13) but have now lost that place.[741]

What to make of Christ's specific promise that He will **make them come and bow down before your feet** is difficult. One may say it is unlikely that any person will be made to **bow down before** Christians *alone*, but that instead those enemies of Christ who reject Him (which included and continues to include those of the Jewish faith per John 1:11 and 5:23) will be made to bow down to Him (Philippians 2:10) and that Christians will be alongside Him since He promises that we will be in some sense seated with Him on the throne (Revelation 3:21). More preferrable is the position of J. Barton Payne, who sees in this a prophetic hope of Christians, that those Jewish individuals to be saved at the Second Coming will attribute "particular honor" to Christians in the millennial kingdom, turning the Jewish expectation of exaltation in the Messianic period on its head, as they recognize the foolishness of their rejection of Jesus and the honorability of those who worshipped Him for so long.[742] Schreiner and Ladd agree with this interpretation, seeing in this verse an inversion of what the Jews anticipated in light of passages like Isaiah 49:23 and 60:14, where it was promised that those who oppressed and despised them would come and bow at their feet.[743] Here, they are presented as the oppressors, and can expect to bow at the feet of those they persecute. Mounce words it

---

[739] Hemer notes that "there is no early record of the presence of a community of Jews in Philadelphia." This solidifies the argument that this phrase refers to those diaspora Jews fleeing in the aftermath of the destruction of Jerusalem. Hemer, *Letters to the Seven Churches*, 175.

[740] Ladd, *Revelation*, 60.

[741] Ladd, *Revelation*, 59.

[742] Payne, *Encyclopedia of Biblical Prophecy*, 606.

[743] Schreiner, *Revelation* BECNT, 191.; Ladd, *Revelation*, 60-61.

perfectly, saying, "what the Jews fondly expected from the Gentiles, they themselves will be forced to render to the Christians."[744]

In this, they will **learn that I have loved you**. This is the accomplishment of Christ's prayer in John 17:23 that the whole world would know that God has loved His people. In this one can see the true context of the bowing down that occurs in this instance. Rather than bowing in worship, it is appropriate to see in the bowing of these enemies the contrition of individuals who are forced to reckon with their own error. They had persecuted God's people and slandered them with false accusations, even blaspheming the name of Christ Himself, but in that moment they will be left without any recourse and will only be able to bow their heads in shame and repentance. While they believed they were the only beloved of God (as Is. 43:3-4 asserts God's love for the Jews), here they discover that "believers in Jesus Christ are the objects of God's electing love" and that it was their faith in the coming Messiah that identified them as the recipients of God's love.[745] But in this last day, they will see and realize that the love that God had for them has been outpoured on others as well, and their rejection of this equally beloved group was heinous. This is precisely what Charles Spurgeon described in his 1 July 1877 sermon, "Mourning for Christ." He said,

> There will come a day when the ancient people of God, who have so long rejected Jesus of Nazareth, will discover him to be the Messiah, and then one of their first feelings will be that of deep humiliation and bitter regret before God… And we and they shall rejoice together in him who hath made both one, and broken down the middle wall or partition, so that there is now neither Jew nor Gentile, barbarous Scythian, bond nor free, but we are all one in Christ Jesus.[746]

Of a similar persuasion was George Caird, who wrote of the great hope for a final conversion of the Jews rather than strictly a humiliation. He argued that this hope could be based on two facts. First, John's inversion of Old Testament allusions would maintain this hope, as Jews "ever since the exile… had looked forward to the day when God would bring about the reversal of world affairs… and the heathen nations would acknowledge her as the chosen servant of the one true God."[747] In the inverted situation, the Christian Church would anticipate a great reversal in Jewish affairs (that is, the rejection of Jesus as Messiah and Lord), and would look forward to a day when the Jews would acknowledge them as the chosen servants of the one true God. Secondly, Caird points to John's

---

[744] Mounce, *Revelation*, 102.
[745] Schreiner, *Revelation* BECNT, 191.
[746] Charles H. Spurgeon, "Mourning for Christ" *Metropolitan Tabernacle Pulpit* Vol. 23 (1 July 1877).
[747] G.B. Caird, *A Commentary on the Revelation of St. John the Divine*, 52.

"boundless confidence in the power of Christ." John sees Christ as able to open doors that others, even Satan himself, are not able to close. This leads Caird to conclude,

> Repeatedly in the letters we have heard the heavenly Christ issue his summons to repentance, even where the church seemed hopelessly compromised or sunk in lethargy, and the same possibility of renewal is open to the church's Jewish and Gentile enemies. If they respond to the invitation, it will not be for any merit of their own, but because Christ is making them come, as in former days he had transferred both Peter and Paul from the service of Satan to the service of God. [748]

This author agrees with both Spurgeon and Caird, that despite this great history of blasphemy, which would lead most anyone to imagine the Jewish people entirely cast off from the grace of God, they will in the end have an experience like Saul of Tarsus in Acts 9. Christ intervened to convert that angry and malicious man, breathing hatreds against God's people and doing all he could to get others to deny and blaspheme His name. It is said that although Saul was on the ground (Acts 9:8) he was taken and led by the hand, and although he went three days blind and hungry (Acts 9:9) God did not ignore his prayers (Acts 9:11), but told Saul the truth (Acts 9:16) and had him healed, filled with the Spirit, and welcomed into the family of God alongside those he once persecuted and hated. God has done this for those who falsely claimed to be Jews because of their ethnic birthright (like Saul), and He will do it again – but it will come with an unbearable sense of regret and contrition on those experiencing it. Why would God do this for them? Ezekiel 36:22-23 says He will do it, not for their sake, but for the sake of His own holy name, that although they had profaned His name among the nations, He will vindicate His holiness in reserving grace for even them, such that all the nations will know that He is the LORD.

How does this reckon with the shame implied in their **bowing at** the **feet** of the Christians? Would we not rightly imagine a solemn moment of reconciliatory love between the Apostle Paul and Stephen upon Paul's entrance into Heaven? Would we not imagine Paul falling on Stephen in a penitent desire to be harmoniously united in the Spirit of God despite their last meeting being that in which Paul participated in Stephen's grotesque execution (Acts 7:58)? This is not to claim that there is a time of shame or repayment for wrongdoing in the eternal state, but how could it possibly be that those who martyred and persecuted God's people only later to be converted themselves would not lavish loving penitence on those they persecuted when they come to meet them? Such will be the response of the Jewish people when they acknowledge

[748] Caird, *Revelation*, 53.

Christ as Lord, Messiah, God, and King. They will certainly turn to those Christians who they so long derided, persecuted, and loathed with loving penitence. And this is a point of great hope for all Christians living in the inter-advent age, as it means that none are too far gone for God to redeem them. There is no person so lost, so blasphemous, so hardened as to be beyond God's redemptive grasp. Regardless of how they have treated us, we may run into them in the Kingdom of God, and find them vigorously hugging us in penitence, telling of how they only now see the providence of God in how they treated us and how our testimony was used to bring them to repentance.

(3:10)

> "Because you have kept my word about patient endurance, I will keep you from the hour of trial that is coming on the whole world, to try those who dwell on the earth."
>
> "ὅτι ἐτήρησας τὸν λόγον τῆς ὑπομονῆς μου, κἀγώ σε τηρήσω ἐκ τῆς ὥρας τοῦ πειρασμοῦ τῆς μελλούσης ἔρχεσθαι ἐπὶ τῆς οἰκουμένης ὅλης πειράσαι τοὺς κατοικοῦντας ἐπὶ τῆς γῆς."

Christ gives this promise of security in salvation and ultimate vindication before those who persecute them, but that is not all. More than this, He promises that **because you have kept my word about patient endurance** (which itself shows that Christ intends for the letters to the other churches to also be considered binding on those churches to whom it is not directly addressed), He will **keep you from the hour of trial that is coming on the whole world, to try those who dwell on the earth**.

This promise, that Christ will **keep you from the hour of trial that is coming on the whole world** has been effectively used by many Dispensationalists as representing a promise of the Pre-tribulational rapture of the Church.[749] It has frequently been taken as a promise that Christ would remove His people so as to keep them from experiencing the tribulation period. The central problem with that interpretation of this verse is that the words Jesus uses to convey this thought all disagree with that. For example, the Greek term rendered "keep" (τηρήσω) properly means to "carefully observe so as to keep", "to keep watch upon and guard", "to watch over protectively" or "to keep in a condition."[750] These all imply the protective nature of Christ over His people, but nothing of His removal of them from a circumstance (cf. 2 Pet. 2:9).[751] In fact, Jesus uses this word in John 17:14-15 when praying to the Father, "I have given them your word

---

[749] See Newell, *Revelation*, 70-71.; and Walvoord, *The Rapture Question*, 66-67.

[750] Perschbacher, *The New Analytical Greek Lexicon*, 407.; Sophocles, *Greek Lexicon*, 1081.

[751] See also footnote 360.

and the world has hated them because they are not of the world, just as I am not of the world. I do not ask that you take them out of the world, but that you *keep* them from the evil one." He sets God's protective "keeping" of His people in direct contrast to taking them out of the world. So, if there is anything that this phrase *does not mean*, it is the concept that Christ is promising the Philadelphians that He will remove them from the world prior to hardship coming.[752]

Rather, as Hemer says, "God's people shall receive special protection *in the trial* rather than exemption from it."[753] The language that is used (τηρήσω ἐκ; *to keep out of*) is used in Galatians 1:4 to describe how Christ has given Himself for our sins to deliver us *from* (literally, ἐκ, *out of*) this present evil age." Obviously, this does not denote physical removal, but spiritual preservation through this present evil age.[754] This accords with the habit of God throughout the Bible. Noah and his family were not snatched away to Heaven during the flood only to be returned to Earth afterwards – they were provisionally maintained through the flood. The Israelites were not snatched away from Egypt during the plagues – they were provisionally maintained through the plagues. God does not deliver His people by removing them from hardship, God delivers His people by maintaining them through hardship. Thus, Christians of all ages (including that final era of supreme persecution) can know that **the hour of trial** "will purify them rather than destroy them."[755]

Christ promises the Philadelphians that He will maintain them, not allowing them to fall away or lose their faith and perseverance, in **the hour of trial that is coming on the whole world.** As He makes clear that this coming time of hardship is to include **the whole world** rather than being some manner of a localized event, it is crucial to maintain that Christ is not promising His people (strictly) physical protection in this coming time of hardship. He promised the church at Smyrna that the second death (eternal damnation) would not hurt them at all, but in the face of death on Earth He gives them no such comfort, saying rather to them that if they will "be faithful unto death" He "will give you the crown of life." Their physical death was possible, but their spiritual death was impossible. Christ promises this sort of keeping to His people in the times of tribulation and hardship which come upon the whole world, in the time of the Philadelphians directly, the entire Church Age, and in that final tumult which will strike the world. God's people will suffer persecution and even martyrdom – this is part of

[752] For a full repudiation of that interpretation of the text, see Gundry, *The Church and the Tribulation*, 54-61.
[753] Hemer, *Letters to the Seven Churches*, 164. Emphasis added.
[754] Ladd, *The Blessed Hope*, 85-86.
[755] Ashcraft, *Broadman*, 273.

God's will and sovereign decree (Rev. 6:9-11). Indeed, the whole world will experience this **hour of trial**, but it must be noted why it is coming.

While this hardship will be a worldwide event, Christ explains the purpose of this coming hardship as being **to try those who dwell on the earth**. Throughout the Revelation, this phrase "those who dwell on the Earth" is repeatedly used to refer to the unsaved, unredeemed, or antichristian (3:10; 11:10; 13:8, 12, 14; 14:6; 17:8).[756] Why does God bring hardship and tribulation on the Earth? It is to try (πειράσαι; *test*) those who are not God's people. For those who make a profession but do not keep it, the testing proved them to be false religionists. For those who make no profession and grow ever more hateful towards God in times of hardship, the testing proves them to be callous and deserving of wrath, such that at one point in Revelation 16:6 it is explicitly said of these that "they have shed the blood of saints and prophets, and you have given them blood to drink. *It is what they deserve!*" Thus, hardship and tribulation serves this purpose: it purges the false professors of Christ's name, and it firmly validates the condemnation of those who continually reject Him. For His people, however, it serves only as an elevated opportunity to persevere and maintain faithfulness. The Puritans had a saying for this, "The same sun that melts the wax, hardens the clay."[757] This concept, that God would use the same event or tactics to secure His people while purging out the dross, is not foreign to the Scriptures. Daniel 12:10 speaks of an apocalyptic event which will have the following result: "Many shall purify themselves and make themselves white and be refined, but the wicked shall act wickedly. And none of the wicked shall understand, but those who are wise shall understand."

(3:11)

> "I am coming soon. Hold fast what you have, so that no one may seize your crown."
>
> "ἔρχομαι ταχύ· κράτει ὃ ἔχεις, ἵνα μηδεὶς λάβῃ τὸν στέφανόν σου."

Similar to the promise that Christ gave to the church at Thyatira in 2:25, He promises that He is **coming soon** and commands them to **hold fast what you have**. The promise that Christ will come **soon** is nothing to stumble over (see notes on 1:1). It is true that this may refer to some other sense of timing that is in the mind of God (such that a day is a thousand years and a thousand years a single day) as appears to be the case when this term is used in Romans 16:20 to refer to the Church's victory over Satan. It is

---

[756] Hemer, *Letters to the Seven Churches*, 164.

[757] Though much older, this saying is attested in Charles H. Spurgeon, "The Lesson of the Almond Tree" *Metropolitan Tabernacle Pulpit* Vol. 46 (7 April 1881).

also worth maintaining in mind that this promise applies to every Christian of every age, such that our experiencing the glory of Christ is never more than 100 years away. The span of time between our present state and our standing in the presence of Christ is by any standard short. So, whether this refers to Christ coming in glory to rule and reign on the Earth at the end of time, or to His coming to us individually to usher us home at the end of our lives, He can be rightly said to be **coming soon** – and as a result, we all must **hold fast** to **what you have.**

Tied closely to His promise that He would keep us in the time of hardship are His repeated warnings against walking away from Him. Although it is true that our salvation is secure because of the monergistic work of God, our experience of perseverance appears to us very syngergistic. That is, in the same way that we see ourselves participating in the sanctification of our lives (although all holiness brought from within us is the result of the work of God in us), we may also see ourselves as participating in the maintenance of our relationship with God (although the preservation of our salvation is entirely the result of the power of God). With this intricate dynamic in mind, Christ calls His people to **hold fast what you have, so that no one may seize your crown.** Crowns here (and elsewhere in Revelation; see notes on 2:10) represent salvation as conveyed by Christ to us. For those who persevere until the end, they are described as being those who do not allow anyone (or anything for that matter) to **seize** (or take away forcibly) **their crown**, that is their faithful relationship with Christ.

(3:12)

> "The one who conquers, I will make him a pillar in the temple of my God. Never shall he go out of it, and I will write on him the name of my God, and the name of the city of my God, the new Jerusalem, which comes down from my God out of heaven, and my own new name."
>
> "Ὁ νικῶν ποιήσω αὐτὸν στῦλον ἐν τῷ ναῷ τοῦ θεοῦ μου καὶ ἔξω οὐ μὴ ἐξέλθῃ ἔτι καὶ γράψω ἐπ' αὐτὸν τὸ ὄνομα τοῦ θεοῦ μου καὶ τὸ ὄνομα τῆς πόλεως τοῦ θεοῦ μου, τῆς καινῆς Ἰερουσαλὴμ ἡ καταβαίνουσα ἐκ τοῦ οὐρανοῦ ἀπὸ τοῦ θεοῦ μου, καὶ τὸ ὄνομά μου τὸ καινόν."

Having given this church, small but faithful, nothing but encouragement and comfort, Christ now gives them the more standard form of encouragement that is offered to all the other churches and those **who conquer**. To the church at Philadelphia, He promises the conquerors that He will **make him a pillar in the temple of my God.** Without any dignifying argument, suffice it to say this promise has nothing to do with any physical temple. Rather, it refers to the place where God dwells (as He was said to do in the Jewish-Temple era). In Heaven, as well as in the New Heaven and New Earth atmosphere, there is no temple (Rev. 21:22). In fact, it is said that "its temple *is* the Lord God the Almighty and the Lamb." The presence of God is no longer constrained to a building called a temple, but is experienced in all places universally, making Him the temple Himself.[758] This is the fulfillment of that grand vision of Ezekiel 40-48, which concludes with the telling words, "the name of the city from that time on shall be, 'The LORD Is There.'"[759]

For those who conquer, Christ promises that they will be ever in the presence of God the Almighty and the Lamb, just as a pillar is always in the building it supports and **never shall... go out of it**. This might have been a direct encouragement to the Philadelphians who had seen their city fall apart (literally and metaphorically) because of a major earthquake.[760] Pillars do not move. They are solid and cannot be removed without dealing severe damage to the building they are in. In the same way, God will **never** allow any of His people to ever **go out** from His presence. This may be a direct statement of affirmation to the Philadelphians, who had seen many of their co-citizens **go out** of the city after the earthquake.[761] The security experienced in God will never quake or falter – and His people will never flee from Him in fear of calamity.[762]

That is not to say that God's loving and peace-giving presence becomes an all-encompassing possession of all that exists, as universalists may wish to impose. There are explicitly some who are outside the Temple (or the city of New Jerusalem). Whilst not having escaped the presence of God (as if such a thing could be done) they experience only the wrath of God in His presence (Rev. 14:10) because they "are the dogs and sorcerers and the sexually immoral and murderers and idolaters and everyone who loves and practices falsehood." (22:15) These are not God's people. The distinction is clear – God's people will spend eternity with and in His presence, never able to depart from Him, enjoying Him forever in the Temple or the Holy City of New Jerusalem, while those enemies of God will also spend eternity with and in His presence, never able to

---

[758] Schreiner, *Revelation* BECNT, 195.

[759] Payne, *Encyclopedia of Biblical Prophecy*, 607. Literally, the Hebrew term rendered "There" (שָׁמָּה׃) is frequently rendered as "where" or "with" such that the phrase could be rendered "the name of the city from that time on shall be *where the LORD is*." The Temple, then, is simply where God is – rather than being a temple, it is a description of His presence. To be in Him is to be in Ezekiel's Temple.

[760] Mounce, *Revelation*, 104.

[761] Ashcraft, *Broadman*, 273.

[762] This could also be an allusion to the recently destroyed Temple in "old Jerusalem" over against the permanent and immovable Temple in the coming "new Jerusalem." However, this interpretation is unlikely, as it would bear very little significance to the Philadelphian church. A local and recent cataclysmic earthquake is a much more likely referent.

depart from Him, separated only from His people and affection whilst experiencing the righteous wrath of God outpoured on them undiluted in the lake of fire. For the Christians, the promise of remaining forever in God's presence is consolation; but for the damned, the promise of remaining forever in God's presence is only terrifying.

Of similar effect but different image is the promise that Christ will write three things on the conquerors:

1. **The name of my God** is written on those who persevere unto the end. This is referred to in Revelation 7:3 as a "sealing." God's people are said to be sealed "on their foreheads." This is certainly the same thing, as the two images are combined in Revelation 14:1 where it is said they have "His name and His Father's name written on their foreheads." It is hard to ignore the contrast between this and the "mark of the beast." (Rev. 13:16; 14:9; 14:11) The people of God are marked, sealed, or identified by having the name of God on their foreheads while the enemies of God are identified by having the mark of the beast on their foreheads. However, rather than this mark being a physically recognizable "tattoo-like" image literally written on the forehead, it is meant to be understood as a public representation of allegiance which is easily recognized, just as it was when this same attribute was said of the Israelites in the Old Testament (Numbers 6:27). Those who are allegiant to God will be "marked out" so clearly that it will be as though His name is written on their foreheads, while those who are enemies of God will be "marked out" so clearly that it will be as though the beast's symbol was written on their foreheads. In short, every Christian takes God's name with them (bringing great meaning to the third commandment not to "take the name of the LORD your God in vain, for the LORD will not hold him guiltless who takes his name in vain" as well as many other Old Testament passages such as Deut. 28:10 and Isaiah 43:7) everywhere they go.[763] In contrast, every heathen takes the name of the enemy of God with them everywhere they go. They are "marked" or identified by their actions and lifestyles, as if by a large flashing sign indicating "belonging to Satan."[764]
2. **The name of the city of my God, the new Jerusalem, which comes down from my God out of heaven** is also written on God's people. Each of these identifiers serve to attest to possession, and this is nothing different from that which precedes or follows it. God's people belong to Him, Christ's people belong

[763] This idea largely influenced by Ashcraft's single line, "Every Christian wears his name." Ashcraft, *Broadman*, 273.

[764] Cf. Matt. 7:16; John 13:35; John 8:44.

to Him, and the people of the Kingdom belong to the Kingdom. It is said elsewhere in the Bible that God's people have a citizenship in Heaven (Philippians 3:20; Gal. 4:26) but this is even more vividly depicted in Revelation 21:9-10 when God's people are literally depicted as *being* the Kingdom of God.[765] In that passage, John is told that he is about to see "the Bride, the wife of the Lamb" (clearly, this is the Church) but then he looks and sees "the holy city Jerusalem coming down out of Heaven from God." Not only do God's people belong to the Kingdom, **the New Jerusalem, the city of my God**, they actually compose this city. Rather than it being a physical place, it is a people group who bear God's mark of citizenship.[766] It is this group of people who **come down from God out of Heaven** in Revelation 21:9-10 and are identified as **the city**. This would have been particularly meaningful to the people of Philadelphia, as in the rebuilding process of the city after the earthquake of AD 17, Tiberias had given the city a "new name" of Neocaesarea in his own honor.[767] Although the name of their city may be in flux, they could trust that the city of God would never change, and that the name of it was written on them eternally.

3. Finally, Christ promises to write on His people **my own new name.**[768] In this the direct contrast to the "mark of the beast" is seen, in that God's people bear the mark of the Lamb. Again, rather than this being a literal mark, it is a spiritual truth recognized by a lifestyle and allegiance. Elsewhere in the Bible, the seal to be set upon God's people is noted as being the Holy Spirit (Eph. 1:13; 4:30). Thus, the people of God are Biblically said to carry the "mark" or "seal" of the Father, the Son, and the Holy Spirit. And it is this Trinitarian God that we will ultimately stand before and worship in eternity, as Revelation 22:3-4 says, "no longer will there be anything accursed, but the throne of God and of the Lamb will be in it, and His servants will worship Him. They will see His face, and His name will be on their foreheads." We will forever be identified by our being owned by and allegiant to this Trinitarian God such that anytime someone sees us, they see a very public and undeniable commitment to serving God.

---

[765] Schreiner provides a very helpful chart showing the similarities in the language of 3:12, 21:2, and 21:10. Schreiner, *Revelation* BECNT, 196-197. For the citizenship of God's people, see Mounce, *Revelation*, 105.
[766] Ladd, *Revelation*, 63.
[767] Morris Ashcraft, *The Broadman Bible Commentary* Vol. 12, 272.
[768] "New" in this sense (καινόν) carries with it the same sense of newness or freshness as that new name promised to the church at Pergamum (see notes on 2:17). There is a deeper sense, however, in which Christ does seem to have some sort of name which is "new" in being hitherto unknown (see Rev. 19:12).

(3:13)

"He who has an ear, let him hear what the Spirit says to the churches.'"

"Ὁ ἔχων οὖς ἀκουσάτω τί τὸ πνεῦμα λέγει ταῖς ἐκκλησίαις."

This letter is a great encouragement not only to those Philadelphians who underwent great hardship and persecution in their time, but to any **who has an ear** to hear. All Christians down through the ages have been benefitted by hearing **what the Spirit says to the churches**, because persecution will always be a reality with which the Christian community must reckon.[769] It will never be the case that Christians will have ease in Zion, until we reach the very presence of God Himself, in which we will find ourselves eternally at home. Until then, we must persevere, hold fast what we have, and although at times we will be few in number, we must recall the Philadelphians who although having but little power kept God's word and would not deny His name. For their faithfulness, they were promised eternal life, vindication in the sight of their enemies, and an unshakable, unmovable position in the presence of God where they would be acknowledged as His and identified by bearing His name forever. May this be our hope as well.

[769] Schreiner helpfully points out that after all of the signs of divinity attributed to Christ in this letter and others, it is still attributed that these are the words of the Spirit. This, he says, suggests that the Holy Spirit is deity along with Christ and the Father. Schreiner, *Revelation* BECNT, 198.

(3:14-22) *Laodicea: The Complacent Church*

(3:14)

"And to the angel of the church in Laodicea write: 'The words of the Amen, the faithful and true witness, the beginning of God's creation."

"Καὶ τῷ ἀγγέλῳ τῆς ἐν Λαοδικείᾳ ἐκκλησίας γράψον· Τάδε λέγει ὁ ἀμήν, ὁ μάρτυς ὁ πιστὸς καὶ ἀληθινός, ἡ ἀρχὴ τῆς κτίσεως τοῦ θεοῦ·"

The final letter is once more addressed to **the angel of the church**. One should meditate on the reality that even in situations like that which follows here, wherein the message to be read or delivered is one without any commendation but only rebuke, the pastor of the church is expected to deliver it to his people. Pastors would do well to remember that the Word of God for churches is not always encouraging, uplifting, or rejuvenating. It edifies, convicts, and instructs – sometimes in painful ways. Pastors are nonetheless expected to deliver the Word, even when it edifies, convicts, and instructs them, not for the encouragement of the church, but for the sanctification of the church.

The church in Laodicea was located in a relatively new city, as far as the seven written to in the Revelation are concerned. It was quite unlike the others in that it had no natural fortifications (as Sardis) nor was it founded upon some naturally occurring landmark that benefitted the city (as Ephesus). Laodicea was, instead, established at the convergence of several trade routes. While this was beneficial to the city, there was one major problem: there was no natural source of water to feed the city. Six miles south in the city of Denizli, there existed hot springs which were, in time, rerouted using stone pipes three feet in diameter to bring water to the city. Almost an equal distance to their north was the city of Hierapolis, which also had hot springs, but the water here was only available to the Laodiceans when it spilled over a 300-foot calcium-carbonate cliff and dribbled down to them. Thus, while the city was known for its flourishing banking industry and local sheep market that produced a rare and valuable black wool used to make expensive carpets and clothes, the water in the city was always bitter to the taste having come to them either over a calcium-carbonate cliff, or having travelled so far through stone pipes. In fact, the water was so unappealing that the ancient historian Strabo, when writing about Laodicea, makes a point to note that despite everything a passerby would think about the water, "it is fit for the purpose of drinking."[770] His point was that the water was so bitter people assumed it was poisonous, so he affirmed that indeed, it was fit for drinking.

---

[770] Strabo, *Geography*, 13:4:14.

The city, historically, is remembered as being one with great wealth. Cicero recorded having done his personal banking there.[771] The Romans are said to have plundered great sums from other Asian cities and invested it in the banks of Laodicea.[772] Aside from their banking and sheep markets, Laodicea was known for hosting a reputable medical school which had some of the greatest faculty in Asia Minor.[773] At this school they were noted as having produced a world-renowned salve which was rumored to be wondrous for both the eyes and ears of afflicted individuals. Further, although Laodicea (like many other cities in the region) was wrecked by an earthquake in the early AD 60's, they chose to rebuild without government assistance. It took them time to rebuild, but by AD 79 they had rebuilt and even erected a stadium to honor the emperor, Titus.[774]

It should also be noted that **Laodicea** was a sister city of Colossae, which lay ten miles away.[775] In Paul's letter to the Colossians, he mentions Laodicea four times (Col. 2:1; 4:13, 15, 16), and some have even speculated that it was Epaphras of Colossae who planted the church at Laodicea.[776] There are no few parallels between the letter written here to the church at Laodicea and the letter Paul wrote to the Colossians. This is for good reason, as the churches were evidently in some connection with one another as manifested by the fact that Paul closes his letter by calling for the Colossians to allow the church at Laodicea to read it, and for the Colossians to read the letter he sent to the Laodiceans. (Col. 4:16) Unfortunately, whatever Paul wrote to the Laodiceans has been lost to history, but it is likely that Christ references several of the things they were expected to have learned both from that letter and the one Paul wrote to the Colossians.[777]

That Christ refers to these as the **words of the Amen** is only clarified by those words which follow, that He is **the faithful and true witness**. The word **Amen** here holds the same meaning as is intended each time it is used in Isaiah 65:16 to describe God as "the God of truth."[778] In the Hebrew the word rendered as "truth" is אָמֵן (*amen*).[779] Rather

---

[771] Cicero, *Epistulae ad Familiares*, 3:5:4.; *Letters to Atticus,* 5:15:1-2.

[772] This is noted in both Hemer and Mounce, although both refer to W.W. Tarn and G.T.Grifith, *Hellenistic Civilization*, 113. This reference, however, appeals to an unascertainable source. They list "Str. 578" which would only sensibly refer to Strabo, but no such reference can be found in his writings.

[773] Strabo, *Geography*, 12:8:20.

[774] Schreiner, *Revelation* BECNT, 200. See comments on 3:18.

[775] Mounce, *Revelation*, 106.

[776] Ladd, *Revelation*, 64.

[777] Readers should not be fooled by a pseudonymous letter sometimes entitled "The Letter to the Laodiceans." While ancient in origin, being found in early Latin Bibles and mentioned by many ancient authors, this letter is nothing more than a "patchwork of phrases from other letters of Paul." Philip Sellew, "The Letter to the Laodiceans" in Bruce Metzger and Michael Coogan, eds., *The Oxford Companion to the Bible*, 420.

[778] Mounce, *Revelation,* 108. Later in Revelation, God is also referred to as the one who is true (6:10).

than indicating an inverse to false, this usage asserts an attribute of character, so as to say "He is *true.*" While more will be said momentarily about the direct application of His referring to Himself as the **faithful and true witness**, it should immediately be noted that (as in 1:5) Christ identifies Himself with the word *martys* (μάρτυς) from which we gather the English word *martyr.*[780] It is rightly rendered *witness*, but its usage throughout the Revelation will always refer to those of God's people who have faithfully endured suffering to the end. Christ is the exemplar of this, both as the first to do so, and certainly as the best to ever do so, having enduring temptations and obstacles like us but unlike anything any human being will ever endure in terms of magnitude and frequency – yet without failure or sin. (Heb. 4:15)

What precisely is meant when Christ refers to Himself as **the beginning of God's creation** has been a topic of much debate – and unlike many arguments over meaning in Revelation, the meaning of this phrase is very important because of its theological and Christological implications. Some call to mind the parallel between Paul's similar statements in his epistle to the Colossians (Col. 1:15-18) and claim that this statement is meant to call to their minds that letter (which they were expected to have read per Col. 4:16).[781] However, this does not serve much of any explanatory purpose, but rather serves only as a cross-reference or callback to another point that seems to be different from the point Christ is making in this moment.

One very appealing (and widely endorsed) position comes from seeing ἀρχὴ as describing a position, as it is "often used for rulers and princes" in passages like Luke 20:20, 12:11; 1 Cor. 15:24; Rom. 8:38; Eph. 1:21, 3:10, 6:12; Col. 1:16; 2:10, 2:15; and Titus 3:1.[782] Mounce is so confident in this rendering that he, without explanation or apology, renders it as "the final designation, 'the ruler (*arche*) of God's creation.'"[783] However, it is difficult to see this as being John's intent given the similarities between his letter to Laodicea and the Pauline letter to the Colossians.

---

[779] There may also be some connection here with what Paul is conveying when he uses the word "amen" in 2 Corinthians 1:20.

[780] This and the characteristic of Christ pointed out to the church at Philadelphia are noted by Schreiner as being the only ones not directly taken from the first vision. However, the connections are so close that although not verbatim, it is obvious that these qualities are connected to that initial description. Schreiner, *Revelation* BECNT, 201.

[781] Hemer, *Letters to the Seven Churches*, 184-185.; Mounce, *Revelation*, 108.

[782] Endorsed by Koester and Schreiner, but more vividly detailed in Stuart, *Commentary on the Apocalypse* 2, 99.

[783] Mounce, *Revelation*, 108. Schreiner does the same in his BECNT commentary (202).

More likely, though, is the approach taken by Schreiner in his 2018 *Expository Commentary* on Revelation, in which he notes that Jesus is referred to as the *arche* because:

> [B]y his resurrection he is the beginning of God's new creation. Colossians 1:18 points us in the same direction, declaring Jesus to be the 'beginning, the firstborn from the dead.' 'Beginning' (*arche*) in Colossians 1:18 is the same term found in Revelation 3:14. In both instances, the point is that Jesus is the beginning of the new creation as the resurrected and exalted Lord. Such an affirmation does not deny or contradict that as the Son of God he is the eternal one, without beginning or end (cf. Rev. 22:13). Why does Jesus tell the church at Laodicea that the new creation begins with him? Because, as the one in whom God's eschatological promises are fulfilled, he has the resources to grant them everything they need (cf. 3:18, 20).[784]

It is painfully regrettable that he entirely reverses himself in his 2023 commentary after embracing New Creation Millennialism, which requires that the New Creation *begins* with the millennial reign. He writes in that commentary that this must refer, not to Christ being the beginning of the New Creation (which would be devastating to his newfound position) but only to His serving as the beginning of the physical creation, with the only rationale for this reversal being given as "there is not a clear reference here to the new creation."[785]

Contrary to this statement, there is a clear reference to the new creation in that the surrounding phrases all reference resurrection passages in directly linked literature. For example, the only other place in the book of Revelation in which Jesus is referred to as the **faithful witness** is in 1:5 where the phrase is followed by the words, "the firstborn of the dead." His being listed as the *firstborn* of the dead points to the promise of the new creation at the resurrection of the saints. And this phrase, like several others in the letter to the Laodiceans, is likely in reference to Paul's wording in Colossians 1:18 wherein he described Jesus as "the beginning and firstborn from among the dead." As Schreiner noted in his 2018 commentary, the word rendered "beginning" in Col. 1:18 is the exact same Greek word as is here found in Rev. 3:14. But what he evidently neglects is that Paul asserts a present reality in Colossians 1 that is not only related to the creation of the physical world (Col. 1:15-17), but also includes the creation of newness of life (Col. 1:21-22). He seems to signal this by using the contrasting titles, "firstborn of all creation" (Col.

---

[784] Thomas Schreiner, "Revelation" in *ESV Expository Commentary* Vol. 12, 595.

[785] Schreiner, *Revelation* BECNT, 203.

1:15) and "firstborn from the dead" (Col. 1:18). Calling Christ the firstborn of all creation might have spoken to His preeminence over the physical creation while His position as firstborn from among the dead referred to his preeminence over the new creation – but John combines those two images and refers to Christ first as the **faithful and true witness**, reminding readers of His being the "firstborn of the dead" in Revelation 1:5, but then flips the script and shows that His death was the **beginning of God's creation.**

To summarize, the scriptural cross-references almost undeniably being made by John allude to two passages which speak of Jesus in resurrection and newness-of-life-oriented contexts rather than strictly Genesis-type creation assertions. John's combination of the two images used by Paul depicts Christ as both the creator of Heaven and Earth, and the creator of the New Heavens and Earth; the creator of man and the creator of the new man in Christ; the conduit through whom came creation and the conduit through whom has come the new creation.

Finally, regarding application, the characteristics of Christ referenced to each respective church has some specific bearing on them. They need to know *this* characteristic about Christ to address an issue in their congregation. The corrective calls that Christ gives this church are variously that they need to "repent" (3:19), "open the door" (3:20), "buy from me gold refined by fire" (3:18) and in response He promises that the shame of their nakedness would be covered and they would begin to see (3:18), and that Christ Himself would "come in to him and eat with him and he with me." (3:20) All of this beats the drum of the newness of life promised to Christians very loudly. A church hearing all of that is undoubtedly being pointed to see and treasure the new creation that Christ catalyzes in His people. For all of these reasons, Christ is called the **beginning of God's creation** because His resurrection from the dead represents the inauguration of God's new creation.

(3:15-16)

> "'I know your works: you are neither cold nor hot. Would that you were either cold or hot! So, because you are lukewarm, and neither hot nor cold, I will spit you out of my mouth."
>
> "οἶδά σου τὰ ἔργα ὅτι οὔτε ψυχρὸς εἶ οὔτε ζεστός. ὄφελον ψυχρὸς ἦς ἢ ζεστός. οὕτως ὅτι χλιαρὸς εἶ καὶ οὔτε ζεστὸς οὔτε ψυχρός, μέλλω σε ἐμέσαι ἐκ τοῦ στόματός μου."

Being one of the only two churches to receive no commendation, Laodicea receives an initial rebuke in that Christ says he **knows your works.** While certainly true of each church to whom He speaks, Christ's conclusion and judgment of the works at Laodicea is the problem, as they are **neither cold nor hot.** This may be an obvious allusion to the problem caused by the city's lack of a natural water supply. Christ's later statements about their being **lukewarm, and neither hot nor cold** leading to His vomiting them **out of** his **mouth** likely drew vivid images in the minds of the Laodiceans of the response of some unknowing passerby's upon tasting the mineral-rich water they had.[786]

While Christian interpreters have long made arguments about the general distastefulness of lukewarm water serving as an analogy of the spiritual state of the Laodiceans, this understanding becomes very difficult to maintain when considering Christ's comment that He **would** prefer **that you were cold or hot.** What sense would it make that Christ would desire for His people to be spiritually cold? This seems to be an odd statement – that Christ would prefer His people to be either one thing *or* its opposite. Mounce, however, helpfully appeals to the work of M.J.S. Rudwick and E.M.B. Green, the mid-twentieth century Cambridge historical theologians.[787] They masterfully explain in their 1958 treatise,

> At Hierapolis the hot spring water was much prized for its healing properties, and the extensive and opulent remains of the city show the breadth of its popularity and appeal. The mineral matter deposited by the water as it falls to the valley floor has formed a series of terraces edged with spectacular white cascades. These white cliffs are a most conspicuous landmark for miles around, and are clearly visible from Laodicea. Hence the mention of *zestos* would probably have reminded a Laodicean of the curative waters of his city's nearest neighbour. Colossae, of course, less than ten miles away, had a perfectly good supply of cold water, and the adjective *psychros* may well refer to her. But no such specific allusion is requisite. For the greater part of the year this region is very hot and dry. In such a climate cold water is the most valued source of refreshment, and the very word *psychyos* inevitably brings such associations to the mind of any one on the spot.

---

[786] The Greek term rendered "spit" (ἐμέσαι) is defined by Thayer as "to vomit, throw up; to reject with extreme disgust." Thayer, *Thayer's Greek-English Lexicon*, 207.
[787] Mounce, *Revelation*, 109.

> If this reconstruction of the local situation be correct, Laodicea would have been notorious as a city which, for all its prosperity, could provide neither the refreshment of cold water for the weary, as, for example, its neighbour Colossae could, nor the healing properties of hot water for the sick, as its neighbour Hierapolis could. Its lukewarm water was useless for either purpose, and only fit to be 'spewed out of the mouth.' The Church in Laodicea would have been intended to see in itself a similar uselessness. It was providing neither refreshment for the spiritually weary, nor healing for the spiritually sick. It was totally ineffective, and thus distasteful to its Lord. On this interpretation, then, the Church is not being informed of its spiritual temperature; rather it is being called to reflect on the barrenness of its works.[788]

This approach comports well with the fact that Christ prefaces such a criticism with the statement, **I know your *works*.** Rather than referring to their spiritual state, He refers to the displeasure He has with their works.

(3:17)

> "For you say, I am rich, I have prospered, and I need nothing, not realizing that you are wretched, pitiable, poor, blind, and naked."
>
> "ὅτι λέγεις ὅτι πλούσιός εἰμι καὶ πεπλούτηκα καὶ οὐδὲν χρείαν ἔχω, καὶ οὐκ οἶδας ὅτι σὺ εἶ ὁ ταλαίπωρος καὶ ἐλεεινὸς καὶ πτωχὸς καὶ τυφλὸς καὶ γυμνός,"

Having identified His central problem with the church (the worthlessness of their works) Christ expands upon the reason for His dissatisfaction with them. Christ describes them as saying, **"I am rich, I have prospered, and I need nothing"** but points out the reality as being one in which they **are wretched, pitiable, poor, blind, and naked.** If it is accepted that Christ has previously reprimanded them for having useless works, this explains why their works are so useless and worthless to Christ. The attitude and demeanor in which they perform their works is the problem. Hanns Lilje speaks succinctly to this problem, not only in the Laodiceans, but in all people, when he writes, "self-sufficiency leads without exception to self-deception."[789]

Perhaps the Laodiceans were performing many good works, but they did so in a mindset of superiority, prosperity, and only in light of their own lack of need (or in a

---

[788] M.J.S. Rudwick and E.M.B. Green, "The Laodicean Lukewarmness" *The Expository Times* 69:6 (March 1958): 177-178.

[789] Lilje, *The Last Book of the Bible*, 101.

mindset of self-sufficiency as Lilje put it). They are only one of two churches (alongside Smyrna) to have no mention of persecution, and correspondingly no commendation. They are at peace with the community around them, likely because of the good works they do, which are not distinctly Christ-exalting, but are instead man-exalting.[790] There are many passages forbidding this sort of "good work." Jesus explicitly commanded His disciples not to be pompous in their relationship with God – with particular attention to how that attitude impacts their relations with others (Luke 18:9-14). He commanded His people to be humble in how they gave to the poor and in how they prayed in the presence of others (Matthew 6:2-8). And while God calls Christians to give out of their abundance (2 Corinthians 8:14) they are not to give only *because* they have abundance. In fact, Christ reckoned the charity of those who contribute out of their poverty as more valuable than the charity of those who contribute out of their abundance (Luke 21:1-4). Thus, the spiritual state of the Laodiceans, even when doing "good works" made their works worthless to Christ. They did no good for the purpose of building up others, or for the purpose of edifying others. They did "good" only out of a sense of self-satisfaction and convenience.

Christ admonishes them to see themselves as He sees them. If they approached ministry, missions, charity, and evangelism with a mindset of one impoverished person helping another, their work would be acceptable. They had a need to see their true nature, as **wretched, pitiable, poor, blind, and naked.** In short, they needed to see themselves in the eyes of those to whom they ministered. The descriptors **wretched, pitiable,** and **blind** would directly call to mind those maimed and crippled individuals who were unable to provide for themselves. Those **poor** and **naked** would call to mind those individuals who, through various misfortunes of their own fault or otherwise, have lost everything. This is how Christ finds each sinner. Completely unable to provide any good thing for themselves – most supremely salvation – and through great misfortune of their own fault or otherwise, standing before God as poor and naked in need of a Savior. The Christians in the church at Laodicea should have known this about themselves, and treated those enduring physically what they endured spiritually with the same physical mercy that Christ spiritually showed them.

For a matter of application, all Christians of all ages should treat all impoverished individuals in just such a way, for just the same reason. For if we fail to, we have become like the Laodiceans – our works may be as "holy" or "righteous" in our eyes as they always have been, but if our motivation is not found in the redemption wrought in us by Christ and our desire to show His love and mercy to others, our "good works" are

[790] Ladd, *Revelation*, 64.

worthless and will be vomited out by Christ. Of similar importance is the recognition that material growth and blessing is not necessarily equivalent or indicative to spiritual growth and blessing. Many churches, Laodicea perhaps included, grow financially and numerically not by doing God's work, but by doing "good works" while minimizing God.[791] Philanthropy and charity alone are not Christianity.

(3:18)

> "I counsel you to buy from me gold refined by fire, so that you may be rich, and white garments so that you may clothe yourself and the shame of your nakedness may not be seen, and salve to anoint your eyes, so that you may see."
>
> "συμβουλεύω σοι ἀγοράσαι παρ' ἐμοῦ χρυσίον πεπυρωμένον ἐκ πυρὸς ἵνα πλουτήσῃς, καὶ ἱμάτια λευκὰ ἵνα περιβάλῃ καὶ μὴ φανερωθῇ ἡ αἰσχύνη τῆς γυμνότητός σου, καὶ κολλ[ο]ύριον ἐγχρῖσαι τοὺς ὀφθαλμούς σου ἵνα βλέπῃς."

To remedy this error, Christ calls to the Laodiceans saying, **I counsel you to buy from me gold refined by fire, so that you may be rich.** Importantly, Christ must not be mistaken as calling for Christians to in any way "purchase" salvation or His favor through either financial means or good works. As bankers and wealthy tradespeople, they were likely familiar with giving investment or trade advice to others, saying sometimes "I counsel you to buy…" But here, Christ reverses their position. They have trusted in their ability as financiers and traders, rather than in true righteousness. God places no earthly price on His esteem (Isaiah 55:1; Rev. 22:17) but instead repeatedly calls to His people to stop the outward shows of faithfulness and turn to Him with inward faithfulness (Isaiah 58:1-12; Joel 2:12-14).

Rather than Christ demanding some earthly purchase of His favor or esteem, it is precisely the point of this counsel that their "good works" are distasteful to Christ to the degree of causing Him to vomit, and that this can only be corrected through their coming to **buy from** him **gold refined by fire**, which would practically look like orienting their hearts and desires toward Him such that their good works might be acceptable in His sight. This is nothing distinct from what Christ says in Matthew 6:20-21, "Lay up for yourselves treasures in heaven, where neither moth nor rust destroys and where thieves do not break in and steal. For where your treasure is, there will your heart be also." This is true wealth in the sight of God: to have one's eyes and heart always oriented heavenward. It is what the Psalmist directed us to in Psalm 49, when in verses 16-17 we are told not to fear when some become wealthy, for their death with eliminate

---

[791] Ladd, *Revelation*, 66.

all their wealth. Verse 20 sums the whole matter up, saying, "Man in his pomp yet without understanding is like the beasts that perish." That is to say, the heart and orientation of the man is the true judge of the value of his work.

Jesus, in His earthly ministry, sometimes rejected the seemingly pious prayers (Matt. 6:1-8) or gestures (Mark 10:17-27) of people who did righteous deeds for unrighteous purposes, and in contrast, He commended individuals who did small acts of goodness for the right reasons (Luke 21:3; Mark 14:8). The Laodiceans, with all of their self-sufficiency and pride, were known for relying on nothing but themselves. Indeed, when wrecked by an earthquake in AD 61, they refused any assistance from Rome and chose to rebuild themselves without any outside contributions.[792]

Further, Christ calls them to buy from Him **white garments so that you may clothe yourself and the shame of your nakedness may not be seen**. This is almost certainly a direct reference to the famous black wool they were known for producing in their sheepfolds.[793] While the world may have coveted their valuable black wool, Christ is not impressed. Instead, He calls them to buy (again, not literally but through spiritual discipline) white garments – which throughout Revelation (i.e., 4:4 and 19:4; as well as other places in the Bible like Daniel 7:9) always represent holiness and faithfulness. They are to lay down the worldly black clothes they are well-looked-upon for in their region, and in exchange, take up the white garments of a saint surrounded by enemies on earth but by a cloud of witnesses in Heaven.

Finally, they are called to buy of Christ **salve to anoint your eyes, so that you may see.** Once more, this almost certainly refers to the salve the medical school at Laodicea had developed which was well-known for its healing properties on both eyes and ears, although Christ here recalls only the necessity for them to have their eyes healed.[794] This might imply that Christ saw them as still in possession of "ears to hear" (v. 22) but if not, it at least asserts something akin to what Paul called the Colossians (and by

---

[792] Tacitus, *Annals*, 14:27. This detail has been variously argued as rationale for a late date, as the earthquake in AD 61 would have cost the city so much both in funds and human life that they would have been unlikely to refer to themselves as "rich, having become wealthy, needing nothing" by AD 67-69 when the Neronian date is suspected. While this is certainly a strong reason for believing in such, it is far from the strongest.

[793] Hemer, *The Letters to the Seven Churches*, 199-201.

[794] Hemer finds little evidence for this connection, basing his conclusions largely off of a study of the type of medical school found in Laodicea (Herophilean). He supports his criticisms by asserting some skepticism of words used by historical figures like Pliny, Celsus, and Strabo. Mounce, on the other hand, finds support for the conclusion in Strabo and Horace. This author finds the arguments to have equal weight, and returning to the text finds it likely that Christ is in some way referencing this eye salve, given His proclivity to use local allusions to make points to the churches. See Hemer, *The Letters to the Seven Churches*, 196-199.; Mounce, *Revelation*, 111.

effect the Laodiceans) to in Colossians 3:2, that they should set their minds on things above rather than things on earth. The unbeliever cannot see these things, since their mind has been blinded by Satan (2 Cor. 4:4), but those who come to Christ in faith will receive from Him **salve** such **that you may see.**

(3:19)

"Those whom I love, I reprove and discipline, so be zealous and repent."

"ἐγὼ ὅσους ἐὰν φιλῶ ἐλέγχω καὶ παιδεύω· ζήλευε οὖν καὶ μετανόησον."

In this verse, the very actions of Christ speak of His identifying with God the Father. Jurgen Roloff is quick to note this connection, as he points out that this statement combines two characteristics attributed to God in Proverbs 3:12 and Hebrews 12:6.[795] Proverbs 3:16 speaks of God reproving those whom He loves, and Hebrews 12:6 speaks of God disciplining the one He loves. Here, Jesus takes each of those actions of God and assumes them Himself, saying **those whom I love, I reprove and discipline**. This grants greater illumination as to what Christ means when He gives certain threats to other churches, such as that to the Ephesians wherein He said He would come and remove their lampstand. Just as Christ is actively involved in the protection and development of His Church, He is also actively involved in the pruning and reconfiguring of His Church, even if that sometimes means reproving, disciplining, or eliminating unfaithful elements from activity. All the while, though, every rebuke and disciplining from Christ is to be consciously maintained as an act of **love**, nothing else. Perhaps Roloff put it best, writing, "behind the rebuke stands nothing other than the love of its Lord, which seeks and goes after the lost."[796]

While almost cliché to mention, it should be noted that the type of **love** used by Christ is not the typical *agape* form that is frequently attributed to God. In a passage such as this, wherein Christ is pointing readers and listeners to His divinity, it is important to catch that He does not use the most typical word for divine love, but instead uses *philo* (φιλῶ; most commonly recognized in the root form, *phileo*). It has been pointed out that this connotates the love of Christ here as not being love from a father to a child, but from a trainer to an athlete with whom he has been entrusted. William Barclay speaks of this sort of love as being one of the surest signs of God's love and continued care, as he argues "it is, in fact, God's final punishment to leave a man alone" since "there is no surer way of allowing a child or young person to end in ruin, than to allow him to do as he

[795] Roloff, *Revelation*, 65.
[796] Roloff, *Revelation*, 65.

likes."[797] As a faithful witness, Christ presents Himself as the standard by which we should judge ourselves. In the loving kindness He has for us, which prompts Him to stir us forward when we would grow lukewarm, He **reproves and disciplines** His people.

What, specifically, He stirs us to is quite clear in this verse. He pushes His people to **be zealous and repent.** There is still time for them. As Ladd puts it, it is not "too late to replace complacency with zeal, and thereby repent."[798]

(3:20)

> "Behold, I stand at the door and knock. If anyone hears my voice and opens the door, I will come in to him and eat with him, and he with me."
>
> "Ἰδοὺ ἕστηκα ἐπὶ τὴν θύραν καὶ κρούω· ἐάν τις ἀκούσῃ τῆς φωνῆς μου καὶ ἀνοίξῃ τὴν θύραν, [καὶ] εἰσελεύσομαι πρὸς αὐτὸν καὶ δειπνήσω μετ' αὐτοῦ καὶ αὐτὸς μετ' ἐμοῦ."

There are a few verses in Revelation which are widely known to be misunderstood by the vast majority of (at least American if not all) Christians. This is one of them. While many evangelists have powerfully utilized this verse for their own evangelistic purposes, and William H. Hunt will be everlastingly enshrined for depicting this verse in his famous painting *The Light of the World*, the appropriate understanding and application of the verse is much less lovely.

Jesus speaks to someone, saying **I stand at the door and knock.** The natural question, then, is "to whom is He speaking?" Modern evangelists would say something along the lines of "Jesus is knocking on the door of lost hearts." Victorian individuals seeing Hunt's painting might imagine Jesus as standing at the door of their homes. But contextually, Jesus is not standing at a house, but instead **at the door** of a church, which naturally is full of people who are already Christians. This is not a salvific call whatsoever, nor is it intended to depict Jesus coming into homes. Rather, the illustration is that "the self-deluded members of the church" at Laodicea had become so unlike Christ that they have truly evicted Him from His own church.[799] They claim His name, but He is not actually allowed inside. Jesus is depicted here as standing outside of His own church, knocking on the door for someone to let Him come in. The imagery is much closer to the scene of Peter in Acts 12:12-17, wherein a group of gathered Christians were intended to be praying for Peter's deliverance, but upon finding him

---

[797] William Barclay, *The Revelation of John* Vol. 1, 184.

[798] Ladd, *Revelation*, 67.

[799] Mounce, *Revelation*, 113.

delivered failed to let him into the house. This church had become so focused on accomplishing things "in Jesus' name" that they had entirely forgotten what it meant to follow Jesus at all. His will and way of doing this was entirely unwelcome.

The reward for **anyone** who **hears** his **voice and opens the door** is that Christ **will come in to him and eat with him, and he with me**. Several conclusions follow from this simple statement. First, one can again see the necessity of "having ears to hear" as noted in each letter. The universality of this call, however, does grant hope to individuals in unfaithful circumstances that no church or people is ever so far gone that Christ will not receive back the most humbly faithful individual, since **anyone** can receive the reward Christ promises.

This is the second point, that the reward Christ offers, to **come in to him and eat with him and he with me** might be directly identified with the Lord's Table (Communion) but may also refer to Christ's promise in John 14:22, in which He said that the one who keeps His word and loves Him would be rewarded by having God the Father and Son (and Holy Spirit per 14:17) come and "make our home with him."[800] In both ways, the reward for the one who is zealous and repentant of their ways is acceptance with Christ and communion (both physical and spiritual) with God.[801]

(3:21)

> "The one who conquers, I will grant him to sit with me on my throne, as I also conquered and sat down with my Father on his throne."
>
> "Ὁ νικῶν δώσω αὐτῷ καθίσαι μετ' ἐμοῦ ἐν τῷ θρόνῳ μου, ὡς κἀγὼ ἐνίκησα καὶ ἐκάθισα μετὰ τοῦ πατρός μου ἐν τῷ θρόνῳ αὐτοῦ."

For that **one who conquers**, or in the case of the Laodiceans, the one who is zealous, who faithfully repents, and who opens the door to allow Christ back into their church, Christ promises to **grant him to sit with me on my throne**. This is a massive promise if it is true that verse 20 is truly a depiction not of salvation but of faithful endurance until the end in the face of lukewarm accommodations of the world in the church. Indeed, Christ recognizes His people, those who persevere faithfully through

---

[800] Ladd references this text and explains its meaning as being something along the lines of an intimate fellowship with affection, confidence, and intimacy. Ladd, *Revelation*, 67-68.

[801] Caird sees the reference to the Lord's Supper in this text, but fails to make any spiritual connections thereby. Mounce is unconvinced of the connection with the Lord's Table, but entertains an eschatological promise in connection with Christ's promise in Luke 22:30. This seems unlikely, given Christ's change in tensing between this promise and the one that follows (which is clearly aimed more at an eschatological understanding). Caird, *A Commentary on the Revelation*, 58.; Mounce, *Revelation*, 114.

hardship, as being those who not only do good works, but who maintain fervor for Christ and do good works for God-honoring purposes. As Leonard Ravenhill was prone to say, "We will not only be judged for what we did; We will be judged for why we did it!" For those who live their lives seeking the good of others in the motivation of accomplishing the glory of God, Christ will **grant** them **to sit** alongside Him on His throne.

Obviously, this does not carry with it equality in all things, such that those who sit on the thrones assume the duty and sovereignty of Christ. In contrast, the sitting of God's people on this throne depicts to them the honor to be received, as well as the victory accomplished. And while this is spiritually experienced each day in the life of God's people (as we presently see Christ on His throne through the eye of faith), it is also true that Christ will ultimately grant His people to sit on thrones in the physical realm and literally experience the honor and victory promised (Matthew 19:28, 2 Timothy 2:12; cf. Rev. 20:4). This, while a distinct promise, is perfectly in line with the previous promise of Christ eating with His people, as all through His ministry He refers to the communing of His people in that future earthly Kingdom in banquet language (Matthew 8:11; 22:1-4; 26:29; Luke 14:14-15; and especially Luke 22:29-30) and it is again referred to that way in Revelation 19:9.[802] Many of Christ's promises can be seen this way, having an immediate spiritual fulfillment, as well as a future physical fulfillment. This is spelled out in the fact that Christ is said to have **conquered** already, although His Parousia has not yet occurred. His return and subsequent reign on earth have not yet taken place, and yet, He is already a conqueror by His faithful martyrdom. He, as Peter said in Acts 2:36, has already been made Lord and Christ. He reigns now, although His reign is easily denied by those who do not have eyes to see nor ears to hear because of its spiritual nature. But in that day, the glorious day of Christ's coming, He will bring His spiritual reign into physical appearance, and He will put every enemy under His feet.[803] (1 Cor. 15:25)

In this way, just as Christ **conquered and sat down with** His **Father on his throne**, we will also conquer and sit down with God (as Christ's throne and God's throne are one and the same; 22:1). There will be no more work to do in any attempt to please God, for Christ has accomplished the full satisfaction of God's will and law, having perfectly imputed His righteousness to our account, bringing us justification instantaneously and eternally. This is no less than what it is to sit on His throne: salvation and eternal security.

---

[802] Ladd points out this connection, but ultimately declines it. Ladd, *Revelation*, 67.
[803] This line of thinking largely to the credit of Ladd, *Revelation*, 68-69.

(3:22)

"He who has an ear, let him hear what the Spirit says to the churches.'"

"Ὁ ἔχων οὖς ἀκουσάτω τί τὸ πνεῦμα λέγει ταῖς ἐκκλησίαις."

Fittingly, Christ finishes these seven letters with the standard greeting, **He who has an ear, let him hear.** He used this phrase all through His ministry; He has used it repeatedly in these letters; and He concludes this most solemn letter with nothing more or less than that which was given before. God's Word does not change and He is not subject to our passions and worries. He knows those who will hear His voice and follow Him, and there seems to be no worry in the voice of Christ. He calls to those who have ears to hear, **hear what the Spirit says to the churches.** May all of God's people hear and heed what the Holy Spirit of God has said, and in an ongoing way, **what the Spirit *says* to the churches.**[804]

Conclusion

Each of these seven letters accomplishes what John was commissioned to do in Revelation 1:19, which was to write the meaning of what He had seen in the first vision. Each has a characteristic of Christ as described in that vision, and each of these characteristics played a vital part in the life of those local churches to whom John wrote.

Preterists will be glad to read that these letters were truly written to churches in Asia Minor, although they will loathe the fact that they were written in the late first century. Nevertheless, it is the case that when Christ dictated these letters and John wrote them, there were immediate and direct applications to be made to those churches in the era in which they lived based on the information in each letter.

On the other hand, it is also true that the historicists can find similarities between each church and different eras in the church age. That is not evidence of the idea that each church represents a different generation of Christian heritage, but rather shows that the prohibitions and promises written in these letters can be seen and shown to occur all throughout history – not just once but several times.

Idealists will appreciate the understanding that while these were actual churches in the late-first century who engaged hardships and conflicts, the proper responses to those hardships are still the proper responses for Christians to conceptually affirm

[804] Mounce's conveyance of this thought is very good. "We are reminded that the messages to the seven historic churches in Asia are at the same time a composite word to the church universal throughout time." Mounce, *Revelation*, 114.

spiritually throughout the inter-advent age. As a result, they will see a direct application, which is that we must maintain faithful devotion to Christ in order to avoid the plagues and curses Christ threatened on us through the words He said to those other individuals millennia ago.

And finally, futurists will appreciate the understanding that these churches, while literal historical churches, are not to be taken as depicting some early Christian event alone wherein the letters to the churches have no bearing to modern or inter-advent age Christians at all. All readers, of all ages and eras, should read these seven letters in the same way they read Galatians or Hebrews – they are epistolary in nature, but despite having a direct audience also bear widespread application for both the present and the future.

Thus, a proper approach (*eclecticism*) presents readers with a balanced understanding of what pertinence the seven churches have in regard to the modern church, both in triumph and hardship. Whether things get better, worse, or are the worst they have ever been, all Christians can hear the words of Christ: Conquer. Faithfully endure, as Christ did, and conquer all that you can. Conquer sin; Conquer death; Conquer fear and discouragement. And to those who conquer, know that you have followed in the steps of your exemplary Savior, and will receive the rewards He promises.

Bibliography

Ancient Sources

Apringius of Beja. *Tractate on the Apocalypse.*

Athenagoras. *A Plea for the Christians.*

Augustine. *City of God.*

Bede. *Explanation of the Apocalypse.*

Caesarius of Arles. *Exposition of the Apocalypse.*

Cassius Dio. *History of Rome.*

Cicero. *Epistulae ad Familiares.*

Cicero. *Letters to Atticus.*

Clement of Alexandria. *Exhortation to the Heathen.*

Clement of Alexandria. *Paedagogus.*

Clement of Alexandria. *Salvation of the Rich Man.*

Clement of Alexandria. *Stromata.*

Clement of Rome. *1-2 Clement.*

The Didache.

Eusebius. *Historia Ecclesiastica.*

Herodotus. *Histories.*

Hippolytus. *Commentary on Daniel.*

Hippolytus. *Refutation of All Heresies.*

Ignatius. *Epistle to the Ephesians.*

Ignatius. *Epistle to the Magnesians.*

Ignatius. *Epistle to the Smyrnaeans.*

Irenaeus. *Against Heresies.*

Jerome. *De Viris Illustribus.*

Justin Martyr. *Dialogue With Trypho.*

Justin Martyr. *First Apology.*

Juvenal. *Satires.*

Lactantius. *Divine Institutes.*

Letter to Diognetus.

Martyrdom of Polycarp.

Minucius Felix. *Octavius.*

Origen. *Commentary on the Gospel of John*.
Origen. *Contra Censum*.
Pliny the Elder. *Natural History*.
Polybius. *Histories*.
Polycarp. *Epistle to the Philippians*.
Primasius. *Commentary on the Apocalypse*.
Seutonius. *Domitianus*.
Seutonius. *The Lives of the Twelve Caesars*.
Strabo. *Geography*.
Tacitus. *Annals*.
Tertullian. *Adversus Gnosticos Scorpiace*.
Tertullian. *De Resurrectione Carnis*.
Tertullian. *On Flight During Persecution*.
Tertullian. *Prescription Against Heretics*.
Tertullian. *Scorpiace*.
Theophilus of Antioch. *To Autolycus*.
Tyconius. *Commentary on the Apocalypse*.
Victorinus of Petovium. *Commentary on the Apocalypse*.

Revelation Commentaries

Andrew of Caesarea, *Commentary on the Apocalypse.* Eugenia Scarvelis Constantinou, translator. Washington, DC: Catholic University of America Press, 2011.

Ashcraft, Morris. *The Broadman Bible Commentary* 12. Nashville: Broadman Press, 1972.

Barclay, William. *The Revelation of John* 1. Edinburgh: Saint Andrew Press, 1960.

Beale, G.K. *The Book of Revelation.* New International Greek Testament Commentary. Grand Rapids: Eerdmans, 1999.

Beasley-Murray, G.R. *Revelation* New Century Bible Commentary. Grand Rapids: Eerdmans, 1981.

Beckwith, Isbon. *The Apocalypse of John*. New York: MacMillan Co., 1919.

Caird, G.B. *A Commentary on the Revelation of St. John the Divine.* New York: Harper & Row, 1966.

Charles, R.H. *A Critical and Exegetical Commentary on the Revelation of St. John* I. Edinburgh: T&T Clark, 1920.

Collins, Adela Y. *The Apocalypse.* New Testament Message: Biblical-Theological Commentary. Wilmington, DE: Michael Glazier, 1979.

Duff, Paul B. *Who Rides the Beast?* Oxford: Oxford University Press, 2001.

Feuillet, André. *The Apocalypse*. Staten Island, NY: Alba House, 1965.

Gill, John. *Exposition of the Old & New Testaments* 9. London: Mathews & Leigh, 1810.

Goodwin, Thomas. *Exposition on the Book of Revelation*. London: Simpkin, Marshall, and Co., 1842.

Gregg, Steve. *Revelation: Four Views.* Nashville: Thomas Nelson, 2013.

Hamilton, James. *Revelation: The Spirit Speaks to the Churches.* Wheaton, IL: Crossway, 2012.

Hendrickson, William. *More than Conquerors*. Grand Rapids: Baker, 2015.

Hort, F.J.A. *The Apocalypse of St. John* I-III. London: MacMillan and Co., 1908.

Hughes, Philip E. *Revelation.* Grand Rapids: Eerdmans, 1990.

Keener, Craig. *The NIV Application Commentary: Revelation.* Grand Rapids: Zondervan, 2000.

Kiddle, Martin. *The Revelation of St. John.* New York: Harper and Brothers Publishers, 1951.

Kistemaker, Simon J. *Revelation*. Grand Rapids: Baker Books, 2001.

Koester, Craig R. *Revelation* 38A. The Anchor Yale Bible. New Haven: Yale University Press, 2014.

Ladd, George Eldon. *A Commentary on Revelation*. Grand Rapids: Eerdmans, 1979.

Lenski, R.C.H. *The Interpretation of St. John's Revelation*. Columbus, OH: Wartburg Press, 1957.

Lilje, Hanns. *The Last Book of the Bible.* Olive Wyon, translator. Philadelphia: Muhlenberg Press, 1957.

Lund, Nils W. *Studies in the Book of Revelation*. Chicago: Covenant Press, 1955.

Mede, Joseph. *The Key of Revelation*. Parliament: England and Wales, 1641.

Metzger, Bruce. *Breaking the Code: Understanding the Book of Revelation.* Nashville: Abingdon Press, 2019.

Michaels, J. Ramsey. *Interpreting the Book of Revelation*. Grand Rapids: Baker Academic, 1992.

Mounce, Robert H. *The Book of Revelation.* New International Commentary on the New Testament. Grand Rapids: Eerdmans, 1997.

_______________. *The Book of Revelation*. Grand Rapids: Eerdmans, 1977.

Newell, William R. *The Book of the Revelation.* Chicago: Moody Press, 1981.

Robbins, R.F. *The Revelation of Jesus Christ.* Nashville: Broadman, 1975.

Roloff, Jurgen. *Revelation: A Continental Commentary*. Minneapolis: Fortress Press, 1993.

Schreiner, Thomas. "Revelation." *ESV Expository Commentary* 12. Wheaton, IL: Crossway, 2018.

_______________. *Revelation* Baker Exegetical Commentary on the New Testament. Grand Rapids: Baker, 2023.

Seiss, Joseph. *The Apocalpyse* I. New York: Charles C. Cook, 1901.

Simcox, William Henry. *The Revelation of St. John the Divine.* Cambridge: Cambridge University Press, 1893.

Smalley, Stephen S. *Thunder and Love*. Eugene: OR, Wipf & Stock, 1994.

Stuart, Moses. *A Commentary on the Apocalypse* II. Andover: Allen, Morrill, and Wardwell, 1845.

Sweet, J.P.M. *Revelation*. Philadelphia: Westminster Press, 1979.

Thomas, Robert L. *Revelation 1-7: An Exegetical* Commentary. Chicago: Moody Press, 1992.

Twisse, William. *The Key of the Revelation*. London: Phillip Stephens, 1642.

Vitringa, Campegius. *Anakrisis Apocalypsios Joannis Apostoli*. Amstelodami: Henrici Strickii, 1719.

Weinrich, William, editor. *Ancient Christian Commentary of Scripture* XII. Downers Grove, IL: IVP Academic, 2005.

Wilson, Mark. *Charts on the Book of Revelation.* Grand Rapids, MI: Kregel, 2007.

Winters, Howard. *Commentary on Revelation*. Greenville, SC: Carolina Christian, 1989.

<u>*General Works*</u>

"John Wesley to Dr. Conyers Middleton" (1749). *Wesley's Works* X.

Acta Apostolicae Sedis 36:2:11 (Vatican).

Allert, Craig. *Revelation, Truth, Canon and Interpretation*. Leiden: Brill, 2002.

Alnor, William. *Soothsayers of the Second Advent*. Old Tappan, NJ: Fleming H. Revell, 1989.

Anderson, David R. "The Soteriological Impact of Augustine's Change from Premillennialism to Amillennialism: Part One." *Journal of the Grace Evangelical Society* (Spring 2002): 25-36.

Bacon, B.W. *The Making of the New Testament*. New York: Henry Holt & Co., 1912.

Barclay, William. *Letters to the Seven Churches.* New York: Abingdon, 1957.

Baxter, Richard. *A Reply to Mr. Tho. Beverley's Answer to My Reasons Against His Doctrine of the Thousand Years Middle Kingdom and the Conversion of the Jews*. London: Thomas Parkhurst, 1691.

___________. *The Glorious Kingdom of Christ, Described and Clearly Vindicated*. London: Snowden, 1691.

Becerra, Daniel. "The Canonization of the New Testament." *New Testament History, Culture, and Society*, Lincoln Blumell, editor. Provo, UT: Deseret Book, 2019.

Bengel, Johan Albrecht. *Gnomon Novi Testamenti*. Tubingae, 1742.

Bernier, Jonathan. "From Papias to Hegesippus." *Theoforum* 42:1 (2011): 37-46.

Bevan, Edwyn R. *The House of Seleucus* 1. New York: Barnes & Noble Inc., 1902.

Beverley, Thomas. *An Appeal Most Humble Yet Most Earnestly by the Coming of Our Lord Jesus Christ*. London: John Salusbury, 1697.

Boeft, Jan Den. "Christ and Asklepios." *Euphrosyne* 25 (1997): 337-342.

Boehringer, Erich. *Altertümer von Pergamon* 8. Berlin: Walter de Gruyter & Co., 1969.

Bonar, Andrew. *Redemption Drawing Nigh*. London: James Nisbet and Co., 1847.

Bonar, Horatius. *Prophetical Landmarks*. London: James Nisbet and Co., 1847.

Bradstock, Andrew. "Millenarianism in the Reformation and the English Revolution." Stephen Hunt, editor. *Christian Millenarianism from the Early Church to Waco*. Indianapolis, IN: Indiana University Press, 2001.

Brownlee, W.H. "The Priestly Character of the Church in the Apocalypse" *New Testament Studies* 5 (1958).

Bruce, F.F. "The Earliest Latin Commentary on the Apocalypse." *The Evangelical Quarterly* 10 (1938): 352-366.

_________. *Peter, Stephen, James, and John*. Grand Rapids: Eerdmans, 1979.

Bunyan, John. *One Thing Is Needful: Serious Meditations on the Four Last Things* 3. London: Francis Smith, 1680.

C.G. Williamson, "Heroes in the Asklepieion of Pergamon." University of Groningen.

Calvin, John. *Institutes of the Christian Religion*. Henry Beveridge, translator. Peabody, MA: Hendrickson Publishers, 2007.

Carson D.A., and Douglas Moo. *An Introduction to the New Testament* 2. Grand Rapids: Zondervan, 2005.

Cartledge, Samuel A. *A Conservative Introduction to the New Testament* 7. Grand Rapids: Zondervan, 1941.

Casey Jay Smith. "Exodus Typology in the Book of Revelation." PhD. Dissertation: Southern Baptist Theological Seminary, 1981.

Catechism of the Catholic Church. Libreria Editrice Vaticana: Catholic Conference, 1994.

Cedrenus, Georgius. *Corpus Scriptorum Historiae Byzantinae.* Bonnae: 1838.

Chapman, Ben, editor. *Three Views on the Rapture.* Grand Rapids: Zondervan, 1996.

Charlesworth, Scott D. "A Reused Roll or a 'Curious Christian Codex'? Reconsidering British Library Papyrus 2053." *Buried History* 53 (2017): 35-44.

Cobern, Camden M. *The New Archaeological Discoveries and Their Bearing Upon the New Testament.* London: Funk & Wagnalls Co., 1917.

Combs, William W. "Erasmus and the Textus Receptus." *Detroit Baptist Seminary Journal* 1:1 (Spring 1996): 35-53.

Cuchet, Jean-Claude Larchet de Guillaume. *Comment notre monde a cessé d'être chrétien: Anatomie d'un effondrement.* Paris: Seuil, 2018.

Culpepper, Alan. *Anatomy of the Fourth Gospel: A Study in Literary Design*. Philadelphia: Fortress Press, 1983.

Deissmann, Adolf. *Light from the Ancient East.* Lionel Strachan, translator. New York: Hodder and Stoughton, 1910.

Delitzsch Franz. *Handschriftliche Funde: Die Erasmischen Entstellungen des Textes der Apokalypse, Nachgewiesen aus dem verloren geglaubten Codex Reuchlins.* Leipzig: Dorffling und Franke, 1861.

Dewar, Michael. "Spinning the *Trabea*: Consular Robes and Propaganda in the Panegyrics of Claudian." Jonathan Edmonson and Alison Keith, editors. *Roman Dress and the Fabrics of Roman Culture.* Toronto: University of Toronto Press, 2008.

Donnelly, Mark, and Daniel Diehl. *The Big Book of Pain: Torture and Punishment Through History.* Gloucestershire: History Press, 2011.

Eamon, William C. "Kingdom and Church in New England; Puritan Eschatology John Cotton to Jonathan Edwards." (1970) The University of Montana: *Graduate Student Theses, Dissertations, & Professional Papers*.

Edmondson, Jonathan. "Public Dress and Social Control in Late Republican and Early Imperial Rome" *Roman Dress and the Fabrics of Roman Culture*. Toronto: University of Toronto Press, 2008.

Ehrman, Bart D., editor. *The Apostolic Fathers* II. Cambridge: Harvard University Press, 2003.

Elliott, James K. "Revelations from the *Apparatus Criticus* of the Book of Revelation." *Union Seminary Quarterly Review* 63 (2012): 1-23.

Fant, Clyde, and Mitchell Reddish. *A Guide to Biblical Sites in Greece and Turkey*. New York: Oxford Academic, 2020.

Farnell, Lewis R. *Greek Hero Cults and Ideas of Immortality*. Oxford: Clarendon Press, 1921.

Ferguson, Everett. *Backgrounds of Early Christianity*. Grand Rapids: Eerdmans, 1987.

Fiorenza, Elisabeth S. "Composition and Structure of the Book of Revelation." *The Catholic Biblical Quarterly* 39:3 (July 1977): 344-366.

Forsythe, Gary. *A Critical History of Early Rome: From Prehistory to the First Punic War.* Berkeley, CA: University of California Press, 2005.

Fortin, John R. "Saint Anselm and the Four Last Things." *The American Benedictine Review* 61:2 (2010).

Franklin, Robert. *Rediscovered Early Church Premillennialism*. Arlington, TX: Word Lamp Productions, 2014.

Friesen, Steven J. "Satan's Throne, Imperial Cults and the Social Settings of Revelation." *Journal for the Study of the New Testament* 27:3 (2005): 351-373.

Frost, Henry W. *Matthew Twenty-Four and the Revelation.* New York: Oxford University Press, 1924.

Gallus, Laslo. "The Exodus Motif in Revelation 15-16: It's Background and Nature." *Andrews University Seminary Studies* 46:1 (2008): 21-43.

Garrigou-Lagrange, Reginald. *Life Everlasting and the Immensity of the Soul*. Rockford, IL: TAN Books, 1952.

Gentry, Kenneth L. "Book Review: The Avenging of the Apostles: A Commentary on Revelation by Arthur M. Ogden." *The Counsel of Chalcedon* (April 1995): 11-12.

_______________. *Before Jerusalem Fell: Dating the Book of Revelation*. Tyler, TX: Institute for Christian Economics, 1989.

George, Michele. "The 'Dark Side' of the Toga." *Roman Dress and the Fabrics of Roman Culture*. Toronto: University of Toronto Press, 2008.

Gerhold, Victoria. "The Legend of Euphratas." *Dumbarton Oaks Papers* 74 (2020): 67-124.

Gervais, Timothy. "The Fragments of Hegesippus and 1 Clement." *Intermountain West Journal of Religious Studies* 8:1 (Fall 2017): 2-24.

Giblin, Charles H. "Recapitulation and the Literary Coherence of John's Apocalypse" *The Catholic Biblical Quarterly* 56 (1994): 81-95.

Gifford, David S. *The Exodus Motif in Revelation 12: Divine Deliverance for the 21st Century.* Virginia Beach, VA: Regent University, 2018.

Griffith, Lee. *The War on Terrorism and the Terror of God*. Grand Rapids: Eerdmans, 2002..

Gumerlock, Francis. "Millennialism and the Early Church Councils." *Fides et Historia* 36:2 (Fall 2004): 83-95.

Gundry, Robert H. "The New Jerusalem People as Place, Not Place for People." *Novum Testamentum* 29 (1987): 254-264.

_______________. *The Church and the Tribulation: A Biblical Examination of Posttribulationism.* Grand Rapids: Zondervan, 1973.

Gunn, Grover. "Book Review: Before Jerusalem Fell: Dating the Book of Revelation by Ken Gentry." *The Counsel of Chalcedon* (March 1990): 22-23.

Guthrie, Donald. "The Christology of Revelation." *Jesus of Nazareth Lord and Christ: Essays on the Historical Jesus and New Testament Christology*. Joel Green and Max Turner, editors. Grand Rapids: Eerdmans, 1994.

Halkin, Francois. *Bibliotheca Hagiographica Graeca.* Bruxelles: Societe des Bollandistes, 1957.

Harrill, J. Albert. "Coming of Age and Putting on Christ: The *Toga Virilis* Ceremony, Its Paraenesis, and Paul's Interpretation of Baptism in Galatians." *Novum Testamentum* 44 (2002): 255-266.

Havssleiter, Johannes, editor. *Victorini Episcopi Petavionensis Opera.* New York: Johnson Reprint Co., 1965.

Hemer, Colin J. *The Letters to the Seven Churches of Asia in their Local Setting*. Sheffield, England: Sheffield Academic Press, 1989.

Henry, Matthew. *Matthew Henry's Commentary on the Whole Bible.* Peabody, MA: Hendrickson, 2021.

Henschenius, Godefridus and Daniel Papebrochius. *Acta Sanctorum der Bollandisten*. Antwerp: 1675.

Herman, Bruce. "Making and Breaking: Art, Hospitality, and Eucharist." *Boisi Center for Religion and American Public Life* (2016).

Hill, C.E. "The Debate Over the Muratorian Fragment and the Development of the Canon." *Westminster Theological Journal* 57:2 (Fall 1995): 437-452.

Hill, Charles E. *The Johannine Corpus in the Early Church*. Oxford: Oxford University Press, 2004.

Hitchcock, Mark L. "A Defense of the Domitianic Date of the Book of Revelation." PhD Dissertation, Dallas Theological Seminary, 2005.

Hjelde, Sigurd. *Das Eschaton und die Eschata: Eine Studie uber Sprachgebrauch und Sprachverwirrung in protestantischer Theologie von der Orthodoxie bis zur Gegenwart.* Munich: Kaiser, 1987.

Hodge, Bryan C. *Problems with Preterism*. Eugene, OR: Wipf & Stock, 2022.

Hoekema, Anthony. "Amillennialism." Robert G. Clouse, editor. *The Meaning of the Millennium*. Westmont, IL: InterVarsity Press, 1977.

Holmes, Michåel W., editor. *The Apostolic Fathers* 3.Grand Rapids: Baker Academic, 2007.

Hudson, Winthrop. *Baptists in Transition: Individualism and Christian Responsibility*. King of Prussia, PA: Judson Press, 1979.

Hurtado, Larry W. *The Earliest Christian Artifacts*. Grand Rapids: Eerdmans, 2006.

Ice, Thomas D. "Mathers, Richard, Increase, and Cotton." *Dictionary of Premillennial Theology.* Mal Couch, editor. Grand Rapids: Kregel, 1996.

___________. "The Date of the Book of Revelation." *Article Archives* (May 2009):75-79.

Ireland, Corydon. "Revelations on Revelation" *The Harvard Gazette* (7 December 2009).

Jauhiainen, Marko. "Recapitulation and Chronological Progression in John's Apocalypse: Towards a New Perspective." *New Testament Studies* 49 (2003): 543-559.

Justinian. *The Digest of Justinian*. Charles H. Monro, translator. London: Cambridge University Press, 1904.

Keach, Benjamin. *A Golden Mine Opened.* London: Keach and Marshall, 1694.

Keathley III, Hampton J. *Studies in Revelation*. Spokane, WA: Biblical Studies Press, 1997.

Kim, Chul Hae. "Ecclesiology and Christology in the First Three Chapters of the Book of Revelation." *Torch Trinity Journal* 6:1 (2003).

Kohlberg, Etan. "Taqiyya in Shi'i Theology and Religion." *Secrecy and Concealment: Studies in the History of Mediterranean and Near Eastern Religions*. Hans G. Kippenberg and Guy G. Stroumsa, editors. Leiden: Brill, 1995.

Kostenberger, Andrea J., L. Scott Kellum, Charles L. Quarles. *The Cradle, The Cross, and the Crown.* 2 Brentwood, TN: B&H Academic, 2016.

Krans, Jan. *Beyond What is Written: Erasmus and Beza as Conjectural Critics of the New Testament.* Boston: Brill, 2006.

Kruger, Michael J. "The Book of Revelation: How Difficult Was Its Journey into the Canon?" *Canon Fodder* (12 February 2014). Accessed 28 March 2023.

______________. *The Question of Canon*. Downers Grove: InterVarsity Press, 2013.

Kummel, Werner G. *Introduction to the New Testament.* Howard C. Kee, translator. Nashville: Abingdon, 1981.

Ladd, George Eldon. *The Blessed Hope.* Grand Rapids: Eerdmans, 1979.

________________. *A Theology of the New Testament*. Grand Rapids: Eerdmans, 1993.

Lawlor, Hugh J. *Eusebiana: Essays on the Ecclesiastical History of Eusebius Bishop of Caesarea*. Oxford: Clarendon Press, 1912.

Lietzmann, Hans, editor. *Das Muratorische Fragment und die Monarchianischen Prologue zu den Evangelien* 2. Berlin: Klein Text, 1933.

Louth, Andrew. "The Date of Eusebius' *Historia Ecclesiastica.*" *Journal of Theological Studies* 41:1 (1990): 111-123.

Lund, Nils W. "The Presence of Chiasmus in the New Testament." *The Journal of* Religion 10:1 (Jan., 1930): 74-93.

MacArthur, John. *The MacArthur Bible* Commentary. Nashville: Thomas Nelson, 2005.

Mainardus, Otto F.A. "The Christian Remains of the Seven Churches of the Apocalypse." *The Biblical Archaeologist* 37:3 (September 1974): 69-82.

Malik, Peter. "Another Look at P.IFAO II 31: An Updated Transcription and Textual Analysis." *Novum Testamentus* 58 (2016): 204-217.

Mather, Increase. *The Mystery of Israel's Salvation.* Boston: 1669.

Mathison, Keith. *From Age to Age: The Unfolding of Biblical Eschatology*. Phillipsburg, NJ: P&R Publishing, 2014.

McBeth, H. Leon. *The Baptist Heritage*. Nashville, TN: Broadman & Holman Publishers, 1987.

McGrath, Alister. *Iustitua Dei* 2. Cambridge: Cambridge University Press, 1998.

McKelvey, R.J. *The Millennium and the Book of Revelation*. Cambridge: Lutterworth, 1999.

Mealy, J. Webb. *After the Thousand Years: Resurrection and Judgment in Revelation 20.* Sheffield: JSOT Press, 1992.

___________. *New Creation Millennialism.* Independently Published, 2019.

Mede, Joseph. *The Works.* London: Roger Norton, 1620.

Menn, Jonathan. *Biblical Eschatology*. Eugene, OR: Resources Publications, 2013.

Metzger, Bruce M. *A Textual Commentary on the Greek New Testament* 3. London: United Bible Societies, 1971.

_____________. *The Canon of the New Testament.* Oxford: Clarendon Press, 1989.

Metzger, Bruce M., and Bart D. Ehrman. *The Text of the New Testament: It's Transmission, Corruption, and Restoration* 4· Oxford: Oxford University Press, 2005.

Moulton, James H. *A Grammar of New Testament Greek* 1. Edinburgh: T&T Clark, 1906.

Mueller, Ekkehardt. "Christological Concepts in the Book of Revelation – Part 1: Jesus in the Apocalypse." *Journal of the Adventist Theological Society* 21:1 (2010): 276-305.

______________. "Christological Concepts in the Book of Revelation – Part 3: The Lamb Christology." *Journal of the Adventist Theological Society* 22:2 (2011): 42-66.

______________. "Introduction to the Ecclesiology of the Book of Revelation." *Journal of the Adventist Theological Society* 12:2 (Autumn 2001): 199-215.

Mueller, Ekkehardt. "Recapitulation in Revelation 4-11." *Journal of the Adventist Theological Society* 9:1 (1998): 260-277.

Muhling, Markus. *T&T Clark Handbook of Christian Eschatology.* Jennifer Adams-Massman and David A. Gilland, translators. London: Bloomsbury, 2015.

Nicoll, W. Robertson, editor. *The Expositor's Greek Testament* 5. New York: Dodd, Mead, and Co., 1910.

Oort, Johannes van, and Einar Thomassen, editors. *The Panarion of Epiphanius of Salamis* 2. Boston: Brill, 2013.

Parker Jr., Floyd O. "'Our Lord and God' in Rev 4,11: Evidence for the Late Date of Revelation?" *Biblica* 82:2 (2001): 207-231.

Parker, T.H.L. *Calvin's New Testament Commentaries* 2. Louisville, KY: Westminster/John Knox Press, 1993.

Pausaniua. "Description of Greece." *Pausanias' Description of Greece with an English Translation in Four Volumes.* W.H.S. Jones, translator. London: Harvard University Press, 1918.

Payne, J. Barton. *Encyclopedia of Biblical Prophecy.* Grand Rapids: Baker, 1997.

Perschbacher, Wesley J., editor. *The New Analytical Greek Lexicon*. Peabody, MA: Hendrickson, 1990.

Peters, George N.H. *The Theocratic Kingdom.* New York: Funk & Wagnalls, 1884.

Piper, John. *Come, Lord Jesus*. Wheaton, IL: Crossway, 2023.

_________. *Counted Righteous In Christ*. Wheaton, IL: Crossway, 2002.

Plummer, Alfred. "The Revelation of St. John the Divine." *The Pulpit Commentary* 22. Grand Rapids: Eerdmans, 1950.

Poythress, Vern S. "Johannine Authorship and the Use of Intersentence Conjunctions in the Book of Revelation." *Westminster Theological Journal* 47 (1985): 329-336.

Price, Walter. *The Coming Antichrist*. Chicago: Moody, 1974.

Publius Aelius Aristides. "Orations." *P. Aelius Aristides: The Complete Works* I. Charles A. Behr, translator. Leiden: Brill, 1986.

Quintern, Jason L, and H. Michael Shultz Jr. *Revelation in Focus: Two Perspectives on Its Meaning and Timing*. Longview, TX: Grace and Truth Press, 2026.

Raja, Rubina. "In and Out of Contexts: Explaining Religious Complexity through the Banqueting Tesserae from Palmyra." *Religion in the Roman Empire* 2:3 (2016): 340-371.

Ramsay, William. *The Letters to the Seven Churches of Asia and Their Place in the Plan of the Apocalypse*. London: Hodder and Stoughton, 1904.

Rengstorf, Karl H. *Die Anfänge der Auseinandersetzung zwischen Christusglaube und Asklepiosfrömmigkeit* 30. Münster: Schriften der Gesellschaft zur Förderung der Westfälischen Landesuniversität zu Münster, 1953.

Reuss, Eduardus. *Bibliotheca Novi Testamenti Graeci.* Brunsvigae: C.A. Scwetschke, 1872.

Reynolds Benjamin, and Loren Stuckenbruck, editors. *The Jewish Apocalyptic Tradition and the Shaping of the New Testament Thought*. Minneapolis, MN: Fortress Press, 2017.

Reynolds, Edwin. "The True and the False in the Ecclesiology of Revelation." *Journal of the Adventist Theological Society* 17:2 (Autumn 2006): 18-35.

Robertson, A.T. *Word Pictures in the New Testament* VI. Grand Rapids, MI: Baker Book House, 1933.

Robinson, John A.T. *Redating the New Testament*. Philadelphia: Westminster Press, 1976.

Robinson, Sarah. "The Origins of Jewish Apocalyptic Literature: Prophecy, Babylon, and 1 Enoch." M.A. Thesis, University of South Florida, 2005.

Rossing, Barbara. "Apocalyptic Violence and Politics: End Times Fiction for Jews and Christians." *Contesting Texts* (2007): 67-77.

Rudwick M.J.S., and E.M.B. Green. "The Laodicean Lukewarmness." *The Expository Times* 69:6 (March 1958): 177-178.

Rummel, Erika. *Erasmus' Annotations on the New Testament.* Toronto: University of Toronto Press, 1986.

Ryrie, Charles C. *The Basis of the Premillennial Faith.* Neptune, NJ: Loizeaux Brothers, 1953.

Sabourin, Leopold. *Christology: Basic Texts in Focus*. New York: Alba House, 1984.

Schnabel, Eckhard. *New Testament Theology.* Grand Rapids: Baker, 2023.

Schneemelcher, Wilhelm. *New Testament Apocrypha* I. R. McL. Wilson, translator. Louisville, KY: Westminster John Knox Press, 2003.

Scrivener, Frederick H.A. *A Plain Introduction to the Criticism of the New Testament* 1-2. London: George Bell and Sons, 1894.

Sellew, Philip. "The Letter to the Laodiceans." Bruce Metzger and Michael Coogan, editors. *The Oxford Companion to the Bible.* Oxford: Oxford University Press, 1993.

Sequeira, Aubrey, and Samuel Emadi. "Biblical-Theological Exegesis and the Nature of Typology." *SBJT* 21:1 (2017): 11-34.

Servetus, Michael. *The Restoration of Christianity.* Marian Hillar and Christopher Hoffman, translators. Lewiston, NY: Edwin Mellen Press, 2007.

Seutonius. *The Lives of the Twelve Caesars*. New York: Modern Library, 1931.

Sherwin, William. *The World to Come*. London: Unidentified Publisher, 1671.

Shultz Jr., H. Michael. "Review of The Rise and Fall of Dispensationalism" *Ecclesia Militans* 1:1 (Winter 2023).

Silcock, Jeffrey G. "A Lutheran Approach to Eschatology." *Lutheran Quarterly* 31 (2017): 373-395.

Silver, Jesse Forrest. *The Lord's Return*. London: Fleming H. Revell Co., 1914.

Smith, Geoffrey. "The Willoughby Papyrus: A New Fragment of John 1:49-2:1 (P134) and an Unidentified Christian Text." *Journal of Biblical Literature* 137:4 (Winter 2018): 935-958.

Smith, William. *Dictionary of Greek and Roman Antiquity.* Boston: Little, Brown, and Co., 1859.

Sophocles, E.A. *Greek Lexicon of the Roman and Byzantine Periods*. New York: Charles Scribner's Sons, 1900.

Spurgeon, Charles H. "Mourning for Christ." *Metropolitan Tabernacle Pulpit* 23 (1 July 1877).

________________. "The Lesson of the Almond Tree." *Metropolitan Tabernacle Pulpit* 46 (7 April 1881).

Stepenberg, Maia. "Dostoevsky's *Crime and Punishment* in the Light of Eschatology." *Quaestio Rossica* 7:4 (2019): 1160-1171.

Strand, Kenneth. "The Eight Basic Visions in the Book of Revelation." *Andrews University Seminary Studies* 25 (1987): 107-121.

Svigel, Michael J. *The Fathers on the Future*. Peabody, MA: Hendrickson Publishers, 2024.

Tarn, W.W., and G.T.Grifith. *Hellenistic Civilization.* New York: Meridian Books, 1952.

Telfer, William. "Was Hegesippus a Jew?" *Harvard Theological Review* 53:2 (April 1960): 143-153.

Thayer, Joseph H. *Thayer's Greek-English Lexicon of the New Testament.* Peabody, MA: Hendrickson Publishers, 2000.

Berry, George Ricker. *The Interlinear Literal Translation of the Greek New Testament with the Authorized Version*. New York: Arthur Hinds and Co., 1965.

Thomas, Robert L. "The Structure of the Apocalypse: Recapitulation or Progression?" *The Masters Seminary Journal* 4:1 (Spring 1993): 45-66.

______________. "Theonomy and the Dating of Revelation." *The Masters Seminary Journal* (Fall 1994): 185-202.

Thomassen, Einar, and Johannes van Oort, editors. *The Panarion of Epiphanius of Salamis.* Frank Williams, translator. Boston: Brill, 2009.

Thompson, Robin. "Healing at the Pool of Bethesda: A Challenge to Asclepius?" *Bulletin for Biblical Research* 27:1 (2017): 65-84.

Toon, Peter. *Puritans, The Millennium and the Future of Israel: Puritan Eschatology 1600 to 1660*. London: James Clarke, 1970.

Tregelles, Samuel P. *An Account of the Printed Text of the Greek New Testament*. London: Samuel Bagster and Sons, 1854.

Tse, Caley. "Unity Between the Book of Revelation and the Gospel of John." MTS Essay, Taylor Seminary, 2018.

Underwood, Grant. *The Millenarian World of Early Mormonism*. Chicago: University of Illinois Press, 1993.

Vincent, Marvin R. *Word Studies in the New Testament* 2. Grand Rapids: Eerdmans, 1973.

Wagemakers, Bart. "Incest, Infanticide, and Cannibalism: Anti-Christian Imputations in the Roman Empire" *Greece & Rome* 57:2 (October 2010): 337-354.

Waldron, Sam. *MacArthur's Millennial Manifesto.* Owensboro, KY: RBAP, 2008.

Walvoord, John. *The Rapture Question.* Grand Rapids: Zondervan, 1979.

Walzer, Richard. *Galen on Jews and Christians*. London: Oxford University Press, 1949.

Ward-Perkins, J.B. *Roman Imperial Architecture.* London: Yale University Press, 1981.

Warfield, B.B. "The Formation of the Canon of the New Testament." *The Inspiration and Authority of the Bible*. Phillipsburg, NJ: P&R Publishing, 1948.

Watson, Thomas. *A Body of Practical Divinity.* Philadelphia, James Kay, Jun. & Co., 1833.

Weber, Eugene. *Apocalypses: Prophecies, Cults, and Millennial Beliefs through the Ages*. Cambridge, MA: Harvard University Press, 1999.

Weima, J.A.D. *The Sermons to the Seven Churches of Revelation: A Commentary and Guide*. Grand Rapids: Baker Academic, 2021.

Weinrich, William, editor. *Latin Commentaries on Revelation*. Downers Grove: InterVarsity Press, 2011.

West, Nathaniel. *The Thousand Years in Both Testaments*. Fincastle, VA: Scripture Truth Book Company, 1970.

Whitby, Daniel. *A Treatise of Traditions* I. London: Awnsham Churchill, 1688.

White, James. *The King James Only Controversy.* Minneapolis, MN: Bethany House, 1995.

White, R. Fowler. "Making Sense of Rev 20:1-10? Harold Hoehner Versus Recapitulation." *Journal of the Evangelical Theological Society* 37:4 (December 1994): 539-551.

Wilson, J. Christian. "The Problem of the Domitianic Date of Revelation." *New Testament Studies* 39:4 (October 1993): 587-605.

Winkle, Ross E. *Clothes Make the (One Like a Son of) Man): Dress Imagery in Revelation 1 as an Indicator of High Priestly Status*. Andrews University: PhD Dissertation, 2012.

Wright, N.T. *Paul and the Faithfulness of God*. Minneapolis, MN: Fortress Press, 2013.

Scriptural Index

Alphanumerically Arranged

About the Author

H. Michael Shultz Jr. is the husband of Storm. Together, they have three children on Earth and two others awaiting them in Heaven. Since 2019, Dr. Shultz has served as Pastor of Antioch Baptist Church, and in 2022, he became Associate Professor of Church History at Forge Theological Seminary, where he also now serves as Director of Institutional Advancement.

Dr. Shultz has published extensively, with his most recent book being a co-authored dialogical book on interpreting Revelation entitled *Revelation in Focus: Two Perspectives on Its Meaning and Timing* (Grace and Truth Press, 2026). His M.Div. Thesis was one of the top-25 most widely-read anthropology resources worldwide in 2021, exploring the influence Mennonites had on ending Russian Serfdom. His D.Min. Dissertation was published in 2024, entitled "Defending the Fixed-Period Perspective of 'Generation' in Matthew 24:34: An Engagement with the Dispensational-Ethnic Approach of J.B. Hixson." In 2026, Shultz is set to complete his Ph.D., publishing his dissertation on the Historical Theology of Universal Salvation for Infants Dying in Infancy.

Formerly a Chaplain (*Captain*) in the United States Air Force Auxiliary, Shultz now spends his time split between pastoring, writing, reading, and playing with his children.

www.ingramcontent.com/pod-product-compliance
Lightning Source LLC
LaVergne TN
LVHW020706110826
845149LV00012B/2124

* 9 7 9 8 9 9 5 1 5 9 8 1 0 *